In Defense of Doctrine

In Defense of Doctrine

Evangelicalism, Theology, and Scripture

Rhyne R. Putman

Fortress Press
Minneapolis

IN DEFENSE OF DOCTRINE

Evangelicalism, Theology, and Scripture

Cover design: Alisha Lofgren

Library of Congress Cataloging-in-Publication Data

Hardcover ISBN: 978-1-4514-9971-1

Paperback ISBN: 978-1-4514-7216-5

eBook ISBN: 978-1-4514-9670-3

The paper used in this publication meets the minimum requirements of American
National Standard for Information Sciences — Permanence of Paper for Printed
Library Materials, ANSI Z329.48-1984.

Manufactured in the U.S.A.

This book was produced using PressBooks.com, and PDF rendering was done by
PrinceXML.

For Micah, *"Who is like the LORD."*

Contents

Acknowledgments

If I took the time to thank the entire list of mentors, family members, friends, church members, and colleagues who helped bring me to this point, the orchestra would surely play me off the platform. First and foremost, I am indebted to professors Anthony Thiselton and Kevin Vanhoozer, whose respective works in theological prolegomena served as a catalyst for this book. They have been valuable dialogue partners and critics of my work, and I hope that I have represented them fairly and that my readers will be driven to their much more substantial works. It has been a pleasure on my part to work with Michael Gibson, Lisa Gruenisen, and the team at Fortress Press.

I am very grateful for Dr. Charles Kelley Jr. and Dr. Steve Lemke, the president and provost at New Orleans Baptist Theological Seminary, who gave me the opportunity to fulfill my calling under their leadership. I am also thankful for members of the Division of Theological and Historical Studies with whom I serve: Dr. Daniel Holcomb, Dr. Michael Edens, Dr. Lloyd Harsch, Dr. Rex Butler, Dr. Page Brooks, and Dr. Adam Harwood.

My past and present administrative and teaching assistants, Hyuna Choe Franklin, James Franklin, Kimberly Steinmetz, Edward T.

Wright, and Patrick Cochran have been invaluable aides throughout this process, organizing my books, making countless library runs, crosschecking bibliographic information, and grading stacks of papers so I could have time to write. Dr. Mark Foster and Tim Walker deserve special recognition for being a sounding board for my ideas.

Special thanks are due to my doctoral committee, Dr. Robert Stewart and Dr. Jeff Riley. Beyond their services in aiding me in this book when it was a dissertation, these men made significant investments in my life for which I am eternally grateful. Bob, *mein Doktorvater*, has been my pastor, my academic advisor, my spiritual mentor, and one of my most faithful friends. As my teacher, my division chair, and one of my closest allies, Jeff has modeled a brand of Christian character, godly leadership, and academic excellence I strive to emulate. He has been a source of sage wisdom whenever I have needed it.

Whenever I think about them, I praise my heavenly Father for the parents with whom he entrusted me: Glen and Diane Putman. I would not be who I am today apart from their love for the Lord, for one another, and for me. As husband and wife, parents, and ministers of the gospel, they are my exemplars. I am also indebted to my in-laws, Collin and Marcia Elder, who have also been faithful supporters throughout this journey.

I affectionately dedicate this work to my wife, Micah, who has made this journey with me as my helpmeet and my co-laborer. "You have captivated my heart, my sister, my bride; you have captivated my heart with one glance of your eyes. . . . How beautiful is your love, my sister, my bride!" (Song of Sol. 4:9a, 10a). Micah's constant encouragement and countless sacrifices helped me fulfill this calling. Since I completed the dissertation on which this book is based, we have been blessed by a son, Bennett Roberts Putman. God has been so faithful to us. I echo the sentiments of the psalmist: "The LORD has done great things for us, and we are filled with joy!" (Ps. 126:3).

Soli Deo gloria
Rhyne Putman

Introduction

thesis? (handwritten annotation with arrow)

"If we have the Bible, why do we need theology?" That is, if Christian believers truly possess the written word of God in the biblical canon, why do they need *critical, contemporary,* and *constructive theologies* that go beyond the explicit wording of written revelation in Scripture? What value are creeds or confessions of faith, and what use are appeals to our traditions and spiritual forebears? Doesn't an authoritative appeal to postcanonical doctrine call into question commonly held Christian convictions about biblical inspiration, clarity, and sufficiency?

For many in the broader ecumenical climate, these kinds of questions are bewildering, if not absurdly naïve. Those in the Roman Catholic, Anglo-Catholic, or Eastern Orthodox traditions may find the biblicist posture assumed in these types of questions unsettling because of their respective commitments to the longstanding tradition of the Church. Progressive and liberal Protestants who reject traditional views of biblical inspiration may regard the Bible as a remarkable literary collection that represents the best attempts of human authors to describe their distinctly Christian experiences of transcendence but by no means count it as the final word on faith and practice, especially in a pluralistic and post-critical culture. Questions about the necessity of constructive or systematic theology

1

may be atypical for the traditionalist and the progressive alike, but I encounter questions like these on a regular basis from students in my introductory theology courses and from laypeople in the churches where I serve.

I am an evangelical. Specifically, I belong to a particular brand of confessional evangelicalism shaped by historic Christianity, the Protestant Reformation, the Great Awakening, Baptist distinctives, and twentieth-century "neo-evangelicalism." The term *evangelical* might give some readers caution or unease, but I embrace it as a central part of my identity and theological heritage. However, evangelical conviction can prompt particular challenges for how one understands the relationship between Scripture and theology, especially when addressing how the Bible relates to the historical phenomena of postcanonical doctrinal developments. This book is a positive examination of this theme—an apologia for the ongoing development of doctrine—written from a distinctly evangelical perspective.

The descriptor "evangelical" means different things for different hearers. It can take on theological, ecclesial, or sociological connotations. For some, "evangelical" is synonymous with American Christian fundamentalism. While "fundamentalism" can describe a historically significant American evangelical movement of the early twentieth century—a movement to which I am indebted in many ways—the term can also be used as a pejorative to describe a particular anti-intellectual and separatist mindset. Most evangelical theologians have gone to great lengths to distance themselves from this

[handwritten margin annotation: thesis]

perception.[1] It is my recommendation to refrain using this term unless describing those who apply the term to themselves.

For others, "evangelical" is associated with religiously motivated political activism, typically of the most politically and socially conservative variety. For many, evangelicals represent everything wrong with American religious culture: hackneyed conceptions of piety, judgmental attitudes, cultural and intellectual obtuseness, and high cholesterol from gorging themselves on Chick-fil-A sandwiches. Even among themselves, evangelicals disagree about how to define the term, as theologians, historians, churchmen, and sociologists within the broader tradition devote entire tomes to the question "What is an evangelical?" On occasion, these conversations deteriorate into ecclesial playground fracases over which evangelical group is the "most evangelical" or rousing rounds of "My favorite theologian could beat up your favorite theologian." Those sorts of debates, though always entertaining and sometimes even worth having, are not my primary concern in this study.

When I use the term "evangelical," I mean those who prioritize the proclamation of the gospel (good news, *euangelion*) of Jesus Christ.[2]

---

1. The formal distinction between early twentieth-century Christian fundamentalism and evangelicalism (or neo-evangelicalism) inaugurated with Carl F. H. Henry, *The Uneasy Conscience of Modern Fundamentalism* (Grand Rapids, MI: Eerdmans, 1947). Helpful histories of and introductions to American Christian fundamentalism include George M. Marsden, *Fundamentalism and American Culture*, rev. ed. (New York: Oxford University Press, 2006); idem., *Understanding Fundamentalism and Evangelicalism* (Grand Rapids, MI: Eerdmans, 1990); Joel A. Carpenter, *Revive Us Again: The Reawakening of American Fundamentalism* (New York: Oxford University Press, 1999); D. G. Hart, *That Old-Time Religion in Modern America: Evangelical Protestantism in the Twentieth Century* (Chicago: Ivan R. Dee, 2003); and Richard J. Mouw, *The Smell of Sawdust: What Evangelicals Can Learn From Their Fundamentalist Heritage* (Grand Rapids, MI: Zondervan, 2000).

2. This definition takes its basic shape from the "Bebbington Quadrilateral" presented in David W. Bebbington, *Evangelicalism in Modern Britain: A History from the 1730s to the 1980s* (London: Routledge, 1989), 2–3 and other models found in Alister E. McGrath, *Evangelicalism and the Future of Christianity* (Downers Grove, IL: InterVarsity, 1995), 55–56; R. Albert Mohler, "Confessional Evangelicalism," in *Four Views on the Spectrum of Evangelicalism*, ed. Andrew David Naselli and Collin Hansen (Grand Rapids, MI: Zondervan, 2011), 68–96.

With historic Christianity, evangelicals insist that all human persons are sinners in need of salvation, and that this great salvation comes exclusively through repentance and personal faith in Christ and his *atoning work* on the cross. Evangelicals stress the need for *conversion*, the need for persons to turn from a life of displeasing a holy God to a life of being remade in Christ's likeness. With an inherited theological legacy from the Protestant Reformers, evangelicals deem *justification by faith* an essential tenet of their shared communion. Throughout their history, evangelicals have also stressed the importance of *activism*, of putting their belief in the gospel's transforming power into action. Evangelicals believe that God is in the business of redemption and reconciliation through Christ's atoning work on the cross and personal and social transformation through the *power and presence of the Holy Spirit*. Simply put, we have a share in the ministry of reconciliation as "ambassadors for Christ" through whom "God is making his appeal" (2 Cor. 5:20).

Most importantly for the present study, evangelicals uniformly embrace some variety of *biblicism*. This term, as we shall see, can have both positive and negative connotations depending on the type of "biblicism" utilized. Here, I am simply using the term in a general sense to describe an *unwavering commitment to the authority of the Bible* practiced by evangelicals. To say that Scripture is important for evangelicals is a serious case of understatement. A "high" view of Scripture is an essential identity marker and social marker for confessional evangelicalism. Evangelicals contend that the biblical canon is the written word of God and the supreme and unrivaled authority in matters of faith and practice. Yet there is a lot of confusion about what evangelicals mean by terms like *authority*, *sufficiency*, *inspiration*, *infallibility*, and *inerrancy*. There is also a lot of misunderstanding about how evangelicals read and interpret

secondary purpose

Scripture] Throughout this book, I hope to clarify some of these issues for readers both inside and outside of evangelicalism, but a few preliminary remarks here might be helpful.

First, all evangelicals affirm the supreme authority of Scripture in faith and practice. We likewise agree on the material and formal sufficiency of Scripture. This doctrine (designated *sola scriptura* in the Protestant Reformation) does not mean that the Bible is the only tool in a theologian's belt or that it is a depository of all human knowledge. Clearly, as a collection of ancient Semitic literature devoted to religious instruction, the Bible was not intended to detail contemporary economic theory, the history of the Spanish-American War, neuroscience, or quantum mechanics. But evangelicals insist that the Bible contains the most important information that can possibly be known: all the revelatory "material" necessary for knowledge of salvation and a vibrant, personal relationship with God. Namely, the Bible gives its readers or hearers access to the gospel of Jesus Christ. With its histories, its precepts, its oracles, its songs and prayers, its sage advice, its letters, and its dreams and visions, Scripture supplies Christian believers with the overarching story that shapes their collective worldview: a story of creation, fall, covenant, redemption, and consummation. Evangelicals believe that the Bible is the principal means by which people can know and understand God's will for their lives.[3]

The evangelical commitment to biblical authority is not, as many of its critics often decry, "bibliolatry." We do not serve a "paper pope" or attribute to the inspired texts any kind of independent authority. Books cannot "possess" or "exercise" authority, nor can

---

3. Some evangelicals in the Reformed tradition take this one step further, embracing a form of *cessationism* that denies any and all revelation apart from the written word of God in Scripture. The divines of the Westminster Confession express an early form of this cessationism when they write that "those former ways of God's revealing His will unto His people [particularly prophecy] being now ceased" (The Westminster Confession of Faith, 1.1).

they "speak." When the ink hits the page at Bible printing presses, no transubstantiation occurs; the letters do not take on magical qualities. Words and sentences are merely instruments, complex aggregates of spoken and written signs utilized by a speaker or author to address hearers or readers. The Bible does not "say" anything of its own accord. Such personification makes for strange syntax and even stranger doctrines of revelation. Rather, evangelicals, with the consensus of Christian believers for the past two millennia, recognize that *biblical authority is God's authority.* The divinely inspired and human words of Scripture serve as the primary instrument or vehicle of divine authority in the world today.

Second, most American evangelicals, particularly in the strand of confessional evangelicalism to which I subscribe, affirm explicitly or affirm something akin to the plenary-verbal inspiration of Scripture. This theory is more about the *nature of Scripture* itself than it does the *process or mode of inspiration*: "all Scripture" is "inspired by God" (2 Tim. 3:16). Evangelicals ground their understanding of God's mediated authority in Scripture in their idea that "the whole of Scripture and all its parts, down to the very words of the original, were given by divine inspiration."[4] This does not mean, as some might erroneously assume, that evangelicals believe the Bible dropped out of heaven, inscribed on golden plates. Nor does this mean, as many of our fundamentalist brothers and sisters confidently assert, that the authors of Scripture were merely amanuenses or secretaries jotting down what God audibly told them (though there are specific occasions in prophetic literature where this appears to be the case). Rather, evangelicals assert that God utilized "the distinctive personalities and literary styles of the writers whom He had chosen and prepared" and deny "that God, in causing these writers to use the

---

4. International Council on Biblical Inerrancy, *The Chicago Statement on Biblical Inerrancy* (1978), Article VI.

very words that He chose, overrode their personalities."[5] Evangelicals reject a revelatory docetism that denies the human personalities, literary conventions, and life situations of biblical texts. We believe that the Bible, though verbally the written word of God, is concurrently and concursively a very human collection of writings, shaped by its time and place in history.[6] God providentially has inspired all of the human words of the Bible through various means and methods.

Advocates of the plenary-verbal theory recognize (1) the use of ① historically-bound human personalities and literary conventions to convey a perfect divine disclosure and (2) the sovereign, guiding ② hand of God working in and through the process to produce results that can truly be called the written word of God. As John Calvin (1509–1564) notes, the "hidden God" (*deus absconditus*) has spoken through human languages, personalities, and concepts.[7] Calvin further compares this revelatory act of self-abasement to the overly simplistic and nuanced way that young mothers and fathers talk *helpful* to their babies (an image that this new parent finds particularly amusing).[8] This act of divine accommodation is not an ✳ accommodation to error, but rather a necessary revelatory accommodation to "bridge the gap if communicator and audience do not share the same language, the same culture or the same experiences."[9]

Plenary-verbal theorists stress that the God who inspired these texts may have used different methods with different authors (e.g., audible speech or visions in prophetic literature, historical research

---

5. ICBI, *The Chicago Statement on Biblical Inerrancy*, Article VIII.
6. J. I. Packer, *"Fundamentalism" and the Word of God* (Grand Rapids, MI: Eerdmans, 1958), 80–83.
7. John Calvin *Institutes of the Christian Religion* 1.13.1.
8. John Calvin *Commentary on Genesis* 1.16
9. John H. Walton and D. Brent Sandy, *The Lost World of Scripture: Ancient Literary Culture and Biblical Authority* (Grand Rapids, MI: InterVarsity, 2013), 43.

and testimony in the composition of the four Gospels and in Acts) but ultimately contend the final forms of biblical books are tantamount to the written word of God. Unlike those in theological streams influenced by neo-orthodoxy, most confessional evangelicals hold that the Bible is not merely a record of revelation but also the primary means of God's self-revelation today.[10] Yes, evangelicals believe that readers can experience the revelation of Christ in a subjective, personal sense when reading Scripture, but they also believe that the Bible is the primary location of revelation because it is an objective preservation of God's spoken and written word. The Bible is the unique locus of God's revelation because of the Spirit's work of inspiration.

On this point, some might object that grounding all Christian belief in a notion of biblical inspiration is circular reasoning, or a very subjective foundation at best. Belief in the plenary-verbal inspiration of the Bible is a common, if not essential, identity marker for many evangelical forms of biblicism, but belief in verbal inspiration is not the cornerstone on which all other evangelical beliefs rest. B. B. Warfield (1851–1921), one of the most important voices in framing the modern evangelical doctrine of plenary verbal inspiration, makes this point emphatically:

> Let it not be said that thus we found the whole Christian system upon the doctrine of plenary inspiration. We found the whole Christian system on the doctrine of plenary inspiration as little as we found it upon the doctrine of angelic existences. Were there no such thing as inspiration, Christianity would be true, and all its essential doctrines would be credibly witnessed to us in the generally trustworthy reports of the teaching of our Lord and of His authoritative agents in founding the

10. As the 2000 revision of *Baptist Faith and Message* statement makes clear, the Bible is not merely a human record of revelation but a form of direct revelation as well. For an explanation and analysis of this revision, see Joseph D. Wooddell, "Article I: The Scriptures," in *Baptist Faith and Message 2000: Critical Issues in America's Largest Protestant Denomination*, ed. Douglas K. Blount and Joseph D. Wooddell (Lanham, MD: Rowman and Littlefield, 2007), 4–6.

Church, preserved in the writings of the apostles and their first followers, and in the historical witness of the living Church. Inspiration is not the most fundamental of Christian doctrines, nor even the first thing we prove about the Scriptures. It is the last and crowning fact as to the Scriptures. These we first prove authentic, historically credible, generally trustworthy, before we prove them inspired. And the proof of their authenticity, credibility, general trustworthiness would give us a firm basis for Christianity prior to any knowledge on our part of inspiration, and indeed apart from the existence of inspiration.[11]

In other words, Warfield recognizes that even if we did not have a divinely inspired Bible, we could establish the general credibility of the Christian faith by testing the historical witnesses to Jesus in the Gospels and the early church. As Michael S. Horton observes, "The historical facts of creation and redemption would be true regardless of whether God chose to report them through inspired Scripture."[12] *important!* The notion of inspiration attested to by biblical authors (e.g., 2 Tim. 3:16–17; 2 Pet. 2:21) and affirmed historically by the church simply gives greater assurance that God has spoken—and still speaks—to his people.

Finally, most self-identifying evangelicals, particularly within my strand of confessional evangelicalism, affirm a doctrine of biblical inerrancy. As evangelical theologian Millard Erickson defines it, inerrancy is the view that the "Bible, when correctly interpreted in light of the level to which culture and the means of communication had developed at the time it was written, and in view of the purposes for which it was given, is fully truthful in all that it affirms."[13] Inerrancy is primarily a theological claim about the nature of Scripture deduced from belief in (1) the plenary-verbal inspiration

11. Benjamin Breckenridge Warfield, *The Inspiration and Authority of the Bible*, ed. Samuel G. Craig (Philadelphia: Presbyterian and Reformed, 1948), 210.
12. Michael Horton, *The Christian Faith: A Systematic Theology for Pilgrims on the Way* (Grand Rapids, MI: Zondervan, 2011), 173.
13. Millard J. Erickson, *Christian Theology*, 2nd ed. (Grand Rapids, MI: Baker, 1998), 259.

of the Bible and (2) the trustworthy character of God. Disagreement over inerrancy spurred much infighting among evangelical scholars in the latter half of the twentieth century, and while the number of vocal detractors of this doctrine within evangelicalism has diminished, some animated intramural discussions about the implications of this doctrine for biblical interpretation continue to the present day. Some evangelicals, especially among those voices outside of North America, express some concern about the modernistic implications of the term *inerrancy* but still hold to some *de facto* form of the doctrine.[14] By biblical inerrancy, I mean a commitment to the full *truthfulness* and *trustworthiness* of the word of God in what biblical authors affirm to be true.[15] This definition has both objective and subjective dimensions: objective in the sense that we affirm that biblical assertions correspond to reality and subjective in the sense that we subject ourselves to the divine guarantor of those assertions.

Despite popular claims to the contrary, the evangelical commitment to inerrancy does not mean that interpreters should read everything in the Bible in a wooden, literalistic fashion. The Bible is a treasure trove of metaphors, poems, songs, and figures of speech that can express truth without an absurd literalism.[16] Inerrantists can and should pay careful attention to the pluriform literary genres

14. See Michael F. Bird, "Inerrancy is Not Necessary for Evangelicalism Outside the USA," in *Five Views on Biblical Inerrancy*, ed. J. Merrick and Steven M. Garrett (Grand Rapids, MI: Zondervan, 2013), 145–73.

15. As a member of the Evangelical Theological Society—a professional organization consisting of over four-thousand evangelical scholars, ministry professionals, and students—I subscribe in writing annually to its Doctrinal Basis, which states that the "Bible alone, and the Bible in its entirety, is the Word of God written and is therefore inerrant in the autographs." That is, the Bible is completely trustworthy in so far as the texts we have today correlate to the original, inspired autographs. With other ETS members, I affirm the definition of inerrancy described in *The Chicago Statement on Biblical Inerrancy* (1978). See *Evangelical Theological Society Constitution* (as adopted Dec. 28, 1949, and amended in 1950, 1951, 1959, 1976, 1985, 1990, 2008), article 3.

16. Packer, *"Fundamentalism" and the Word of God*, 104; Carl F. H. Henry, *God, Revelation, and Authority*, vol. 4, *God Who Speaks and Shows—Fifteen Theses, Part Three* (Waco: Word, 1979), 201–02.

of Scripture in interpretation. While the whole of Scripture should not be read in a literalistic fashion, an affirmation of inerrancy does mean that everything the human authors of Scripture present as true is literally true. (Note the important distinction between made here between "truly literal" and "literally true.") Furthermore, as evangelical New Testament scholar D. A. Carson observes, "Inerrancy does not mean that every conceivable sequence of linguistic data in the Bible must be susceptible to the term *inerrant*, only that no errant assertion occurs."[17] Inerrancy has to do with the assertions biblical writers make, not every statement made in Scripture. For instance, biblical writers do not affirm the lies told by characters in narrative passages to be true, nor do they necessarily affirm the bad advice of Job's friends. While biblical authors write within the culturally conditioned literary conventions of antiquity, they are faithful in their presentation of the world as they see it. The divinely inspired authors of Scripture were neither deceptive nor deceived in what they present as truth.[18]

Given these assumptions about the Bible, it might seem remarkable to some that I would argue for the *ongoing need to develop doctrine*, to give *new and creative expressions of ancient ideas*, and to *offer constructive solutions for contemporary settings*. But that is exactly what I intend to do with this book: write a defense of constructive theology and doctrinal development from within a confessional evangelical tradition and respective of evangelical biblicism. I do so with two distinct audiences in mind: evangelicals who are skeptical about the need for systematic and constructive formulations of Christian doctrine (those who would say things like "no creed but the Bible!")

---

17. D. A. Carson, *Collected Writings on Scripture*, ed. Andrew David Naselli (Wheaton, IL: Crossway, 2010), 88.
18. See ICBI, *The Chicago Statement on Biblical Inerrancy*, Article XII. The framers of *The Chicago Statement* describe the Bible as "from all falsehood, fraud, or deceit."

and critics of evangelicalism who contend that historical developments of Christian doctrine embraced by evangelicals are fundamentally incompatible with first-century Christian origins and evangelical understandings of Scripture (those who would say that the earliest followers of Jesus did not espouse "traditional" Christian beliefs). My treatment of what has been called the "problem of doctrinal development" is explicitly hermeneutical, meaning I give considerable attention to the nature of interpretation in general and biblical interpretation in particular.

In Defense of Evangelical Biblicism

The commitment to biblical authority, inspiration, inerrancy, and sufficiency espoused by evangelicals like myself is often thought to be incompatible with postcanonical doctrinal development, as sociologist Christian Smith (b. 1960) suggested in his recent work, *The Bible Made Impossible: Why Biblicism Is Not a Truly Evangelical Reading of Scripture* (2011). Smith argues, as the subtitle of his book makes clear, that evangelical biblicism is an incoherent and internally inconsistent theological and interpretive framework. After all, biblicists cannot claim Scripture as the sole authority for doctrine and practice and continue to utilize postcanonical doctrinal formulations such as the Trinity, biblical inerrancy, and the exclusivity of Christ, can they? In his argument for the internal incoherence of evangelical biblicism, Smith defines the "biblicism" of his critique with a list of ten assumptions allegedly held by its adherents:

1. Biblicists hold to *the plenary-verbal inspiration of the Bible*—the idea that the human words of Scripture are God's words in written form. The logical inference of this belief is that the Bible is also *inerrant* or trustworthy in every aspect.

2. The Bible alone communicates God's will for humanity.

3. Everything relevant to Christian doctrine and ethics is contained within the pages of Scripture.

4. Biblicists hold to the *perspicuity* of the Bible—the notion that the Bible is clear enough that any intelligent human being can rightly interpret its meaning.

5. Because the Bible is so clear, the best way to read it is to look for *literal, plain meaning*. This use of "commonsense hermeneutics" means that readers do not necessarily have to understand the specific cultural, historical, or literary background of a passage.

6. The Bible can be understood without any reference whatsoever to creeds, confessions, church traditions, or ecclesial authorities.

7. The canon of Scripture contains no genuine contradictions, and any apparent inconsistencies can be explained away.

8. The message of the Bible is universally applicable for all Christian believers in every era.

9. All the truths of the Bible can be discerned through an inductive reading strategy.

10. The Bible is a "handbook" for every present-day facet of living, including apparel, cooking, dating, dieting, finances, health, marriage, politics, sex, and science.[19]

Clearly, I affirm some of these propositions, but many of them, while reflective of some strands of popular or even folk evangelicalism, do not represent my views or the views of the broader evangelical movement. Smith recognizes that biblicists do not universally acknowledge all of these points and suggests that, despite points of difference, biblicists are united by a common appeal to statements about the nature of Scripture.[20] So, at least by Smith's

19. Christian Smith, *The Bible Made Impossible: Why Biblicism Is Not a Truly Evangelical Reading of Scripture* (Grand Rapids, MI: Brazos, 2012), 4–5.

definition, my affirmation of biblical inspiration and biblical inerrancy would put me square in his definition of incoherent biblicism.

According to Smith, evangelical biblicists tend to ignore the reality of "pervasive interpretive pluralism," the way in which biblical interpreters can present numerous options for understanding biblical texts.[21] He lists several examples of this phenomenon: disagreements about doctrine among like-minded evangelicals, the historic use of the Bible to support competing ethical viewpoints (e.g., pro-slavery and anti-slavery positions, just war and pacifist interpretations, etc.), and looking to the Bible in support of differing forms of church government.[22] He also accuses biblicists of ignoring certain teachings (e.g., the "holy kiss" in Rom. 16:16; 1 Cor. 16:20) and strange passages (e.g., Paul's instruction about Cretan Jews in Titus 1:10–14), as well as arbitrarily labeling some biblical instructions as culturally relative ideas no longer relevant to contemporary audiences (e.g., Levitical law, Paul's wine remedy in 1 Tim. 5:23).[23] Smith concludes that these patterns of interpretive pluralism and selective application in evangelical biblicism are at odds with its primary assumptions, namely notions of verbal inspiration, inerrancy, and perspicuity. Hence, he claims that evangelical biblicism is not only an untenable position but an "impossible" one.[24]

Many of these criticisms feel like potshots directed at a crude caricature of evangelical biblicism that I suspect many of my first-semester seminary students could answer with reasonable clarity, charity, and conviction. First, as evangelical systematic theologian Kevin J. Vanhoozer observes, we must be able to make a distinction

20. Ibid., 5.
21. Ibid., 16–17.
22. Ibid., 27–42.
23. Ibid., 68–74.
24. Ibid., 26.

between *uncritical* or *naïve biblicism* and *critical* or *nuanced biblicism*.[25] Naïve biblicists are those whom Smith describes as giving little or no attention to the cultural, historical, and social specificity of individual biblical texts. The tendency to treat the Bible like a "handbook" or "instruction manual" for all aspects of contemporary life, from dating to dieting, is a hallmark of naïve or uncritical biblicism. One may expect to find this approach to Scripture in the "Christian Living" section of Barnes & Noble, but this is not generally the case in evangelical scholarship.

Critical biblicism, by contrast, entails an affirmation of biblical inspiration and inerrancy *without* resorting to the hermeneutical naïveté of uncritical biblicism. The critical biblicist strives to avoid the kind of biblical or revelatory docetism found in naïve biblicism that ignores the human, phenomenal, and historically-contingent aspects of Scripture. The critical biblicist likewise admits that the Bible does not explicitly address every imaginable issue in Christian life and interaction with culture because she sees the Bible for what it is: an ancient literary collection of religious texts. [She recognizes that interpreters must, to the best of their ability, attempt to understand the social, historical, cultural, and literary contexts of biblical writings. A failure to do so can have disastrous consequences for biblical interpretation.]

Critical biblicists affirm the general perspicuity of Scripture, but they also recognize varying degrees of hermeneutical diversity. With the doctors of the Westminster Confession of Faith (1646) critical biblicists recognize that "all things in Scripture are not alike plain in themselves, nor alike clear unto all."[26] Interpretive pluralism is

---

25. See Kevin J. Vanhoozer, "May We Go Beyond What Is Written After All? The Pattern of Theological Authority and the Problem of Doctrinal Development," in *"But My Words Will Never Pass Away": The Enduring Authority of the Christian Scriptures*, ed. D. A. Carson (Grand Rapids, MI: Eerdmans, forthcoming).
26. The Westminster Confession of Faith 1.7.

a reality that has been long acknowledged in the Reformation tradition, but it is not nearly as "pervasive" as Smith seems to think. In his review of Smith's work, Bible scholar Craig Blomberg points out that evangelicals (and most within the broader, historic Christian tradition) universally agree about issues like the true humanity and divinity of Jesus, his bodily resurrection, human sinfulness, the character of God, and the basic content of the gospel.[27]

Yet Smith is right on several fronts. For some theological conservatives (particularly those within fundamentalism or quasi-fundamentalism), there is a lingering temptation to resort to a naïve or uncritical biblicism that conflates one's interpretation of Scripture with the inspired text itself. Oftentimes these uncritical biblicists perceive disagreement with their understanding of a biblical text's meaning as a rejection of biblical authority or trustworthiness. Sometimes you might hear the naïve biblicist argue like this: "If you don't agree with my doctrine of eschatology, you must not believe the Word of God!" This response occurs because many uncritical biblicists neglect the *interpretive nature of theology*. Evangelicals do not claim the same kind of inspiration or inerrancy for their doctrines, which come about as a result of interpreting the inspired biblical texts. Most troubling for the problem at hand, some naïve biblicists tend to ignore or reject the need for postcanonical doctrinal development—the ongoing practice of articulating new doctrinal formulations that go beyond the explicit wording of Scripture. I agree with Smith that this kind of uncritical biblicism can pose significant problems for the evangelical theological enterprise.

27. Craig L. Blomberg, review of *The Bible Made Impossible: Why Biblicism is Not a Truly Evangelical Reading of Scripture*, by Christian Smith, *Review of Biblical Literature* (August 2012): 3–4; available at http://www.bookreviews.org/pdf/8205_8969.pdf (accessed May 17, 2013).

In Defense of Developing Doctrine

An unexamined belief about the relationship between the Bible and belief is only one of the challenges evangelical theology faces. Naïve biblicists are not the only ones raising serious questions about the legitimacy of postcanonical doctrinal development. I did not grasp the significance of this issue for non-Christian skeptics until I was well into the initial research stage of this book and found myself sharing a meal with one of those famous, cultured despisers of religion. This celebrity scholar, author of multiple New York Times bestselling books, and frequent guest on *The Colbert Report* has gained much notoriety popularizing the idea that what we now know as "traditional" or "orthodox" Christianity constitutes a significant departure from its earlier, more primitive historical forms. During this dinner conversation, he inquired about my research project, and I told him that I was working with an issue that theologians traditionally call the "problem" of doctrinal development.

Because theology is not his primary field, I had to explain what I meant by the problem—that I was attempting to deal with the tension between the nature of doctrine purportedly grounded in closed biblical revelation and its frequently changing forms throughout history. His initial reaction was one of confusion: "You mean to tell me that a Southern Baptist would acknowledge that Christian doctrine has grown or developed in history?" For a moment, I was flustered (but not surprised) by his caricaturizing of everyone within my denomination as fideistic, world-denying fanatics. Upon further reflection, however, I began to suspect that he was advocating his own unique brand of world-denying fanaticism.

This scholar has made a career out of challenging traditional Christian beliefs by demonstrating their shifting verbal expression and conceptual reformulation at various stages of their historical development: in the transition from oral traditions to biblical texts, in the scribal transmission of biblical texts, and in the later production of doctrines allegedly based on these biblical texts. He frequently makes assertions like "The author of Mark's Gospel did not believe in the divinity of Jesus because he did not expressly say so" or "The formulation of trinitarian doctrine at Nicaea would have been impenetrable to the apostle Paul." Much like a card-carrying fundamentalist smitten with modernistic reductionism, he assumes that Christian texts, doctrinal expressions, and concepts must be *verbally* or *conceptually identical* in order to retain their essential identity throughout time. Just like the uncritical biblicist, this type of historical skepticism suggests that we can't go beyond the explicit wording and conceptual framework of the Bible and still be faithful to it. Because the doctrines of the Christian faith have developed over time, some scholars argue, orthodox Christianity is incapable of demonstrating continuity with the past—especially with the authors of the biblical canon. As I hope to demonstrate, this guiding assumption could not be further from the truth.

Christians believe God to be *constant* and *faithful*. As the prophets testify, "I, YHWH, do not change" (Mal. 3:6). In God, "the Father of lights . . . there is no variation, or shifting shadow" (James 1:17). Christ is the "same yesterday, today, and forever" (Heb. 13:8). The gospel proclaimed by the apostles provides a stable core for Christian identity that must be protected at all costs (Gal. 1:6-10). [Christianity is in some sense unchanging, but in quite another sense, *it always changes*. It must do so in order to be what it is supposed to be.] The essential message of the gospel does not change, but its forms of expression and particular implications do. The gospel of Christ presents us with a challenge to mature as individuals: God has called us to be *new* creatures (2 Cor. 5:17) and has called us into a process that *transforms* us into the likeness of Christ (Rom. 8:29). Christ may not change but his followers are called to do so—to *grow* in their respective understandings of things of God (Phil. 1:9; Heb. 5:11-12) and in their love for one another (Eph. 4:16). God will ultimately make "all things new" (Rev. 21:5). This observation brings us to an important question: Should we not expect for the macrocosm (the *good point?* received faith practiced throughout history) what we expect of the microcosm (the faith of an individual believer)? Should we not expect the people of God, the household of faith, or the body of Christ to grow in their collective understanding of the things of God?

Evangelicals have practical concerns tied up in the issue of doctrinal development. We are named for our commitment to the gospel message (*euangelion*). We take the risen Lord's instruction to "make disciples of all nations" (Matt. 28:19) as serious marching orders for the church. But how exactly can we expect to relate the gospel of Christ to a constantly changing world apart from presenting it in new ways? How do we preach an ancient message to a contemporary audience on a weekly basis without a fresh means of articulation and delivery? Then the fear factor sets in. How do we know we haven't gone too far in trying to be relevant? Can we be confident we haven't exchanged our "eternal inheritance" (Heb. 9:15) for a meaningless tryst with the cultural *zeitgeist*? We live in the tension created by our desire to be faithful to the past horizon of the biblical text and a desire to communicate its divinely inspired, life-changing message to present horizons. The following study is an exploration of this tension, which I hope will serve as an apologetic for the evangelical theological task and the living Christian tradition.

Where We Are Going

This book is an exploration of the so-called problem of doctrinal development from an evangelical perspective. The historical development of doctrine may raise significant questions for many under the broader ecumenical tent, particularly when attempting to distinguish between distortions of and legitimate developments within the received tradition. The issue grows even more complicated for evangelicals who highlight the primacy of Scripture and who downplay the necessity of external authorities. In what way, if any, are doctrinal statements, confessions, and creeds binding on evangelicals? Perhaps more pressing: Is adherence to the sufficiency of Scripture compatible with the need for evangelical Christians to speak to contemporary crises and ethical quandaries unaddressed and unforeseen by the human authors of Scripture? The historical phenomenon of doctrine is more than *a* problem for evangelical theology; I dare say it is *the* problem of evangelical theology. Development is also more than an academic concern; it is a concern for Christian preaching, ministry, missions, and the proclamation of the gospel message—all things essential to the evangelicalism.

I begin this book by acquainting readers with basic issues in the problem of postcanonical doctrinal development and their importance for Christian theology, faith, and practice. I will also attempt to paint a big picture of contemporary hermeneutical theory and the theological interpretation of Scripture—two fields of academic inquiry that I suggest are particularly helpful in explaining the historical phenomenon of doctrinal development. I will argue that postcanonical doctrinal development, is for evangelicals, a historical phenomenon best explained through the tools of contemporary hermeneutical theory. In chapter 2, I will proceed by describing noteworthy Roman Catholic and Protestant models of doctrinal development, giving special attention to nineteenth- and twentieth-century advances in this area. Along the way, I will trace threads and influences common to the development of contemporary hermeneutical theory and the problem of doctrinal development in the nineteenth century and the following century.

The analyses of the models of theological hermeneutics provided by Anthony Thiselton (b. 1937) and Kevin Vanhoozer in chapters 3 and 4 constitute the nucleus of this project. In each analysis, I will examine the selected works of the representative scholar in order to address the guiding questions. Critical evaluation follows each analysis, examining the strengths and weaknesses of each respective model. Whereas Thiselton's theological hermeneutic is primarily descriptive, Vanhoozer's is primarily normative.

Both scholars are also in a broad, emerging group of theologians and biblical scholars calling for *theological hermeneutics* and the *theological interpretation of Scripture* (TIS). Despite their shared interests and connection to the TIS movement, Thiselton and Vanhoozer also have considerably different influences and methodologies, making them choice interlocutors. Thiselton, professor emeritus of Christian theology at the University of Nottingham, is an Anglican New Testament scholar, hermeneutics specialist, and theologian. His sustained engagement with the works of Hans-Georg Gadamer, Martin Heidegger, and Ludwig Wittgenstein has resulted in a revolution of sorts in biblical and theological studies. Vanhoozer is a Presbyterian theologian (PCUSA) who presently serves as research professor of systematic theology at Trinity Evangelical Divinity School.[28] Throughout his corpus, Vanhoozer interacts with various influential continental and postmodern thinkers such as Paul Ricoeur, Jacques Derrida, Roland Gérard Barthes, Richard McKay Rorty, and Stanley Eugene Fish.

---

28. In addition to his three stints on the faculty of Trinity (1986–1990, 1998–2008, 2011–present), Vanhoozer has served as Blanchard Professor of Theology at Wheaton College and Graduate School (2008–2011) and senior lecturer in theology and religious studies at New College in the University of Edinburgh (1990–1998).

In chapters 5–7, I identify three central problems or questions for models of doctrinal development that I believe hermeneutical theory is in a privileged position to help answer: (1) the problem of authority, (2) the problem of reality depiction, and (3) the problem of continuity. While other questions are important for models of doctrinal development, these questions relate specifically to the use of Scripture in developing doctrine.

The question of authority in the problem of doctrinal development is in focus in chapter 5. Who or what is the arbiter of meaning in doctrinal formulation and development? This question has both theological and hermeneutical dimensions. Theologically, a model of doctrinal development must address the standards or channels by which doctrine is formed, modified, or amended. In contemporary hermeneutical theory, the term *authority* has come to represent the person or object responsible for producing meaning in the interpretive process. Who controls the meaning of texts? Is it the author, the autonomous text, the reading community, the isolated reader, or some combination thereof? How one answers these hermeneutical questions of authority will have considerable impact on how one answers the theological dimension of this problem.

We explore the question of reality depiction in doctrinal development in chapter 6. Once more, this problem has both theological and hermeneutical dimensions. If genuine doctrinal development or change is occurring, what does that say about the ability of doctrinal statements to depict reality, particularly those depicting a God who is, according to classical theism, immutable? The theologian must address how, if at all, doctrinal statements depict transcendent reality. When development or reformulation does occur, do these refined or modified doctrinal statements cease to correspond to reality, correspond more closely to reality, or does the reality to which they refer, namely God, change? Again, hermeneutics and the philosophy of language can assist in addressing the theological issue.

Chapter 7 addresses the question of continuity or identity in doctrinal development. How does Christian doctrine maintain identity with the past throughout development and change? In other words, how do Christian doctrinal statements remain essentially Christian with progress and transformation? This chapter, in turn, will address how doctrines, despite their development and modification, can retain essential meaning in the hands of different faith communities in varying contexts.

The final chapter of this book presents general conclusions about how contemporary hermeneutical theory aids in answering key questions related to doctrinal development and offers practical suggestions for the ongoing Christian practice of doctrinal development. These suggestions are tentative and by no means comprehensive or exhaustive.

If the Bible and theology are closely intertwined, as evangelicals customarily argue, then it is important to evaluate how biblical interpretation leads to the formation of doctrine. Yet oftentimes practitioners of biblical hermeneutics overlook some of the "big picture" questions raised and addressed by hermeneutical philosophers: questions about the nature of texts, the role of readers, and the experience of interpretation. Contemporary hermeneutical theory has remarkable explanatory power over the historical development of all ideas and cultural traditions. In this book, I intend to extend these explanatory tools to Christian theology, *to explain the historical phenomenon of doctrinal development in hermeneutical terms.* In other words, hermeneutical theory provides a way of understanding the development of Christian doctrine in history. Insights from hermeneutical philosophy and the philosophy of language can aid theologians in constructing explanatory theses for particular theological problems associated with the facts of doctrinal development, namely, questions related to textual authority, reality depiction, and theological identity. Hermeneutics can aide theologians in *describing* the nature and scope of Christian doctrine and in *prescribing* the ongoing practice of doctrinal development. This is an especially important endeavor for evangelical theology because evangelical theologians prioritize the interpretation of Scripture in the formulation and articulation of Christian belief and practice.

In the same way that philosophical hermeneutics is concerned with elucidating the nature of human understanding, this project in theological hermeneutics and doctrinal criticism seeks to explain the nature of theological understanding in doctrinal development. I am not concerned with creating a "how-to" book in theological method. Theology grounded in the truth of Scripture and relevant to contemporary concerns requires more than a paint-by-numbers reading of biblical texts. The theological task involves more *Spirit-led wisdom* than interpretive science. So, readers hoping to find a one-size-fits-all, systematic process for formulating doctrine will be sorely disappointed because no such step-by-step method is articulated here. Instead, I am primarily interested in addressing the tension between evangelical commitment to the biblical canon as the supreme, normative rule of Christian belief and the need for critical, constructive theology that addresses contemporary crises and needs.

1

Reading Scripture and Developing Doctrine

For Christian believers, no one captivates the attention, moves the affections, or stirs the imagination like Jesus of Nazareth. He is the visible display—the perfect icon—of the inexhaustible love and power of an invisible God (Col. 1:15). What we know of this Jesus we have read in the writings of the New Testament. These first-century texts are the gateway to Christ, the "primary sources" on which we base our historical, theological, and practical beliefs about him. Through the theologically flavored biographies, ecclesial missives, and dream-like visions contained within, we can get to know him and get a glimpse of the impact he had on his earliest followers.

Yet nowhere do the texts that reveal him reduce their description of him to a systematic description or an orderly set of facts. Nowhere does the New Testament resemble a question-and-answer catechism. New Testament writers attribute to him many names: "Messiah," "Lord," "Savior," "Son of God," "Son of Man," "King," "the image of the invisible God," "the Head of the church," "the firstborn from the dead," "the Way, the Truth, and the Life," "the Good Shepherd," "the True Vine," and many others. But no one of these titles or metaphorical descriptions fully encompasses his significance for Christian belief and practice.

While our words can never exhaust the embarrassment of riches that comes with knowing Christ, believers do need a shorthand way of describing him, a way of talking about him "on-the-go." As an evangelical concerned with sharing the gospel or *evangel* of Jesus Christ, I want to tell everyone I can about his person and work in the most effective way I can. Whether I am preaching a sermon or engaged in personal evangelism, I need a concise way of talking about him that does not feel like an extended seminary curriculum on the historical Jesus and New Testament Christology. As invaluable as that kind of extended treatment may be, I don't always have the time or the patient hearing that such a detailed description would require. I need to "cut to the chase," to get to the main point. I need a way of expressing the historical and theological meaning of Jesus' life and mission for those who do not have a comprehensive background in the religious and political history of early Judaism. In sharing the good news of Jesus, I need to get to the matter of *who* Jesus is and *why* people should care.

So how do I give a contemporary and concise expression to the message of the Bible in terms that they can understand without oversimplifying the complexities and nuances of the historical record or without diminishing the theological richness of the biblical witness? The short answer is *doctrine*. Doctrine (from the Latin term *doctrīna*, meaning "teaching") is *the verbal articulation of Christian beliefs*. Doctrine is an expression of "what we believe" in summary statements, most often appearing in the form of propositional statements.

As New Testament scholar N. T. Wright aptly describes them, the doctrines expressed in Christian creeds and theology function like "portable narratives." Doctrines are like the biblical story packed in a suitcase, ready to go. They

> consciously tell the story—precisely the scriptural story!—from creation to new creation, focusing particularly, of course, on Jesus and summing up what Scripture says about him in a powerful, brief narrative (a process that we can already see happening within the New Testament itself). When the larger story needs to be put within a particular discourse, for argumentative, didactic, rhetorical, or whatever other purpose, it makes sense, and is not inimical to its own character, to telescope it together and allow it, suitably bagged up, to take its place in that new context—just as long as we realize that it will collect mildew if we leave it in its bag forever.

As the portable expressions of biblical teaching, "doctrines" or "doctrinal formulations" are not synonymous with revealed ideas or the inspired teachings of the Bible.

Biblical authors certainly model the practice of doctrine for us with *biblical doctrine*. Doctrines, as I use the term in this book, are primarily *postcanonical expressions of the content of Christian belief* and *interpretations of Scripture* shaped by particular historical and conceptual frameworks. Though they take their shape and substance from Scripture, doctrinal constructs are not necessarily semantically or conceptually identical to the particular teachings expressed by biblical authors. The Holy Spirit may have "fixed" the meaning or substance of biblical texts in the process of inspiring biblical authors, but the articulation of that substance in postcanonical Christian doctrine is an ongoing process.

Theology, a term derived from the Greek terms *theos*, meaning "God," and *logos*, meaning "word" or "reason," describes the broad category of disciplines committed to explicating these Christian

1. N. T. Wright, "Reading Paul, Thinking Scripture," in *Scripture's Doctrine and Theology's Bible: How the New Testament Shapes Christian Dogmatics*, ed. Markus Bockmuehl and Alan J. Torrance (Grand Rapids, MI: Baker, 2008), 64.

doctrines or teachings. One such discipline, *biblical theology*—the study of the particular expressions of biblical doctrine found in the Old and New Testaments that gives specific attention to the arguments, historical situations, and nuances of individual units of text—has a crucial and proper role in the church and academy.[2] In addition to biblical theology, there is also a need for *systematic theology*. Systematic theology or constructive theology is a discipline committed to articulating the message of the Christian faith in such a way that it addresses the particular questions and concerns that contemporary hearers may have along the way. Whenever we try to explain a biblical doctrine in our own words or relate it to a new situation, we have moved from biblical doctrine toward postcanonical doctrinal formulation.

While the formal, academic discipline of systematic theology is a later historical development, the habit of developing doctrine in a way that is both orderly and germane to its context is an ancient practice. With their liturgical functions, creeds are by no means "systematic theologies" in the academic sense, but they did emerge as postcanonical attempts to articulate and express the meaning of Scripture for their contemporary audiences. For example, the fathers who penned the Nicene Creed (325/381) and the Chalcedonian Creed (451) proffered their own confessions or "portable narratives" in the fourth and fifth centuries in order to address particular questions pertinent the internal conflicts of the church. These developments were more than products of insatiable intellectual curiosity; they emerged in a context of devotion and prayer. As Thomas F. Torrance observes, "We have found in these centuries

---

2. The definitions of "biblical theology" are legion. Where two or three biblical scholars have gathered, there are probably five or six different ways to conceive of the nebulous task that is "biblical theology." A recent, helpful introduction to these various models of biblical theology comes in Edward Klink III and Darian R. Lockett, *Understanding Biblical Theology: A Comparison of Theory and Practice* (Grand Rapids, MI: Zondervan, 2012).

a continuing tradition characterised by a deep intertwining of faith and godliness, understanding and worship, under the creative impact of the primary evangelical convictions imprinted upon the mind of the Church in its commitment to God's self-revelation through the incarnate Son and in the Holy Spirit."[3]

Yet in order to develop these creedal formulations, the theologians of the fourth and fifth centuries did take on the task of constructive doctrinal development in order to give fuller expression to their understanding of Christian revelation. As R. P. C. Hanson observes in his magisterial study on the Arian controversy of the fourth century, the "theologians of the Christian Church were slowly driven to a realization that the deepest questions which face Christianity cannot be answered in purely biblical language, because *the questions are about the meaning of biblical language itself.*"[4] While much of the language of these creeds is puzzling to contemporary hearers with little or no interest in Greco-Roman metaphysics, these portable narratives were quite fitting to the particular intellectual climate in which they grew (a place so culturally saturated with Platonist and Neo-Platonist philosophical presuppositions that it could have been called "the Platonic belt").

The Nicene bishops describe Christ as being God, having the "same essence as the Father" (*homoousios*). They insisted that Jesus is not merely similar to God in his essence (*homoiousios*). Christ is not

---

3. Thomas F. Torrance, *The Trinitarian Faith: The Evangelical Theology of the Ancient Catholic Church* (Edinburgh: T&T Clark, 1988), 44.

4. See R. P. C. Hanson, *The Search for the Christian Doctrine of God: The Arian Controversy, 318-381* (London/New York: T&T Clark, 1988), xxi. Hanson does distinguish between *genuine* doctrinal development and doctrinal distortion. See R. P. C. Hanson and Reginald Fuller, *The Church of Rome: A Dissuasive* (London: SCM, 1948), 102. Hanson and Fuller (1915–2007) write, "Genuine development of Christian doctrine . . . has taken place only in the enunciation of certain formulae necessary to protect the original tradition of the Church from error. These formulae are only *de fide*, necessary to salvation, in as far as points of controversy have been raised to which they could be the only answer if the witness of the Bible to God's revelation in Jesus Christ was to be maintained in its truth."

a created being who has "God-like" qualities. For the Nicene fathers, Christ is the very same God "by whom all things were made," and the person of the Godhead "who for us . . . and for our salvation, came down and was incarnate and was made a human being." In the incarnation, Jesus Christ is the one who "suffered" on the cross for sins and the one who "rose again on the third day." He "ascended into heaven," and he will return "to judge both the living and the dead." The Nicene fathers were trying to sum up the great narrative of the New Testament regarding Christ in a portable way and a way that would address those, like the Arian party, who they felt fundamentally misunderstood and misrepresented the biblical portrait of Christ.

Over a century later, when wrestling through the implications of what it meant for Jesus to be human and divine, the divines at Chalcedon described him as "the one and only Son" who is "truly God and truly man." Christ shares the very essence of God in his divine nature and is truly human in every way according to his human nature, save for the absence of personal sin in his life. Against the Nestorian teaching that divided Christ into two persons or the Eutychian notion that he is a *tertium quid* (i.e., a "third thing") who is neither truly divine nor truly human, these fathers contended that in the Messiah of Israel, divine and human natures are united in one person, without separation or confusion.

Both of these creeds neatly and tidily express the "raw material" of biblical Christology, and they were also profitable expressions of Christian belief for their particular time and context. Yet they also represent considerable advancements in understandings of Christian ideas developed long after the events of the New Testament. Out of historical carelessness we may be tempted to think that just because these early confessions are ancient (a relative term, I might add) that they were basically contemporaneous with Jesus and the early church.

But to put things in perspective, these creeds, written approximately three to four centuries after the life of the historical Jesus, have a greater time span between them and the life of their subject matter than we do with William Shakespeare or George Washington. It took a lot of time and a lot of thought to formulate clear expressions of what we call historic, orthodox Christian beliefs. As Alister McGrath notes, these formulations "can be seen as the climax of a long, careful, and exhaustive process of theological reflection and exploration." And while early Christians had "always recognized that Jesus of Nazareth embodied God," "the intellectual exploration of what this [recognition] implied took more than three centuries, involving the critical examination of a wide range of intellectual frameworks for making sense of what the church had already discovered to be true."[5]

For some, the realization of the great gulf of time between the writing of the New Testament and the later formation of creeds can be quite unsettling. Some might say that these later church fathers were in no better place to establish the identity of Jesus as God than a twenty-first century person would be establishing the identity of George Washington as America's first monarch. Many would also argue (correctly, to some degree) that this later, creedal language of Christian belief would have been quite alien to biblical authors themselves. On the other side of the spectrum, there are Christians who would deny any genuine historical development at all, who would contend that creeds and confessions formulated along the way at places like Nicaea or Chalcedon did nothing to grow understanding of God's work in Christ but merely gave new expression to clear biblical concepts. For these, there is "no creed but the Bible." The Bible is so self-explanatory and perspicuous that

5. Alister E. McGrath, *Heresy: A History of Defending the Truth* (San Francisco: HarperOne, 2009), 25–26.

any open-minded reader from any cultural or historical context can understand it if they simply heed its words. As Millard J. Erickson astutely observes, not many preachers stand behind their pulpits, read the text, and sit down without giving some kind of explanation.[6] Doctrine, as explanation of the biblical teaching, is an inescapable outgrowth of the faithful proclamation of the written word. Others might admit some degree of development in early Christianity, a making explicit of what was already implicit in biblical texts, and then suggest that the theological task is basically finished. For these, there is no further need for doctrinal construction or re-evaluation, and the only theologian we need to read is (fill-in-the-blank).

These critiques bring us to a larger question and one that will occupy us throughout this study: Is there an ongoing role for contemporary theologians other than *historical theology*, the rehearsal of theological formulations from the past? Can evangelical theology retain its commitment to the normative supremacy of Scripture and simultaneously provide new and constructive solutions for issues unforeseen by ancient authors—issues like abortion, climate change, cloning, drone warfare, gay marriage, gender reassignment surgery, gun control, internet pornography, nuclear proliferation, online gambling, overpopulation, and stem-cell research? These are questions related to the so-called "problem of doctrinal development."

The Historical Phenomenon of Doctrinal Development

New Testament writers repeatedly warn their readers about doctrinal downgrades and religious or philosophical trajectories that would lead believers away from the Christ proclaimed by the apostles. With

---

6. Millard J. Erickson, *Christian Theology*, 3d. ed. (Grand Rapids, MI: Baker, 2013), 74.

a figure of speech drawn from Greek athletic contests, Jude pled that his audience would "carry on the fight" for the "faith which was once and for all delivered to the saints" against the devices of antinomian teachers who infiltrated the church (Jude 3–4). John warned of teachers who possessed the spirit of antichrist and who rejected the truth revealed to them (1 John 2:18–24; 4:1–6). Paul likewise admonished Galatian and Corinthian Christians for exchanging the gospel proclaimed by the apostles with a contrary gospel of their own devices (Gal. 1:6–9; 2 Cor. 11:3–4). The same kind of plea appears throughout the Pastoral Epistles: "Maintain the standard of sound teaching that you have heard from me. . . . Protect the good thing that was entrusted to you" (2 Tim. 1:13–14; cf. 1 Tim. 6:20a). The first followers of Jesus were insistent that their message was pure and without the corruption of "cleverly fabricated myths" or the pretense of "personal interpretation" (2 Pet. 1:16, 21). Concern for maintaining a faithful, unadulterated gospel message has been with the Christian tradition since its inception.

While distortion of the apostolic proclamation always has been cause for alarm, the ongoing development of doctrine has been a fixture of the Christian tradition since the first century. Simply stated, doctrinal development is the ongoing task of advancing the teachings of the Christian faith. The term "doctrinal development" can describe (1) the ongoing process of reconstructing and reordering doctrines into *systematic theologies* that offer both conceptual clarity and internal consistency. This common practice, as John B. Webster observes, is a post-apostolic, postcanonical enterprise shaped by a desire to develop a comprehensive understanding of unorganized New Testament teaching that is predominately *ad hoc* or situational in nature.[7]

---

7. John B. Webster, "Introduction: Systematic Theology," in *The Oxford Handbook of Systematic Theology*, ed. John B. Webster, Kathryn Tanner, and Iain Torrance, 1–18. Oxford: Oxford University Press, 2009.

Development may also describe (2) attempts to *contextualize* or "translate" the substance of Christian teaching for new settings and new cultures. On occasion, and of central concern for the present study, development means (3) the introduction of new *theological concepts and expressions*. These developments, which go beyond the verbal and conceptual bounds of previously received revelation, are attempts to amplify or shed new light on established ideas and themes. All three of these uses of development are interrelated and can be difficult to distinguish.

[The biblical canon itself is a witness to these kinds of historical developments, either in making explicit what is implicit in previous texts, shifting theological emphases, mutating older beliefs, or in some cases, introducing completely new ideas.] While an inspired, revelatory act of God, the Bible is itself a collection of historically situated documents, and the beliefs of biblical authors were themselves shaped by their time and place in history. A few things are worth noting when looking at these historical developments. First, several crucial theological developments in Second Temple Judaism set the stage for the New Testament: the rise of apocalypticism, the expansion of eschatological beliefs about afterlife and judgment, a more developed understanding of the spirit world of angels and demons, a more explicit commitment to monotheism, and the expansion of the synagogue model. Second, the New Testament itself is a witness to several developments within the framework of Jewish belief, including (1) the new emphasis on God as Father, (2) the concept of the threefoldness of God, (3) the inclusion of Gentiles under the rubric of the people of God, (4) and the decentralization of Torah,[8] and (5) the new centrality of resurrection belief.[9]

---

8. Ian Howard Marshall, *Beyond the Bible: Moving from Scripture to Theology* (Grand Rapids, MI: Baker, 2004), 48–50.

Other developments or shifts appear within the early Christian movement itself. Even with broad similarities between the teaching of Jesus and his followers, the earliest disciples of Jesus move their explicit focus away from his kingdom of God motif in the gospels to the kerygma about the crucified and risen Lord.[10] When it became apparent to some late first-century Christians that the Lord's return may not happen in their lifetime, they began formulating distinctively Christian praxis and gave new attention to the codification of their doctrines.[11] One might call these instances of intracanonical developments evidence of "progressive revelation" within the canon,[12] but the pressing difficulty, especially for evangelicals like myself committed to the material and formal sufficiency of Scripture,[13] is that the normative tradition of the faith community continued to grow even after this unique period of divine revelation was complete.[14]

9. For example, in his *The Resurrection of the Son of God* (Minneapolis: Fortress Press, 2003), N. T. Wright identifies at least six Christian "mutations" of Jewish resurrection belief. Wright notes several Christian "mutations" of antecedent Jewish resurrection belief: (1) the centrality of resurrection belief for Christians, (2) the explicit description of the resurrection as immortal physicality, (3) the universality of resurrection belief, (4) the division of the resurrection into two stages (1 Cor. 15:23), (5) its metaphorical association with baptism (Rom. 6:4–5), and (6) the resurrection of messiah. Following his dialogue with John Dominic Crossan (b. 1934) at the 2005 Greer-Heard Point-Counterpoint Forum in New Orleans, Wright added a seventh mutation: "collaborative eschatology." See also N. T. Wright, *Surprised by Hope: Rethinking Heaven, the Resurrection, and the Mission of the Church* (San Francisco: HarperOne, 2008), 45–46; cf. Robert B. Stewart, ed., *The Resurrection of Jesus: John Dominic Crossan and N. T. Wright in Dialogue* (Minneapolis: Fortress Press, 2006), 26–27, 31–32.

10. Marshall, *Beyond the Bible*, 50–52.

11. See Albert Schweitzer, *The Quest of the Historical Jesus: A Critical Study of Its Progress from Reimarus to Wrede*, trans. William Montgomery (London: Adam and Charles Black, 1910), 21. As Albert Schweitzer (1875–1965) states, "The main problem of primitive dogmatics was the delay of Parousia." For an examination of this change of practice and doctrine following eschatological shifts in early Christianity, see R. P. C. Hanson, *The Continuity of Christian Doctrine* (New York: Seabury, 1981), 34–50.

12. For a critical, evangelical treatment of this theme, see Daniel B. Wallace, "Is Intra-Canonical Development Compatible with a High Bibliology?" (paper presented at the Evangelical Theological Society Southwestern Regional Meeting, Dallas, TX, March 1, 2002).

13. I.e., the need for no other revelation than that which is preserved in Scripture. Material sufficiency denotes the sufficiency of the content of Scripture for knowledge of God and the Christian life.

Christian history is a witness to the ongoing development of postcanonical doctrine. Thus far, I have used the word "canon" only as a general term to describe the thirty-nine books of the Old Testament and the twenty-seven of the New.[15] The notion of canon

---

14. The precise nature of revelation (particularly special revelation) has been another contentious issue in the area of theological prolegomena, especially in the nineteenth and twentieth centuries. A traditional evangelical defense of God's revelation as supernatural, propositional self-disclosure and intervention in the affairs of humanity can be found in Benjamin Breckenridge Warfield, *The Inspiration and Authority of the Bible*, ed. Samuel G. Craig (Philadelphia: Presbyterian and Reformed, 1948), 71–102. Yet more can be said about what this self-disclosure constitutes and how it functions. See also John Baillie, *The Idea of Revelation in Recent Thought* (New York: Columbia University Press, 1956); Carl F. H. Henry, *God, Revelation, and Authority*, vol. 3, *God Who Speaks and Shows: Fifteen Theses, Part Two* (Wheaton, IL: Crossway, 1999); and Avery Dulles, *Models of Revelation*, rev. ed. (Maryknoll, NY: Orbis, 1992), 3–115. Avery Dulles (1918–2008) identifies five basic models of revelation in nineteenth- and twentieth-century theologies: revelation as propositional doctrine, as modeled by evangelicals like Carl F. H. Henry (1913–2003); revelation as history as seen in the works of biblical theologians like George Ernest Wright (1909–1974); revelation as the inner experience to which Friedrich D. E. Schleiermacher (1768–1834) testified; revelation as dialectical presence in Karl Barth (1886–1968) and Emil Brunner (1889–1966); and revelation as new awareness in the works of Pierre Teilhard de Chardin (1881–1955). Much of the modern debate over revelation hinges on a false dichotomy made between revelation as personal encounter and revelation as propositional revelation. As many evangelicals under the influence of contemporary speech-act theory have argued, special revelation does not have to be either personal or propositional. It can be *both* personal *and* propositional. See Kevin J. Vanhoozer, "God's Mighty Speech-Acts: The Doctrine of Scripture for Today," in *A Pathway into the Holy Scripture*, ed. P. E. Satterthwaite and David F. Wright (Grand Rapids, MI: Eerdmans, 1994), 143–82, esp. 178–80; Millard J. Erickson, *Christian Theology*, 2nd ed. (Grand Rapids, MI: Baker, 1998), 216–221; and Michael Scott Horton, *The Christian Faith: A Systematic Theology for Pilgrims along the Way* (Grand Rapids, MI: Zondervan, 2011), 115–26. An extensive treatment of revelation is beyond the scope of the present study, but many of these themes will appear in the discussion of the nature of Christian doctrine. Sufficient for the present discussion is the common acknowledgment among Christians that God's revelation of himself in Christ has been preserved supernaturally through the activity of the Holy Spirit in the inspired texts of the Old and New Testaments. Furthermore, I assume that the closure of the canon and the traditional criteria for canonicity (apostolicity, orthodoxy, catholicity, and antiquity) mean that this process of inscripturation is complete. Without this assumption, the historical development of doctrine poses no real "problem."

15. In so doing, I do not mean to indicate that every biblical author possessed a "canonical consciousness," that all of these authors were aware of the fact that they were in process of inscripturating the word of God, which, for them, was primarily the inspired, living, oral message of God. This may have been the case for some (e.g., 2 Pet. 3:15–16), but, as Ben Witherington III observes, the move from an understanding of the word of God as the spoken proclamation of God to Scripture as the written word of God was itself a doctrinal development that took some time to transpire. See Ben Witherington III, *The Living Word of God: Rethinking the Theology of the Bible* (Waco, TX: Baylor University Press, 2007), 1–14;

as an authoritative list of books was an even later development, and much like the development of other early dogmas, this codification of the canon required some prodding from heretical factions along the way.[16] In the same way that believers eventually gave formal articulation to their beliefs about Jesus after long, creative contemplation and reflection on Scripture, it seems that, as Bruce Metzger observes, the church "did not create the canon, but came to recognize, accept, affirm, and confirm the self-authenticating quality of certain documents that imposed themselves as such upon the Church."[17] To be clear, when I use the term "postcanonical doctrinal developments," I am referring to all historical developments in Christian teaching after the unique period of apostolic revelation ended at the close of the first century, not simply doctrines that emerged after the fourth-century solidification of the canonical list.

New situations in the centuries that followed writing of New Testament books demanded innovative formulas, expressions, and even new conceptual tools. Second and third century Christians faced formidable threats from religious philosophies like Gnosticism, which utilized characters and vocabulary familiar to readers of Scripture, but in ways very different from their canonical counterparts. In many ways, it was heresy—not orthodox belief—that gave birth to the practice of systematic theology. Early Christian apologists felt an obligation to offer formal responses to the complex philosophical and theological systems advocated by these religious groups. These apologists even employed vocabulary and concepts borrowed from

idem, "The Truth Will Win Out: An Historian's Perspective on the Inerrancy Controversy," *Journal of the Evangelical Theological Society* 57/1 (March 2014): 22–24.

16. Bruce M. Metzger, *The Canon of the New Testament: Its Origin, Development, and Significance* (New York: Oxford University Press, 1987), 75–112. Metzger identifies three basic non-orthodox groups that spurred on the orthodox development of the canon: Gnosticism, Marcionism, and Montanism.

17. Ibid., viii.

Greco-Roman philosophy to defend the Christian tradition from opponents deemed heretical or hostile to the faith.[18]

Even with Trinitarian, christological, and pneumatological dogma virtually settled for the larger Christian tradition in the creeds formulated at the ecumenical councils of Nicaea (325), Constantinople (381), Ephesus (431), and Chalcedon (451), theologians would devote the next millennium to formulating doctrines of creation, providence, salvation, the church, and last things. Doctrinal development did not stop with the first four ecumenical councils. Christians still wrestle through issues like these today, debating one another over the meaning of pertinent biblical texts. Even the Protestant reformers who contended for the supreme authority of Christian Scripture continued to formulate their own confessions and distinctive doctrines, often relying on extra-biblical patristic and medieval formulations of doctrine in the process.[19]

If history is any indication, postcanonical doctrinal development is an inevitable reality in the Christian theological tradition. But such development can also serve as a significant threat to the identity and continuity of the received tradition. Can theology present new expressions of belief and remain faithful to the unique authority and sufficiency of the Bible? More practically, can the contemporary

---

18. Anticipating Jewish and Christian objections to this use of philosophical concepts, Clement of Alexandria (c. 150–215 c.e.) argues that Hellenistic philosophy "came into existence . . . for the advantages reaped by us from knowledge" (*The Stromata* 1.2) and provides a "preparatory culture" for Christian doctrine (*The Stromata* 1.5.4). Clement calls Plato's dialogues "divinely inspired" (*The Stromata* 1. 8) and describes Aristotle as "assenting to Scripture" (*The Stromata* 1.17). Following the second-century Syrian philosopher Numenius, Clement believes the works of Plato were historically dependent upon the Law of Moses (*The Stromata* 1.23) and that Greek philosophers in the Socratic school were guilty of "plagiarizing . . . dogmas from the Hebrews" (*The Stromata* 1. 21).

19. For an example of this unconscious acceptance of extrabiblical dogmatic formulations, see Martin Luther, "On the Councils and the Church," trans. Charles M. Jacobs and Eric W. Gritsch, in *Luther's Works*, vol. 41, ed. Jaroslav Pelikan (Philadelphia: Fortress Press, 1966), 95–106; Dennis Ngien, "Chalcedonian Christology and Beyond: Luther's Understanding of the *Communicatio Idiomatum*," *The Heythrop Journal* 45 (2004): 54.

systematic theologian address current crises and still maintain continuity with biblical faith? The theologian who takes up the so-called *problem of doctrinal development* assumes that God has once and for all revealed himself through the medium of human language in Scripture and must by some means explain how Christian doctrines, which purport to be grounded in this revelation, continue to grow or develop even after the epoch of canonical revelation is closed. As Jan Hendrik Walgrave aptly observes, "No one who accepts both presuppositions can possibly get round the problem" when faced with the facts of development in history.[20]

The Nature of the Theological Problem

Extensive, critical reflection on the problem posed by postcanonical development is a more recent feature in the history of Christian thought, sparked largely by the rise of historical consciousness in the nineteenth century. Among the first to produce a systematic theory of development was the Anglican Oxford Movement leader who eventually became a Roman Catholic cardinal, John Henry Newman (1801–1890), and other Catholic theologians quickly followed suit. Reasons for Roman Catholic attention to development are clear. First, extra-biblical traditions play a crucial, normative role in the formation of distinctive Catholic doctrines such as the doctrine of purgatory or the perpetual virginity of Mary.[21] Second, many

---

20. Jan Hendrik Walgrave, *Unfolding Revelation: The Nature of Doctrinal Development* (Philadelphia: Westminster, 1972), 6.

21. Matthew explicitly states that Joseph did not "know" Mary until (*heós*) the birth of Jesus (1:25). However, the second-century apocryphal gospel *The Protoevangelium of James* (also known as *The Birth of Mary*) is an ascetic apology for Mary's ongoing sexual purity. According to this text, Mary is not the mother of Jesus' brothers and sisters but their stepmother. Joseph is a widower who is several years Mary's senior—so much older that he is concerned that his fiancée-ward will be perceived as his daughter (*Prot. Jas.* 9:2). According to this text, Mary's virginity is preserved even in the birth of Jesus. The author graphically depicts the midwife Salome—who initially doubts Mary's virginity and purity—testing Mary by inserting her finger in her birth

distinctive Catholic doctrines like the doctrines of papal infallibility, the Immaculate Conception of Mary, and her bodily assumption into heaven became "official" church dogma only in recent history.[22] Some Catholic theologians continue to suggest that dramatic doctrinal changes, such as the ordination of females and married males into the priesthood, are in the near future of their Church.[23]

Development is not simply a "Catholic problem" or a "Catholic thing." It is as significant a concern for Protestants and evangelicals, though theologians in these traditions must deal with the issue differently than their Roman Catholic counterparts. The Jesuit theologian John Courtney Murray (1904–1967) suggests that the central point of disagreement between Catholics and Protestants is the issue of doctrinal development. He adds, "That development has taken place in both communities cannot be denied. The question is, what is legitimate development . . . and what, on the other hand, is accretion, additive increment, adulteration of the deposit, distortion of true Christian discipline?"[24] Evangelicals in particular must address the relationship between their convictions about Scripture and the historical processes through which their distinctive doctrines emerged.

---

canal in order to see if her hymen remains intact (*Prot. Jas.* 19:3—20:1). When Salome removes her hand, flames consume it (*Prot. Jas.* 20:1). See also Ronald F. Hock, *The Infancy Gospels of James and Thomas* (Santa Rosa, CA: Polebridge Press, 1995), 14–15.

22. Pius IX (1792–1878) defined the immaculate conception of Mary as infallible doctrine in his 1854 *Ineffabilis Deus*. Nearly a century later, in 1950, Pius XII (1876–1958) defined the assumption of Mary as infallible dogma in his *Munificentissimus Deus*.

23. For more about these debates within contemporary Catholicism, see Arturo Cattaneo, Manfred Hauke, André-Marie Jerumanis, and Ernesto William Volonté, eds., *Married Priests? 30 Crucial Questions about Celibacy* (San Francisco: Ignatius, 2012); Anthony P. Kowalski, *Married Catholic Priests: Their History, Their Journey, Their Reflections* (New York: Crossroad, 2005); and Kelley A. Raab, *When Women Become Priests: The Catholic Women's Ordination Debate* (New York: Columbia University Press, 2000).

24. John Courtney Murray, *The Problem of God: Yesterday and Today* (New Haven: Yale University Press, 1964), 53.

Protestants and evangelicals who contend that there is an ongoing need for their communities to express implicit biblical ideas for their contemporary context acknowledge (at least in their praxis) that development is a staple in their own respective traditions.[25] Many doctrines cherished by Protestants and evangelicals lack explicit expression in the first several centuries of Christianity. [Even the *true* foundational Reformation principle of *sola scriptura* is a postcanonical development!] The question remains, Does the practice of postcanonical doctrinal development contradict evangelical adherence to canonical Scriptures as the sole normative authority of the Christian faith? Is such adherence logically possible, or is it a performative contradiction? Furthermore, what place is there for postcanonical doctrine if Scripture is sufficient for faith and practice? Protestants in general and evangelicals in particular need a theory of development that reconciles their notion of the sufficiency of Scripture and their need for contemporary expressions of doctrine.

How one understands the development of doctrine relates to how one understands *the nature of doctrine itself.* Much is at stake here. First, a theory of development serves to demonstrate continuity across different stages of the Christian tradition. For instance, skeptics and historical critics often raise concerns about the absence of explicit Trinitarian thought in the New Testament, bemoaning the lack of Trinitarian vocabulary and the vast differences in conceptual frameworks between first-century Jewish writers and Nicene-era theologians. [By illuminating the nature and function of theology, theories of development can aid in ascertaining a stable tradition across very different conceptual worlds, as in the case of the development of Trinitarian doctrine.] Second, a theory of doctrinal

---

25. George A. Lindbeck, "The Problem of Doctrinal Development and Contemporary Protestant Theology," in *Man as Man and Believer*, ed. Edward Schillebeeckx and Boniface Willems (New York: Paulist, 1967), 133–35.

development is valuable in distinguishing between *fitting and unfitting developments* or between good doctrines and erroneous doctrines. Finally, without the possibility of doctrinal development devoid of distortion, theology cannot realize its central task in seizing and translating the ideas of past for an ever-changing contemporary climate. Attention to this question thus becomes a necessary component in an apologetic for contemporary systematic theology.

The examination of the development problem in this book is limited to theologians who have dealt with development as a theological problem and thus will circumnavigate the more historically oriented studies of development, such as those from the "history of religions school" (*religionsgeschichtliche Schule*) like Adolf von Harnack (1851–1930), Wilhelm Bousset (1865–1920), and Walter Bauer (1877–1960). Scholars in this tradition may lament the Hellenistic or "orthodox corruption" of the Christian tradition, but they do not see historical development as a theological problem because of their rejection of Christian Scripture as a unique, divine depository of revelation.[26] On the other hand, evangelicals

---

26. For a small but important sampling of the so-called "History of Religions School," see Adolf von Harnack, *History of Dogma*, 3d ed., 7 vols., trans. E. B. Speirs and James Millar (Eugene, OR: Wipf and Stock, 1997); Wilhelm Bousset, *Religionsgeschichtliche Studien: Aufsätze zur Religionsgeschichte des Hellenistischen Zeitalters*, ed. Anthonie F. Verheule (London: Brill, 1979); *Kyrios Christos: A History of the Belief in Christ from the Beginnings of Christianity to Irenaeus*, trans. John E. Steely (Nashville: Abingdon, 1970); and Walter Bauer, *Orthodoxy and Heresy in Earliest Christianity*, ed. Robert Kraft and Gerhard Krodel, trans. P. J. Achtemeier (Philadelphia: Fortress Press, 1971). In *Orthodoxy and Heresy*, first published in German in 1934, Bauer rejects the traditional view that orthodox truth preceded heretical corruption. He surmises that many groups later dubbed "heretics" were in fact the earliest Christian groups in many regions.New Testament scholar Bart Ehrman (b. 1955) is a contemporary heir of the *religionsgeschichtliche Schule* who applies the "Bauer thesis" to New Testament textual criticism, biblical studies, and early church history. See Bart D. Ehrman, *The Orthodox Corruption of Scripture* (New York: Oxford University Press, 1993); idem, *Lost Christianities: The Battles for Scripture and the Faiths We Never Knew* (New York: Oxford University Press, 2003). For a critical evaluation of the Bauer-Ehrman thesis from an evangelical perspective, see Andreas J. Köstenberger and Michael J. Kruger, *The Heresy of Orthodoxy: How Contemporary Culture's Fascination with Diversity Has Reshaped Our Understanding of Early Christianity* (Wheaton, IL: Crossway, 2010), 23–103.

committed to some form of biblicism face significant theological challenges in light of the phenomena of historical development.

While postcanonical doctrinal development is a phenomenon observed in history, the problem does not belong primarily to the historian. The problem as stated since the nineteenth century does not belong to historical theology, nor is it about the historical development of any particular doctrine.[27] In a sense, concern over doctrinal development is a *transhistorical* and *transcontextual* theological problem. By describing the problem as transhistorical and transcontextual, I do not mean to imply that doctrines grow outside of specific historical and cultural contexts but that questions about the nature of development need not hinge on any particular instances of it. Specific theories about how development *can* and *should* work are not necessarily contingent on tracing the history of a particular doctrine.

The problem of development is also a second-order question that properly belongs to theological prolegomena, theological method, doctrinal criticism, or fundamental theology.[28] The term *second-order* indicates the philosophical distinction between first-order language and second-order language. Simon Blackburn defines first-order language as a "language in which the quantifiers contain only variables ranging over individuals and the functions have as their arguments only individual variables or constants." In second-order language, on the other hand, "the variables of the quantifiers may

27. The study of development as a theological problem is an area distinct from historical theology, although the former may borrow insights from the latter. See Peter Toon, *The Development of Doctrine in the Church* (Grand Rapids, MI: Eerdmans, 1979), xii.

28. The term *fundamental theology* reflects Heinrich Fries, *Fundamental Theology*, trans. Robert J. Daly (Washington, DC: Catholic University of America Press, 1996), 4. Fries notes, "The term 'fundamental theology' is intended to express that the apologetic task can and should be integrated into a comprehensive theological reflection: in the believing reason's self-examination of its foundations and presuppositions." Fundamental theology is the primary way contemporary Roman Catholic theologians describe what Protestant and evangelical theologians label "theological prolegomena."

range over functions, properties, relations, and classes of objects, and in yet higher-order languages over properties of properties."[29] In simpler terms, first-order language describes the *content* of beliefs and ideas and second-order language is a description of *how* such first-order language works. Whereas first-order theological studies address specific doctrines, second-order theology is structural and organizational, answering "meta" questions about the nature and method of theology.

The Role of Hermeneutical Theory

This particular study of the problem of development gives significant attention to another second-order discipline that is of no small consequence for history and theology: hermeneutics. When most people in Bible colleges, churches, and seminaries hear the word "hermeneutics" (from the Gk. *hermeneuō*, meaning "to interpret"), they usually assume the term describes "the art" or "the rules" of biblical interpretation. When used this way, "hermeneutics" is practically synonymous with biblical *exegesis* (i.e., to "draw out" meaning from the biblical text). On the other hand, those in university humanities departments who hear "hermeneutics" might think of a rather obscure branch of continental philosophy that addresses the interpretation of all texts—a discipline very close to or the same as literary theory or literary criticism. This book uses "hermeneutics" in both senses: *general hermeneutics* (sometimes called "philosophical hermeneutics")—the philosophical exploration of the nature of interpretation—and *special hermeneutics*—the application of interpretive rules or theory to a specific texts like the Bible. This study

---

29. Simon Blackburn, *The Oxford Dictionary of Philosophy* (Oxford: Oxford University Press, 1994), 140.

also calls on the insights of literary criticism and the philosophy of language, sister disciplines of hermeneutics.

Philosophical hermeneutics or general hermeneutics is a discipline that formally dates back to the work of Friedrich D. E. Schleiermacher (1768–1834), who, in addition to developing hermeneutical philosophy, has been called the "father of modern liberal theology."[30] While hermeneutics emerged principally as rules for interpreting texts in general and biblical texts in particular, hermeneutics extends far beyond biblical interpretation and has since the nineteenth century broadened its focus to include the very nature of human understanding (*Verstehen*).[31] The study of hermeneutics extends to every aspect of human communication and interpretation. Sure, I use hermeneutics in my personal Bible reading and sermon preparation, but the discipline can also aid in describing my "reading" of all "texts," whether they are Shakespeare or *Seinfeld*, a Baroque sonata or *SportsCenter*, Fitzgerald or Facebook, the latest summer blockbuster or a late night pillow talk with my wife. Hermeneutics is relevant whenever human beings attempt to inform, entertain, direct, or persuade one another.[32]

30. Friedrich D. E. Schleiermacher, *Hermeneutics and Criticism: And Other Writings*, Cambridge Texts in the History of Philosophy, ed. Andrew Bowie (Cambridge: Cambridge University Press, 1998); idem., *Hermeneutics: The Handwritten Manuscripts*, American Academy of Religion Texts and Translation Series, ed. Heinz Kimmerle, trans. James Duke and Jack Forstman (Atlanta: Scholars Press, 1999).

31. Some Christian critics challenge the common narrative that it was post-critical, post-Enlightenment philosophical hermeneutics in the German tradition that moved interpretation from texts to universal concepts of human understanding. In his *Recovering Theological Hermeneutics* (Grand Rapids, MI: Baker, 2004), Jens Zimmermann (b. 1965) argues that this particular narrative of hermeneutic history ignores many of the same elements that appear in the pre-Enlightenment Christian tradition, particularly encapsulated in the Anselmian catchphrase "faith seeking understanding." Seeing that the shared insights of philosophical and theological hermeneutics are what are important for this present study, this is not a debate I will concern myself with here.

32. Kevin J. Vanhoozer, *Is There a Meaning in This Text? The Bible, the Reader, and the Morality of Literary Knowledge* (Grand Rapids, MI: Zondervan, 1998), 22–23.

While it bears certain similarities to epistemology (i.e., the philosophical study of how we obtain knowledge) and ontology (i.e., the philosophical study of reality), contemporary philosophical hermeneutics probably is best understood as a branch of philosophical anthropology (i.e., the philosophical study of humanity). It is a philosophical exploration of the whole human being, her worldview, and her interpretive experience. Texts may serve as the primary focus of this "art" of understanding, but hermeneutics also encompasses the *entire communicative process*, including understanding how texts are read, understood, and applied by their individual and communal interpreters.[33] Hans-Georg Gadamer (1900–2002) summarizes the task of hermeneutics as

> the opening up of the hermeneutical dimension in its full scope, showing its fundamental significance for our entire understanding of the world and thus for all the various forms in which this understanding manifests itself: from interhuman communication to manipulation of society; from personal experience by the individual in society to the way in which he encounters society; and from the tradition as it is built of religion and law, art, and philosophy, to the revolutionary consciousness that unhinges the tradition through emancipatory reflection.[34]

The study of hermeneutics then constitutes an interpersonal, dialogical engagement between the inquirer and the text, whatever that text may be. To this end, hermeneutics is by its very nature an interdisciplinary enterprise that draws from epistemology, history, linguistics, literary theory, philosophy of science, sociology, and theology.

So, what hath the Continent to do with Jerusalem, or philosophical hermeneutics with the problem of postcanonical doctrinal

---

33. See Friedrich D. E. Schleiermacher, *Hermeneutics: The Handwritten Manuscripts*, ed. Heinz Kimmerle, trans. James Duke and Jack Forstman (Atlanta: Scholars Press, 1997), 95–117.

34. Hans-Georg Gadamer, *Philosophical Hermeneutics*, 2nd ed., trans. and ed. David E. Linge (Berkeley: University of California Press, 2008), 18.

development? New Hermeneutic proponent Gerhard Ebeling (1912–2001) once described church history as the "history of the interpretation of Holy Scripture."[35] Likewise, one may regard the history of doctrinal development as a story of the Christian struggle to understand biblical texts and the identity of their community of interpreters. The faith may have been once delivered, but it has been many times interpreted—and reinterpreted. Such reinterpretation is necessary in new situations because, as Ebeling notes, "the same word can be said to another time only by being said differently."[36] Contemporary hermeneutics provides a means to describing how this interpretation of biblical texts, tradition, experience, and reason come together in the process of doctrinal development.

Contemporary hermeneuticists point to the historical nature of all human knowledge and interpretation. Gadamer belabors the point that all human understanding takes its shape under the influence of history. As interpreters, we cannot escape history or having presuppositions influenced by our time and place in history. We can never be fully aware of the impact of our milieu on the presuppositions through which we read texts.[37] The same is true of our scriptural reading and formulation of Christian doctrine. God may dwell in eternity, but doctrine develops in the particular locations in time and space.[38] If doctrinal development is the product of history, then awareness of its potential problems is a product of this hermeneutical and historical consciousness.

The philosophical alarm systems might be ringing in some of the minds of more attentive readers at this point, especially those among

---

35. See Gerhard Ebeling, *The Word of God and Tradition: Historical Studies Interpreting the Divisions of Christianity*, trans. S. H. Hooke (London: Collins, 1968), 11–31.

36. Gerhard Ebeling, "Time and Word," in *The Future of Our Religious Past: Essays in Honour of Rudolf Bultmann*, ed. James M. Robinson (London: SCM, 1971), 265.

37. Hans-Georg Gadamer, *Truth and Method*, 2nd rev. ed., trans. Joel Weinsheimer and Donald G. Marshall (New York: Continuum, 2004), 278.

38. Kevin J. Vanhoozer, *The Drama of Doctrine* (Louisville: Westminster/John Knox, 2005), 345.

my fellow evangelical readers who eschew all things philosophical or who suffer from an acute case of *pomophobia* (i.e., the fear of all things "postmodern"). Continental philosophy rarely if ever graces the pages of my Southern Baptist Sunday School quarterlies—and probably with good reason. For one thing, a lot of it can be laborious, pretentious reading. But the more profound concerns for evangelical theologians are both epistemological and practical: Are we granting undue epistemic authority to sin-distorted reason by allowing ourselves to be subjected to the philosophies of unbelievers? Are not all postmodern thinkers relativists who reject the notion of absolute truth? Most importantly, doesn't the New Testament warn against "hollow and deceptive philosophy" (Col. 2:8, NIV) and "irreverent babble and contradictions of what is falsely called 'knowledge'" (1 Tim. 6:20b)?

Let me try to alleviate some of these concerns by assuring readers that the truthfulness and reality-depicting nature of Scripture and Christian doctrine is of the utmost concern for me. I have enough "modern" (or common sense) in me to know that theology without a robust means of explicating "the way things are" is a pretty futile exercise. "God-talk" not grounded in divine realities is as existentially and practically useful as catching up on *Downton Abbey* or *The Walking Dead* spoilers at the office water-cooler. Such chatter may be amusing and even emotionally satisfying, but it is also a way of wasting everyone's time at work. The question of God-talk will be the central theme in chapter 6, but for the moment, it is important to advise more skittish readers against informal fallacies such as *guilt by association* or the *genetic fallacy* that would cause them to discount these postmodern thinkers altogether because of some of their conclusions or the philosophical company that they keep. These are types of *ad hominem* ("against the person") fallacies that result in a failure to take other voices in the conversation seriously, and worst still, in the language of the Christian tradition, are *a priori* refusals to see the others with different perspectives as those created in the image of God and endowed with common grace.

A theological assumption that undergirds this entire project, and one that I believe enables truly interdisciplinary conversations between the church and the academy, is a simple premise, oft repeated but too often ignored in evangelicalism: all truth belongs to God.[39] Truth is—forgive the tautology—truth, no matter who ascribes to it or verbalizes it. The Christian apologist in me believes it important to have a two-way conversation if we are going to have a hearing in proclaiming and defending the faith. If there are truths found in non-Christian sources, they will ultimately reflect the supreme truth we believe to be exclusively available in the gospel of Christ.[40] Moreover, if the gospel is true, it can stand on its own two feet in the face of any intellectual adversity. Though they often come from those who are ambivalent about or even hostile to the faith, many of the valuable insights from contemporary hermeneutical theory stem from the common grace and general revelation given by God to all of humanity.

There is, nevertheless, an important place for a theological criticism shaped by the authority of Scripture to correct or amend the trajectories that some of these thinkers take with the truth that they have from general revelation or common grace. Human beings are more than the sum of the true propositions they hold, and people often hold worldviews that are counterintuitive to the truths they do possess. Gadamer, Wittgenstein, and Austin have some very helpful things to say about the way we read texts and use language, but they also have fundamentally different world pictures. For that reason, where there is helpful insight from the God-given common grace in

---

39. ICBI, "The Chicago Statement on Biblical Hermeneutics," Article XX.
40. ICBI, "The Chicago Statement on Biblical Hermeneutics," Article XXI.

contemporary hermeneutical theory, evangelicals should cautiously embrace it. Paul's admonition to Thessalonian Christians about prophecy appears applicable to the semblances of truth found in the non-believing academy: "Do not despise prophecies, but *test everything* and *hold fast to what is good*. Reject everything evil" (1 Thess. 5:20–22). [Evangelicals also recognize that our aim is not knowledge for knowledge's sake. Our academic exercises should have the ultimate end of glorifying God](1 Cor. 10:31).

Philosophy can be a vital means to accessing public and shared truth, but such recognition need not result in its uncritical usage. Philosophy and special revelation often have overlapping spheres of ideas. As Thomas Aquinas (c. 1225–1274) explains, the truths of reason never contradict special revelation, though such revelation often goes beyond the limits of human reasoning.[41] But philosophy divorced from a theistic framework is an assault on reason and its source. Philosophical hermeneutics isolated from revelation is incapable of adequately describing the human experience, because, as even as hermeneutical philosophers admit, their human finitude makes complete self-understanding impossible.[42] This hermeneutical observation is itself consistent with the Christian theological tradition. As Calvin observes, "It is certain that man never achieves a clear knowledge of himself unless he has first looked upon God's face, and then descends from contemplating him to scrutinize himself."[43] Blaise Pascal (1623–1662) offers similar wisdom in his *Pensées*: "Not

---

41. Thomas Aquinas, *Summa Theologica* I, q. 1, a. 1. For example, one can reasonably argue their way to the existence of God, but it is only through special revelation that one can known about God's acts in history or the Trinity.

42. As Jean Grondin, Gadamer's biographer and one of his most reliable expositors, summarized his program, "the whole of Gadamer's philosophy serves to remind us . . . that we are not gods, but human beings." Jean Grondin, *The Philosophy of Gadamer*, trans. Kathryn Plant (Montreal: McGill University Press, 2003), 116.

43. John Calvin, *Institutes of the Christian Religion*, 1.1.

only is it through Jesus Christ alone that we know God, but it is only through Jesus Christ that we know ourselves."[44]

Doctrinal Development and Theological Interpretation

While general hermeneutics provides valuable insight into the relationship between texts and readers, critical reflection on the relationship between Scripture and doctrine entails a more focused examination on how Christians read the sacred texts of the church. The fledgling academic discipline of theological hermeneutics or the theological interpretation of Scripture—a marriage of biblical interpretation, hermeneutical theory, and theology—seeks to serve that role. Though the movement is not without its evangelical critics,[45] it does have the potential to give evangelicals insight into their reading practices and the nature of doctrinal development. The terms *theological hermeneutics* and *theological interpretation of Scripture* can be used interchangeably but can also mean two different things: (1) a theological shaped theory of textual interpretation and (2) a theologically-motivated reading of Scripture.

Advocates of "theological interpretation of Scripture" (hereafter, TIS) believe that God is the primary subject matter of Scripture and that the Bible belongs primarily to God's people. TIS advocates want to read the Bible the same way Christians have instinctively read it for two millennia: as the living and active word of God (Heb. 4:12). TIS is not a rejection of critical scholarship per se, nor is it a rejection of the exegetical theology that should have precedence in biblical interpretation. The movement is simply a calling to go beyond the

---

44. Blaise Pascal, *Pensées* 1.36.
45. D. A. Carson, "Theological Interpretation of Scripture: Yes, But . . ." in *Theological Commentary: Evangelical Perspectives*, ed. R. Michael Allen (London: T&T Clark, 2011), 187–207.

mere historical evaluation of biblical texts and to think about the uniqueness of Christian readings of Scripture. More importantly, TIS advocates want to understand and apply the theological content of Scripture in the context of the church because they believe that God is still speaking through these texts. Evangelical TIS advocates in particular are concerned with how we best *apply* the established historical meaning of the text to new settings with new theological and ethical questions.

While evangelical voices have been important voices in the TIS movement, they are certainly not alone in embracing this trend.[46] Academicians from every corner of Western Christianity—charismatic, evangelical, "mainline" Protestant, or Roman Catholic—have joined in the discussion. Some hold to rather traditional views about biblical authorship and the nature of texts, and some are thoroughgoing deconstructionists and/or postcolonialists.[47]

TIS advocates of every confessional stripe share four common points of concern. First, TIS advocates seek to understand the nature

---

46. The past decade has proved to be a fruitful time for scholars working in the area of the theological interpretation of Scripture. Significant monographs in this pioneering field include Werner G. Jeanrond, *Theological Hermeneutics: Development and Significance* (New York: Crossroad, 1991); Stephen E. Fowl, *Engaging Scripture* (Oxford: Blackwell, 1998); Francis Watson, *Text, Church, and World* (Grand Rapids, MI: Eerdmans, 1994); and Nicholas Wolterstorff, *Divine Discourse* (Cambridge: Cambridge University Press, 1995). A few essay collections worth mentioning are Joel B. Green and Max Turner, eds. *Between Two Horizons: Spanning New Testament Studies and Systematic Theology* (Grand Rapids, MI: Eerdmans, 2000); Markus Bockmuehl and Alan J. Torrance, eds., *Scripture's Doctrine and Theology's Bible* (Grand Rapids, MI: Baker, 2007), A. K. M. Adam, Stephen E. Fowl, Kevin J. Vanhoozer, and Francis Watson, *Reading Scripture with the Church* (Grand Rapids, MI: Baker, 2006); Gary T. Meadors, ed., *Four Views on Moving from the Bible to Theology* (Grand Rapids, MI: Zondervan, 2009); Stephen E. Fowl, ed., *Theological Interpretation of Scripture* (Cambridge, MA: Blackwell, 1997), and the eight volumes from the Scripture and Hermeneutics Series (Grand Rapids, MI: Zondervan, 2000–2009).

47. For a sampling of the TIS movement outside of evangelicalism, see George A. Lindbeck, "Postcritical Canonical Interpretation: Three Modes of Retrieval," in *Theological Exegesis: Essays in Honor of Brevard Childs,* ed. Christopher Seitz and Kathryn Green-McCreight (Grand Rapids, MI: Eerdmans, 1999), 26–51; Dale B. Martin, *Pedagogy of the Bible: An Analysis and Proposal* (Louisville: Westminster/John Knox, 2008), 71–91.

and role of biblical discourse in theology and interpret the Bible through the lens of theological discourse.[48] For those outside the academy, this is not a shockingly novel concept. For those outside the academy, this is not a shockingly novel concept. Christians throughout history have read the Bible in order to foster a meaningful relationship with God. TIS supporters simply want to analyze and encourage this practice at an academic level. By encouraging this kind of theological reading, TIS advocates are not necessarily promoting interpretive proof-texting or the reading of a systematic theological framework back into the text. Rather, they express a desire to read the Bible in a manner consistent with ancient and traditional readings, as books with real-world theological concerns written for people who share similar interests and frameworks of belief.

Second, TIS advocates reject the historical-critical method as the dominant hermeneutical paradigm of biblical interpretation.[49] In other words, TIS is an attempt to go beyond the critical study of literary composition and historical backgrounds. This aversion to the supremacy of historical criticism by no means conveys a desire to return to pre-critical or pre-modern methods of interpretation. While historical-critical study is crucial for biblical interpretation, it is certainly not the end goal or even the primary purpose of its authorship. Like Barth before them, whom many TIS representatives

---

48. See Kevin J. Vanhoozer, "Introduction: What Is Theological Interpretation of the Bible?" in *Dictionary for Theological Interpretation of the Bible*, ed. Kevin J. Vanhoozer (Grand Rapids, MI: Baker, 2005), 19–25; Daniel J. Treier, *Introducing Theological Interpretation of Scripture: Recovering a Christian Practice* (Grand Rapids, MI: Baker, 2008); idem, "Theological Hermeneutics, Contemporary," in *Dictionary for Theological Interpretation of the Bible*, ed. Kevin J. Vanhoozer (Grand Rapids, MI: Baker, 2005), 787–93; and J. Todd Billings, *The Word of God for the People of God: An Entryway to the Theological Interpretation of Scripture* (Grand Rapids, MI: Eerdmans, 2010).

49. See Max Turner, "Historical Criticism and Theological Hermeneutics of the New Testament," in *Between Two Horizons: Spanning New Testament Studies and Systematic Theology*, ed. Joel B. Green and Max Turner (Grand Rapids, MI: Eerdmans, 2000), 44–70.

identify as a progenitor of their movement, they understand the importance of critical methods while recognizing the even greater importance of theology as the Bible's subject matter.[50] In his (in)famous theological commentary *The Epistle to the Romans* (rev. ed., 1923), Barth laments that many biblical scholars limit their so-called commentaries to historical-critical remarks about the text without ever commenting on the significance or application of the text for Christian belief. He contends that with historical-critical issues, they have only taken "the first step towards a commentary."[51] Exegesis ending with historical analysis stops short of what biblical authors expect from their readers. TIS advocates believe that the Bible addresses the people of God in Israel and in the church in order that they may know and love this God on a deeper level. The proposed alternative of TIS to historical criticism, which Vanhoozer calls "theological criticism," is a hermeneutical approach to the Bible characterized by a desire to *"enable the church better to hear what God is saying to the church and world today."*[52]

Third, TIS advocates share a desire to reconcile the long-estranged disciplines of biblical studies and systematic theology.[53] The divorce of biblical studies and systematic theology in the late eighteenth century and the overspecialization in research that ensued regrettably resulted in a kind of academic apartheid or disciplinary segregation, even within seminaries, divinity schools, and religion departments. Biblical scholars and theologians may be collegial colleagues, but

50. For more on Barth's theological exegesis, see Daniel J. Treier, *Introducing Theological Interpretation*, 14–20; Richard E. Burnett, *Karl Barth's Theological Exegesis: The Hermeneutical Principles of the Römerbrief Period* (Grand Rapids, MI: Eerdmans, 2004).

51. Karl Barth, *The Epistle to the Romans*, rev. ed., trans. Edwyn C. Hoskyns (New York: Oxford University Press, 1968), 6.

52. Vanhoozer, "Introduction," 22.

53. See Joel B. Green, "Scripture and Theology: Uniting the Two So Long Divided," in *Between Two Horizons: Spanning New Testament Studies and Systematic Theology*, ed. Joel B. Green and Max Turner (Grand Rapids, MI: Eerdmans, 2000), 23–43.

they often seem to be from different planets. They often speak in different scholarly languages and have great difficulty understanding one another. Biblical scholars in particular are suspicious about the way that theologians seem to rush to easy answers or neglect the hard work of history and exegesis. Theologians, by contrast, grow weary of a tendency in biblical scholarship to ignore the unity of the Bible assumed in divine authorship and the inability of many within the field to draw out implications for contemporary readers of Scripture. Biblical theologians charge systematic theologians with forcing their presuppositions and dogmatic categories on the text while theologians counteract by claiming that the Bible guys are often oblivious to their own presuppositions in interpretation. This sort of scholarly trench warfare tends to go on *ad nauseam*.

While some welcome this disciplinary stalemate, others, like TIS advocates, are striving for reconciliation. Even within evangelicalism, there is a temptation for biblical scholars and theologians, equally committed to the normative authority of the Bible, to operate in isolation from and suspicion of one another. Many evangelical theologians believe that their more historically oriented colleagues in biblical studies lack the ability and/or concern to create coherent, contemporary expressions of faith, and many evangelical biblical scholars fear the tendency of systematic theologians to resort to proof-texting and forcing theological frameworks on the text rather than do the hard, slow work of exegesis and historical research.

Taking a page from the playbook of humanities specialists in American universities,[54] TIS advocates see *interdisciplinarity* as a necessary step toward bridging the great divide between systematic

54. For a small sampling of this movement, see Julie Thompson Klein, *Humanities, Culture, and Interdisciplinarity: The Changing American Academy* (New York: State University of New York Press, 2005); idem, *Interdisciplinarity: History, Theory, and Practice* (Detroit: Wayne State University Press, 1991); Joe Moran, *Interdisciplinarity*, The New Critical Idiom (New York: Routledge, 2001).

theology and biblical studies first forged by Johann Philipp Gabler (1753–1826)[55] and later perpetuated by modern biblical scholars such as Krister Stendahl and James Barr.[56] Some scholars take this interdisciplinary effort even further than the relationship between biblical studies and systematic theology. Kevin Vanhoozer, for instance, believes that TIS is a call for *all* theological disciplines—even practical theological fields such as preaching, missions, ethics, Christian counseling, and Christian education—to heed.[57]

Finally, and most importantly for our present concern, TIS advocates frequently employ the insights of the philosophy of language and contemporary hermeneutical theory.[58] The evangelical scholars represented in this book share a commitment to the unique authority of the Bible, even if they frame this belief differently, but they also recognize that the valid insights of reason—whether found in an analytic or a continental philosophical tradition, whether modern or postmodern—can be useful aides in the theological task. A biblically and theologically directed theory of interpretation like that found in the TIS movement offers a substantial dimension that a purely philosophical hermeneutics cannot, because apart from

---

55. See Johann Gabler, "An Oration on the Proper Distinction between Biblical and Dogmatic Theology and the Specific Objectives of Each," in *The Flowering of Old Testament Theology: A Reader in Twentieth-Century Old Testament Theology, 1930-1990*, ed. Ben C. Ollenburger, E. A. Martens, and Gerhard F. Hasel (Winona Lake, IN: Eisenbrauns, 1992), 493–502.

56. See Krister Stendahl, "Biblical Theology, Contemporary," in *Interpreter's Dictionary of the Bible*, ed. G. A. Buttrick, vol. 1 (New York: Abingdon, 1962), 418–32; Ben C. Ollenburger, "What Krister Stendahl 'Meant'—A Normative Critique of 'Descriptive Biblical Theology,'" *HBT* 8 (1986): 61–98; James Barr, *The Bible in the Modern World* (London: SCM, 1973); idem, *The Concept of Biblical Theology: An Old Testament Perspective* (Minneapolis: Fortress Press, 1999).

57. Vanhoozer, "Introduction," 21–22.

58. See Anthony C. Thiselton, "Biblical Studies and Theoretical Hermeneutics," in *The Cambridge Companion to Biblical Interpretation*, ed. John Barton (Cambridge: Cambridge University Press, 1998), 95–113; idem, *Thiselton on Hermeneutics: Collected Works with New Essays* (Grand Rapids, MI: Eerdmans, 2006), 32–50, esp. 36–39; and Kevin J. Vanhoozer, "The Spirit of Understanding: Special Revelation and General Hermeneutics," in *Disciplining Hermeneutics: Interpretation in Christian Perspective*, ed. Roger Lundin (Grand Rapids, MI: Eerdmans, 1997), 131–65.

knowledge of God in Christ, there is no true knowledge of the human condition.

In order to address how hermeneutics can provide explanatory theses for the historical phenomenon of development, we will engage with the works of biblical scholars, systematic theologians, and hermeneutics specialists. At the focus of this analysis are the works of two scholars who have dedicated their respective careers to the implications of hermeneutical theory for biblical studies and Christian theology: Anthony Thiselton and Kevin Vanhoozer. Interaction with contemporary hermeneutical philosophy and the philosophy of language shapes their respective understandings of the nature of doctrine and its usage in the church. Thiselton and Vanhoozer are suitable for this investigation because of (1) their extensive and influential works in hermeneutics and theological prolegomena, (2) their pairing of critical scholarship and a commitment to biblical authority, (3) their mutual concern for the practicality of Christian doctrine, and (4) their shared influence on evangelical academia.

Thiselton and Vanhoozer offer *descriptive* and *normative* options for explicating the phenomenon of doctrinal development. Perhaps at the risk of oversimplifying their respective projects and agendas, Thiselton tends to focus on the descriptive features of theological formation while Vanhoozer more readily highlights the normative dimension. Neither provides a step-by-step process for how doctrine should develop. The descriptive aspects of a hermeneutics of development demonstrate how later formulations of doctrine *can* retain continuity with an earlier tradition. The normative aspects of a hermeneutics of development highlight *how* and *why*. Before we approach their respective models of theological interpretation and evaluate their significance for doctrinal development, we will explore the history of the problem, highlighting the hermeneutical qualities of past treatments.

2

Historical Consciousness, Development, and Hermeneutics

Doctrinal development may be an inevitable, even essential element of the theological task as it has been practiced for nearly two millennia, but explicit theoretical reflection on the nature of this phenomenon is a relatively recent feature in Christian thought. The history of evangelical attention to the problem of development is much shorter, because, as we shall see, Roman Catholic theologians began addressing the issue much earlier than their Protestant and evangelical counterparts. The study of general hermeneutics or hermeneutical theory, a discipline concerned with understanding the relationship between interpreters and texts (i.e., written texts or any other complex aggregate of signs employed in interpersonal communication), also has a short history, and as is the case with the history of the development problem, evangelicals were tardy to the discussion.

A detailed historical account of either hermeneutics or the problem of doctrinal development is far beyond the scope of the present study.[1] Space mandates sidestepping many important contributions to these fields. Furthermore, some studies of doctrinal development devote much space to the cataloging of various models of development, such as Jan Walgrave's oft-cited typology of logical theories, transformistic theories, and theological theories.[2] Such typologies can be heuristically and pedagogically useful, but they also tend to subject these theories to hermetically sealed categories which reflect the biases of their architects and which are often alien to the intentions of the theologians they describe. For these reasons, no such typology appears in this historical outline.

The purpose of the present chapter is to survey hermeneutical features in a few notable theories of doctrinal development throughout three stages of the history of the problem: pre-critical approaches from early medieval Christianity to the Protestant and Catholic Reformations, nineteenth-century approaches following the rise of historical consciousness, and twentieth-century approaches

1. A few comprehensive histories of the theory of doctrinal development worth noting are Owen Chadwick, *From Bossuet to Newman*, 2nd ed. (Cambridge: Cambridge University Press, 1987); Jan Hendrik Walgrave, *Unfolding Revelation: The Nature of Doctrinal Development* (Philadelphia: Westminster, 1972); and Aidan Nichols, *From Newman to Congar: The Idea of Doctrinal Development from the Victorians to the Second Vatican Council* (Edinburgh: T&T Clark, 1990). Helpful introductory histories of hermeneutics include Josef Bleicher, *Contemporary Hermeneutics: Hermeneutics as Method, Philosophy and Critique* (London: Routledge, 1980); Jean Grondin, *Introduction to Philosophical Hermeneutics*, trans. Joel Weinsheimer (New Haven: Yale University Press, 1994); Richard E. Palmer, *Hermeneutics* (Evanston, IL: Northwestern University Press, 1969); David Jasper, *A Short Introduction to Hermeneutics* (Louisville: Westminster/John Knox, 2004); Anthony C. Thiselton, *New Horizons in Hermeneutics*; idem, *Hermeneutics: An Introduction* (Grand Rapids, MI: Eerdmans, 2009).

2. Walgrave, *Unfolding Revelation*, 135–347. A more recent and more refined typology appears in Rolf J. Pöhler, *Continuity and Change in Christian Doctrine: A Study of the Problem of Doctrinal Development*, Friedensauer Schriftenreihe, Reihe A: Theologie, Band 2 (Berlin: Peter Lang, 1999), 51–116. Pöhler (b. 1949) applies the typology he develops to his own Adventist tradition in *Continuity and Change in Adventist Teaching*, Friedensauer Schriftenreihe, Reihe A: Theologie, Band 3 (Berlin: Peter Lang, 2000). See also John E. Thiel, *Senses of Tradition: Continuity and Development in Catholic Faith* (Oxford: Oxford University Press, 2000), 57–76.

since the Second Vatican Council. Roman Catholic theologians have dominated this conversation historically, and many of the representative Protestant and evangelical approaches to the topic have been reactionary. In this chapter, many features common to critical studies in hermeneutics and doctrinal development will be observed, as conscious, critical reflection on each of these issues shares a common ancestry in the impact of Romanticism and post-Enlightenment historicism on biblical and theological studies. The history of the problem of development shows that its theorists, like philosophers of hermeneutics, mostly wrestle with questions about the nature of historical understanding and interpretation.

Hermeneutics and Development
in Pre-Critical Approaches

Some of the most noteworthy and most universally recognized examples of postcanonical doctrinal development appeared during the first five centuries of Christianity. Amid centuries of theological, political, and social turmoil, the church developed the confessional statements that came to be associated with "orthodoxy" (or "right belief"). The parameters of the Christian canon were drawn, and the traditional doctrines of the Trinity and the two natures of Christ were established. Yet it was only in retrospect that Christian theologians started reflecting on the nature of these historical developments or the growth of Christian doctrine.

Before the advent of historical criticism in the nineteenth century, there were two basic approaches to the phenomenon of development. One approach, seen throughout medieval theology, was a growing awareness of the need to defend the ecclesial interpretation of doctrine and the authoritative role of extracanonical tradition. Medieval theologians were greatly concerned about advancing their understanding of the Christian faith and assumed that doctrinal development was essentially the "unpacking" of fixed biblical truth. Historical theologian Malcolm Yarnell calls this the "classic thesis."[3] Another approach, represented by Protestant and Roman Catholic voices during the Reformation and post-Reformation era, was to deny any true development in the history of the church. Reformers on both sides seemed to take one step forward and two steps back, as they simultaneously acknowledged the need for ecclesial reformation and theological critique but also denied the historical phenomena of a growing tradition. Approaches to development in the pre-critical era generally regard true doctrine as *immutable* or unchanging.

Early and Medieval Theology

The anathematization of Nestorianism at the First Council of Ephesus (431) was a recent memory when the Gallic monk Vincent of Lérins (d. 445 C.E.) penned his *Commonitorium* (or "memory aid"). In this classic work on theological method, Vincent defends the church's authoritative tradition over against what he perceives to be the doctrinal innovations of heretics. Vincent does not address the particular theological issues that concern him, though some have suggested he is responding to the pessimistic theological anthropology and predestinarianism of Augustine of Hippo (354–430).[4] Although he warns against excessive theological speculation, Vincent insists that individual Christians and the entire

---

3. See Malcolm B. Yarnell III, *The Formation of Christian Doctrine* (Nashville: Broadman & Holman, 2007), 107–13.

4. See Karl Barth, *Church Dogmatics* vol. 1, no. 2, *The Doctrine of the Word of God*, trans. G. T. Thomson and Harold Knight (Edinburgh: T&T Clark, 1956), 550; Jaroslav Pelikan, *The Emergence f the Catholic Tradition (100-600)*, The Christian Tradition 1 (Chicago: University of Chicago Press, 1971), 333. For an evaluation of arguments for and against this position, see Thomas G. Guarino, *Vincent of Lérins and the Development of Christian Doctrine* (Grand Rapids, MI: Baker, 2013), xxii–xxvi.

church alike should progress in their understandings of doctrine: "There should be a great increase and a vigorous progress, in individuals and in the whole group, in the single man as well as in the entire church, as the ages and centuries march on, of understanding, knowledge, wisdom, but, at least in its own kind, in the same doctrine, that is, in the same sense, in the same meaning."[5]

For Vincent, doctrinal progress does not mean transformation of the gospel's essence; it means organic, continuity-preserving growth in knowledge of divine truth. In the same way that a human being retains his or her identity from infancy through childhood into adulthood and old age while growing and maturing, so too "the doctrine of the Christian religion must follow the laws of progress, so as to be strengthened by the years, amplified by time, grow taller with age, yet remain uncorrupted and unimpaired, complete and perfect in . . . its proper senses, permitting . . . no change, no wasting of its distinctive character, no variation in its outline."[6] This analogy from anthropological identity is the first of many like it in the history of the problem of doctrinal development.

Vincent likewise compares the development of doctrine to the process by which seedlings sown are cultivated, nurtured, blossomed, and ripened. This growth is appropriate as long as there is no essential transformation: "It is right that those ancient doctrines . . . should in the progress of time be given complete care, be refined, polished, but it is wrong for them to be changed . . . to be mutilated, to be marred. Let them get proof, illumination, definition, but they still must retain their fullness, their integrity, their natural characteristics."[7]

---

5. Vincent of Lérins *The Commonitory* §23.28. This translation appears in George E. McCracken and Allen Cabaniss, eds., *Early Medieval Theology*, The Library of Christian Classics 9 (Philadelphia: Westminster, 1957), 69.

6. Vincent of Lérins *The Commonitory* §23.29; McCracken and Cabaniss, 70.

7. Vincent of Lérins *The Commonitory* §23.30; McCracken and Cabaniss, 71. Jerome (c. 347–420) offers a similar illustration in his commentary on the parable of the mustard seed (*Comm. in Matt.*). See also Walgrave, *Unfolding Revelation*, 85–86.

Vincent maintains that the biblical canon is "complete" and "sufficient for every purpose" but notes that there is need for the church to interpret Scripture as safeguard against the various interpretive errors of heretics. His defense of postcanonical doctrinal development is explicitly hermeneutical: "By its very depth the Holy Scripture is not received by all in one and the same sense, but its declarations are subject to interpretation, now in one way, now in another, so that, it would appear, we can find almost as many interpretations as there are men."[8] So how should believers discriminate between doctrines that are the result of spurious heretical innovation and those that are genuine developments? Vincent formulates his well-known rule for biblical interpretation and doctrinal evaluation: "We hold to that which has been believed everywhere, always, and by all people" (*quod ubique, quod semper, quod ab omnibus creditum est*).[9] This threefold test for orthodoxy, which Thomas Oden calls the "classic ecumenical method," evaluates doctrinal teaching on the basis of its usage in cross-cultural space (universality), across intergenerational time (antiquity), and its development through fair deliberation among believers (consensus).[10] Well over a millennium later, the Vincentian rule would become a major catalyst in the discussion of doctrinal development.

After Vincent, most medieval theologians did not give special attention to the problem of development. Many medieval developments, however, would contribute to future discussions. Anselm's (c. 1033–1109) method of "faith seeking understanding" (*fides quaerens intellectum*) *would shape Roman Catholic responses to*

---

8. Vincent of Lérins *The Commonitory* §2.2; McCracken and Cabaniss, 38.

9. Vincent of Lérins *The Commonitory* §2.3. For the explicit application of this rule to the interpretation of Scripture, see §§24.33–25.40.

10. For Oden's contemporary evaluation of Vincent's rule and the *Commonitorium*, see Thomas C. Oden, *The Rebirth of Orthodoxy: Signs of New Life in Christianity* (San Francisco: HarperCollins, 2003), 156–86; cf. Vincent of Lérins *The Commonitory* §2.3.

development in the nineteenth century.[11] *Many medieval theologians during this time became aware of discrepancies in the theological tradition, especially when* collections of early Christian writings began to appear. Collections of canon law, such as *Concordia Discordantium Canonum* by the twelfth-century Benedictine jurist Gratian (d. 1179), were attempts to harmonize these contradictory statements of the fathers and the councils.[12] The acknowledgement of discrepancies in the tradition showed cracks in the foundation of an allegedly immutable tradition and demonstrated not all within orthodoxy shared beliefs held "everywhere, always, and by all."

The Protestant and Catholic Reformations

Development became a critical issue again during the Protestant and Catholic Reformations, when Protestants and Catholics alike accused one another of corrupting the apostolic depository. Martin Luther (1483–1546) challenged the Catholic narrative of developing doctrine by arguing that if true doctrine is immutable and apostolic, as suggested by Vincent's rule, then it seems unnecessary to go beyond the apostolic writings found in Scripture.[13] Luther's most explicit treatment of development is in his 1539 pamphlet "On the Councils and the Churches" (*Von den Consiliis und Kirchen*), in which Luther provides his assessment of the first four ecumenical councils

---

11. Recently, some scholars have explored the implicit issue of theological development in the works of Thomas Aquinas. See Christopher Kaczor, "Thomas Aquinas and the Development of Doctrine," *Theological Studies* 62 (2001): 283–302.

12. See Gratian, *The Treatise on the Laws* (with *The Ordinary Gloss*), Studies in Medieval and Early Modern Canon Law, no. 2, trans. Augustine P. Thompson and James Gordley (Washington, DC: Catholic University of America Press, 1993). See also Luther, "On the Councils and the Church," 21. Luther contended that the "paper-clippers" [*Papirklicker*] who collected these harmonies were uncritical ("when they think that whatever they read and imagine must be so") and biblically and theologically illiterate (as "they neither know the *a-b-c*['s] of Scripture, nor are they versed in the councils and the fathers.").

13. Yarnell, 111.

and his own views on the nature of the church. Luther here rails against the necessity of conciliar authority. In part one, Luther judges the propriety of ecumenical councils and surmises that the decrees of councils and church fathers were insufficient for reforming the church. In part two, he evaluates the first four ecumenical councils, from Nicaea to Chalcedon. Luther concludes the volume with an exposition detailing the biblical concept of the church in part three.

Luther believes the first four ecumenical councils were helpful when *restating* apostolic belief in the face of heretical opposition but ineffective (and often contradictory) in establishing binding authoritative precedents. While most contemporary Protestant and evangelical scholars cite Nicaea as a clear example of the doctrinal development within Christianity, Luther himself rejected any such idea out of hand:

> No council ever did it or can do it; the articles of faith must not grow on earth through the councils, as from a new, secret inspiration, but must be issued from heaven through the Holy Spirit and revealed openly; otherwise, as we shall hear later, they are not articles of faith. Thus the Council of Nicaea (as was said) did not invent this doctrine or establish it as something new, namely, that Christ is God; rather, it was done by the Holy Spirit. . . . It remained unchanged since the days of the apostles until this council, and so on until our own day—it will remain until the end of the world.[14]

Here Luther explicitly rejects the possibility of positive development. All postcanonical developments are corruptions of the apostolic depository.

The original champion of *sola scriptura* is often naïve about the way tradition colors his own thinking. For example, he propounds that the fundamental mistake of both Nestorius (c. 386–451) and

---

14. Martin Luther, "On the Councils and the Church," trans. Charles M. Jacobs and Eric W. Gritsch, in *Luther's Works*, vol. 41, ed. Jaroslav Pelikan (Philadelphia: Fortress Press, 1966), 58.

Eutyches (c. 380–456) was their rejection of the doctrine of the "communication of attributes" (*communicatio idiomatum*) between the two natures of Christ.[15] Of course, such judgment seems premature, as this medieval doctrine was the result of conscious reflection on the Chalcedonian definition of the hypostatic union, which of course developed in response to Nestorius and Eutyches. Nonetheless, Luther assumes that this doctrine is axiomatic and can be discovered simply through a *plain reading of Scripture*. For the Reformer, the Council of Ephesus's pronouncement on *Theotokos* was not so much a development as much as it was a simple affirmation of biblical truth (Luke 1:23, 43; 2:11; Gal. 4:4).[16] The council "only defended the old faith against the new notion of Nestorius" and no one—especially those claiming conciliar or papal authority—can "take any examples from it" that "give the councils authority to establish new or different articles of faith." In Luther's estimation, true doctrine is fixed and immutable; it has "remained unchanged" since the apostolic era.[17]

---

15. Ibid., 100–1. An *idioma* is an attribute inherent in a nature. *Idiomatum* in human nature include death, suffering, sadness, speech, humor, eating, drinking, having a mother and a father, sleeping, working, and the like. *Idiomatum* in the divine nature include eternality, aseity, omnipotence, omniscience, omnibenevolence, holiness, etc. For Luther, the doctrine of the *communicatio idiomatum* means that an *idioma* describing the human nature of Christ likewise describes his divine nature and vice versa. For this reason, Luther affirmed the propriety of the term *Theotokos*, because if God and man truly are united in one person, everything that can be said about the human nature of Jesus also can be said of his divine nature. Luther adds, "Mary is the true natural mother of the child called Jesus Christ, and that she is the true mother of God and bearer of God, and whatever else can be said of children's mothers, such as suckling, bathing, feeding—that Mary suckled God, rocked God to sleep, prepared broth and soup for God, etc."

16. Luther, "On the Councils and the Church," 101, cf. 105. Luther cited 1 Cor. 2:8 as a biblical affirmation of this description. Luther does note that too much emphasis was put on Mariological concerns at this council because the primary issue is christological and pertains to the doctrine of *communicatio idiomatum*. Luther believes that the council also should have resolved "that Pilate and the Jews were the crucifiers and murderers of God." The term *Theotokos* initially was intended to affirm the deity of Jesus but gradually became an honorific title for Mary. See Harold O. J. Brown, *Heresies: The Image of Christ in the Mirror of Heresy and Orthodoxy* (Grand Rapids, MI: Baker, 1988), 173.

17. Luther, "On the Councils and the Church," 105.

Some Catholic Reformers (or Counter-Reformers) made very similar cases for doctrinal immutability but pronounced that Protestants, not Roman Catholics, were the ones who were truly guilty of transforming the articles of faith. In his 1688 anti-Protestant polemic *A History of the Changes in Protestant Churches* (*Histoire des variations des Églises Protestantes*), Jacques-Bénigne Bossuet (1627–1704), then the bishop of Meaux, concretized Vincent's rule with this provocative slogan:

> The Church's doctrine is always the same (*semper eadem*). . . . The Gospel is never different from what it was before. Hence, if at any time someone says that the faith includes something which yesterday was not said to be of the faith, it is always *heterodoxy*, which is any doctrine different from *orthodoxy*. There is no difficulty about recognizing false doctrine: there is no argument about it: it is recognized at once, whenever it appears, merely because it is new.[18]

Bossuet contrasted the array of divergent Protestant sects of the late seventeenth century with his vision of a unified, monolithic Roman Church and alleged that Protestant variations of doctrine were indicators of corruption in the Church's received, static tradition.[19] Bossuet, like his *bête noire* Luther before him, would challenge any positive notion of doctrinal development aside from the logical inference or explication of what is already established in revelation.

Bossuet considers the Catholic Church faithful to Scripture and the Church's interpretation of Scripture necessary for preventing

---

18. Jacques-Bénigne Bossuet, *Première Instruction Pastorale sur les promesses de l'Eglise* 28, *Oeuvres complètes de Bossuet* 22 (Besançon, 1815), 418–19; quoted in Chadwick, *From Bossuet to Newman*, 17.

19. Chadwick, *From Bossuet to Newman*, 5–6. Recently Bossuet's Roman Catholic defenders have challenged Chadwick's portrait of Bossuet as overconfident and unwavering to the notion of development through ecclesial consensus, arguing that it is far too dependent upon *Histoire des variations des Églises Protestantes*. See Richard F. Costigan, "Bossuet and the Consensus of the Church," *Theological Studies* 56 (1995): 652–72.

doctrinal corruption. The bishop describes the relationship between heresy and orthodoxy in hermeneutical terms:

> When our opponents would like to look at things in a more humanly way, they would be forced to admit that the Catholic Church, far from wishing to become a mistress of her [doctrines], as they have accused, has, on the contrary, done everything in her power to bind her hands, and to deprive herself of the means of innovation. For she not only submits to Holy Scripture, but in order to banish for ever these arbitrary interpretations, which would substitute Scripture for men's fleeting thoughts, she has committed herself to interpret it, especially in regards to [doctrines] and morals, in the same way as the Holy Fathers, to whom she professes fidelity. . . . [She declares fidelity] by all the Councils, and by all the professions of faith which she has published, that she receives no doctrine which is not consistent with the tradition of all the preceding centuries.

Doctrinal corruption is the product of the "arbitrary interpretations" of individual readers, and the Church alone is capable of interpreting Scripture faithfully.[20]

Whether Catholic or Protestant, many of these pre-critical theologians assumed that true doctrine was immutable in nature. These theologians failed to acknowledge the way in which their places in time and history influenced their interpretations of the Christian tradition. Neither Luther nor Bossuet could anticipate the way in which critical historical methodology and advances in hermeneutics would spell certain change for the understanding of history, doctrine, and biblical interpretation.

---

20. Jacques-Bénigne Bossuet, *Exposition de la doctrine de L'église Catholique sur les matières de controverse* (Paris, 1686), 187–89.

Hermeneutics and Development
in the Nineteenth Century

Critical studies in hermeneutics and the problem of doctrinal development emerged in the ideological fallout of the Enlightenment and within the context of "Romanticism." Romanticism, much like "postmodernism," is notoriously difficult to define. As one of its most significant early representatives, Friedrich Schlegel (1772–1829) once opined in a letter to his brother and fellow romanticist, August Wilhelm Schlegel (1767–1845): "I cannot send you my explanation of the word 'romantic' because it would be 125 sheets long."[21] Contemporary critical theorists observe that "attempts to summarize Romanticism inevitably end up over-systematising and simplifying the phenomenon."[22] It is sufficient for our purposes to say that discontent with rationalism and the mechanistic worldview that dominated eighteenth-century natural sciences resulted in the rise of numerous romantic movements across Europe. These broad-sweeping movements affected architecture, art, history, literature,

---

21. Frederick C. Beiser, *Enlightenment, Revolution, and Romanticism: The Genesis of Modern German Political Thought 1790–1800* (Cambridge, MA: Harvard University Press, 1992), 410 n. 67.

22. Aidan Day, *Romanticism*, The New Critical Idiom (Oxford: Routledge, 1996), 5. See also Arthur O. Lovejoy, *Essays in the History of Ideas* (Baltimore: John Hopkins University Press, 1948), 228–53. In a seminal 1924 article, Arthur Oncken Lovejoy (1873–1962), the progenitor of contemporary history of ideas studies, observed the seemingly countless ways literary historians and philosophers describe the history, nature, and character of "Romanticism." Lovejoy garnered much controversy when he gave a virtual cease-and-desist order to scholars using the term to describe a single, monolithic movement spread throughout Europe. The term is used best in the plural to describe numerous movements, not merely variations of the same philosophy drawn by geopolitical boundaries. Lovejoy, however, suggests limiting the term's use to those figures who describe themselves with it. He contends that the late eighteenth- and early nineteenth-century movement of German idealists is "the only one which has an indisputable title to be called Romanticism, since it invented the term for its own use" (235). The term "Romanticisms" is used here in the plural sense to describe reactionary sentiments to Enlightenment rationalism common to the German idealists and Victorian-era theologians, which in turn resulted in critical reflection on the nature of understanding (hermeneutics) and doctrinal development.

music, philosophy, politics, and theology, thus revitalizing the humanities.

Against this backdrop, Friedrich Schleiermacher "deregionalized" hermeneutics—moving "the art of understanding" out of the realm of biblical exegesis and whatever auxiliary function it served for other fields of study into its own distinct philosophical discipline.[23] Schleiermacher's theological methodology and study in hermeneutics had a strong influence on early German Catholic discussions of doctrinal development. A romantic spirit similar to but not directly linked to the German Romantic *Geist* imbued certain Victorian-era theologians as they clamored for an Anglo-Catholic revival, the movement from which sprang the most prominent theologian in the history of the problem of development, the British theologian John Henry Newman.[24]

Attention to development and hermeneutics is a product of the rise of "historical consciousness" (*geschichtliches Bewußtsein*) in the nineteenth century.[25] Whereas the Enlightenment of the seventeenth

23. "Deregionalisation" is Paul Ricoeur's terminology for Schleiermacher's move toward general (as opposed to special or biblical) hermeneutics. See Paul Ricoeur, *Hermeneutics and the Human Sciences: Essays on Language, Action and Interpretation*, ed. and trans. John B. Thompson (New York: Cambridge University Press, 1981), 43–48.

24. For an evaluation of the impact of English Romanticism on the Anglo-Catholic revival, see Michael H. Bright, "English Literary Romanticism and the Oxford Movement," *Journal of the History of Ideas* 40 (1979): 385–404. The standard treatment of English Romanticism, highlighting features distinctive from the continental movement, is Marilyn Gaull, *English Romanticism: The Human Context* (New York: W. W. Norton, 1988).

25. Philosophers of history continue to vary considerably in their usage of this term, as some consider it simply to be the "collective memory" of the past while others, such as Gadamer, use it to describe consciousness of our own historicity and the relativity of our beliefs. For an examination of this debate, see Peter C. Seixas, "Introduction," in *Theorizing Historical Consciousness*, ed. Peter C. Sexias (Toronto: University of Toronto Press, 2004), 5–10; cf. idem, "Collective Memory, History Education, and Historical Consciousness," in *Recent Themes in Historical Thinking: Historians in Conversation*, ed. Donald A. Yerxa (Columbia: University of South Carolina Press, 2008), 28–34. Seixas accuses the latter position of an implicit Eurocentrism that favors Western critical ideology over and against other forms of communal memory and practice. Gadamer gives explicit attention to his definition in Hans-Georg Gadamer, "The Problem of Historical Consciousness," trans. Jeff L. Close, *Graduate Faculty Philosophy Journal* 5 (1975): 8–52.

and eighteenth centuries had profound effects on the natural sciences, politics, and philosophy, it was the "rise" of historical consciousness in the nineteenth that produced both an explicit awareness of the historical particularities of past and present and a critical methodological stance toward the sources and subject matter of history. History, in the sense of written history, emerged as a reflective science focusing on the course of human events by means of the critical evaluation of evidence. [26]

With this newfound approach to history came "a determination to seek the truth for its own sake and not for the sake of demonstrating some preconceived dogmatic opinion."[27] The two figures most often associated with the rise of the historical consciousness are Johann Herder (1744–1803) and Leopold von Ranke (1795–1886). Herder sought to produce a critical history, independent of received tradition. Von Ranke took this initiative one step further and encouraged history as an objective science capable of describing history as it actually occurred.

Just as this historical revolution breathed new life into the critical study of history, so too did this historical revolution have enormous consequence for the emergence of hermeneutical theory. Gadamer asserts that this rise of historical consciousness makes philosophical reflection on hermeneutics possible:

> It seems, rather, to be generally characteristic of the emergence of the "hermeneutical" problem that something *distant* has to be brought close, a certain strangeness overcome, a bridge built between the once and the now. Thus hermeneutics, as a general attitude over against

26. See R. G. Collingwood, *The Idea of History*, rev. ed. (Oxford: Oxford University Press, 1993), 7–13.
27. Alan Richardson, *The Bible in the Age of Science* (London: SCM, 1961), 54–55. This critical approach often resulted in an anti-dogmatic position, as illustrated in the various *Leben von Jesu* of the First Quest of the Historical Jesus. See Robert B. Stewart, *The Quest of the Hermeneutical Jesus: The Impact of Hermeneutics on the Jesus Research of John Dominic Crossan and N. T. Wright* (Lanham, MD: University Press of America, 2008), 9–16.

the world, came into its own in modern times, which had become aware of the temporal distance separating us from antiquity and of the relativity of the life-worlds of different cultural traditions. . . . Its true unfolding only came about when a "historical consciousness" arose in the Enlightenment . . . and matured in the romantic period to establish a relationship (however broken) to our entire inheritance from the past.[28]

Historical consciousness is no less important for special or biblical hermeneutics, as an awareness of the "pastness of the past" is necessary for understanding the worlds of difference between the worlds of Jesus and Paul and those of contemporary interpreters.[29]

Historical consciousness is also crucial to the problem of doctrinal development, as there can no such "problem" without it.[30] With regard to the relatively new awareness of the problem of development, Walgrave points out that

> problems about facts do not arise *ante factum*. Development of doctrine could not present itself to the Christian mind as a problem as long as time had not created a sufficient distance from the epoch of beginnings and nothing had happened that could invite a reflection. . . . The idea of a post-apostolic development of doctrine did not [and could not] emerge into consciousness except after a sufficient lapse of time and under the stress of relevant circumstances.[31]

---

28. Hans-Georg Gadamer, *Philosophical Hermeneutics*, 2nd ed., trans. and ed. David E. Linge (Berkeley: University of California Press, 2008), 22–23. One could argue that Gadamer's entire hermeneutical program, especially in his notion of the "historically effected consciousness" (*wirkungsgeschichtliches Bewußtsein*), is a response to the (mis)use of the historical consciousness by historicists such as Wilhelm Dilthey (1833–1911). See Jean Grondin, *The Philosophy of Gadamer*, trans. Kathryn Plant (Montreal: McGill-Queen's University Press, 2002), 66–70.

29. Anthony C. Thiselton, *The Two Horizons: New Testament Hermeneutics and Philosophical Description with Special Reference to Heidegger, Bultmann, Gadamer, and Wittgenstein* (Carlisle: Paternoster, 1980), 51–53. This observation is foundational to contemporary social-scientific studies of the New Testament, such as the work produced by the Context Group. See Bruce J. Malina, *The New Testament World: Insights from Cultural Anthropology*, 3d ed. (Louisville: Westminster/John Knox, 2001); Richard L. Rohrbaugh, ed., *The Social Sciences and New Testament Interpretation* (Grand Rapids, MI: Baker, 2003).

30. Pöhler, *Continuity and Change in Christian Doctrine*, 29–31.

31. Walgrave, *Unfolding Revelation*, 65–66.

The recognition of religious plurality by philosophers of religion such as Wilfred Cantwell Smith is likewise possible because of this historical consciousness.[32]

The Development Theory of Johann Sebastian von Drey

The historical revolution of the nineteenth century had a relativizing effect on religion in general, but Catholic intellectuals especially felt the burden of this new emphasis on historical criticism. This newfound historical awareness and attention to historical method seemed to affirm what Protestants had been claiming all along: several uniquely Roman Catholic doctrines and practices (e.g., the sacramental system, purgatory, the veneration of Mary and the saints, etc.) developed long after the close of the apostolic era.[33] Consequently, many early nineteenth-century Catholic thinkers came to an ideological crossroads. For these thinkers, the choice was either to concede to Protestant historical critics—effectively downplaying distinctively Catholic doctrines and praxis and producing a new, liberal Catholicism—or to retreat into some kind of fideistic isolationism. Some Catholic theologians, such as Johann Sebastian von Drey (1777–1853), the founder of the so-called

---

32. George A. Lindbeck, *The Nature of Doctrine* (Louisville: Westminster/John Knox, 1984), 79, italics mine. Smith details his pluralistic philosophy of religion in Wilfred Cantwell Smith, *The Meaning and End of Religion: A New Approach to the Religious Traditions of Mankind* (New York: Macmillan, 1963).
33. Gustav Voss, "Johann Adam Möhler and the Development of Dogma," *Theological Studies* 4 (1943): 420–21.

"Catholic Tübingen School,"[34] attempted to forge a new way forward that would avert both extremes of liberalism and fideism.

Drey was an apologist, a specialist in theological method, and a pioneer in the critical study of doctrinal development.[35] Sustained engagement with the thinkers of the German Enlightenment (*Aufklärung*)[36] and his own research into the historical development

34. "The Catholic Tübingen School" (*Die Katholische Tübinger Schule*) is the traditional designation for the Catholic theological faculty at the University of Tübingen in the mid-nineteenth century. Initially part of an independent Catholic seminary established in Ellwangen five years earlier, these theologians were transferred to Tübingen in 1817. There Drey and the others, many of whom were once his students at Ellwangen, served alongside the Protestant theological faculty and forged a century-long Catholic theological tradition. Other early members included Johann Baptist von Hirscher (1788–1865); Johannes Evangelist von Kuhn (1806–1887); and Drey's better-known student, Johann Adam Möhler (1796–1838). The majority of critical studies of the Catholic Tübingen School are in German, and the contribution of Josef Rupert Geiselmann (1890–1970) is among the most influential works in this area. See Josef Rupert Geiselmann, "Die Glaubenswissenschaft der katholischen Tübinger Schule in ihrer Grundlegung durch Johann Sebastian v. Drey," *Tübinger Theologische Quartalschrift* 111 (1930): 49–117; idem, *Lebendiger Glaube aus geheiligter Überlieferung: Der Grundgedanke der Theologie J. A. Möhlers und ker katholischen Tübinger Schule* (Freiburg: Herder, 1964); idem, *The Meaning of Tradition*, Quaestiones Disputatae, no. 15, trans. W. J. O'Hara (New York: Herder and Herder, 1962), 39–78. The most thorough treatment of Drey and the Catholic Tübingen School in English is Wayne L. Fehr, *The Birth of the Catholic Tübingen School*, AAR Academy Series, no. 37 (Ann Arbor, MI: American Academy of Religion, 1971). The Catholic Tübingen School is also notably distinct from the Protestant group of the next generation led by Baur and the Old Tübingen School of the previous generation led by rational supernaturalists Gottlob Christian Storr (1746–1805) and Friedrich Gottlieb Süskind (1769–1829). For an excellent introductory survey of Baur's Tübingen School and its significance for biblical and theological studies, see Horton Harris, *The Tübingen School: A Historical and Theological Investigation of the School of F. C. Baur* (Oxford: Clarendon, 1975). The dispute between the second-generation Catholic Tübingen School and Baur's Tübingen School is outlined in Joseph Fitzer, *Möhler and Baur in Controversy, 1832-1838* (Tallahassee, FL: American Academy of Religion, 1974).

35. Drey's primary works include Johann Sebastian Drey, *Die Apologetik als wissenschaftliche Nachweisung der Göttlichkeit des Christentums in seiner Erscheinung*, 3 vols. (Mainz: Fl. Kupferberg, 1838–1847); idem, *Kurze Einleitung in das Studium der Theologie, mit Rücksicht auf den wissenschaftlichen Standpunct und das katholische System* (Tübingen: Heinrich Laupp, 1819). All English translations of *Kurze Einleitung* cited here appear in Johann Sebastian Drey, *Brief Introduction to the Study of Theology with Reference to the Scientific Standpoint and the Catholic System*, Notre Dame Studies in Theology, vol. 1, trans. Michael J. Himes (Notre Dame: University of Notre Dame Press, 1994).

36. As James C. Livingston demonstrates, the early German Enlightenment was very different from its English and French counterparts. See James C. Livingston, *Modern Christian Thought*, vol. 1, *The Enlightenment and the Nineteenth Century* (Minneapolis: Fortress Press, 2006), 28–30, 186–87. The early *Aufklärung* did not yet resemble the atheism of Paul-Henri d'Holbach

of the practice of sacramental confession sparked Drey's interest in the problem of development.[37] Drey also was conversant with the idealistic philosophies of Immanuel Kant (1724–1804), Johann Gottlieb Fichte (1762–1814), Friedrich Wilhelm Schelling (1775–1854), and Georg Wilhelm Friedrich Hegel (1770–1831); but Schleiermacher helped form his understanding of the nature of theology, revelation, history, and hermeneutics.[38]

German Romanticism animated the worldviews of Drey and the Catholic Tübingen School in three particular ways. First, the Catholic Tübingen School shared in the "organicism" popular in Romantic literature. Organicism describes an anti-mechanistic worldview prominent in the Romantic period in general and German idealism in particular. Over and against the popular eighteenth- and nineteenth-century Newtonian worldview that saw all of the universe as an orderly mechanism operating according to discernible natural laws, organicists saw the world more like living organisms—interrelated wholes that cannot be understood by the division of their parts. These metaphors stress the interconnected

(1723–1789) or even the slightly milder religious skepticism of Voltaire (1694–1778). While they were often critical of traditional Christianity and religious naiveté, these German thinkers were not anti-religious. Deism, not atheism, was the predominant religious perspective at work. Perhaps the most considerable difference was epistemological. Whereas many of the thinkers of the English and French Enlightenments gravitated toward the empiricism of John Locke (1632–1704) and David Hume (1711–1776), the German *Aufklärung* was built upon the rationalism of Gottfried Leibniz (1646–1716) and Christian Wolff (1769–1754).

37. See Johann Sebastian von Drey, *Dissertatio Historico-Theologica Originem et Vicissitudinem Exomologeseos in Ecclesiâ Catholicâ ex Documentis Ecclesiasticis Illustrans* (Ellwangen: Typis Johann, Georg Ritter, 1815). Drey not only rejected the Council of Trent's stance that Christ himself instituted the sacrament of private confession; he rejected the practice's apostolicity as well. Despite rejecting its claims to antiquity, Drey believed the practice of private confession is an important part of church discipline that is a result of Spirit-led doctrinal development. Rome later refused Drey the bishopric of Rottenburg partly on the basis of this then-controversial investigation.

38. See Bradford E. Hinze, *Narrating History, Developing Doctrine: Friedrich Schleiermacher and Johann Sebastian Drey* (Atlanta: Scholars Press, 1993). Here Hinze (b. 1954) traces a number of common points between Schleiermacher and Drey in the German Romantic tradition, including Schleiermacher's affective-experiential understanding of religion but central to his thesis is their shared theology of history.

nature of reality, which is beyond mechanical dissection. During this time, organic metaphors became wildly popular in literature, history, philosophy, and theology.[39]

Second, the Catholic Tübingen School shared approaches to religion and religious consciousness similar to the Romantic theology of Schleiermacher.[40] In this scheme religion is viewed primarily as a strong sense of religious affection and an awareness of one's dependence on the divine reality. Theology, then, is not so much an ordering of cognitive propositions as much as it is the task of describing the feelings evoked by this religious consciousness. Third, the Catholic Tübingen School shared an inclination with Romantic writers to relate to the past in an idealized manner.[41]

In order to showcase their own academic freedom and, in turn, create their own unique brand of apologetics for Roman tradition and authority, Drey and the Catholic Tübingen faculty employed many of the same historical-critical methods practiced by their esteemed Protestant colleagues but without capitulating to their often anti-

39. Herder was an early representative of this organicist spirit. See also Johann Gottfried Herder, "Vom Erkennen und Empfinden der menschlichen Seele," *Herders Werke* (Berlin: Aufbau-Verlag, 1982), 3:331–405; idem, *Reflections on the Philosophy of History of Mankind*, trans. F. E. Manuel (Chicago: University of Chicago Press, 1968); Edgar B. Schick, *Metaphorical Organicism in Herder's Early Works: A Study of the Relation of Herder's Literary Idiom to His World-View* (The Hague: Mouton, 1971). A more recent work chronicling the history of organicism from German Idealism to deconstructionism is Charles I. Armstrong, *Romantic Organicism: From Idealist Origins to Ambivalent Afterlife* (New York: Palgrave Macmillan, 2003).

40. See Drey, *Kurze Einleitung*, §§4–11. In a Schleiermachian vein, Drey here defines religion as the "experience and [the] accompanying feeling" of dependence and notes that "the *experience* of connectedness and dependence is not separable from consciousness" (*Kurze Einleitung*, §6; cf. idem, *Brief Introduction*, 2). For Schleiermacher's own exposition of religion as the consciousness of "absolute dependence," see Friedrich D. E. Schleiermacher, *The Christian Faith*, 2nd ed., trans. and ed. H. R. Mackintosh and J. S. Stewart (Edinburgh: T&T Clark, 1928), §§4–6, §§32–35.

41. Chadwick, *From Bossuet to Newman*, 102. German Catholics impacted by Romanticism showed renewed interest in Catholic theology from the Middle Ages. For similar revivals of medieval interest throughout romanticism, see R. R. Agarwal, *The Medieval Revival and Its Influence on the Romantic Movement* (New Delhi: Abhinav, 1990), 154–60. Literary critics often point to the resurgence of the medieval aesthetic—particularly related to architecture, art, and literature—as evidence of this phenomenon, but it also extended to politics and theology.

dogmatic conclusions.[42] Like Schleiermacher and Hegel before him, Drey desired to produce a defense of Christian theology that could withstand the lingering threat of rationalism, which endangered positive religion with a religion of pure reason.[43] *Positive religion* is a term used to describe any religion that is based on what has been "posited" (from the Latin participle *positivus*, meaning "something given") through historical particulars or, in this case, based on revelation. A positive religion such as Christianity is but one among many historically and culturally conditioned forms of natural religion.[44] For Drey, this meant that theology should begin with history, not reason independent of historical accidents, because God is revealed throughout history to the consciousness of humanity.[45] Christianity stands as the most complete positive religion because the incarnation of Christ represents the most complete self-revelation of God.[46] Unlike Schleiermacher, Drey primarily envisioned the apologetic task as defending the "divine positivity" (i.e., the revelatory character) of the Christian faith.[47]

---

42. Chadwick, *From Bossuet to Newman*, 102–3. Chadwick highlights the significance of this apologetic when he says that this period was "the first time Catholic theologians were having to frame a doctrine of authority and tradition which allowed the partial justice of Protestant historical criticism while it denied any theological deductions which Protestants sought to draw from it." See also Fehr, *The Birth of the Catholic Tübingen School*, 127; Drey, *Kurze Einleitung*, §§107–73.

43. Drey describes Christianity as a religion of a "wholly *positive kind*" contingent upon both "historical foundation" and the "immediate intervention by God in the course of religious evolution" (*Kurze Einleitung*, §34; *Brief Introduction*, 14). See also Drey, *Die Apologetik*, vol. 1, §1.

44. See Francis Schüssler Fiorenza, *Foundational Theology: Jesus and the Church* (New York: Crossroad, 1992), 251–64; cf. Hinze, *Narrating History, Developing Doctrine*, 21–30.

45. Johann Sebastian Drey, "Toward the Revision of the Present State of Theology," in *Romance and the Rock: Nineteenth-Century Catholics in Faith and Reason*, Fortress Texts in Modern Theology, ed. and trans. Joseph Fitzer (Minneapolis: Fortress Press, 1989), 70–71; cf. idem, *Kurze Einleitung*, §§107–8. The centrality of history in Christian theological study also appears in Schleiermacher. See Friedrich D. E. Schleiermacher, *Brief Outline of Theology as a Field of Study*, 3d ed., trans. Terrence N. Tice (Louisville: Westminster/John Knox, 2011), 31–35.

46. Drey, *Kurze Einleitung*, §32; idem, *Brief Introduction*, 13.

47. Hinze, *Narrating History, Developing Doctrine*, 143–61, esp. 153–55; cf. Bradford E. Hinze, "Johann Sebastian Drey's Critique of Schleiermacher's Theology," *The Heythrop Journal* 37

Drey formulated a theory of doctrinal development that contrasted essential, unchanging Catholic dogma with its changing particular forms throughout history.[48] Even if the essence of dogma is in fact immutable, the practices and organization of the church can and must change frequently in order to meet the needs of generational shifts.[49] Doctrinal development is not only an inevitable historical phenomenon but also is the central task of the systematic theologian. Doctrinal revision is often a necessary means to ecclesial reform. Christianity is a living organism, an organic unity that must grow in order to survive. One of Drey's most striking ideas is his assumption that development is an *inevitable* feature in the *living church*. Organic metaphors such as a "living" church were a common staple in the German Romantic tradition and a regular feature in Schleiermacher and Drey's theologies.[50]

As the Christian tradition grows and develops, so too do its authoritative sources. Drey believes that the Protestant principle of *sola scriptura* deviates from theology's central task as it reduces theology to biblical interpretation and binds theology to a dead tradition. He contends that interpretation requires a living tradition as well:

(1996): 1–23. For the later Drey, the task of apologetics thus becomes to demonstrate "the positive basic character [of Christianity] as perfect revelation." See Johann Sebastian Drey, *Die Apologetik*, vol. 1, §18.

48. Drey, *Brief Introduction*, 29; idem, *Kurze Einleitung*, §69.

49. Chadwick, *From Bossuet to Newman*, 105. The distinction between a permanent essence of doctrine and changing praxis is similar to the outmoded scholastic distinction made between "proximate" and "remote" norms of faith. This position, abandoned in 1965 in the Second Vatican Council's *Dogmatic Constitution on Divine Revelation* (Boston: St. Paul Books and Media, 1965), gave more authority to the more "proximate" contemporary *magisterium* than earlier, more "remote" traditions. See also Lash, *Change in Focus*, 7–8.

50. Chadwick, *From Bossuet to Newman*, 108. For an evaluation of this romantic metaphor in Schleiermacher's thought, see Jack Forstman, *A Romantic Triangle: Schleiermacher and Early German Romanticism* (Missoula, MT: Scholars Press, 1977), 97–99. Schleiermacher also conceived of the church as an organic unity. See Martin Redeker, *Schleiermacher: Life and Thought*, trans. J. Wallhauser (Philadelphia: Fortress Press, 1973), 189.

> If Scripture alone is accepted as the means of the tradition of ideas of religious belief, then construction proceeds by way of scriptural interpretation; then the whole of theology is exegesis. But if there exists a *living objective reality* which is generally recognized as the continuance of the originating event and therefore as its most authentic tradition, then the historical witness is found in and through it. *This reality is the church.*

Individual interpretation of Scripture is "wholly and entirely open to subjectivism," and theology "can only be made *positive* and *effective* by a church."[51]

If God providentially guides the church in history, then ecclesial tradition must be an important source for theology. Drey insists that if inspiration is a supernatural event, grammatical-historical exegesis alone—a "naturalistic" exercise—will not suffice in establishing a positive or divinely revealed theology. However, if the church, God's living institution on the earth, interprets Scripture, it ensures that the interpretation of Scripture is supernatural as well. The same Spirit that inspires the text continues to guide the church. The church is for Drey "the true basis of all theological knowledge" and the theologian's primary source for "the empirically given content of that knowledge."[52] While the Catholic Church is the unique teaching authority of God on earth, the Spirit of God himself is guiding the process. "God himself unfolds in the course of history what He had planted in its soil at the time of revelation," meaning that "revelation and the subsequent tradition together form one continuous process."[53]

For Drey, the development of doctrine occurs through a dialectical process that occurs when the "internal history" or "inner history"

---

51. Drey, *Brief Introduction*, 20; idem, *Kurze Einleitung*, §47. Elsewhere, Drey equates rationalistic deism with "naturalism." See Drey, *Die Apologetik*, vol. 1, §32.

52. Drey, *Kurze Einleitung*, §54; idem, *Brief Introduction*, 22.

53. Walgrave, *Unfolding Revelation*, 285.

(*innere Geschichte*) of Christianity intersects with the "external history" (*äussere Geschichte*) of Christianity's engagement with the world. Christianity's internal history is its essence, its living history.[54] This internal history is the organic, ongoing history of Christian thought. In describing the history of Christian developments this way, Drey aims to demonstrate the continuity of Christian thought across the ages.[55]

The external history of Christianity, by contrast, is its struggle with culture and ideologies foreign to itself.[56] External history partly consists of conflicts such as heresy or religious opposition that result in forcing a clearer, more articulate expression of Christianity's essence. Christianity's external history also entails the "history of its effects" (*Geschichte seiner Wirkungen*) on culture.[57] This history of effects is a two-way street. Scripture plays a vital role in the development of doctrine, but external tradition and history also play extensive roles in how Scripture is interpreted:

> Scripture, which begins and is preserved along with living tradition, must be external to that tradition and thus act on the development of doctrine as an external factor. Throughout its history, the study of the Bible has had an impact on doctrine and has had that impact in those respects in which it was energetically pursued. . . . But all ideas, and so Christian ideas as well, mutually affect one another, and so whatever ideas, especially of a philosophical or scientific character, have existed or have recently been discussed among people must act on Christian doctrines as external stimuli.[58]

---

54. Drey, *Kurze Einleitung*, §177; cf. §179. Drey also divides the internal history of Christianity into the "history of Christian ideology" (*Geschichte der christlichen Ideologie*) or doctrine and the "history of the Christian church's institutions" (*Geschichte der christlichen Kirchengesellschaft*).

55. Drey, *Brief Introduction*, 88; idem, *Kurze Einleitung*, §190.

56. Drey, *Kurze Einleitung*, §177.

57. Drey, *Kurze Einleitung*, §§187–88.

58. Drey, *Brief Introduction*, 88–89; idem, *Kurze Einleitung*, §192.

Nevertheless, Drey warns that not every doctrinal development of biblical or speculative theology is a constructive development. Schisms and heresies arise when developments are alien to the inner history of Christianity.[59]

The introduction of external ideas such as philosophical speculation does not necessarily produce corruption, as Christianity must translate that which is essential into the present zeitgeist; but corruption can occur when biblical interpretation or philosophical speculation contradicts the spirit of Christianity present in the universal church in every age. For Drey, like Schelling before him, *Vernunft* and revelation are two sides of the same coin.[60] Drey writes, "All revelation comes from God's eternal absolute reason and proceeds from that reason and so cannot be totally alien to human reason in which the divine reason is preeminently revealed."[61] Consequently, Drey equates the evolution of human ideas with continuous revelation, and all genuine developments of reason stem from God's purpose to educate humanity.[62]

Later developments of dogma, such as the post-apostolic practice of sacramental confession, do not originate with the historical Jesus or the apostles. But if such developments are (1) reasonable and (2) consistent with the inner spirit of Christianity in the church, then they constitute God's unfolding and ongoing process of revelation in history. The church as an organic institution has the responsibility of

59. Drey, *Kurze Einleitung*.
60. Fehr, *The Birth of the Catholic Tübingen School*, 23–72, esp. 45–66. Drey's theology of revelation is itself an apologetic against deistic rationalism. Rather than conceiving of the God-world relationship in terms of radical transcendence over-and-against nature, he has a panentheistic conception of God as a personal creator who is intrinsic to the created order. Creation and history comprise this ever-present revelation of God, and this revelation is received through the divinely initiated processes of human reason.
61. Drey, *Kurze Einleitung*, §97; idem, *Brief Introduction*, 44.
62. Drey, *Kurze Einleitung*, §65; cf. Fehr, *The Birth of the Catholic Tübingen School*, 58–63. Drey borrows from Gotthold Ephraim Lessing (1729–1821) the conception of revelation as "the education of the human race." See also Gotthold Ephraim Lessing, *The Education of the Human Race* (London: Smith, Elder, and Co., 1858), §1.

governing the process of development and preventing individualistic errors and schisms; it is responsible for the maintenance of religious life in its various forms.[63] This evaluation of dogmatic developments comes in two stages. First, in what Drey calls the "Historical Propaedeutic" (*Historische Propädeutik*), the church's theologians must do the work of historians. This task entails biblical interpretation and historical theology because both disciplines are means of investigation into God's revelatory processes in history.[64] Drey understands revelatory history to be organic and devoid of clearly distinguishable epochs. Once the historical task is complete, theologians of the church are tasked with distinguishing between true development and heretical corruption by testing doctrines to see whether they are in the same "spirit" as biblical Christianity and the universal church throughout its history.[65]

Like Schleiermacher before him, Drey defined hermeneutics as "the art of interpretation."[66] This discipline of general hermeneutics is of first importance because it has the power to "form the scriptural interpreter . . . most directly."[67] Drey offers this broad definition of its task: "By nature it is wide as criticism and must be based on the laws through which the human mind arrays its thoughts in words or actually thinks in words."[68] Words have a "polysemic quality" in which "the author is able to display endless variety in his thoughts" and so "*his meaning*" must be "discovered."[69] Drey, in the vein of Schleiermacher, divides hermeneutics into universal, *grammatical* interpretation and particular, *historical* and *individual*

---

63. Chadwick, *From Bossuet to Newman*, 107–8.

64. See Drey, *Kurze Einleitung*, §§107–220.

65. Drey, *Kurze Einleitung*, §193.

66. Drey, *Brief Introduction*, 71–72; idem, *Kurze Einleitung*, §153.

67. Drey, *Brief Introduction*, 72; idem, *Kurze Einleitung*, §154.

68. Drey, *Brief Introduction*, 71; idem, *Kurze Einleitung*, §153.

69. Drey, *Brief Introduction*, 71; idem, *Kurze Einleitung*, §153.

interpretation. Grammatical interpretation addresses the nature of language and linguistic expression in the universal reading of texts. Individual and historical forms of interpretation address particular expressions in history, the mind of the author, and the development of new ideas.[70] The interpreter may begin with individual texts, but his or her goal is to interpret the whole in its organic relationship to the ideas of the author.[71] For Drey, hermeneutics cannot be limited to a set of rules and principles. This discipline "requires special talent" because the "interpreter must put himself completely in the author's position, must transform himself into the author, so to speak, and then reconstruct anew what the author created originally."[72]

With Schleiermacher, Drey asserts that biblical exegesis is only one special application of general hermeneutics. He recognizes that exegesis is a "universal discipline" employed in all disciples with written texts.[73] Drey's departure from Schleiermacher comes with the special attention he gives to Catholic exegesis. Though Drey declines further elaboration, he suggests that the Catholic Church has a special interpretative power that individuals do not have. Someone who knows the deceased has a better place of understanding to interpret his or her words than do those who did not know the deceased. The Church, as a living organism in continuity with the past, is in a better place to interpret Scripture than those outside of apostolic succession.[74]

In the end, Drey's theory of development is an apologetic for traditional Catholic views of ecclesial authority couched in the hazy language of German idealism. This model bears the influence of Schelling's dialectic; but Schleiermacher shapes Drey's

---

70. Drey, *Brief Introduction*, 73–74; idem, *Kurze Einleitung*, §§156–58.
71. Drey, *Kurze Einleitung*, §160; idem, *Brief Introduction*, 75.
72. Drey, *Kurze Einleitung*, §161; idem, *Brief Introduction*, 75.
73. Drey, *Kurze Einleitung*, §70; cf. §127.
74. Drey, *Kurze Einleitung*, §155.

understandings of theology, religious consciousness, and hermeneutics. If Christianity is a positive religion, it can be explained historically and through biblical exegesis. The tension between Schleiermacher's notion of hermeneutics and the Church's special authority in interpretation goes relatively unaddressed. Nevertheless, Drey does make a plain connection between the task of historical interpretation and the ongoing development of doctrine.

The Contribution of John Henry Newman

No single figure has been more influential on theories of doctrinal development in Anglo-American theology than John Henry Newman, whose name has become virtually synonymous with the problem. In his seminal work *An Essay on the Development of Christian Doctrine*, Newman offers a "hypothesis to account for a difficulty" of "the apparent variation and growth of doctrine," as well as providing normative criteria that can discriminate between genuine, "faithful" developments and corruptions of divine truth.[75] Despite a passing reference to Drey's student and better-known successor, Johann Möhler,[76] Newman's theory of development seems to have formed independently of the Catholic Tübingen School, as Owen Chadwick painstakingly argues.[77] Moreover, as Bradford Hinze points out,

75. John Henry Newman, *An Essay on the Development of Christian Doctrine* (London: James Toovey, 1845), 26–27. The first edition of the *Essay* was published in 1845, shortly after Newman's reception by Rome. The second edition, published in 1878, is a more nuanced, slightly rearranged revision of the previous edition and typically is considered the standard edition by Newman scholars. All following citations from the *Essay*, unless otherwise indicated, come from John Henry Newman, *An Essay on the Development of Christian Doctrine*, rev. ed. (London: Basil Montagu Pickering, 1878).

76. Newman, *An Essay on the Development of Christian Doctrine*, 29. Newman comments that he believes the ideas of doctrinal development are implicit in the works of "distinguished writers of the continent" such as Möhler and Joseph-Marie Maistre (1753–1821). For more on Möhler's theory of development, see Johann Adam Möhler, *Symbolik: Oder Darstellung der Dogmatischen Gegensätze der Katholiken und Protestanten* (Mainz, 1833); cf. Voss, "Johann Adam Möhler and the Development of Dogma," 420–44.

Newman, unlike the Tübingen Catholics, is not concerned with ongoing theological revision as much as he is defending the established Catholic tradition.[78]

For the Anglican divine who became a Roman Catholic cardinal, the cords of theology and biography seem to braid seamlessly. Personal experience and critical reflection went hand in hand with the evolution of his insights.[79] As a leading defender of the English "via media" ("middle way") in the Anglo-Catholic Oxford Movement, Newman attacked the doctrines he perceived as Roman corruptions of the depository of faith.[80] He gradually became convinced that the Anglican Communion was beyond the

77. Chadwick, *From Bossuet to Newman*, 111–19. Lord John Dalberg-Acton (1834–1902), who personally knew both Newman and Möhler's colleague Johann Joseph Ignaz von Döllinger (1799–1890), believed that Newman derived his theory from Möhler. This speculation is the object of Chadwick's dispute here. Newman, who did not know German, likely came into contact with Möhler's works through French editions. See also Henry Tristam, "J. A. Moehler et J. H. Newman. La pensée allemande et la renaissance catholique en Angleterre," *Revue des sciences philosophiques et théologiques* 27 (1938): 184–204.

78. Hinze, *Narrating History, Developing Doctrine*, 11.

79. Newman details this journey in his classic spiritual autobiography, *Apologia Pro Vita Sua* (London: Longmans, Green, and Co., 1864). Newman supporter Wilfrid Philip Ward (1856–1916) published a two-volume biography largely drawn from Newman's journals and his own personal correspondence with the cardinal. See Wilfrid Ward, *The Life of John Henry Newman*, 2 vols. (London: Longmans, Green, and Co., 1912). Other notable and more critical biographies include Owen Chadwick, *Newman* (Oxford: Oxford University Press, 2005); Avery Dulles, *John Henry Newman* (London: Continuum, 2009); Ian Ker, *John Henry Newman: A Biography*, 2nd ed. (Oxford: Oxford University Press, 2010); Roderick Strange, *John Henry Newman: A Mind Alive* (London: Darton, Longman and Todd, 2008).

80. The Oxford Movement gained widespread recognition with the publication of *Tracts for the Times*, a ninety-volume series of theological writings published between 1833 and 1841 which eventually led to their designation as "Tractarians." Newman, along with John Keble (1792–1866), Edward Bouverie Pusey (1800–1882), and several others, offered social, political, and theological critiques of an increasingly secularized church-state relationship. Their own ecclesiologies gradually came to reflect predominant Roman Catholic doctrines of authority, apostolic succession, and sacramentalism. While the Movement waned after Newman's conversion to Roman Catholicism, it continued to have influence on Anglicanism throughout the nineteenth century under the leadership of figures such as Richard William Church (1815–1890) and Henry Parry Liddon (1829–1890). See Richard William Church, *The Oxford Movement: Twelve Years, 1833-1845* (London: Macmillan, 1892); Eugene R. Fairweather, ed., *The Oxford Movement* (New York: Oxford University Press, 1964); Owen Chadwick, *The Mind of the Oxford Movement* (Stanford: Stanford University Press, 1967); Marvin R. O'Connell, *The Oxford Conspirators: A History of the Oxford Movement* (New York: Macmillan, 1969);

reformation he once desperately longed to see within it, largely because of its sectarian and anti-Catholic tendencies. While he eventually came to believe that the Roman Church is a truly apostolic institution from antiquity, he initially had great difficulty reconciling the historical realities of the Church's later, transformed tradition with its earliest apostolic stages. His long-term engagement with the problem of development culminated in his conversion to Rome. On 9 October 1845, after years of struggling with questions about ecclesial authority, antiquity, and catholicity, Newman was received into the Roman Church. The first edition of his *Essay on the Development of Christian Doctrine* was published the next month.[81]

The Development of Newman's Theory

While development is an implicit theme in Newman's earlier works, such as his 1833 *The Arians of the Fourth Century*,[82] its first explicit mention in his corpus is in disparaging remarks made toward Roman

and Geoffrey Rowell, *The Vision Glorious: Themes and Personalities of the Catholic Revival in Anglicanism* (Oxford: Oxford University Press, 1983).

81. Chadwick, *From Bossuet to Newman*, 160–63.

82. In opposition to the scholarly consensus of earlier generations, Newman proposed that Arius of Alexandria's (c. 250–336) doctrine was a thoroughgoing biblical literalism with little or no philosophical sophistication. See John Henry Newman, *The Arians of the Fourth Century*, 3d ed. (London: E. Lumney, 1871), 207–249, cf. 413–425. Newman describes a Syrian-Antiochene tradition that "devoted itself to the literal and critical interpretation of the Scripture" and "gave rise first to the Arian and then to the Nestorian heresy" (414). He paints Arius as a disciple of Paul of Samosata (c. 200–275) and Lucian of Antioch (c. 240–312) in a literalist Antiochene hermeneutical tradition—a heterodox school that stood in opposition to the spiritual, allegorical hermeneutic of the Alexandrian church. Some have described Newman's interpretation of Arius as an unbalanced portrait reflecting his own ecclesial and theological agendas. See Rowan Williams, *Arius: Heresy & Tradition*, rev. ed (Grand Rapids, MI: Eerdmans, 2002), 4–5. Williams (b. 1950) calls Newman's thesis an argument "built upon a foundation of complacent bigotry and historical fantasy" and an apologia for "what the early Oxford Movement thought of as spiritual religion and authority" (4). According to Williams, the Tractarian theologian held up the Alexandrians "as the very exemplar of traditional and revealed religion" in their commitment to spiritual readings of text, extra-biblical tradition, and an ecclesial view of progressive revelation (4–5).

Catholic doctrinal innovations. In his 1837 *Lectures on the Prophetical Office of the Church*, Newman describes Romanism as "an unnatural and misshapen development of the Truth."[83] Despite the fact that he acknowledges both Roman Catholics and high-church Anglicans profess Vincentian rule as the measuring rod of apostolic fidelity, he avers that historical evidence plainly indicates that Catholics are inconsistent in their application of it.[84] Newman alleges that uniquely Roman doctrines such as papal infallibility, purgatory, and transubstantiation fail the threefold test of antiquity, universality, and consensus and are therefore corruptions of received tradition.[85] According to this earlier Tractarian Newman, the only way in which distinctively Roman doctrines could possibly be justified is on the basis of the historically dubious first principle of ecclesial infallibility—a principle that the later Catholic Newman would employ to justify Roman Catholic developments.[86]

In the final years of Newman's Tractarian period, his understanding of development was in flux, as a series of impassioned university sermons on the relationship between faith and reason preached before Oxford staff and undergraduates attest.[87] The most

83. John Henry Newman, *The Via Media of the Anglican Church*, vol. 1 (London: Longman, Green, and Co., 1891), 41. See also Ker, *John Henry Newman*, 269–81. Newman formally retracted statements of this nature in an anonymous, yet discernibly Newman-like letter that appeared in the *Conservative Journal* on 28 January 1843. A similar retraction serves as a preface to his *Essay*, dated 6 October 1845. See also John Henry Newman, *The Via Media of the Anglican Church*, vol. 2 (London: Basil Montagu Pickering, 1877), 411–19.

84. Newman, *The Via Media of the Anglican Church*, vol. 1, 49. See also Adian Nichols, *From Newman to Congar: The Idea of Doctrinal Development from the Victorians to the Second Vatican Council* (Edinburgh: T&T Clark, 1990), 35–37. Adian Nichols (b. 1948) notes that Newman is here unaware that nineteenth-century Catholic apologists such as the Austrian Jesuit Johann Baptist Franzelin (1816–1886) were presenting more nuanced formulations of the Vincentian rule that give more serious attention to the historical critiques of Roman Catholic doctrine that were appearing during the Enlightenment.

85. Newman, *The Via Media of the Anglican Church*, vol. 1, 51. Newman here summarizes Vincent's rule as the standard by which doctrinal fidelity should be measured: "Catholicity, Antiquity, and consent of Fathers, is the proper evidence of the fidelity or Apostolicity of a professed Tradition."

86. Newman, *The Via Media of the Anglican Church*, vol. 1, 48.

noteworthy of these was his sermon "The Theory of Developments in Religious Doctrine," which he preached on 2 February 1843 at St. Mary's University Church.[88] Newman's central text was Luke 2:19: "But Mary kept all these things, and pondered them in her heart" (KJV). Newman believes the Lord's mother to be a model theologian because she is an exemplar of faith

> both in the reception and in the study of Divine Truth. She does not think it enough to accept, she dwells upon it; not enough to possess, she uses it; not enough to assent, she develops it; not enough to submit the Reason, she reasons upon it; not indeed reasoning first, and believing afterwards, with Zacharias, yet first believing without reasoning, next from love and reverence, reasoning after believing. And thus she symbolizes to us, not only the faith of the unlearned, but of the doctors of the Church also, who have to investigate, and weigh, and define, as well as to profess the Gospel; to draw the line between truth and heresy; to anticipate or remedy the various aberrations of wrong reason.[89]

In true Augustinian and Anselmian fashion, Newman suggests that faith, or the volitional reception of divine revelation, is a necessary albeit insufficient condition for true understanding. The *telos* of faith is not merely the acquiescence of divine truth. Rather, faith in received revelation should be the genesis of an ongoing process of reflection and application. For Newman, doctrinal development in the church macrocosmically reflects this critical, reasonable faith in the lives of individual believers.

---

87. These sermons are available in John Henry Newman, *Fifteen Sermons Preached before the University of Oxford* (New York: Scribner, Welford, and Co., 1872). University sermons relevant to but not explicitly descriptive of Newman's developing theory of development include "Faith and Reason, Contrasted as Habits of the Mind" (6 January 1839), "The Nature of Faith in Relation to Reason" (13 January 1839), and "Explicit and Implicit Reason" (29 June 1840). Many of the ideas in these sermons would be developed further in Newman's *An Essay in Aid of a Grammar of Assent* (London: Burns, Oates, and Co., 1870).
88. See Newman, *Fifteen Sermons*, 312–51.
89. Newman, *Fifteen Sermons*, 313.

By his own admission, the study of the problem of development was the crucial final step in Newman's conversion to Roman Catholicism. In his *Apologia* he writes, "I determined to write an Essay on Doctrinal Development; and then, if, at the end of it, my convictions in favour of the Roman Church were not weaker, to make up my mind to seek admission into her fold."[90] The first edition of the *Essay* met with no small controversy from high-church and low-church Anglicans alike, as well as disagreement from some Roman Catholics. Blandished by Romantic ideals, Newman advances the notion that doctrines not only grow or change over time, but also that such growth is evidence of a living body of doctrine. As Newman commentator Nicholas Lash observes, Newman's theory presents no detailed explanation of how doctrines develop or how they should develop. Newman simply acknowledges that doctrines have developed, which was a remarkable admission for nineteenth-century Roman Catholics, and makes a case that such development need not contradict the divine deposit of revelation.[91]

The later, Catholic Newman shares many similar apologetic interests with Drey and the Tübingen Catholics. They all reject the claims of rationalists who would separate the essential truths of Christianity and its historical particulars, and they contest the liberal opinion that all Christian denominations fundamentally misrepresent the original intentions of Christ and his apostles by assimilating doctrines and practices from alien philosophical and religious traditions.[92] Newman is also in step with Drey and Möhler in the way he defends the infallibility of the Catholic Church in interpreting

---

90. Newman, *Apologia Pro Vita Sua*, 360.
91. Nicholas Lash, "Literature and Theory: Did Newman Have a 'Theory' of Development?" in *Newman and Gladstone*, ed. James D. Bastable (Dublin: Veritas, 1978), 161–62.
92. Newman, *An Essay on the Development of Christian Doctrine*, 4–5.

and developing doctrine.[93] Nevertheless, Newman's philosophical genealogy is very different from his German counterparts.[94]

The English Protestant audience Newman addressed was poles apart from the Protestant scholarship the Tübingen Catholics encountered. Ahistorical biblicism, not skeptical historical criticism, was Newman's primary complaint with the Protestant position. He contests the refusal of Protestants such as William Chillingworth (1602–1644) to acknowledge authentic historical doctrinal development and alleges a naiveté on their part about the nature of Christian history: "This one thing at least is certain; whatever history teaches, whatever it omits, whatever it exaggerates or extenuates, whatever it says and unsays, at least the Christianity of history is not Protestantism. If ever there were a safe truth, it is this. . . . To be deep in history is to cease to be a Protestant."[95] Taking his argument for the importance of historical study one step further, Newman suggests that many cherished Protestant doctrines, including the "doctrine of the divine efficacy of the Scriptures as the one appointed instrument of religious teaching," are also dependent upon the later development

93. See Voss, "Johann Adam Möhler and the Development of Dogma," 437–43; cf. Möhler, *Symbolik*, §§39–42.

94. See Thomas K. Carr, *Newman and Gadamer: Toward a Hermeneutics of Religious Knowledge* (Atlanta: Scholars Press, 1996), 84–87. Newman eventually encountered German speculative idealism in an English translation of a secondary source by Heinrich Moritz Chalybäus (1796–1892) but dismissed the philosophy and criticized it for attempting to produce a "scientific metaphysics." See also Heinrich Moritz Chalybäus, *Historical Development of Speculative Philosophy from Kant to Hegel*, trans. Alfred Edersheim (Edinburgh: T&T Clark, 1854). Newman's theory of ideas is greatly indebted to John Locke's (1632–1704) *Essay Concerning Human Understanding*, even if he is highly critical of Locke's empiricism and rationalistic religion. See also Carr, *Newman and Gadamer*, 63–83. Newman's most profound influences, however, were classical: the Platonic ideas he encountered in the Alexandrian Fathers Clement (c. 150–215) and Origen (c. 184–253), as well as in the works of Joseph Butler, and later as a Catholic, a Thomistic version of Aristotelianism.

95. Newman, *An Essay on the Development of Christian Doctrine*, 7–8. Chillingworth denounced Catholic tradition largely on the basis of its variations. See William Chillingworth, *The Religion of Protestants a Safe Way to Salvation* (Oxford: Leonard Lichfield, 1638), 131. Chillingworth writes, "There have been Popes against Popes, Councells against Councells, Councells confirmed by Popes, against Councells confirmed by Popes: Lastly the Church of some Ages against the Church of other Ages."

of tradition.[96] The new historical consciousness seized Newman, and the Protestantism of his youth no longer satisfied his understanding of Christian history.

Newman's Critique of Traditional Models of Development

Newman distinguishes his position on doctrinal development from the Vincentian canon that he previously cherished as a member of the Anglican via media. As a Tractarian he believed that Catholics abused Vincent's rule, and as a Catholic he came to believe that the Anglicans could not employ it consistently either. He then believes Vincent's notion that the only true doctrine is doctrine that is "believed everywhere, always, and by all men" is incapable of clear demonstration because "always" and "everywhere" are ambiguous and imprecise terms.[97] He also asserts that even the commonly held Nicene Creed cannot be supported by Vincent's ecumenical method because explicit language regarding the Trinity and the divinity of the Holy Spirit is unaccounted for in most Ante-Nicene creeds and writings.[98]

Newman finds some value in the more enigmatic appeal of some Catholics to the *Disciplina Arcani*, or secret disciplines, to explain the appearance of later postcanonical developments.[99] In the late second or early third century, churches felt it necessary to segregate worship services for two groups of believers: catechumens—new (or potential) converts receiving instruction but deemed not yet ready for baptism—and the "faithful ones"—baptized, instructed converts.

96. Newman, *An Essay on the Development of Christian Doctrine*, 9.
97. Ibid., 11–12. The first hint of discontent with the imprecision of Vincent's rule comes in his 1837 *Lectures on the Prophetical Office*. See Newman, *The Via Media of the Anglican Church*, vol. 1, 55–56.
98. Newman, *An Essay on the Development of Christian Doctrine*, 15–18.
99. Ibid., 27–29.

Only the faithful ones could hear of certain doctrines or participate in particular rites; these doctrines and practices withheld from catechumens acquired the name "secret disciplines." Some early Eastern and Western apologists thought this practice necessary for engagement with Jewish and pagan nonbelievers, making a distinction between public or exoteric doctrines and private or esoteric doctrines. The preaching and the reading of Scripture was a public practice, but the sacraments were largely a private practice. Secret disciplines virtually ceased around the close of the fifth century when pagan threats against Christianity began to wane.[100]

Many who appeal to the secret disciplines as an explanation for the later appearance of certain Christian doctrines assume that doctrine is indeed immutable and that many seemingly later developments of doctrine were doctrines explicitly held by the church from the apostolic period forward but not taught in public until circumstances demanded such disclosure.[101] An appeal to the *Disciplina Arcani* was a popular apologetic 150 years earlier, but, again, as a testament to the nineteenth-century rise of historical consciousness, many of the texts once thought evidence of this phenomenon, such as the works of Pseudo-Dionysius (c. 6th century c.e.), were by this point widely considered forgeries. One of the most influential arguments for the *Disciplina Arcani* as a means to explaining the later public appearance of privately held apostolic doctrines such as transubstantiation, the veneration of saints, and other Catholic distinctives comes from the Jesuit theologian Emmanuel Schelstrate (1649–1692).[102] Newman

---

100. See Philip Schaff, *History of the Christian Church*, vol. 2 (New York: Charles Scribner, 1910), 232–35.

101. Chadwick, *From Bossuet to Newman*, 140–41.

102. See Emmanuel Schelstrate, *Antiquitas Illustrata Circa Concillia Generalia* (Antwerp: Marcelli Parys, 1678); idem, *De Disciplina Arcani* (Rome: Sac. Congregat. de Propagandâ Fide, 1685). The latter volume is a response to the Lutheran apologist Wilhelm Ernst Tentzel (1659–1707), whose *Dissertatio de Disciplina Arcani* (Leipsic, 1683) is a response to Schelstrate's 1678 argument for the *Disciplina Arcani*.

recognized that secret disciplines may explain the later emergence of some ceremonial aspects of Christian doctrine and practice but maintained that this hypothesis cannot account for the seemingly slow nature of development and the continued presence of doctrinal variations after allegedly secret doctrines became manifest to the public eye.[103]

What Chillingworth's biblicism, the Vincentian canon, and the theory of secret disciplines all hold in common is a desire to demonstrate a doctrine's credibility by defending its antiquity and its immutability. As a theologian entrenched in the new historical consciousness, Newman ultimately considered such theses untenable; and with impinging Romantic inclinations, he began to find such cold, lifeless conceptions of doctrine unappealing. Historical study reveals that no contemporary Christian tradition is a perfect, untouched image of the Christianity of antiquity—either in Roman Catholicism or in Protestantism. Newman thus exchanges his earlier arguments for doctrinal immutability and antiquity for arguments of genuine development based on historical identity and continuity.

Newman's Descriptive Model of Development

Following Vincent, Newman likens the development of Christian belief to organic growth. Doctrine may grow in the church, unfolding from the initial seed of revelation, but it maintains its essential identity in the process. Yet Newman's organic understanding of the relationship between doctrines is a product of Romantic influences. He insists that the acceptance of early developments, such as later Trinitarian and christological formulations, necessarily entails the acceptance of all other later

103. Newman, *An Essay on the Development of Christian Doctrine*, 29.

Roman Catholic developments, which are "members of one family . . . illustrative of each other."[104] Doctrines such as the sacraments, the mass, the mediation and merits of the saints, the unity of the Catholic Church, the veneration of relics, transubstantiation, the celibate priesthood, and purgatory all relate organically to the doctrine of the Incarnation. Their organic life means that one "must accept the whole or reject the whole; attenuation does but enfeeble, and amputation mutilate."[105]

Newman likewise compares the Church's development of doctrine to the mind's reception and enlargement of an idea. The continuous identity of an idea is demonstrated in its growth and maturation throughout time and in public engagement. To be sure, if immutability and antiquity are no longer the central criteria of doctrinal truth, corruption is a viable threat to the tradition, especially if theology is brought into the marketplace of ideas. This risk of corruption is a small price to pay

> if a great idea is duly to be understood, and much more if it is to be fully exhibited. [The idea] is elicited and expanded by trial, and battles into perfection and supremacy. . . . [The development of an idea] necessarily arises out of an existing state of things, and for a time savours the soil. Its vital element needs disengaging from what is foreign and temporary, and is employed in efforts after freedom which become more vigorous and hopeful as the years increase. . . . From time to time, it makes essays which fail, and are in consequence abandoned. It seems in suspense which way to go; it wavers, and at length strikes out in one definite direction. In time, it enters upon strange territory; points of controversy alter their bearing; parties rise and fall around it; dangers and hopes appear in new relations; and old principles reappear under new forms. *It changes with them in order to remain the same.* In a higher world it is

104. Ibid., 96. Newman's organicism is more pronounced elsewhere, where he describes ideas or doctrines as "mutually connected and growing out of one another . . . all parts of a whole" (56).
105. Newman, *An Essay on the Development of Christian Doctrine*, 94; cf. 169. For Newman, the distinctively Catholic developments of doctrine represent "legitimate growth" and "the natural and necessary doctrine of the early church."

otherwise, but here below to live is to change, and to be perfect is to have changed often.[106]

Moreover, Newman portends later discussions about the need for theological contextualization: "If Christianity be a universal religion, suited not simply to one locality or period, it cannot but vary in its relations and dealings toward the world around it, that is, it will develop."[107] The development of an idea is not only the unavoidable consequence of changing times and cultural expression, it is essential to its vitality and reproduction in ever-changing horizons.

The Hermeneutical Features of Newman's Model

The explanation of this growth of ideas has clear hermeneutical qualities. First, as Newman observes, "Time is necessary for the full *comprehension* and perfection of great ideas; and that the highest and most wonderful truths, though communicated to the world once for all by inspired teachers, *could not be comprehended all at once by the recipients*, but, as being received and transmitted by minds not inspired and through media which are human, have required only the longer time and deeper thought for their full *elucidation*."[108] This "full comprehension" comes in several stages. First, an idea makes an impression on the mind.[109] The mind then apprehends the idea

---

106. Newman, *An Essay on the Development of Christian Doctrine*, 39–40, italics mine.
107. Newman, *An Essay on the Development of Christian Doctrine*, 58. Newman frequently refers to this inevitability as an "antecedent probability."
108. Newman, *An Essay on the Development of Christian Doctrine*, 29–30, italics mine. Some describe Newman's approach as a "noetic model" of development. See Thiel, *Senses of Tradition*, 67–72.
109. Chadwick deems that Newman is inconsistent with his use of the term *idea*, but the term as it used in his discussion of development is "the object itself as it is capable of being apprehended in various notions." See Chadwick, *From Bossuet to Newman*, 149. Chadwick adds that "an idea will in this sense be more complex and many-sided than the individual notions about it, and perhaps never fully 'perceptible' in such notions as human language is capable of expressing." The idea that is central to Newman's theory of doctrinal development is the revelation given by God to the Church.

through definition and description. Newman describes the final phase of understanding much like Schleiermacher's hermeneutical circle: "whole objects do not create in the intellect whole ideas, but are, to use a mathematical phrase, thrown into a series, into a number of statements, strengthening, interpreting, correcting each other, and with more or less exactness approximating, as they accumulate, to a perfect image. There is no other way of learning or teaching."[110] The understanding of any idea or doctrine demands the labor of interpretation, and interpretation takes place within a matrix of other ideas and concepts.

Second, the finitude of the interpreter and the greatness of the revealed ideas of Scripture make development a never-ending process. For his time, Newman is remarkably sensitive to the way that culture and tradition impel the reading of texts. In one of his Tractarian sermons on faith and reason he writes, "Texts have their illuminating power, from the atmosphere of habit, opinion, usage, tradition, through which we see them."[111] He also recognizes that Scripture is a deep, multifaceted collection of different genres and interests that lacks the organization and systematization of dogmatics. Scripture will never be understood fully in the present age, but even if it could, "it must be [understood] in the same way as natural knowledge is come at, by continuance and progress of learning and liberty, and by particular persons attending to, comparing, and pursuing intimations scattered up and down it, which are overlooked and disregarded by the generality of the world."[112]

---

110. Newman, *An Essay on the Development of Christian Doctrine*, 55.
111. Newman, *Fifteen Sermons*, 191.
112. Newman, *An Essay on the Development of Christian Doctrine*, 71–72. Newman credits the interpretation of obscure biblical texts for later explicit developments in early and medieval Christianity. He suggests doctrines such as purgatory (Acts 14:22; 1 Cor. 3:15), the imputation of saintly merit (Matt. 10:41), the real presence (Luke 22:19), and extreme unction (James 5:14) are present in Scripture. He implies that many additional truths in Scripture remain undiscovered.

Third, Newman challenges the possible objection that the text of Scripture set the limits for doctrinal development because "ideas are in the writer and reader of revelation, not the inspired text itself."[113] The segregation of the ideas of Scripture from the text itself is troubling, but perhaps more confusing is how an idea moves from an ancient author to a contemporary reader without a medium to transmit it. Perhaps Newman is defending authorial intent over and against some notion of an autonomous text, but he is unclear at this point. For Newman the most important concern is not where meaning is located in textual interpretation but "whether those ideas which the letter conveys from the writer to reader reach the reader at once in their completeness and accuracy on his first perception of them, or whether they open out in his intellect and grow to perfection in the course of the time."[114]

Fourth, Newman describes developments within the canon, such as the fulfillment of Old Testament prophecies in the New, in hermeneutical terms: "The event which is the development is also an interpretation of the prediction; it provides a fulfillment by imposing a meaning."[115] He admits that the christological interpretation of some prophecy, such as Matthew's reading of Hosea 11:1 in Matthew 2:15, initially seems contrary to proper hermeneutical procedure, but this reading can be accepted as appropriate when and only when "we readily submit our reason on competent authority." Building a case for an interpretive authority, Newman adds,

> We receive such difficulties on faith, and leave them to take care of
> themselves. Much less do we consider mere fulness in the interpretation,
> or definiteness, or again strangeness, as a sufficient reason for depriving
> the text, or the action to which it is applied, of the advantage of such
> interpretation. We make it no objection that the words themselves come

113. Newman, *An Essay on the Development of Christian Doctrine*, 56.
114. Ibid.
115. Ibid., 102.

short of it, or that the sacred writer did not contemplate it, or that a previous fulfilment satisfies it.

Just as the Anglican apologist Joseph Butler (1692–1752) defends the messianic interpretation of these difficult texts on the basis of acquaintance with the history of Jesus, Newman contends for Roman doctrinal developments that also profess "to have been derived from Revelation" and which present "no strong opposition to the sacred text."[116] Chadwick's compelling criticism of Newman applies here: "In what meaningful sense may it be asserted that these new doctrines are not 'new revelation'?"[117]

Ultimately, Newman appeals to ecclesial infallibility as a necessary, divinely appointed authority that can "secure the validity of inferences" in the interpretation of divinely deposited ideas.[118] Newman believes that "modern Catholicism is nothing else but simply the legitimate growth and complement, that is, the natural and necessary development, of the doctrine of the early church, *and that its divine authority is included in the divinity of Christianity.*"[119] However, as many of his Protestant and evangelical critics note, even if Newman contends that revelation is itself immutable despite its varying interpretations, his appeal to the Catholic Church as an ever-present, infallible interpreting authority on par with the apostles seems to conflate interpretation with new revelation.[120] Despite these

---

116. Ibid., 104–5; cf. Joseph Butler, *Analogy of Religion: Natural and Revealed to the Constitution and Course of Nature*, ed. Robert Emory and G. R. Brooks (New York: Harper and Brothers, 1860), 284–85.

117. Chadwick, *From Bossuet to Newman*, 195.

118. Newman, *An Essay on the Development of Christian Doctrine*, 78–83.

119. Ibid., 169.

120. Chadwick, *From Bossuet to Newman*, 195; cf. Yarnell, 121–23. Some Protestants have taken up the position of development as new revelation. See David Brown, *Tradition and Imagination: Revelation and Change* (Oxford: Oxford University Press, 1999); idem, *Discipleship and Imagination: Christian Tradition and Truth* (Oxford: Oxford University Press, 2000).

issues, Newman's discussion of development remains one of the most significant contributions to the problem.

The hermeneutics of development in the *Essay* are more descriptive than prescriptive. Newman provides little help in distinguishing between a faithful interpretation of a revealed idea and a corruption. Though he offers seven criteria for generally "ascertaining the correctness of developments," he admits that they are not useful for individual interpreters or valuable for producing final judgments on a doctrine's development.[121] Chadwick observes that these tests, "which convinced no one," could just as easily be applied to Luther, Calvin, Schleiermacher, or critics of traditional Christianity like David F. Strauss (1808–1874).[122]

Newman's Protestant and Evangelical Critics

Nineteenth-century Protestant discussions about doctrinal development were largely reactionary to the opposition their theologians faced on two fronts: the Anglo-Catholic apologetic of John Henry Newman and the more formidable threats of F. C. Baur (1792–1860), Harnack, and the *religionsgeschichtliche Schule*, whose radical revision of early Christian history defied traditional orthodoxy.[123] Concerns about impinging Catholicism fueled the former responses, the growing feud between modernism and orthodox belief directed the latter. In response to Harnack and the classic liberals utilizing comparative religion methodologies to discredit traditional Christian interpretations of Scripture,

---

121. Newman, *An Essay on the Development of Christian Doctrine*, 78; cf. 169–206. The tests include (1) the preservation of a type or idea, (2) continuity of principles, (3) assimilative power, (4) early anticipation, (5) logical sequence, (6) preservative additions, and (7) chronic continuance.
122. Chadwick, *From Bossuet to Newman*, 143–44.
123. Peter Toon (1939–2009) outlines these responses in *The Development of Doctrine in the Church* (Grand Rapids, MI: Eerdmans, 1979), 17–35, 55–73.

Presbyterian apologist James Orr (1844–1913) used evolutionary theory to reconcile the progress of doctrinal development with fixed revelation.[124]

Among Newman's contemporary critics were James Bowling Mozley (1813–1878), the brother-in-law of Newman who was also a leader in the Oxford Movement, and William Archer Butler (1814–1848), who was himself a former Catholic.[125] On the other side of the pond, Princeton theologian Charles Hodge (1797–1878), who was highly influential in shaping the direction of nineteenth- and twentieth-century evangelical theology in America, offered another reaction to the nineteenth-century theories of development proffered by Roman Catholic theologians. Hodge affirmed the notion of doctrinal development, but went to great lengths to distinguish a Protestant or evangelical theory of development from the Roman Catholic apology for the material and/or formal insufficiency of Scripture. He writes,

> The Romish doctrine of tradition is not to be confounded with the modern doctrine of development. All Protestants admit that there has been, in one sense, an uninterrupted development of theology in the Church, from the apostolic age to the present time. All the facts, truths, doctrines, and principles, which enter into Christian theology, are in the Bible. . . . No addition has been afforded to their nature or relations.[126]

For Hodge and the old Princeton School tradition, the Bible is a "store-house of facts" in which the interpreter-theologian works.[127] Hodge understands doctrinal development to be the simple identification of propositions already contained implicitly in the

---

124. See James Orr, *The Process of Dogma*, 3d ed. (London: Hodder and Stoughton, 1908), 1–32.
125. See James Bowling Mozley, *The Theory of Developments* (London: Rivingtons, 1878); William Archer Butler, *Lectures on Romanism in Reply to Mr. Newman's Essay on Development*, 2nd ed., ed. Charles Hardwick (Cambridge: Macmillan, 1858).
126. Charles Hodge, *Systematic Theology*, vol. 1 (Peabody, MA: Hendrickson, 2003), 116.
127. Ibid., 9–12.

Bible. In this sense, even this early evangelical approach to development was explicitly hermeneutical.

Hermeneutics and Development in Recent Protestant Approaches

Events leading up to and following the Second Vatican Council (1962–1965) sparked renewed interest in the problem in Catholic and Protestant quarters. In the previous decade, Catholics witnessed Pius XII define the Assumption of Mary as infallible dogma. This 1950 exercise of *ex cathedra* came nearly a century after Pius IX defined the Immaculate Conception as infallible dogma, the only other exercise of papal infallibility confirmed by the magisterium. With this new dogma, Catholic theologians found themselves addressing the problem of development once more. For example, Karl Rahner (1904–1984) uses this doctrine to set the stage for his discussion of the development of dogma.[128]

The spirit of ecumenicism sparked by Vatican II also fostered new Protestant approaches to the problem. Then-Lutheran theologian Jaroslav Pelikan (1923–2006) initially addressed the problem of development at the St. Thomas More Lectures at Yale University in the autumn of 1965, where he was the first non-Catholic to give those lectures. Pelikan believes this problem to be the crucial difference between Catholics and Protestants, and he warns against extreme approaches that neglect either history or theology.[129]

---

128. See Karl Rahner, *Theological Investigations*, vol. 1, trans. Cornelius Ernst (New York: Seabury, 1961), 39–77. For a summary of theories from mid-twentieth-century Catholic scholars like Rahner, Yves Congar (1904–1995), and Edward Schillebeeckx (1914–2009), see Herbert Hammans, "Recent Catholic Views on the Development of Dogma," *Concilium* 1 (1967): 109–31.

129. See Jaroslav Pelikan, *Development of Christian Doctrine: Some Historical Prolegomena* (New Haven: Yale University Press, 1969); and *Historical Theology: Continuity and Change in Christian Doctrine* (Philadelphia: Westminster, 1971).

Development was a considerable theme throughout Pelikan's career, as evidenced by the subtitle of his magisterial five-volume history of Christian thought: *A History of the Development of Doctrine*.[130]

Oxford theologian Maurice Wiles represents a liberal twentieth-century response to the problem. He offers a model of doctrinal development that leaves little room for doctrinal identity or any stable norm of Christian doctrine.[131] Irish church historian Richard P. C. Hanson offers harsh criticism of Wiles: "The idea that the development of Christian doctrine should be reduced to *Religionsgeschichte*, to a story of activity without reference to criteria, to a picture of what one might coarsely describe as 'one damn thing after another,' is intolerable, and could only have occurred to someone who is dangerously divorced from serious Christian pastoral or theological concern."[132]

The Scottish Protestant theologian Thomas F. Torrance also offers helpful insights into the issue in his analysis of theological reflection. While Torrance does not address the "problem" of development directly, many of the issues he raises in his treatment of the relationship between theological method and the philosophy of science overlap with development issues. Shaped by his interaction with the work of Michael Polanyi in the formulation of scientific theories, Torrance offers a three-leveled model for how theological reflection works. Torrance then in turn applies these insights to the historical development of Trinitarian doctrine, suggesting that the historical process of development reflects the individual experience of theological reflection.

---

130. See Jaroslav Pelikan, *The Christian Tradition: A History of the Development of Doctrine*, 5 vols. (Chicago: University of Chicago Press, 1975–1991).

131. See Maurice Wiles, *The Making of Christian Doctrine: A Study in the Principles of Doctrinal Development* (Cambridge: Cambridge University Press, 1967); idem, *The Remaking of Christian Doctrine* (London: SCM, 1974); idem, *Working Papers in Doctrine* (Naperville, IL: Allenson, 1976).

132. R. P. C. Hanson, *The Continuity of Christian Doctrine* (New York: Seabury, 1981), 32.

According to Torrance, doctrinal formulation begins with the *"incipient theology"* of every Christian believer,[133] the "basic level of experience and worship . . . in which we encounter God's revealing and reconciling activity in the Gospel."[134] This level embodies the regular, "day-to-day" practice of theological reflection in the life of the Christian believer living in the Scriptures and in a local faith community. At this level of doctrinal formulation, reason and experience are closely intertwined; reflection on belief and the experience of worship are virtually indistinguishable.

Theological reflection then proceeds with a secondary level—the *"theological level"* in which believers wrestle with the meaning and scope of God's self-revelation in Scripture.[135] The second level is basic orientation into the concepts of the tradition and Christian revelation. Here the Christian theologian moves toward something resembling a "general theological structure" or framework.[136] Torrance places the development of the "economic trinity" in this category of theological reflection because the earliest reflections on this issue were simple analyses of the activity of God revealed in Christ, not advanced, critical reflections on his *ad intra* Being.[137]

In the third level, which Torrance calls the *"higher theological level,"* significant postcanonical developments take place.[138] These postcanonical developments go beyond the explicit wording of Scripture, often resulting in the use of new terminology, new uses of older vocabulary, new metaphors, and a newly critical approach

---

133. Thomas F. Torrance, *The Christian Doctrine of God, One Being Three Persons* (Edinburgh: T&T Clark, 1996), 89.

134. Thomas F. Torrance, *The Ground and Grammar of Theology* (Charlottesville: University Press of Virginia, 1980), 156.

135. Torrance, *The Christian Doctrine of God*, 91.

136. Alister E. McGrath, *A Scientific Theology*, vol. 2, *Reality* (Grand Rapids, MI: Eerdmans, 2002), 235.

137. Torrance, *The Ground and Grammar of* Theology, 158; idem, *The Christian Doctrine of God*, 91–98.

138. Torrance, *The Ground and Grammar of* Theology, 157–58.

to our analysis of doctrine.[139] Torrance sees this level of reflection operating in later discussions of the immanent or ontological Trinity. Torrance's model, helpful as it may be for evangelical reflection of belief formation, does not directly address the tension between closed revelation and ongoing development. Nor does he explain in detail what role biblical interpretation has in the process of constructive theology.

The hermeneutical features of two late twentieth-century Protestant approaches are the foci of this section. The scholars represented here demonstrate varying degrees of engagement with contemporary hermeneutical theory and the philosophy of language. With his postliberal model of doctrinal development, George A. Lindbeck offers a mainline or progressive Protestant approach shaped by postmodern thought. The British evangelical theologian Alister McGrath offers a model of development shaped by dialogue with postmodernism and the philosophy of science.

George A. Lindbeck on Development

Yale theologian and Protestant ecumenicist George Lindbeck's interdisciplinary engagement with the problem of doctrinal development, hermeneutics, and the philosophy of language makes him one of the most important interlocutors in this study.[140] His

---

139. Torrance, *The Christian Doctrine of God*, 102–03.

140. Lindbeck has long been considered one of the leaders of the so-called "Yale School," but this designation has fallen out of favor with postliberal theologians in recent years. Furthermore, some postliberals question the propriety of the designation in reference to Lindbeck. See George Hunsinger, "Postliberal Theology," in *The Cambridge Companion to Postmodern Theology*, ed. Kevin J. Vanhoozer (Cambridge: Cambridge University Press, 2003), 42–45. George Hunsinger contends that Lindbeck's cultural-linguistic theory is mislabeled as postliberal when in reality it is neoliberal—a new road to the conclusions of classical liberalism. Hunsinger concedes that Lindbeck's cultural approach may be labeled postliberal even if his understanding of doctrine as regulative and truth as pragmatist—"defined as to make them significantly non-cognitive"—is a telltale sign of the modern liberal repugnance for propositional truth.

postliberal, narrativist hermeneutic stems from engagement with the later Wittgenstein, Ricoeur, and biblical scholars such as Hans Wilhelm Frei.[141] The number of Lindbeck's published works is remarkably disproportionate to his significance in doctrinal studies. His slender 1984 volume, *The Nature of Doctrine*, initially intended to serve as prolegomena to a larger work on agreements and disagreements in the larger Christian tradition, is an inventive, influential monograph on theological method that is in a class with works like Newman's *Essay*. While Lindbeck addresses many of the questions about development raised by Newman, he also acknowledges that issues in the ecumenical movement enlarged his focus.[142] This broader scope includes a number of issues related, but not limited to, development: intramural doctrinal disagreements, the prospect of unity, and the change of doctrine over time.[143]

Development and the Early Lindbeck

Before *The Nature of Doctrine*, development was a pronounced theme in Lindbeck's earlier work in Protestant-Catholic dialogue.[144] In a 1967 article, he concedes that Protestants have not given adequate attention to the problem of development. He rejects organicist analogies like those from Vincent and Newman and advocates an approach to doctrinal development that he calls "historical

---

141. See Hans W. Frei, *The Eclipse of Biblical Narrative: A Study in Eighteenth and Nineteenth Century Hermeneutics* (New Haven: Yale University Press, 1974).
142. Lindbeck, *The Nature of Doctrine*, 8–9, 13.
143. Ibid., 9.
144. See George A. Lindbeck, *The Future of Roman Catholic Theology: Vatican II—Catalyst for Change* (Philadelphia: Fortress Press, 1970); idem, *Infallibility* (Milwaukee: Marquette University Press, 1972); idem, "The Problem of Doctrinal Development and Contemporary Protestant Theology," in *Man as Man and Believer*, ed. Edward Schillebeeckx and Boniface Willems (New York: Paulist Press, 1967), 133–49; idem, "Protestant Problems with Lonergan on Development of Dogma," in *Foundations of Theology*, ed. Philip McShane (Notre Dame: University of Notre Dame Press, 1972), 115–23.

situationalism" or "decision theory."[145] According to this model, which Lindbeck calls the implicit "Protestant consensus," development is the result of a conversation between God and the church as they wrestle through the implications of Scripture for their time and place in history.[146]

Like Newman before him, Lindbeck says that doctrinal reformulation is often necessary because "traditional formulations, when repeated in novel situations, take on different—sometimes radically different—meanings." On occasion, repetition of traditional formulations betrays the apostolic deposit rather than protecting it or defending it.[147] Unlike Newman, however, Lindbeck denies that the church is always in need of new dogmas for deeper understanding of revealed truth but believes its established doctrines need frequent restatement in light of the church's continually changing historical situation.[148] As the historical situation changes, Christians seek answers to the questions that the ancient authors of Scripture do not address or expect. Through this process, which Lindbeck likens to Paul Tillich's (1886–1965) method of correlation, Christians formulate new doctrinal expressions to answer their situation.[149]

The hermeneutic that Lindbeck promotes here anticipates what would eventually become known as the theological interpretation of Scripture. In one sense, the theological interpretation of Scripture is a hermeneutical practice concerned with how the Bible functions

145. Ibid., 139; cf. Lindbeck, *The Future of Roman Catholic Theology*, 101. Lindbeck defends this rejection of growth metaphors: "This does not mean that there are no advances of any sort in the understanding of faith. It means rather that whatever development there must be understood not as analogous to a process of cumulative growth . . . but rather as similar to the much weaker type of 'progress' in comprehension which comes from viewing the same object from different perspectives as one moves away, around, or towards it."

146. Lindbeck, "The Problem of Doctrinal Development," 139.

147. Ibid.

148. Lindbeck, *The Future of Roman Catholic Theology*, 101.

149. Lindbeck, "The Problem of Doctrinal Development," 139; cf. 139 n. 14. See also Paul Tillich, *Systematic Theology*, vol. 1 (Chicago: University of Chicago Press, 1951), 3–68.

theologically. In this use, theological interpretation has premodern concerns. In quite another sense, theological interpretation is a practice of understanding how the Bible has functioned historically in believing communities. This use of theological interpretation is more postmodern in its ethos.[150]

He encourages a theological reading of Scripture that is mindful of the history of interpretation because he believes that such a reading can provide a valuable aid in determining the present application of the text. Lindbeck insists that this does not mean that traditional interpretations supplement the apostolic deposit, as they do in Catholicism, but rather these past interpretations serve as voices of wisdom or guides in the interpretive task.[151] Every generation attempts to read the Bible for itself, but contemporary readers are often unaware of the way in which previous generations affect their interpretations. For this reason, Lindbeck pleads, it is crucial that the contemporary readers of Scripture correct "partiality and distortions" in their doctrine "by studying and learning how our forefathers in the faith through the whole of history have understood the Gospel."[152] Doctrinal formulations are incapable of exhausting the content of Scripture, and they are often incorrect. Ultimately, for the early Lindbeck anyway, "all teachings of the Church must be constantly tested by Scripture and thus kept open to review, revision or perhaps even repeal."[153]

---

150. Paula Gooder, *Searching for Meaning* (Louisville: Westminster/John Knox, 2009), 120–26.

151. Lindbeck, "The Problem of Doctrinal Development," 139–40, n. 15; cf. 140–41. Even if the early Lindbeck questions the propriety of the term of *sola scriptura* in the Protestant tradition, as Protestants use a number of other "subjective" sources like experience and tradition, he does deem Scripture as "materially sufficient" and the decisive norm by which all other theological sources are measured.

152. Lindbeck, "The Problem of Doctrinal Development," 140.

153. Ibid., 141–42. Lindbeck admits that this test is difficult to apply to post-apostolic developments such as the practice of infant baptism. He also holds all doctrinal formulations—even the Nicene and Chalcedonian creeds—provisionally. See also Lindbeck, "Protestant Problems with Lonergan," 121–22. Here the young Lutheran theologian is unclear about whether he is

Development in *The Nature of Doctrine*

With the same ecumenical impulse that defined his earlier career, the Lindbeck of *The Nature of Doctrine* envisions "doctrinal reconciliation without capitulation"—that is, intra-Christian discourse without the sacrifice of convictions and distinctives—by conceiving a new way of understanding doctrine: what he calls the "cultural-linguistic" approach.[154] He here addresses an often-neglected question: "What is doctrine?"[155] While the definition of theology has been a contentious issue since the Enlightenment, the once-tacit definition of doctrine, from the Latin term *doctrīna* meaning "teaching," "instruction," "training," or "branch of learning,"[156] remained virtually unquestioned until the twentieth century. Lindbeck asks whether doctrines cognitive-propositional truth claims about the nature of divine reality, merely affective expressions that give linguistic expression to the feelings of religious experience,[157] or second-order, "cultural-linguistic" grammatical statements or "rules" that guide a particular faith community in life and praxis? He is the first to demonstrate that how one answers this query is of enormous consequence for the development problem.

Without question, cognitive-propositionalist accounts of doctrine make agreement between contrary doctrinal positions difficult, if not impossible. For example, one cannot logically affirm and reject transubstantiation simultaneously.[158] Lindbeck adds that development

---

advocating a more traditional *sola scriptura* position or entertaining a hermeneutic more like his later view of "faithfulness as intratextuality."

154. Lindbeck, *The Nature of Doctrine*, 15–16, 32–41.

155. Ibid., 15–19.

156. *The Oxford Latin Dictionary* (Oxford: Clarendon, 1968), s.v. "*doctrīna*."

157. Lindbeck, *The Nature of Doctrine*, 16. The experiential-expressive approach "interprets doctrines as noninformative and nondiscursive symbols of inner feelings, attitudes, or existential orientations." Lindbeck designates Schleiermacher as the father of this theory of doctrine, though Schleiermacher's emphasis on a positive theology calls this description into question. See also Alister E. McGrath, *The Genesis of Doctrine: A Study in the Foundation of Doctrinal Criticism* (Grand Rapids, MI: Eerdmans, 1990), 16.

is only a serious "problem" for theologians committed to some kind of a propositionalist theory.[159] Because the propositionalist holds doctrine to be timeless truth, the propositionalist must have difficulty conceiving of new formulations of Christian doctrine.[160] Contextualization thus becomes an insoluble undertaking because "propositionalist accounts of how old doctrines can be reinterpreted to fit new circumstances are unconvincing; they have difficulty in distinguishing between what changes and what remains the same."[161]

The experiential-expressivist approach fares no better in doctrinal development. For Lindbeck, this approach, represented to some degree by Rahner and Lonergan, is "weak in criteria for determining when a given doctrinal development is consistent with the sources of faith."[162] Whereas propositional theories have difficulty with diversity in doctrine, affective theories do little to demonstrate unity in doctrinal reformulation. As Lindbeck asks, "How can a religion claim to preserve 'the faith which was once for all delivered to the saints' . . . as all religions in some sense do, when it takes so many forms in both the past and the present?"[163] Development may present a serious challenge to the propositionalist, but the expressionist may not see it as an issue at all because doctrine presents "no self-identical core [that] persists down through the centuries" and because all religious traditions, including Christianity, are in flux.[164]

Neither of these approaches, Lindbeck argues, allows for both doctrinal development and fidelity to the received tradition. In his

---

158. Lindbeck, *The Nature of Doctrine*, 16. To do so would violate the law of non-contradiction: something cannot be A and not-A in the same time and in the same way.

159. Lindbeck, *The Nature of Doctrine*, 80; cf. 89, n. 11. Lindbeck looks to the narrative described in Chadwick's *From Bossuet to Newman* for anecdotal evidence of this suggestion.

160. Ibid., 16.

161. Ibid., 78.

162. Ibid., 17. Lindbeck presents the model of doctrinal development given by Wiles as an example of experiential expressivism (50).

163. Lindbeck, *The Nature of Doctrine*, 78.

164. Ibid., 78–79.

"rule theory" or cultural-linguistic approach, an approach shaped by interaction with Wittgenstein and cultural anthropology, religions are treated like cultures and language games.[165] Lindbeck's notion of religion as a socially and culturally constructed framework through which reality is interpreted is based on the work of sociologists of knowledge Peter Berger and Thomas Luckmann, who contend that there "can be no social reality apart from man" despite the fact that "man is a product of society."[166] Religions for Lindbeck are akin to social structures that Berger calls "sacred canopies," social constructs that shield us from an unlivable kind of nihilism.[167] Where religion is likened to a language game, doctrines are neither propositional truth claims nor mere symbolic expressions of an inner experience, but rather grammatical rules of belief with a primarily regulative or normative function.[168] Rather than constituting the cognitive content of a narrative framework, doctrines are merely like grammatical rules that shape the way the narrative is interpreted.[169] In sum, doctrines do not depict extra-linguistic realities; they guide the beliefs of the religious community.

The rule theory presented here shifts the focus of the problem of development. Tracing a theme he covers in his earlier work, Lindbeck insists that the theological task does not consist of mere

165. Lindbeck, *The Nature of Doctrine*, 18; cf. 20, 27, n. 10.
166. See Peter L. Berger, *The Sacred Canopy: Elements of a Sociological Theory of Religion* (New York: Doubleday, 1967), 3; Peter L. Berger and Thomas Luckmann, *The Social Construction of Reality* (New York: Anchor, 1966), 26–27. Berger and Luckmann derive this dialectic of social construction from Karl Marx (1818–1883), who observes that "it is not the consciousness of men that determines their being, but on the contrary, their social being that determines their consciousness." See Karl Marx, "Preface to *A Contribution to the Critique of Political Economy*," in *The Marx-Engels Reader,* ed. Robert C. Tucker (New York: Norton, 1978), 4. Philosopher of social science and Wittgenstein specialist Peter Winch (1926–1997) and cultural anthropologist Clifford Geertz (1926–2006) also inform Lindbeck's model. See Peter Winch, *The Idea of a Social Science and Its Relationship to Philosophy*, 2nd ed. (London: Routledge, 1990), 24–62; Clifford Geertz, *The Interpretation of Cultures* (New York: Basic, 1973), 87–125.
167. Berger, *The Sacred Canopy*, 25.
168. Lindbeck, *The Nature of Doctrine*, 18.
169. Ibid., 80.

verbal regurgitation. Oftentimes new formulations of doctrines are needed in order to adhere faithfully to the regulations of earlier expressions. As a linguistic grammar is impaired by its limitations, so too is theological grammar that guides religion because every rule has its exceptions.[170] If doctrines are second-order rules and not first-order descriptions, then changing expressions and descriptions should be of little concern.[171]

Lindbeck suggests that religions are not part of a worldview per se, but rather interpretive schemes that guide and direct worldviews. With changing worlds, worldviews frequently shift, but religious grammar remains a constant. The grammar of the Christian faith, found in the narrative of Jesus, can maintain its identity as it orders new articulations in new situations. New situations or forms of life entail different conceptual frameworks by which Jesus' story is read. For first-century Jews, Jesus may have been interpreted as Israel's Messiah and as *Homoousion* for fourth-century Eastern Christians. For some twenty-first century Christians, Jesus may be the community organizer par excellence. According to Lindbeck, the story of Christ recorded in the Gospels provides the stable grammar for whatever theological or conceptual framework in which the story is read.[172] When Christians "read" their situation by the narrative of Jesus, the story will transform their worldview, and each successive generation will need to formulate new expressions.

Lindbeck's hermeneutic steers his rule-theory model of doctrinal development. With an "intratextual" hermeneutic, he suggests that the systematic theologian's task is to "give a normative explication

---

170. Ibid., 81.
171. Language has a constant, common structure across various dialects and grammar systems. While the specific rules may change contextually, language depends on common structural elements that are stable across the spectrum. Michael Steinmetz has made this insight from structuralism clear to me in his criticism of Lindbeck.
172. Lindbeck, *The Nature of Doctrine*, 82–83.

of the meaning a religion has for its adherents."[173] He differentiates this cultural-linguistic reading of the Bible from cognitive-propositionalists' and experiential-expressivists' "extratextual" approach that "locates religious meaning outside the text . . . either in the objective realities to which it refers or in the experiences it symbolizes."[174] The temptation of extratextual hermeneutics is to translate the Bible into extra-biblical categories (such as concepts of historicity or metaphysical identity).[175] "Intratextual theology," on the other hand, "redescribes reality within the scriptural framework rather than translating Scripture into extrascriptural categories. It is the text, so to speak, which absorbs the world, rather than the world the text."[176]

For Lindbeck in *The Nature of Doctrine*, "the normative or literal meaning must be consistent with the kind of text it is taken to be by the community of faith for which it is important." This meaning is "not something behind, beneath, or in front of the text; not something that the text reveals, discloses, implies or suggests to those with extraneous metaphysical historical, or experiential interests."[177] Attempts to describe Jesus in historical reconstructions or Christ in metaphysical terminology are alien to the internal interpretive framework of the text. With Frei, Lindbeck describes the Bible as "history-like" narrative written not to disclose God's being but to

---

173. Ibid., 113. For more on Lindbeck's intratextual hermeneutics, see George A. Lindbeck, "The Bible as Realistic Narrative," *Journal of Ecumenical Studies* 17 (1980): 80–85; idem, "The Story-Shaped Church: Critical Exegesis and Theological Interpretation," in *Scriptural Authority and Narrative Interpretation*, ed. Garret Green (Philadelphia: Fortress Press, 1987), 161–78; idem, "Toward a Postliberal Theology: Faithfulness as Intertexuality," in *The Return to Scripture in Judaism and Christianity*, ed. Peter Ochs (New York: Paulist Press, 1993), 83–103; idem, "Atonement and the Hermeneutics of Intratextual Social Embodiment," in *The Nature of Confession*, ed. Timothy Phillips and Dennis Okholm (Downers Grove, IL: InterVarsity, 1996), 221–40.
174. Lindbeck, *The Nature of Doctrine*, 114.
175. Ibid., 118, 120–22.
176. Ibid., 118.
177. Ibid., 120.

inform those who are in covenant with God as his people how they are to live their lives.[178] Doctrinal development is to be expected with a changing setting, as there is no permanent or fixed meaning in the text itself.[179]

Alister McGrath's Multifaceted Approach to Doctrinal Development

One of Lindbeck's most important evangelical dialogue partners is the British theologian Alister McGrath. Few evangelical scholars have made the kinds of contributions to public theology and theological method as noteworthy as McGrath's. While his monograph on doctrinal development theory is still forthcoming,[180] he has addressed the issue numerous times in his capacities as a historical theologian, a systematic theologian, a natural theologian, and a popular Christian writer. His histories of the doctrine of justification, medieval and Reformation thought, and contemporary German christologies all cast light on the historical particularities of doctrinal development.[181]

---

178. Ibid., 121.
179. Lindbeck is more open to authorial-discourse in a more recent article. See George A. Lindbeck, "Postcritical Canonical Interpretation: Three Modes of Retrieval," in *Theological Exegesis: Essays in Honor of Brevard Childs,* ed. Christopher Seitz and Kathryn Green-McCreight (Grand Rapids, MI: Eerdmans, 1999), 26–51. See also Kevin J. Vanhoozer, *The Drama of Doctrine: A Canonical Linguistic Approach to Christian Theology* (Louisville: Westminster/John Knox, 2005), 166–67. Even still, Vanhoozer notes, "Lindbeck has made no attempt to explain whether, or how his openness to authorial-discourse interpretation squares with his earlier proposal concerning the nature of doctrine."
180. Alister E. McGrath, *A Scientific Theology*, vol. 3, *Theory* (Grand Rapids, MI: Eerdmans, 2003), 213. Here McGrath promises two "larger books" dedicated to the related themes of doctrinal development and heresy. His popular-level *Heresy: A History of Defending the Truth* (New York: HarperOne, 2009) takes Bauer's thesis to task.
181. Alister E. McGrath, *Iustitia Dei: A History of the Christian Doctrine of Justification*, 3d ed. (Cambridge: Cambridge University Press, 2005); idem, *The Intellectual Origins of the European Reformation*, 2nd ed. (Oxford: Blackwell, 2004); idem, *The Making of Modern German Christology: From the Enlightenment to Pannenberg* (Oxford: Basil Blackwell, 1986). In *Iustitia Dei*, McGrath describes the development of the doctrine of justification as a "paradigm for the study of ideological interaction in the development of doctrine, illustrating how theological and

Most consequential for theoretical discussions of doctrinal development are McGrath's contributions to the topic in his work in systematic theology and natural theology.

Gadamer's philosophical hermeneutics, particularly Gadamer's critique of the Enlightenment rejection of tradition, plays a pivotal role in McGrath's theory of doctrinal formulation.[182] Christian tradition is a necessary vehicle of the transmission of information concerning Jesus, but this observation need not mean that the tradition is beyond critical examination.[183] McGrath believes that the genesis of doctrine and the future of doctrine are linked inextricably by the same historical conditions that give rise to doctrinal development: the need for historically contingent faith communities to articulate their respective worldviews in their own given contexts. Despite the best efforts of movements within Protestant theological liberalism to purge doctrine from Christianity, McGrath trusts that it will continue to play a significant role because of its relationship to the perceived needs of faith communities in their attempts to distinguish themselves from the secular culture and to maintain their association with the historical Jesus.[184]

McGrath considers a wide array of possible analogies from nature, life science, and psychology in constructing his model of doctrinal development. He considers organic models but reiterates the criticism of Dominican theologian Ambroise Gardeil (1859–1931) toward the metaphor, noting that the organic model "fails to identify and account for the fundamental impulse which drives the process of evolution."[185] McGrath also rejects theories of doctrinal development

secular concepts were related as theologians responded to the cultural situation of their period" (vii).

182. The impact of Gadamer's hermeneutics on McGrath's earlier theory of development is observed in Steven L. Oldham, "Alister E. McGrath and Evangelical Theories of Doctrinal Development" (Ph.D. diss., Baylor University, 2000), 115–26.

183. McGrath, *The Genesis of Doctrine*, 179–85.

184. Ibid., 193–98.

based on analogies drawn from biological evolution.[186] He also offers an analogy based on the developmental psychology of Jean Piaget.[187] Ultimately, McGrath finds each of biological and psychological analogies such as these deficient because none specifically addresses the development of human ideas nor are they equipped to "capture the observable complexities of human intellectual and cultural progress."[188]

Presently, the most systematic presentation of McGrath's concept of doctrinal development is in his *A Scientific Theology* trilogy (2001–2003). Unlike past natural theologies like those of William Paley (1743–1805), the scientific theology of which McGrath conceives is not dependent on any first-order scientific theory because a theology grounded in provisional scientific theory can be dismissed and outmoded with advances in science. Instead, McGrath aims to base his scientific theology "upon the methods and working assumptions which underlie [natural] sciences—supremely a belief in the regularity of the natural world, and the ability of the human mind to uncover and represent regularity in a mathematical manner."[189] In other words, his scientific theology is a second-order way of reflecting on the relationship between scientific thinking and theological thinking rather than establishing theological claims in contemporary scientific data or theories. Here, McGrath shows clear

185. McGrath, *A Scientific Theology*, vol. 3, *Theory*, 216; cf. Ambroise Gardeil, *Le donné révélé et la théologie* (Paris: Editions Du Cerf, 1932). For an overview of Gardeil's criticisms of Newman and his own model of doctrinal development, see Nichols, *From Newman to Congar*, 155–76.

186. For an example of an evolutionary theory of development, see Hastings Randall, *The Idea of the Atonement in Christian Theology* (London: Macmillan, 1919). Also see Alister E. McGrath, "The Evolution of Doctrine? A Critical Examination of the Theological Validity of Biological Models of Doctrinal Development," in *The Order of Things: Explorations in Scientific Theology* (Oxford: Blackwell, 2006), 117–65.

187. McGrath, *The Genesis of Doctrine*, 194–95. For a fuller examination of Piaget's significance for McGrath's model of development, see McGrath, *The Order of Things*, 169–82.

188. McGrath, *The Genesis of Doctrine*, 195.

189. Alister E. McGrath, *A Scientific Theology*, vol. 1, *Nature* (Grand Rapids, MI: Eerdmans, 2001), 50.

indebtedness to the similar enterprise of Thomas Torrance in the previous generation of British theology, as Torrance sought to show the "relationship between *science* and *theology* . . . and between the philosophy of natural science and the philosophy of theological science in the common struggle for scientific method on their proper ground and their own distinctive fields."[190]

McGrath here likens doctrinal development to the process of scientific theorizing. Scientific theories, like doctrines, develop sometimes to "the displacement of those [theories] which were once widely accepted and regarded as the best available explanation of the known evidence."[191] Following the course charted by Thomas S. Kuhn (1922–1996),[192] McGrath presumes that doctrinal theories, like scientific theories, can undergo paradigm shifts whereby "theories . . . once judged to be successful by the criteria of their contemporaries . . . have now been abandoned."[193] Even so, doctrinal theories, like scientific theories, take their shape in engagement with a dynamic tradition. Even "'new departures' are actually modifications to a tradition, which allow and propose new and unexpected ways of maintaining continuity with that tradition."[194]

Unlike Kuhn, McGrath does not believe that acknowledgment of paradigm shifts necessitates a rejection of scientific or epistemic realism.[195] Echoing philosopher of science Lawrence Sklar, McGrath finds scientific anti-realism an untenable position because, regardless of changing theories and provisional conclusions, science operates

---

190. T. F. Torrance, *Theological Science* (Oxford: Oxford University Press, 1969), xiii.

191. McGrath, *A Scientific Theology*, vol. 3, *Theory*, 214.

192. See Thomas S. Kuhn, *The Structure of Scientific Revolutions*, 3d ed. (Chicago: The University of Chicago Press, 1996), esp. 66–135. See also Toon, *The Development of Doctrine*, 113–15.

193. McGrath, *A Scientific Theology*, vol. 3, *Theory*, 215–16.

194. McGrath, *The Genesis of Doctrine*, 181.

195. McGrath, *A Scientific Theology*, vol. 3, *Theory*, 216. For McGrath's critique of the Kuhnian program, see Alister E. McGrath, *A Scientific Theology*, vol. 2, *Reality* (Grand Rapids, MI: Eerdmans, 2002), 161–66.

with the working assumption that there is regularity in the natural world that can be ascertained and represented. Science cannot function with the belief that "our current best theories are ultimately headed for the scrap-heap that has welcomed their predecessors."[196] Nevertheless, the value of Kuhn's observations for McGrath's model of doctrinal development is in the alternative that it presents to models dependent upon linear development. McGrath writes, "The authenticity of theoretical advance is determined not by the linearity of the process, but by the empirical adequacy and intratheoretical excellence of the outcome of that process. . . . The validity of the ensuing theories is dependent not upon the process by which they evolved, but upon their empirical credentials."[197]

McGrath takes the metaphor of "Neurath's Boat" out to sea in order to explain how these doctrinal paradigm shifts take place. This metaphor, first put forward by "left-wing" member of the Vienna Circle Otto Neurath (1882–1945) and later popularized by W. V. O. Quine, is primarily a critique of foundationalism. Against foundationalism Neurath protests, "We are like sailors who on the open seas must reconstruct their ship but are never able to start afresh from the bottom."[198] McGrath stresses that doctrinal development occurs *in via* (not *de novo* or *ab initio*) with three "specific pressures . . . implicit in Neurath's original metaphor." First, those at sea must learn to *unpack*, or learn "to live within the boat's confines" and understand "what is already incorporated within its structures."[199] For McGrath,

---

196. Ibid., 166.

197. McGrath, *A Scientific Theology*, vol. 3, *Theory*, 216.

198. See Otto Neurath, "Protokollsätze," *Erkenntnis* 3 (1932): 204–14; reprinted in Otto Neurath, *Philosophical Papers 1913-1946*, Vienna Circle Collection 16, ed. and trans. Robert S. Cohen and Marie Neurath (Dordecht: D. Reidel, 1983). For a detailed critical examination of this illustration and its application, see Nancy Cartwright, Jordi Cat, Lola Fleck, and Thomas E. Uebel, *Otto Neurath: Philosophy between Science and Politics* (Cambridge: Cambridge University Press, 1996), 89–165.

199. McGrath, *A Scientific Theology*, vol. 3, *Theory*, 219.

this means that members of the faith community learn to make use of the elements of the Christian tradition available to them.

Second, the sailors must learn to *reconstruct* or rebuild "parts of the ship from what is already present . . . in response to damage caused by adverse conditions . . . which threaten to capsize or swamp the ship."[200] McGrath cites the Reformation as a primary example of doctrinal development as reconstruction using resources available aboard the ship. For Luther, reformation "was renovation, not innovation."[201] His initial interests were restoring the Catholic Church to what he believed was a more biblically faithful doctrine of grace, not abandoning or replacing the ship altogether.[202] Luther proposed a return to the biblical texts themselves and a rejection of the hierarchical interpretation imposed on believers by the magisterium.[203]

Finally, sailors must learn how to *incorporate driftwood*, i.e., use "material which is at hand in the environment to strengthen the boat."[204] McGrath writes, "The history of the Christian tradition demonstrates a marked propensity to avail itself of intellectual and cultural resources it encountered around it, floating in the water of history. Such driftwood is not part of the original fabric of the boat, and its incorporation must be temporary, not permanent."[205] Although reconstructed at sea with driftwood, Neurath's boat cannot entirely escape the paradox of Theseus's ship.[206] Presently, McGrath has yet to address the additional problems for identity or continuity in doctrinal development that the use of Neurath's boat as a model might create.

200. Ibid., 219–20.
201. Ibid., 220.
202. McGrath, *Heresy*, 212.
203. Ibid., 211.
204. McGrath, *A Scientific Theology*, vol. 3, *Theory*, 219.
205. Ibid., 220.
206. Plutarch *Theseus*.

Though McGrath describes the process of development as "a process of *interpretation* of a complex biblical witness to the identity and significance of Jesus Christ,"[207] the philosophy of science plays a larger role than explicit hermeneutical theory in his model. Nevertheless, many of his resources are from hermeneuticists, and many of his ideas relate to hermeneutical theory. Some of his conservative critics confront McGrath for neglecting to produce a more robust view of the role Scripture plays in development.[208] McGrath, however, does not intend to provide a prescriptive account of doctrinal development, as he explains in his *Scientific Theology*.[209] Like Lindbeck, McGrath is also concerned with producing a theory of development that considers the nature of doctrine itself.

Summary

This chapter was an exploration of the historical relationship between the practice and theory of hermeneutics and the problem of doctrinal development in pre-critical, modern, and contemporary settings. Many nineteenth- and twentieth-century theories of development share certain family resemblances with hermeneutical theory. Newman, for instance, indicates that many of the same questions relating to doctrinal development relate to the understanding of any complex idea and require critical reflection that is similar to the attempt to understand a text.

All of these models stress the importance of bridging the biblical world with the present, which is an important hermeneutical

---

207. McGrath, *A Scientific Theology*, vol. 3, *Theory*, 234, italics mine.
208. Yarnell, 126–27.
209. McGrath, *A Scientific Theology*, vol. 3, *Theory*, 219. McGrath describes his theory as "descriptive, not prescriptive . . . [and] based on the historical study of Christian theology without reference to any preconceived notions of what form development ought to have taken."

concern. Yet these theorists disagree about the precise nature of interpretation and debate whether it is the magisterium, the local faith community, or the individual reader who has supreme authority in the interpretive process. In the chapters that follow, we will explore the relationship between contemporary hermeneutical theory and the problem of development in the works of two evangelical theologians. We shall also return to important questions about authority in development, religious language, and continuity.

3

Doctrinal Development in the Descriptive Theological Hermeneutics of Anthony Thiselton

The previous chapter highlighted some of the shared themes and influences between hermeneutical theory and the problem of doctrinal development throughout their respective histories. The present chapter begins to build a more constructive case, utilizing the insights of evangelical scholars engaged in conversation with contemporary hermeneutical theory for constructing a hermeneutical model of doctrinal development. Here, we will explore the theological hermeneutics of Anglican New Testament scholar and theologian Anthony C. Thiselton, whose descriptive approach to theological hermeneutics has remarkable explanatory power for the phenomenon of growing doctrinal traditions.

Few figures loom larger in evangelical hermeneutics than Thiselton, who virtually introduced conservative Anglo-American biblical scholarship to contemporary hermeneutical theory. By all accounts, his April 1977 presentation at the Second National Evangelical Anglican Conference in Nottingham was a major turning point in the history of evangelical biblical scholarship. In this much-talked-about address, Thiselton ventured to show how philosophers like Gadamer, Heidegger, and Wittgenstein could be valuable aids in appropriating biblical texts for contemporary settings.[1] The 1980 publication of *The Two Horizons*, a revision of Thiselton's doctoral thesis, gave even more currency to hermeneutical theory among evangelical biblical scholarship.[2] With this monograph, like his NEAC address, Thiselton displayed a gift that would characterize the next thirty years of his scholarship: the unique ability to employ the often-esoteric concepts of the Continental philosophical tradition in biblical interpretation and Christian theology with both conceptual clarity and pastoral concern.

Even his critics on the right and the left essentially divide the recent history of evangelical biblical interpretation into two distinct epochs: before Thiselton and after Thiselton. On the right, evangelical scholars like Robert L. Thomas bemoan what they perceive to be a dramatic departure from grammatical-historical exegesis and authorial intent in evangelical biblical hermeneutics. Thomas holds Thiselton personally responsible for this shift: "[Thiselton's *The Two*

1. This presentation is available in Tony (Anthony) Thiselton, "Understanding God's Word Today," in *Obeying Christ in a Changing World*, vol. 1, *The Lord Christ*, ed. John Stott (Glasgow: Fountain Books, 1977), 90–122. For an assessment of Thiselton's speech and its impact on evangelicals, see Robert Knowles, *Anthony C. Thiselton and the Grammar of Hermeneutics: The Search for a Unified Theory, A Study Presented to Anthony C. Thiselton in Recognition of Fifty Years of Outstanding Contribution to the Discipline of Hermeneutics* (Milton Keynes, UK: Paternoster, 2012), 50–54; Alister E. McGrath, "Evangelical Theological Method: The State of the Art," in *Evangelical Futures: A Conversation on Theological Method* (Grand Rapids, MI: Baker, 2000), 29; idem, *J. I. Packer: A Biography* (Grand Rapids, MI: Baker, 1997), 215–17.
2. See Anthony C. Thiselton, *The Two Horizons: New Testament Hermeneutics and Philosophical Description with Special Reference to Heidegger, Bultmann, Gadamer, and Wittgenstein* (Carlisle: Paternoster, 1980).

Horizons] radically altered the way many evangelicals interpret the Bible. . . . Thiselton transformed the search for propositional truth into a search for subjective human bias. From the 1960s, home Bible studies had pooled the ignorance of untrained Christians as each participant shared 'what the passage means to me.' That sort of approach was now to be the basis for discussions at meetings of evangelical theologians."[3] Thiselton's conservative detractors have (often unfairly) accused him of popularizing hermeneutical relativism among evangelicals.

By contrast, some of Thiselton's non-evangelical critics charge him not with relativism but an incoherent and naïve biblicism. In her *Fundamentalism and Evangelicals* (1998), Harriet A. Harris principally reiterates James Barr's claim that neo-evangelicals unwittingly embrace a kind of outmoded fundamentalism, especially in their adherence to a "high" view of Scripture. In her penultimate chapter, Harris responds to the claim of R. T. France that the label "fundamentalist" does not apply to evangelicals who engage with contemporary hermeneutical theory.[4] Harris credits Thiselton for introducing evangelical scholars to hermeneutics, noting that while "Thiselton's work is highly technical, it is trusted by evangelicals who know him to be of their general theological orientation."[5] Nevertheless, Harris accuses evangelicals and, by extension, Thiselton himself, of a fundamentalist and inconsistent usage of Gadamerian and phenomenological hermeneutical theory, "drawing on philosophically incompatible traditions" in order to preserve "biblical authority."[6]

---

3. Robert L. Thomas, *Evangelical Hermeneutics: The New Versus the Old* (Grand Rapids, MI: Kregel, 2002), 18.
4. Harriet A. Harris, *Fundamentalism and Evangelicals* (Oxford: Oxford University Press, 1998), 278.
5. Ibid., 287.
6. Ibid., 311.

Attempts to shelve Thiselton by locating him in a school of thought will prove equally difficult, as he borrows widely from within the Christian tradition and without. While he appropriates insights about the nature of texts and language from figures like Gadamer and Wittgenstein, he is sensitive to the accusation that he is a "Gadamerian" or a "Wittgensteinian." Thiselton rejects this notion out of hand: "I do not intend to 'follow' anyone. It is a trait of many British scholars, unlike their counterparts elsewhere in the world, to abhor any notion of belonging to a 'school.' I draw upon Moltmann, Pannenberg, Gadamer, Ricoeur, Wittgenstein, *and many other thinkers*, where I find in their writings resources that facilitate what I want to say, or sometimes ideas that inspire further vision."[7] Thiselton ultimately shares Tillich's concern that organizing theologians into "schools" or "categories" can be "a cheap and clumsy way . . . of shelving somebody."[8]

The descriptive presentation of his encyclopedic knowledge of hermeneutics and interaction with a wide range of scholarship can at times leave readers scratching their heads about what Thiselton himself thinks on some of these matters. Some of this ambiguity is pedagogical, and some stems from his earnest desire to create open-ended dialogue. Thiselton is primarily interested in driving readers to creative thought, not creating Thiseltonites. Some of this ambiguity stems from Thiselton's disdain for oversimplifications and over-generalizations. He frequently echoes Wittgenstein's frustration with "the contemptuous attitude towards the particular case" and

---

7. See Anthony C. Thiselton, *The Hermeneutics of Doctrine* (Grand Rapids, MI: Eerdmans, 2007), xxi.

8. Anthony C. Thiselton, "Authority and Hermeneutics: Some Proposals for a More Creative Agenda," in *Pathway into the Holy Scripture*, ed. Phillip E. Satterthwaite and David F. Wright (Grand Rapids, MI: Eerdmans, 1994), 108; cf. Paul Tillich, *The Protestant Era* (Chicago: University of Chicago Press, 1966), x.

the "craving for generality" found among philosophers, and by extension, theologians.[9]

Some evangelical scholars take a "touch not the unclean thing" (2 Cor. 6:17, KJV) approach to any and all interdisciplinary or integrated approaches in hermeneutics, let alone any attempt to incorporate insights from "postmodern" or "relativistic" Continental philosophy.[10] Thiselton, however, does not shy away from such interdisciplinary engagement. His work represents not only a marriage of philosophical hermeneutics and biblical interpretation but also a valiant effort to decipher the Continental tradition for a largely Anglo-American analytic audience. While he has attempted to utilize insights from philosophers of hermeneutics and language for biblical interpretation, he has never abandoned a high view of biblical authority. Because of his views on Scripture, he has been characterized as an evangelical in the Anglican tradition.[11] As a theologian interacting with the Continental philosophical tradition, Thiselton says is interested in the *"creative exploration"* of "ideas that inspire further vision."[12] As Jens Zimmermann notes, the most difficult task of theological hermeneutics is the critical appropriation of non-theological concepts, but "as so often in the history of the church, non-Christian thinkers [can] provide the most clear-sighted framing of issues and the best conceptual tools."[13] Thiselton typically succeeds in this brand of critical appropriation and even when he does not, he offers his readers new ways to think about old ideas. He

---

9. Ludwig Wittgenstein, *The Brown and the Blue Books: Preliminary Studies for the 'Philosophical Investigations'* (New York: Harper & Row, 1965), 18. See Thiselton, *The Two Horizons*, 430; idem, *New Horizons in Hermeneutics: The Theory and Practice of Transforming Biblical Reading* (Grand Rapids, MI: Zondervan, 1992), 218; idem, *Thiselton on Hermeneutics: Collected Works with New Essays* (Grand Rapids, MI: Eerdmans, 2006), 9, 234.

10. See Thomas, *Evangelical Hermeneutics*, 121–34.

11. For a helpful evaluation of Thiselton's evangelical theological positions and relationship to evangelicalism, see Knowles, 54–59.

12. Thiselton, *The Hermeneutics of Doctrine*, 164, xxi.

13. Jens Zimmermann, *Recovering Theological Hermeneutics* (Grand Rapids, MI: Baker, 2004), 160.

appears to work with the conviction that truth, wherever found, can be helpful in articulating Christian ideas.

This chapter is an exploration and evaluation of Thiselton's theological hermeneutics, highlighting elements that pertain to the so-called problem of postcanonical doctrinal development. The first section serves as an introduction to the descriptive theological hermeneutics of *The Hermeneutics of Doctrine*. The second section highlights Thiselton's interaction with traditional conceptions of the development problem. This chapter closes with an exploration and evaluation of Thiselton's descriptive, hermeneutical dialectic model of doctrinal development.

A "Life-Related" Hermeneutics of Doctrine

Neatly summarizing Thiselton's theological hermeneutics or, for that matter, identifying his central thesis is a daunting task, as his magisterial and deliberately unsystematic work evades tidy and pithy generalizations. In his recent work, *The Hermeneutics of Doctrine* (2007), Thiselton has applied his encyclopedic knowledge of hermeneutics to theological prolegomena. While this newer work represents his most explicit treatment of theological prolegomena, themes that permeate his entire corpus play an essential role in the shape of his descriptive theological hermeneutics. In *The Hermeneutics of Doctrine*, Thiselton is concerned with ways in which specific questions from hermeneutical theory address concerns in theological method, creating an apologia for a hermeneutical theology, and using his method to address specific Christian doctrines. Thiselton applies hermeneutical questions to individual doctrines because, as he aptly observes, most standard works in theological method usually lack exposition of particular doctrines and "often seem like an overture without an opera."[14]

Thiselton's overall approach to theological hermeneutics is reminiscent of the philosophical hermeneutics of Gadamer, whose work he critically appropriates without slavish devotion. The first and most noteworthy way that Thiselton imitates Gadamer's hermeneutics is in his descriptive approach to the hermeneutical task, which is a considerable departure from the normative "how-to" approach to biblical interpretation usually practiced by evangelical scholars. In similar descriptive fashion, Thiselton does not present his readers with procedure for formulating Christian doctrine as much as he provides a hermeneutical description of the nature and use of doctrine in the church.

Gadamer may have titled his magnum opus *Truth and Method* (1960), but he is not concerned with a method for hermeneutics or an explicit theory of truth because he believes that the fundamental problem of hermeneutics goes *beyond method*, at least as method is conceived of in scientific disciplines.[15] As he describes his hermeneutics, his primary task is philosophical description of the process of human interpretation that is always going on, whether or not the interpreters are cognizant of it.[16] For Gadamer, like Heidegger before him, human experience itself is essentially hermeneutical. Interpretation is not something we can plan or deliberate by method; it is an inevitable aspect of our existence. The task of a philosophical hermeneutics thus becomes *critical reflection* on the event of interpretation, which extends to all aspects of human life. Hermeneutics, then, is a type of philosophical anthropology: an

---

14. Thiselton, *The Hermeneutics of Doctrine*, xx.
15. Hans-Georg Gadamer, *Truth and Method*, 2nd rev. ed., trans. Joel Weinsheimer and Donald G. Marshall (New York: Continuum, 2004), xx.
16. Ibid., xxv–xxvi.

exploration of what it means to be human. A descriptive theological hermeneutics takes up a similar task but does so with theological claims about creation, human sinfulness, and the need for God's redemptive activity.

Second, in place of colder, more abstract theological theorizing, Thiselton calls for an "embodied," "life-related" hermeneutics of doctrine.[17] On this point Thiselton echoes Gadamer's concern that understanding must entail *application*, which Gadamer calls the most important issue in hermeneutics.[18] For pre-Romantic hermeneuticists such as Johann August Ernesti (1707–1781), the task of hermeneutics was twofold: the interpreter must first produce "a sound *understanding*" (*subtilitas intelligendi*) and second be "skilful in *explanation*" (*subtilitas explicandi*).[19] Ernesti defines this two-component process as the ability to express "the sense of an author [of the given text], either in words of the same language which are more perspicuous than his, or by translating into another language and explaining by argument and illustration."[20] The Pietist Johann J. Rambach (1693–1735) added a third component with the skill of *application* (what Gadamer calls *subtilitas applicandi*).[21] For Ernesti and the Pietists alike, these "subtleties" were successive stages of the hermeneutical task. According to Gadamer, the romantic hermeneuticists first recognized that interpretation and understanding are in fact two sides of the same coin. Gadamer takes a further step, arguing that interpretation, understanding, and

17. Thiselton, *The Hermeneutics of Doctrine*, xvi–xxii. See also Gadamer, *Truth and Method*, 306–10.

18. Gadamer, *Truth and Method*, 306.

19. Johann August Ernesti, *Elementary Principles of Interpretation*, 4th ed., trans. Moses Stuart (Andover, UK: Allen, Morrill, and Wardwell, 1842), 14. According to Ernesti, "Acute understanding" (*subtilitas intelligendi*) is exhibited in rightly understanding the meaning of a text and in practicing proper methodology to get to this correct meaning (Ernesti, *Elementary Principles*, 14–16).

20. Ernesti, *Elementary Principles of Interpretation*, 17.

21. Johann J. Rambach, *Institutiones Hermeneuticae Sacrae* (Jena, 1723), 2; see also Gadamer, *Truth and Method*, 306.

application all comprise a single, cohesive process.[22] One does cannot make sense of a text or explain it *without applying it.*

For Gadamer, understanding and application are methodologically indistinguishable. In order to become "meaningful," a text must find "application" in the present. Gadamer himself explicitly relates this notion to theology and biblical interpretation: "Even as the scholarly interpretation of the theologian, it must never forget that Scripture is the divine proclamation of salvation. Understanding it, therefore, cannot simply be a scientific or scholarly exploration of its meaning."[23] Thiselton and Gadamer agree that theological hermeneutics must be more than fodder for scholarly journals and professional meetings; it must be life-related.

Thiselton in particular is concerned with the ways in which biblical texts are able to produce *"certain transforming effects"* and is dissatisfied with hermeneutical approaches that limit the Bible to disclosure.[24] Whether he is speaking about biblical hermeneutics or Christian theology, he shows great concern for fidelity to the discourse of Scripture and its enduring ability to transform its contemporary interpreters. This concern is particularly evident in his "hermeneutics of pastoral theology," in which he celebrates the value of a plurality of approaches to biblical interpretation in Christian formation and discipleship.[25] Christian doctrine also plays an important formative role.

Finally, Thiselton's description of doctrine as practical, character-forming wisdom reflects Gadamer's hermeneutical philosophy of education, which was largely a critique of positivistic tendencies in nineteenth- and early twentieth-century hermeneutical philosophy. In the wake of the Enlightenment attack on tradition, many

22. Gadamer, *Truth and Method*, 307.
23. Ibid., 327.
24. Thiselton, *New Horizons in Hermeneutics*, 17.
25. Ibid., 556–619.

academics deemed classical humanistic disciplines far less valuable than practical and scientifically rigorous fields. In response, philosopher and historian Wilhelm Dilthey (1833–1911) sought to create a methodology for the humanities (*Geisteswissenschaften*, "the sciences of the spirit" or "the sciences of the mind") that would provide the same kind of epistemic certainty he believed to be in the natural sciences (*Naturwissenschaften*).[26] Gadamer believed that this pragmatic move for theoretical objectivity dehumanized education and resulted in the loss of the communal, holistic formation of the human being.[27]

Inspired by Aristotle's discussion of practical wisdom (*phronēsis*) and Giambattista Vico's (1668–1774) notion of common sense (*sensus communis*), Gadamer attempts to redirect the humanities away from pseudo-scientific methods toward holistic worldview thinking.[28] He reminds the humanities that truth is more than scientific reductionism and education is more than the acquisition of facts. Rather, education is *Bildung*, the process of personal formation that opens the interpreter up for dialogue with other perspectives.[29] Hermeneutics is for Gadamer a kind of self-reflective philosophy with an eye toward the maturation of the whole person. Thiselton insists that doctrine, like Gadamer's notion of *phronēsis* or *Bildung*, must be practical if it is to be the means for producing "formative change" in Christian character, training, habit, and praxis.[30] Theological hermeneutics must be more than theory building; it results in the completion and maturation of the servant of God so that she may be "equipped for

---

26. See Wilhelm Dilthey, *Introduction to the Human Sciences: An Attempt to Lay a Foundation for the Study of Society and History*, trans. and ed. Ramon J. Betanzos (Detroit: Wayne State University Press, 1988).
27. Gadamer, *Truth and Method*, 10–11, 17–27.
28. See Aristotle, *Nicomachean Ethics* Book VI; Giambattista Vico, *New Science* 1.12 §142–43.
29. Gadamer, *Truth and Method*, 17.
30. Thiselton, *The Hermeneutics of Doctrine*, 96.

every good work" (2 Tim. 3:17). Doctrine is more than possessing "right beliefs" cognitively; it involves the transformation of a person's entire worldview, including her "*habits and practices.*"[31]

Many of the issues Thiselton treats in his descriptive theological hermeneutics are relevant to the so-called problem of postcanonical doctrinal development. His contribution to theological method recognizes communal tradition, changing life contexts, and a dynamic relationship with God. Doctrine must be more than timeless, ahistorical propositional statements extracted from the Bible; it is practical, life-related wisdom grounded in human history and interpretation.

Development Is Not a "Problem"

In some sense, Thiselton does not deem postcanonical doctrinal development to be a genuine "problem" for Christian theology, at least not a problem in the way that some Roman Catholic apologists, historical critics, and evangelical theologians have described it. He offers historical, theological, and hermeneutical critiques of many traditional "problems" related to postcanonical doctrinal development.

First, Thiselton argues that the historical case for the dramatic transformation of Christian doctrine as stated by modern liberal scholarship has been overstated. He identifies a kind of "wedge" historiography in New Testament scholarship since Baur, which surfaces in but is not limited to Baur's Tübingen School and the "History of Religions School" (*religionsgeschichtliche Schule*). These writers "sought to drive a wedge between the proclamation of Jesus and Paul on one side, and the supposedly 'early catholic' . . . writings

---

31. Ibid.

of the later New Testament documents and the subapostolic and early Patristic writings on the other."[32] For Baur, Harnack, Schweitzer, and Martin Werner (1887–1964), the postapostolic turn toward theology was an unfortunate accident of history, ultimately transforming the teachings of the historical Jesus and his earliest disciples into philosophical dogmas quite alien to their sources.[33] Some contemporary New Testament scholars make similar claims, arguing that Paul and other second- and third-generation Christian communities exchanged the original social-political message of Jesus and his earliest followers with confessional Christologies.

Conflating "doctrine" with formal systematic theological teaching, these writers argue that doctrine—an emphasis on the cognitive aspects of Christian belief—was largely absent in the earliest Christian communities. Harnack, for example, accuses the Gnostics of setting a perilous precedent by transforming the "Gospel into a doctrine, into an absolute philosophy of religion."[34] Schweitzer and Werner push the blame back earlier to Paul, alleging that the apostle transformed Jesus' message of the Kingdom into "Hellenizable" beliefs such as the union with Christ, sacraments, and the "belief in the Messiah as the bringer of resurrection."[35] For Schweitzer, the whole history of Christian doctrine "is based on the delay of the Parousia, the abandonment of eschatology, the progress and completion of the 'de-eschatologising' of religion."[36]

---

32. Ibid., 34.
33. Ibid., 34–35.
34. Adolf von Harnack, *The History of Dogma*, vol. 1, trans. Neil Buchanan (Eugene, OR: Wipf & Stock, 1997), 253.
35. Albert Schweitzer, *The Mysticism of Paul the Apostle*, trans. William Montgomery (Baltimore: John Hopkins University Press, 1998), 336.
36. Albert Schweitzer, *The Quest of the Historical Jesus: A Critical Study of Its Progress from Reimarus to Wrede*, trans. William Montgomery (London: Adam and Charles Black, 1910), 358. For Werner's appropriation of Schweitzer's theory to the development of dogma, see Martin Werner, *The Formation of Christian Dogma: An Historical Study of Its Problem*, trans. S. G. F. Brandon (New York: Harper & Brothers, 1957), esp. 9–161.

The evidence for this "wedge" between first century faith communities and Christian doctrine is not particularly compelling for Thiselton. He contends that scholars in the German liberal tradition tend to overlook doctrinal formulations within the New Testament and in the earliest Christian communities.[37] He posits what he calls a "dispositional" account of Christian doctrine, largely drawn from the work of Wittgenstein and Welsh philosopher Henry Habberley Price (1899–1984). This dispositional account of Christian doctrine highlights the nature of implicit belief in the earliest Christian communities and the need for response in the face of later challenges to the faith. Thiselton's dispositional account of belief is, as I will argue in chapter 7, a very helpful tool in addressing the issue of identity in doctrinal development.

Thiselton identifies a second faulty assumption on the other end of the theological spectrum. For some conservative theologians who confuse their interpretations of sacred texts with the sacred texts themselves, the ongoing struggle to develop doctrine in new contexts poses a significant problem. These theologians often treat doctrines as self-evident axioms in Scripture. This kind of assumption appears in the work of the influential contemporary evangelical theologian Wayne Grudem, who describes doctrine simply as "what the whole Bible teaches us today about a particular topic"[38] and systematic theology as "any study that answers the question, 'What does the whole Bible teach us today?' about any given topic."[39] Christian fundamentalists take this assumption one step further, often encouraging strict separation from those with whom they have doctrinal disagreements. For the fundamentalist or uncritical biblicist, such disagreements are not merely differences of interpretation but

---

37. Thiselton, *The Hermeneutics of Doctrine*, 36–37.
38. Wayne Grudem, *Systematic Theology* (Grand Rapids, MI: Zondervan, 2000), 25.
39. Ibid., 21.

likely are rooted in one party or the other's refusal to believe the word of God in Scripture.

Uncritical biblicists might have great difficulty with the development of doctrine and diverse interpretations of biblical texts. They do so, Thiselton suggests, because of their failure to recognize the finitude of interpreters and the constructive nature of interpretation. While the tension between a closed period of revelation and the progressive growth of doctrinal formulations customarily defines the development problem, the real tension for Thiselton is between the doctrine of posited special revelation and a hermeneutics of finitude. Revelation is wholly God's prerogative, made possible only by his sovereign, gracious abasement. Doctrine can only find its epistemic footing in this revelatory action.[40] By contrast, hermeneutics is an imprecise art colored by human limitations, pre-understandings, and the very creaturely struggle to understand "that which is other," or in the case of Christian doctrine, the God who is, in Barth's terms, "Wholly Other."[41]

The "creaturely" dimension of hermeneutics that Thiselton describes is implicit in the philosophical hermeneutics of Heidegger and Gadamer. For Heidegger, the limits of human knowledge relate to the human experience of being-in-the-world, of our "thrownness" (*Geworfenheit*)[42] and "situatedness" (*Befindlichkeit*).[43] Human beings do

---

40. On this point, Thiselton cites Barth's maxim: "God is known through God alone." See Thiselton, *The Hermeneutics of Doctrine*, 62; see also Karl Barth, *Church Dogmatics*, vol. 2, no. 1, *The Doctrine of God*, trans. G. T. Thomson and Harold Knight (Edinburgh: T&T Clark, 1957), 179.

41. See Karl Barth, *The Epistle to the Romans*, 6th ed., tran. Edwyn C. Hoskyns (New York: Oxford University Press, 1968), 380ff.

42. Martin Heidegger, *Being and Time*, trans. John Macquarrie and Edward Robinson (New York: Harper & Row, 1962), 174, 219–24.

43. Ibid., 172–82. Macquarrie and Robinson translate *Befindlichkeit* as "state-of-mind," which Heideggerian scholar Einar Øverenget laments is an "unfortunate" translation because it seems to indicate that Heidegger is only referring to a mental state or mood when the term is far more involved than this. See Einar Øverenget, *Seeing the Self: Heidegger on Subjectivity* (Norwell, MA: Kluwer Academic, 1998), 116.

not choose their existence, nor do they choose their time and place in history or their primary socialization.[44] Even in his non-theistic or religiously agnostic framework, Gadamer tenders implicitly theological ideas. As Jean Grondin, Gadamer's biographer and one of his most reliable expositors, summarizes his program, "the whole of Gadamer's philosophy serves to remind us . . . that we are not gods, but human beings."[45]

Therein lies the problem for Thiselton: "If doctrine is founded upon a definitive revelation from God, what room is there for the ambiguities, provisionality, contingencies, and particularities that characterize hermeneutical inquiry?"[46] How does the revelation relate to a hermeneutics of finitude? Thiselton makes a distinction that only the naïve realist would reject as blatantly obvious: doctrine may be impossible to formulate without revelation, but doctrine is not tantamount to revelation.[47] Doctrine is the result of interpretation, and if it is debatable, it is "capable of diverse interpretations."[48] Only God makes doctrine possible through his self-revelation; but doctrine, as a critical, provisional reflection on this revelation, is a fallible human enterprise fashioned within the limits of human interpretation. Thiselton here again follows Barth, who describes theology as a "fallible human work . . . [that] must be obedience to grace if it is well done."[49]

44. Gadamer, *Truth and Method*, xv–xvi, 295.

45. Jean Grondin, *The Philosophy of Gadamer*, trans. Kathryn Plant (Kingston, ON: McGill-Queens University Press, 2003), 116.

46. Thiselton, *The Hermeneutics of Doctrine*, 63.

47. Ibid. Thiselton here appeals to church historian Justo L. González (b. 1937), who writes that one of the "most common errors in the life of the church . . . has been to confuse doctrine with God." See Justo L. González, *A Concise History of Christian Doctrine* (Nashville: Abingdon, 2005), 7.

48. Thiselton, *The Hermeneutics of Doctrine*, 63.

49. Karl Barth, *Church Dogmatics*, vol. 1, pt. 1, *The Doctrine of the Word of God*, trans. G. T. Thomson and Harold Knight (Edinburgh: T&T Clark, 1975), 4.

Consequently, many arguments against the propriety of doctrinal development and hermeneutics lose much of their force when their proponents resist the temptation to conflate revelation with its interpretations. Theology is a critical, constructive exercise shaped by the interpretation of Scripture, tradition, reason, and experience. If theology is an imprecise, corrigible science, then one should expect that doctrinal expressions can and often do change, taking new forms either with advancements or impediments in biblical and theological understanding. One should also expect a plurality of legitimate readings of biblical texts. To recognize such plurality is not to deny "truth," the role of authors in shaping textual meaning, or the inspiration of the Holy Spirit. The plurality of legitimate interpretations simply serves to remind Christians what they elsewhere affirm in their theological anthropologies and doctrines of God: God is God, and human beings are human beings. Humans lack an Archimedean field of vision, a God's-eye-view. Interpreters have limitations and, despite their attempts to use appropriate "tools" or "methods" in hermeneutics, can be mistaken or disagree about meaning.

Third, doctrinal development becomes problematic when theologians construe doctrine as static, timeless truth abstracted from historical particularity. If Christian theology were in fact "timeless" and universal, presenting new expressions and understandings of doctrine would be quite undesirable. In *The Two Horizons*, Thiselton anticipates an objection to biblical hermeneutics coming from those that would argue that the Bible is a record of timeless truth, unchanging in its interpretation from generation to generation.[50] By rejecting the description of *timeless* for truth or doctrine, Thiselton does not discount a "weak" sense of timelessness in propositional

---

50. Thiselton, *The Two Horizons*, 95; cf. 97.

logic, nor does he mean that the message of the Bible is relegated to the past and incapable of speaking to future generations. Rather, he declines a notion of timelessness applied to doctrine that is ahistorical and *immutable*. He contests that this notion of doctrine is more Platonic than biblical and, foreshadowing a theme that would appear later in his later work in theological method, insists that "a God of 'necessary truth' would be unrelated to human life and experience."[51] To borrow language from nineteenth-century discussions of doctrinal development, Thiselton maintains the "positivity" (i.e., the historical or "posited" character) of doctrine.

In the case of Christianity, positive theology takes its shape from historical and grammatical biblical exegesis. This approach, contingent on the accidents of history, stands in stark contrast to the philosophical theology of medieval scholasticism and the religion of pure reason later advocated by *Aufklärung* rationalists, of which G. E. Lessing was one of the leading proponents. In his "On the Proof of the Spirit and of Power" (1777), Lessing famously argues for a religion grounded in reason over against a religion grounded in historical revelation. Lessing describes an "ugly ditch" between the "necessary truths of reason" (propositional truths that are necessarily, eternally true) and the "accidental truths of history" (truths about historical contingencies) and argues that the "*accidental truths of history can never become the proof of necessary truths of reason.*"[52] For Lessing, positive religion based on historical revelation is an unfortunate, albeit inevitable reality.[53] Positive religions are true only to the extent to which they conform to natural, rational religion, and "the best

---

51. Thiselton, *The Two Horizons*, 95–96; cf. idem, "Truth (*Alēthia*)," in *The New International Dictionary of New Testament Theology*, vol. 3, ed. Colin Brown (Grand Rapids, MI: Zondervan, 1978), 900; cf. idem, *Thiselton on Hermeneutics*, 284–85.

52. Gotthold Ephraim Lessing, *Lessing's Theological Writings*, trans. and ed. Henry Chadwick (London: Adam and Charles Black, 1956), 53.

53. Ibid., 104–5.

revealed or positive religion is that which contains the fewest conventional additions to natural religion, and least hinders the good effects of natural religion."[54] For Lessing, the development of new doctrines—something rooted in one's historical situation—is genuinely problematic because the most important truths are necessary, eternal, and unchanging.

Thiselton has little or no interest in wading through the muck and mire of Lessing's ugly ditch because biblical revelation is contingent upon history as God *acts in history*, the authors of Scripture addressed a particular *historical context*, and interpreters of Scripture in every successive generation undergo *the effects of history*.[55] The temporal and contingent nature of revelation also extends to doctrine grounded in it: "To say that doctrine is derived ultimately from God, far from suggesting that doctrine inhabits an abstract, timeless, conceptually pure domain, underlines the temporal and narrative character of its subject matter."[56] For Thiselton, attempts to divorce doctrine from space and time and to abstract necessary, "timeless truths" from historically situated narratives more closely resemble docetic and gnostic worldviews than the worldview of the biblical authors.

Many biblical scholars are keenly aware of this docetizing propensity in Western theology that tries to extract "timeless" Christian doctrine from historical situations described in the New Testament. N. T. Wright, for instance, criticizes the tendency of many theologians since Chalcedon to short-circuit the narrative and historical features of the Gospels in exchange for prooftexts for Jesus' divinity and/or humanity. In other words, systematic theologians looking for biblical support to buttress their preconceived beliefs

---

54. Ibid., 105.
55. Thiselton, *The Two Horizons*, 96–101; cf. Gadamer, *Truth and Method*, 278.
56. Thiselton, *The Hermeneutics of Doctrine*, 63.

about Christ often ignore larger questions about the historical Jesus, his self-understanding, and his relationship to the larger narrative of Scripture. These attempts to remove Jesus from his historical context and vocation as Israel's messiah ultimately shortchange biblical Christology and apologetics.[57]

The Pauline scholar Johan Christiaan Beker reminds his readers that Paul does not offer an organized, propositional systematic theology but rather personalized theology in the form of an occasional letter:

> The letter form . . . suggests the historical concreteness of the gospel as a word on target in the midst of human, contingent specificity. . . . The coherent center of the gospel is never an abstraction removed from its "address" and audience; it cannot be a *despositum fidei* or doctrinal abstraction that as a universal, timeless substance is to be poured into every conceivable situation regardless of historical circumstance. In other words, the truth of the gospel is bound up with its contingency and historical concreteness. Particularity and occasionality do not constitute a contamination of Paul's "pure thought"; rather, they serve to make the truth of the gospel the effective word of God.[58]

What Beker says about Pauline epistles is true of every other book in the canon: biblical authors present readers with situational documents, not "timeless" abstract concepts. These authors write from theological frameworks with varying degrees of organization, but these frameworks are conditioned by historicity.

While doctrines as expressions of belief are always shaped by time and place in history, there is a place for recognizing the unchanging

---

57. See N. T. Wright, "Whence and Whither Historical Jesus Studies in the Life of the Church?" in *Jesus, Paul and the People of God: A Theological Dialogue with N. T. Wright*, ed. Nicholas Perrin and Richard B. Hays (Downers Grove, IL: InterVarsity, 2011), 133–37. Wright also impugns the attempts of philosophical theologians to abstract the problem of evil from the cross of Christ (144). He discusses the problem of evil within the narrative framework of the Bible in *Evil and the Justice of God* (Downers Grove, IL: InterVarsity, 2006).

58. Johan Christiaan Beker, *Paul the Apostle: The Triumph of God in Life and Thought* (Philadelphia: Fortress Press, 1980), 24.

nature of propositional truth, what Thiselton calls a "weak" sense of timelessness. Colin Gunton insists that truth must have some kind of timeless quality: "Against the implicit suggestion that propositionalism is a kind of optional and vaguely reactionary or disreputable position, it must be protested in the name of logic that it is as a matter of fact the case that once something is true it is always true."[59] For example, the proposition "John F. Kennedy was killed by an assassin's bullet on November 22, 1963" will always be true in the same way that the proposition "John F. Kennedy was killed by electrocution on November 23, 1963" never was nor ever will be true. The *content* of these propositions (i.e., John F. Kennedy was killed) is contingent upon the events of history. The *statement* of these propositions in the forms of English sentences is likewise contingent on particular, historically bound expressions of this proposition. But the *meaning* of these propositions has a kind of trans-chronological quality.

A fourth, related concern is the conception of God in classical theism. Thiselton challenges a "static" or "mechanistic" understanding of God often presupposed in the standard sketches of the development problem, i.e., the notion that doctrines about an eternal God should not change because God does not experience change. Jürgen Moltmann and Wolfhart Pannenberg are profound influences on his theological vision, particularly in their eschatologies of promise and their respective models of the God-world relationship.[60] Moltmann's model of the God-world relationship,

59. Colin E. Gunton, *A Brief Theology of Revelation: The 1993 Warfield Lectures* (Edinburgh: T&T Clark, 1995), 7.
60. The works of Jürgen Moltmann include *Theology of Hope: On the Ground and the Implications of a Christian Eschatology*, trans. James W. Leitch (New York: Harper & Row, 1967); *The Crucified God*, trans. R. A. Wilson and John Bowden (New York: Harper & Row, 1974); *The Trinity and the Kingdom*, trans. Margaret Kohl (San Francisco: Harper & Row, 1981); and *God in Creation: A New Theology of Creation and the Spirit of God*, trans. Margaret Kohl (San Francisco: Harper & Row, 1985). For a sampling of Wolfhart Pannenberg's works, see *Jesus: God and Man*, 2nd

which John W. Cooper calls his "perichoretic panentheism,"[61] informs Thiselton's belief that "God not only preserves, makes, and perfects, but also indwells, sympathizes, participates in, and delights in, things of creation in a relationship that allows room for 'mutuality.'"[62]

While Thiselton gives favorable consideration to these specific forms of panentheism and open theism, he refrains from explicit affirmation of either position. He is even somewhat ambiguous about his own positions regarding divine attributes. Even if he speaks favorably of the panentheistic and "open" theologies of Pannenberg, Peacocke, John Polkinghorne, and Sallie McFague,[63] Thiselton testifies that God is distinct from creation and "wholly other."[64]

On open theism, Thiselton writes, "It is surprising that today, when so much has been written in criticism of the classical view, so-called 'open theism' appears as an almost daring innovation, when its arguments usually follow not only the biblical narratives but [also] the pioneering insights of Moltmann."[65] He shows also appreciation for Richard Swinburne's modification of classical views of omniscience: "The view that since it is not yet actual, the future may not necessarily 'count' as an object of divine knowledge at least deserves some consideration."[66] Elsewhere, however, Thiselton

ed., trans. Lewis L. Wilkins and Duane A. Priebe (Philadelphia: Westminster, 1977); *Systematic Theology*, 3 vols., trans. Geoffrey W. Bromiley (Grand Rapids, MI: Eerdmans, 1991–1998); and *Theology and the Philosophy of Science*, trans. Francis McDonagh (Philadelphia: Westminster, 1976).

61. For evangelical criticisms of the panentheistic programs of Moltmann, Pannenberg, Peacocke, and Polkinghorne, see John W. Cooper, *Panentheism: The Other God of the Philosophers* (Grand Rapids, MI: Baker, 2006), 237–58, 307–10, 315–17; Stanley J. Grenz and Roger E. Olson, *20th-Century Theology: God & World in a Transitional Age* (Downers Grove, IL: InterVarsity, 1992), 172–86.

62. Thiselton, *The Hermeneutics of Doctrine*, 215.

63. Ibid., 214–22; idem, *Life After Death: A New Approach to Last Things* (Grand Rapids, MI: Eerdmans, 2011), 144.

64. Thiselton, *The Hermeneutics of Doctrine*, 214–22.

65. Ibid., 478.

puzzlingly denies the notion of "temporal everlastingness" that is foundational in many open theistic schemes.[66]

With Moltmann, Thiselton objects to the careless way philosophical theologians often dismiss descriptions of God's emotions and activities in biblical narratives as anthropomorphisms. He accepts that "some references may be anthropomorphic or metaphorical" but offers that these so-called anthropomorphic or anthropopathic descriptions "seem to play too great a part in disclosures of the nature of God to yield an exhaustive explanation of this kind."[68] The God described in the Bible is "living" and "conceived of in more personal and purposive terms." God "makes promises"; he "waits"; and "he even reconsiders and revises plans of action."[69]

Thiselton is apprehensive about many traditional formulations of doctrines in classical theism, including divine impassability, immutability, and timelessness.[70] With Moltmann, Thiselton finds "the classic Patristic doctrines of 'impassability . . . *ousia* . . . immutability' [to] reflect the influence of Platonism more clearly than that of the Bible."[71] He also believes that the traditional doctrine of divine "timelessness" resonates better with Plato than Paul. In his critique of Paul Helm's doctrine of divine timelessness, Thiselton writes, "The most serious criticism of Helm . . . is that he writes entirely as a philosopher, appealing to philosophical works, while the biblical material clearly takes second place, with little careful exegesis

66. Thiselton, *A Concise Encyclopedia*, 214; cf. Richard Swinburne, *The Coherence of Theism*, rev. ed. (Oxford: Clarendon, 1993), 167–83.

67. Thiselton, *The Hermeneutics of Doctrine*, 576–77. See William Hasker, *God, Time, and Knowledge* (Ithaca, NY: Cornell University Press, 1998); Gregory A. Boyd, *God of the Possible: A Biblical Introduction to the Open View of God* (Grand Rapids, MI: Baker, 2000); and Clark H. Pinnock, *Most Moved Mover: A Theology of God's Openness* (Grand Rapids, MI: Baker, 2001).

68. Thiselton, *A Concise Encyclopedia*, 78, cf. 12.

69. Ibid., 78.

70. Ibid., 77–79, 145–46.

71. Thiselton, *The Hermeneutics of Doctrine*, 478

of relevant passages."[72] One may make reasonable philosophical arguments for these positions, but they are not necessarily consistent with the biblical narratives.

The consequence for doctrinal development is that doctrines are "living" because God is "living." As Thiselton explains,

> Doctrines evolve often by responding to new challenges . . . or in the context of changing languages or situations. But they also *assume a living, dynamic, ongoing form, because God is the living, dynamic, ongoing God.* If doctrine reflects the nature of God and derives ultimately from God, *doctrine will be no less 'living' and related to temporality than God*, who acts in human *history*.[73]

Doctrine is not a closed system of static, fixed propositions unrelated to life, but an ongoing, life-related dialectic between revealed truth and expectation that remains open to God's new and future acts in the world.[74] Moltmann and Pannenberg's eschatological emphasis "allows for discontinuity, critique, [and] transcendent reversal" in doctrinal development.[75] Furthermore, the "God of the future remains living and active" and his "presence . . . makes 'glory' an open-ended crescendo, not a full-stop."[76] Theologians are not merely the old guard of the tradition but active participants in the ongoing activity of God in the world.[77]

---

72. Thiselton, *Life after Death*, 140. See also Plato *Timaeus* 37c–38b. For Plato (c. 427–347 B.C.E.) time is an imperfect, moving image or reflection of eternity: "For before the heavens came to be, there were no days or nights, no months or years. . . . But that which is changeless and motionless cannot become either older or younger in the course of time."

73. Thiselton, *The Hermeneutics of Doctrine*, 63.

74. Ibid., 65.

75. Anthony C. Thiselton, "'Behind' and 'in Front of' the Text: Language, Reference and Indeterminacy," in *After Pentecost: Language & Biblical Interpretation*, ed. Craig Bartholomew, Colin Greene, and Karl Möller (Grand Rapids, MI: Zondervan, 2001), 112.

76. Anthony. C. Thiselton, "Signs of the Times: Towards a Theology for the Year 2000 as a Grammar of Grace, Truth and Eschatology in Contexts of So-Called Postmodernity," in *The Future as God's Gift: Explorations in Christian Eschatology*, ed. David Fergusson and Marcel Sarot (Edinburgh: T&T Clark, 2000), 37–38.

77. Thiselton, *The Hermeneutics of Doctrine*, 64–67.

In his fifth and final charge against traditional conceptions of the development problem, Thiselton contests the notion that doctrinal stability and fidelity to Scripture and tradition necessarily entails verbal reiteration of the same doctrinal expressions. The truths of revelation and Christian doctrine may not be timeless in an "atemporal" sense, but they are stable and do endure throughout time. While they continue to be meaningful and significant for subsequent generations of Christians, these truths of Scripture and Christian theology continue to require "hermeneutical reflection" in every era.[78]

On this point, Helmut Thielicke (1908–1986) illuminates the hermeneutical nature of doctrinal development for Thiselton: "The history of theology is fundamentally no other than the history of its various attempts at address."[79] Despite Thielicke's conviction that the "basic truths of the faith are obviously constant and unalterable" and these truths "were well known to our fathers and . . . will still be well known to our grandchildren,"[80] he insists that doctrines must be "re-addressed," "actualized," or reinterpreted in every successive milieu.[81] Thiselton endorses Thielicke's careful distinction between the "actualization" of Christian truth for contemporary audiences and the pragmatic "accommodation" of doctrine.

For Thielicke, actualization is a reinterpretation of truth for the present that is respectful to an authority, namely Scripture or creed, while accommodation asserts the authority of the self in determining what is true for the present. Thielicke defines actualization as a "new interpretation of truth, in its re-addressing" wherein "truth

---

78. Thiselton, *The Two Horizons*, 98.
79. Helmut Thielicke, *The Evangelical Faith*, vol. 1, *Prolegomena: The Relation of Theology to Modern Thought Forms*, trans. and ed. Geoffrey W. Bromiley (Grand Rapids, MI: Eerdmans, 1974), 25; cf. Thiselton, *The Two Horizons*, 98–99.
80. Helmut Thielicke, *How Modern Should Theology Be?* trans. H. George Anderson (Philadelphia: Fortress Press, 1969), 4–5.
81. Thielicke, *The Evangelical Faith*, vol. 1, 23–29.

itself remains intact" and the "hearer is summoned or called 'under the truth' in his own name and situation." On the contrary, accommodation "calls the truth 'under me' and lets me be its norm." Thielicke admits, "Phenomenologically and externally the two outlooks seem to be identical twins. . . . In reality, however, they are as opposite as two antithetical ethical attitudes, namely loyalty and disloyalty."[82]

What need is there for "re-address" or reinterpretation of biblical truth in new contexts? Pannenberg and "new" hermeneutic proponents Ernst Fuchs (1903–1983) and Gerhard Ebeling, who apply Gadamerian hermeneutics to their respective projects, show Thiselton that the contemporary situations of readers—different from the ancient setting in which biblical texts were written—make the mere verbal restatement of doctrines and biblical expressions "*un*faithful to the intention of the New Testament writers."[83] As previously noted, Ebeling says, "The same word can be said to another time only by being said differently."[84] Pannenberg echoes this maxim:

> In a changed situation the traditional phrases, even when recited literally, do not mean what they did at the time of their original formulation. . . . Theology, perhaps, comes closest to material agreement with the biblical witness when it seriously takes up the questions of its own time in order to express relation to them what the biblical writers attested in the language and conceptual framework of their time.[85]

Pannenberg explicitly cites Gadamer's hermeneutics as inspiration for this idea, but this particular explanation appears in earlier models of

---

82. Ibid., 26–27. See also Thiselton, *The Two Horizons*, 98–99; idem, *Thiselton on Hermeneutics: Collected Works with New Essays* (Grand Rapids, MI: Eerdmans, 2006), 38–39.
83. Thiselton, *The Two Horizons*, 99.
84. Gerhard Ebeling, "Time and Word," in *The Future of Our Religious Past: Essays in Honour of Rudolf Bultmann*, ed. James M. Robinson (London: SCM, 1971), 265.
85. Wolfhart Pannenberg, *Basic Questions in Theology: Collected Essays*, trans. George H. Kehm (Philadelphia: Fortress Press, 1970), 9; cf. Thiselton, *The Two Horizons*, 99.

development. In his *Essay* on development, John Henry Newman makes a similar concession about bringing a theological idea into a new context: "[An idea] changes with [its new relations] in order to remain the same. In a higher world it is otherwise, but here below to live is to change, and to be perfect is to have changed often."[86]

The ongoing task of biblical translation is analogous to this ongoing interpretive task in Christian doctrine. Wooden repetition of one translation across cultures and time renders communication ineffective.[87] Similarly, the contexts of biblical interpreters are always changing, some past and present doctrinal expressions inevitably lose their import. For Thiselton, some fourth-century theological terms related to the doctrine of the Trinity, such as *ousia* or *hypostasis*, may be of limited value as a resource for contemporary formulations of the doctrine but were relevant for their own historical context.[88] In the end, this manner of development is not a "problem" for doctrine as much as it is a necessary condition for its continuing vitality.

Development as a Hermeneutical Dialectic

Doctrinal development is an inevitable phenomenon made explicable by the tools of hermeneutical theory. With his hermeneutical-dialectical account of doctrine, Thiselton hopes to "facilitate our understanding of doctrinal development and the relationship between doctrine, life, and action."[89] While his descriptive hermeneutics provides little help in distinguishing between positive

---

86. John Henry Newman, *An Essay on the Development of Christian Doctrine*, rev. ed. (London: Basil Montagu Pickering, 1878), 40.

87. Anthony C. Thiselton, "Communicative Action and Promise in Interdisciplinary, Biblical, and Theological Hermeneutics," in Roger Lundin, Clarence Walhout, and Anthony C. Thiselton, *The Promise of Hermeneutics* (Grand Rapids, MI: Eerdmans, 1999), 138.

88. Thiselton, *The Hermeneutics of Doctrine*, 466.

89. Ibid., 8.

and negative developments, Thiselton's model of development is valuable for second-order reflection on the historical phenomenon of development. He brings together various philosophical, hermeneutical, and theological resources to create a robust, comprehensive theory that has great explanatory power for historical and systematic theologies, as well as Christian apologetics.

In contrast to a notion of fixed, timeless doctrine, Thiselton stresses that doctrines based on divine revelation do not develop in the vacuum of abstracted reason but "arise" in the contingencies of history.[90] They emerge within a "dialogical chain of questions and answers."[91] Here again Thiselton trails Gadamer, for whom the phenomenon of understanding is always a *creative production* which results from the dialectical engagement of the distant horizon of the past and the ever-changing horizon of the present. This hermeneutical dialectic faintly resembles nineteenth-century models of development such as Johann Sebastian Drey's dialectic between Christianity's "inner history" and "outer history" discussed in the previous chapter. But Thiselton's theory, shaped by interaction with twentieth-century phenomenological hermeneutics, lacks the idealistic overtones of Drey's model and gives more focused attention to the historical nature of interpretation. This particular dialectical model is helpful for describing the complex relationship between individuals, ideas, and their respective contexts.

Gadamer and Historical Understanding

Once more, a brief detour into Gadamerian hermeneutical theory is necessary to set the stage for Thiselton's hermeneutical dialectic of doctrinal development. Of particular concern for the issue of

90. Ibid., 3–8.
91. Ibid., 4.

development is Gadamer's critique of objectivism in history and hermeneutics. Some biblical interpreters and theologians may have ambitious aspirations of discovering the theology of the Bible objectively—free of presuppositions that would affect their readings of the texts. Gadamer endeavored to show this kind of "objectivist" thinking, also prevalent in historical and scientific disciplines, to be nothing more than an intellectual pipe dream. Gadamer instead shares Rudolf Bultmann's (1884–1976) belief that exegesis without presuppositions is not only impossible but also undesirable.[92] All interpreters approach texts with "pre-understanding" (*Vorverständnis*) that shapes their interpretations.[93] No interpreter is a blank slate.

Many committed modernists think of science and history as disciplines of "fact" and fields like literature and philosophy as disciplines of opinion, but even ostensibly factual disciplines are subject to interpretation and distortion. Like statisticians who can ask the right questions in order to produce the answers they are seeking, historians can use historical investigation as a means for propaganda.[94] The natural sciences also bear the marks of interpretation, as theories describing natural phenomena come and go. What appears to be "irrefutable proof" one day may end up in the rubbish bin of scientific history on another. To be wrong or disproven is indicative of the reality and inevitability of multiple interpretations, even in "hard" sciences.

Gadamer is particularly critical of the nineteenth-century historicist philosopher Wilhelm Dilthey, who labored to create an objective, non-biased method for textual interpretation and historical research. According to Gadamer, historicists like Dilthey rightly

---

92. See Rudolf Bultmann, *New Testament and Mythology and Other Basic Writings*, trans. and ed. Schubert M. Ogden (Philadelphia: Fortress Press, 1984), 145–54.
93. Gadamer, *Truth and Method*, 268–78; cf. Martin Heidegger, *Being and Time*, trans. John Macquarrie and Edward Robinson (New York: Harper & Row, 1962), 188–95.
94. Gadamer, *Truth and Method*, 299–300.

recognize that historians operate in a particular historical context but wrongly assume that they must attempt to transcend their historicity—their time and place in history—in order to be truly objective in their discipline. No such method can possibly work because one's time and place in history would shape any attempt to develop such a method. Gadamer alleges that historicism, with its uncritical appropriation of the scientific method, its refusal to acknowledge the effects of history, and its failed attempt at objectivity in interpretation leads to an actual "deformation" (*Verformung*) of knowledge.

For Gadamer, the corrective to the kind of naïveté seen in historicism and scientism is what he calls the "historically effected consciousness" or "consciousness of history's effects" (*wirkungsgeschichtliches Bewußtsein*). The German term Gadamer uses is purposely ambiguous, producing a double entendre.[95] In one sense, the "historically effected consciousness" simply means that history affects interpreters by shaping their worldview and ideas. In quite another sense, the term describes the process of the interpreter becoming conscious or aware of history's effects on her. The latter definition is the primary focus of Gadamer's hermeneutical task.[96]

In this sense, the "historically effected consciousness" is a willful or volitional awareness of one's hermeneutical situation—the act of becoming intentionally self-aware of the fact that we cannot be objective about our time and place in history because we cannot transcend it.[97] There is a role for volition in the historically effected consciousness as the interpreter's ongoing assignment is becoming aware of her hermeneutical and historical situation.[98] History affects all minds, but not all persons have an awareness of history's effects

95. Ibid., xx.
96. Ibid., 301.
97. Ibid.
98. Ibid., cf. 269, 303.

on their judgment. On this point Gadamer is at least partially prescriptive: interpreters must become aware of history's effects on us in order to have proper understanding. Interpreters are better off with a critical awareness of their own situation than under some delusion about objectivity.

The "horizon" (*Horizont*) is another important Gadamerian metaphor for *perspective*, *worldview*, and the effects of history on interpreters. This nomenclature comes from the phenomenonological and existential tradition of Edmund Husserl (1859–1938) and Friedrich Nietzsche (1844–1900), and it speaks to the historical conditioning and finitude of all persons. For Gadamer, the horizon is a metaphor for perception from a certain vantage point.[99] Horizons are by definition limited in their vision. Merold Westphal describes the horizon theologically or in terms of our created finitude: "We would have to be either God or dead not to stand in some such particular and contingent place, and in neither case would human understanding be possible."[100] Horizons, then, are part of our essential, innate humanness.

Unlike Nietzsche, Gadamer does not think that this awareness of being bound within a horizon should lead to cynicism about the possibility of understanding. Instead, acknowledgment of one's horizon makes understanding possible because it reveals the otherness of the texts we read and interpret.[101] Moreover, boundedness in one's horizon does not mean that interpretation is fixed.[102] One can change their prejudgments, distinguishing between "true prejudices" and "*false* ones."[103] Horizons can and do continually change—much like

---

99. Ibid., 301.

100. Merold Westphal, *Whose Community? Which Interpretation? Philosophical Hermeneutics for the Church* (Grand Rapids, MI: Baker, 2009), 71.

101. Gadamer, *Truth and Method*, 301. Gadamer calls this awareness of the other "historical alterity."

102. Ibid., 277.

103. Ibid., 298.

the movement of the earth beneath our feet—but this change does not mean escaping the history of effects.[104]

Rightly understanding a text is not in Romanticism's appeal to leave one's own point-of-view behind in order to get in the mind of the author of a text,[105] nor is it in the historicist attempt to transcend one's place in history.[106] Instead, for Gadamer, understanding is the "fusion of horizons" (*Horizontverschmelzung*). Gadamer defines this "fusion" as the intersection of two distinct and historically effected horizons: the past horizon of the text and the present horizon of the reader with all its pre-understandings and prejudices. In the "fusion of horizons," the horizon of the interpreter is always changing with a new understanding that occurs through the "conversation" of past and present horizons.[107] The horizon of the interpreter is not closed or fixed. In fact, in order for understanding to take place, the interpreter must show a willingness to seek understanding of the horizon of the text. When the interpreter seeks to understand the horizon of the past, she will seek to understand it from within her horizon or framework. This fusion of horizons is also an ongoing act that never reaches an omega point; it is an ongoing process wherein the former horizon and the present horizon are continually coalescing to form a new perspective.[108]

Reiterating the charges of relativism in American literary scholar Eric Donald Hirsch Jr.'s critique of Gadamer, many evangelicals vehemently contest Gadamer's notion of the "fusion of horizons" out

---

104. Ibid., 303.

105. Schleiermacher's "psychological" approach, what he called "divination," is the primary example of this romanticist tendency. See Thiselton, *New Horizons in Hermeneutics*, 209–28. For Schleiermacher, the interpreter of a text has a privileged position over the author because the interpreter (1) can recreate the thought-world of the author (thus simulating her subjective view) and (2) can have a more objective frame of reference for evaluating the author's historical context and influences.

106. Gadamer, *Truth and Method*, 338–39; cf. Thiselton, *New Horizons in Hermeneutics*, 317.

107. Gadamer, *Truth and Method*, 305–06.

108. Ibid., 305.

of concern that it leads to a hermeneutical relativism, or something akin to reader-response hermeneutics.[109] For instance, *The Chicago Statement on Biblical Hermeneutics* (1982) explicitly denies "that the 'horizons' of the biblical writer and the interpreter may rightly 'fuse' in such a way that what the text communicates to the interpreter is not ultimately controlled by the expressed meaning of Scripture."[110] As one scholar in my own Southern Baptist tradition describes his understanding of the fusion-event, "when studying those passages where Paul reflects on his past life . . . we do not study Paul but the texts he wrote, and the texts speak to us in our present situation rather than recreate the original author's past situation."[111] As many evangelicals have characterized it, the fusion of horizons appears fundamentally incompatible with traditional grammatical-historical biblical exegesis.

The reason for such concern is justifiable: Gadamer explicitly states that rightly understanding a text is not the same as understanding authorial intent or discovering any meaning fixed within the text. He writes,

> Every age has to understand a transmitted text in its own way, for the text belongs to the whole tradition whose content interests the age and in which it seeks to understand itself. The real meaning of the text, as it speaks to the interpreter, does not depend on the contingencies of

109. See E. D. Hirsch Jr., *Validity in Interpretation* (New Haven: Yale, 1967), 245–64. Hirsch's lasting influence in critiques of Gadamer may have something to do with the fact that his 1965 review of *Truth and Method* (and its republication in his subsequent 1967 volume *Validity in Interpretation*) predates the first English translation of *Truth and Method* by nearly a decade. But as Roger Lundin observes, "For more than three decades, Hirsch's questionable construal of *Truth and Method* has distorted conservative Protestant responses to Gadamer." Roger Lundin, *From Nature to Experience: The American Search for Cultural Authority* (Lanham, MD: Rowman & Littlefield, 2005), 158.

110. International Council on Biblical Inerrancy, *The Chicago Statement on Biblical Hermeneutics*, Article IX.

111. John P. Newport, "Contemporary Philosophical, Literary, and Sociological Hermeneutics," in *Biblical Hermeneutics: A Comprehensive Introduction to Interpreting Scripture*, 2nd ed., ed. Bruce Corley, Steve W. Lemke, and Grant I. Lovejoy (Nashville: Broadman & Holman, 2002), 167.

the author and his original audience. It is certainly not identical with them, for it is always co-determined also by the historical situation of the interpreter and hence by the totality of the objective course of history.[112]

Evangelicals committed to biblical authority believe that God somehow, someway has a matchless authority through the medium of inspired biblical texts. How can the Bible truly mediate God's authority to its readers if its interpreters co-determine the meaning of its sacred pages? Christian believers may be "coheirs with Christ" (Rom. 8:17), but they are not coauthors of Scripture, are they?

For what it's worth, Gadamer is at least sympathetic to a notion of biblical authority shared by many Christians, even if his existentialist worldview and explanation of the fusion event poses additional problems for it. In his discussion of the application of meaning in interpretation, he makes a distinction between legal hermeneutics and theological hermeneutics based on the unique status of the Bible for Christians. While courts and judges have the freedom to create new laws and provisos in their reading and application of the law, readers of biblical texts have no such freedom. Gadamer writes, "The gospel acquires no new content in being preached that could be compared with the power of the judge's verdict to supplement the law. . . . [The preacher] does not speak before the community with the same dogmatic authority that a judge does. . . . Scripture is the word of God, and that means it has an absolute priority over the doctrine of those who interpret it."[113] Gadamer recognizes that Christian preaching (and by extension, doctrinal development) must not (and cannot) be the creation *ex nihilo* of new theological concepts and ideas.

Evangelical critics of Gadamer frequently charge him with a simple kind of relativism and as encouraging a practice of reading akin to

---

112. Gadamer, *Truth and Method*, 296.
113. Ibid., 326.

reader-response criticism.[114] It seems that Gadamer himself would have shuddered at this charge, as he calls this kind of relativism self-refuting.[115] Gadamer is, as Kevin Vanhoozer observes, very conservative on meaning when contrasted with the textual theories of Derrida, Rorty, and Fish.[116] The notion of *alterity* or otherness at the core of Gadamer's philosophy also reveals the crude characterization of many of his critics. Awareness of the "other" results in a dialogue between persons of two *distinct* horizons, and in this conversation, "when we have discovered the other person's standpoint and horizon, his ideas become intelligible without our necessarily having to agree with him; so when someone thinks historically, he comes to understand the meaning of what has been handed down without necessarily agreeing with it or seeing himself in it."[117] Whether or not he is successful, Gadamer desires to *avoid confusing horizons*, insisting that in their fusion, there is a genuine tension between the past and the present made possible by historical consciousness.[118]

For Thiselton, the most important takeaway from Gadamer's notion of fusion for biblical hermeneutics and doctrinal development is that interpreters at every point in history must make sense of ancient texts from their own context and in their own language. Interpreters must recognize that even in their attempts to understand biblical authors, they do not read texts with all the same concerns and situations that the authors of these texts have. Contemporary readers bring new and different concerns to the Bible. Evangelicals may even be insistent that the special revelation of Scripture is God's primary

---

114. See Eduardo J. Echeverria, "Gadamer's Hermeneutics and the Question of Relativism," in *Hermeneutics at the Crossroads*, ed. Kevin J. Vanhoozer, James K. A. Smith, and Bruce Ellis Benson (Bloomington, IN: Indiana University Press), 52.

115. Gadamer, *Truth and Method*, 340.

116. Kevin J. Vanhoozer, *Is There a Meaning in This Text? The Bible, the Reader, and the Morality of Literary Knowledge* (Grand Rapids, MI: Zondervan, 1998), 107.

117. Ibid., 302.

118. Ibid., 305.

instrument of authority in the world today, but many of the moral and theological questions raised in the present climate would be very alien to biblical authors.

For example, contemporary readers with questions about the morality of abortion or embryonic stem-cell research may appeal to biblical prohibitions against murder (e.g., Exod. 20:13; Deut. 5:17, etc.), but in so doing, creative understanding has taken place because *these readers are asking questions of the Bible that its human authorship had no way of anticipating.* This is not to say that biblical authors could not respond in similar fashion if they faced the same historical situation or same questions, but it is an acknowledgement of the contemporary interpreter's need for creative or productive understanding. Interpretation may be a creative act but that need not mean that readers discount the alterity or otherness of the texts. Even when interpreters attempt to apply these texts to their own situation, they need to be aware of the significant historical differences between contexts. Biblical interpreters in particular should recognize the significant cultural differences between the world of the New Testament and twenty-first century Western culture.

The recognition of historical finitude and the contextual, creative nature of interpretation that Gadamer presents is important for Thiselton's descriptive model of development. Thiselton, too, stresses that interpreters operate with pre-understandings and horizons shaped by the effects of history and that reading in new and different horizons always requires creative interpretation. He is, however, critical of much of the ambiguity in Gadamer that has led to pragmatic or relativistic interpretations. The most serious charge he brings against the "fusion of horizons" motif is the danger of ghettoizing interpretation and forestalling action if this process never reaches an omega point or complete knowledge of the text.[119] Thiselton looks to the eschatology of Pannenberg as an important corrective to this Gadamerian tendency. Christian theology looks to a future horizon in which faith will be made sight and provisional understanding will be replaced with a more complete vision of God's overarching activity in history. This theme will reappear in more detail in chapter six.

Development and Hermeneutical "Questions that Arise"

Thiselton seeks to dispel a popular myth that Christian doctrine grows or develops spontaneously and in isolation from real world, everyday concerns. As one version of the myth goes, theologians perched in ivory towers "discover" or invent abstract concepts, most of which are irrelevant to "real" Christian ministry and the life of the church. In another version, theologians extemporaneously concoct doctrinal ideas or statements in order to serve some larger political agenda. A more pietistic yet equally problematic appraisal of postcanonical development may include new revelation or new visions. What all of these conceptions have in common is the idea that advancements in doctrine are not necessarily dependent upon conversation with the past; doctrines seem to fall from the sky or address fixed, "timeless" problems.

The development of doctrine occurs in a conversation between past and present horizons. As in any dialogue, more than one voice is necessary. In describing the nature of this conversation, Gadamer contrasts his own view of the development of philosophical ideas with the view of Immanuel Kant, who he claims approaches "problems" as static, ahistorical abstractions that emerge from reason like fixed, free-floating "stars in sky." Desiring to destroy this "illusion," Gadamer asserts that understanding always begins in the

---

119. See Thiselton, *New Horizons in Hermeneutics*, 331–38.

historical context of dialogue.[120] That is to say, we never explore possible answers to philosophical problems apart from cultural and temporal stimuli. Against Kant's notion of problems, Gadamer deploys philosopher of history R. G. Collingwood's (1889–1943) "logic of question and answer" to describe the *event* of understanding.[121]

Questions affected by history direct the conversation of the interpreter with the past horizon and its "answers." In other words, one attempts to make sense of texts by asking questions of it. These questions are shaped by one's horizon. In this dialogue, horizons "fuse" as new questions and new answers are forged that take the interpreter beyond his or her initial questions. As Gadamer describes this process, "understanding is always more than merely re-creating someone else's meaning. Questioning opens up possibilities of meaning, and thus what is meaningful passes into one's own thinking on the subject. . . . To understand a question means to ask it. To understand meaning is to understand it as the answer to a question."[122]

The "*hermeneutical dialectic* of question and answer" extends to the history of all ideas and attempts at understanding texts, but Thiselton explicitly appropriates it to describe the development of Christian confessions: "Further hermeneutical horizons emerge, most certainly, as controversies, debates, and conflicts that often attend, or lead to, the development of doctrine."[123] Whether in the local church or the

120. Gadamer, *Truth and Method*, 369. Kant never uses this specific metaphor himself but does, as Gadamer observes, describe problems as "ideas produced solely in the womb [of reason]." See Immanuel Kant, *The Critique of Pure Reason*, trans. Werner S. Pluhar (Indianapolis: Hackett, 1996), B23; cf. A763/B791.

121. See R. G. Collingwood, *An Autobiography* (Oxford: Oxford University Press, 2002), 24–43. Here Collingwood summarizes his description of the logic of question and answer that first appeared in his non-extant 1917 work, *Truth and Contradiction*. Gadamer edited and introduced a German translation of Collingwood's *Autobiography*. See R. G. Collingwood, *Denken: Eine Autobiographie* (Stuttgart: K. F. Koehler, 1955).

122. Gadamer, *Truth and Method*, 368.

academy, Christian doctrine—how biblical texts are interpreted and communicated—grows or takes new shapes when faced with new questions that grow out of the interpreter's context. Doctrine results from an ongoing conversation between the theological horizons of the past and present, between that which is *stable*—revelation and the substance of tradition—and that which is *continually transforming*—the historical situation of the church and individual believers. The metaphor of a "chain" of questions and answers also implies a profound sense of historical continuity within the history of ideas.

As Thiselton acknowledges, there are some family resemblances between his dialectical model of development and Paul Tillich's method of correlation, in which theology "answers the questions implied in the 'situation' in the power of the eternal message."[124] Thiselton warns that this similarity is very superficial, because Tillich's "questions" are *"large and generalized ones . . . more akin to Gadamer's 'problems'* than Gadamer's ongoing dialectic." That is, Tillich emphasizes abstract existential questions of ultimate concern, and Thiselton believes theology to be more context-specific. As in the Gadamerian dialogue of question and answer, the questions theologians address are situational and historically contingent than existential and universal.[125] Furthermore, while evangelical theologians usually admit to some sort of dialectic exchange with culture, they are not satisfied with the way in which Tillich's method seems to give the culture control over the conversation.[126] Contra Tillich, culture, composed of selfish and depraved human beings, does not always ask the right questions.

123. Thiselton, *The Hermeneutics of Doctrine*, 7–8.
124. Paul Tillich, *Systematic Theology*, vol. 1 (Chicago: University of Chicago Press, 1951), 6.
125. See Thiselton, *Thiselton on Hermeneutics*, 803.
126. Grenz and Olson, *20th Century Theology*, 119–22.

A hermeneutical dialectic of question and answer provides an important framework for describing the historical processes behind certain doctrinal formulations within the New Testament. A few examples help illustrate its value. First, one may trace christological development within the New Testament along the contours of the history of effects and questions that arise. The Gospels are themselves the results of Jesus' impact on the disciples. Like J. L. Austin's speech-act theory and the later Wittgenstein's philosophy of language, Gadamer's history of effects thesis shows that language does more than disclose information. Jesus' words and actions continued to affect the lives of the disciples in such a way that their devotion to him continued to grow and develop. The history of effects has value in explaining how an event like the resurrection could influence the disciples in such a way that the event's effects on them gave rise to the church and the devotion to him that followed.

Questions within the worldview or horizon of Second Temple Judaism about the identity and vocation of the Messiah shaped Jesus' own self-understanding and those of his followers. With respect to the development of the tradition, the hermeneutical dialectic of question and answer can give insight into the differences in Matthew, Mark, Luke, and the oral tradition.[127] Different historical questions raised in different receptive contexts may give explanation to differences of presentation and historical selection between gospels in the synoptic tradition. The hermeneutic of question and answer may even have explanatory power over the differences between John and the Synoptic Gospels, as Franz Mussner, one of the early adopters of Gadamerian theory in biblical studies, demonstrated over forty years ago.[128] If historical distance is valuable in creating fuller

---

127. For an application of Gadamerian hermeneutics to the oral tradition of the Synoptic Gospels, see James D. G. Dunn, *Jesus Remembered*, Christianity in the Making, vol. 1 (Grand Rapids, MI: Eerdmans, 2003), 99–138.

understanding, as Gadamer suggests, then it is reasonable to suspect a more mature and robust christology from John in his later years than in the time he shared directly with Jesus.

More importantly for the issue at hand, the hermeneutical dialectic of question and answer is valuable for explaining postcanonical developments. New horizons or life situations often invoke new readings and deeper understandings of the Bible and doctrine. Christians facing new questions unaddressed by Scripture require creative reformulations of biblical principles and ideas. New conflicts, many of which were once unimaginable in the biblical world, often transform implicit dispositional beliefs into explicit statements of belief and practice or even lead to the revision of established beliefs.

The developments of Nicaea were not simply impromptu ideas forced by Constantine's hand. They were responses to pressing questions about the validity of Arius's teachings. Third- and fourth-century formulations of Trinitarian doctrine did not emerge as abstract concepts isolated from life but as conversations with Scripture, opposition to the common rule of faith, and the very practical concern of believers to reconcile their worship of Jesus with their desire to keep the first and second commandments. Existential questions about Christ's ability to save, not abstract argumentation for sport, directed discussions about his two natures and personhood

128. Mussner was one of the earliest adopters of Gadamerian theory in biblical studies. Mussner argues that John's distinctive Christology and kerygma is the mature result of his own hermeneutical situation; i.e., the *Wirkungsgeschichte* of Jesus tradition and the developing faith of the church over a considerable period of time resulted in his unique understanding of Jesus. While he believes that the discourse of the Johannine Christ is actually John's own language and ideas, Mussner suggests that the evangelist's particular interpretation stems from his own "remembrance" of the historical Jesus, the church's post-Easter tradition, inspiration from the Paraclete, and the history-affected questions that arose in the face of heresy. See Franz Mußner, *Die Johanneische Sehweise und die Frage nach dem historischen Jesus* (Freiburg: Herder, 1965); cf. idem, *The Historical Jesus in the Gospel of John*, trans. W. J. O'Hara (London: Burns & Oates, 1967). The title of the subsequent English translation lessened the impact of Mussner's thesis that what we really encounter in John the "Johannine vision" of the Jesus of history. See also Thiselton, *The Two Horizons*, 44–46.

at Ephesus and Chalcedon. If Christ's human and divine natures were lost in a new, third kind of nature, as Eutyches (c. 380–456) and the later Monophysites argued, could he truly represent human beings before God?

The historical distance of nearly three hundred years between the Christ-event and Nicaea need not be fodder for historical skepticism about trinitarian claims, as some contemporary critics of orthodoxy have claimed. Gadamer notes that in the conversation between horizons, the passing of time can often lead to a greater understanding and can help distinguish true presuppositions from false presuppositions.[129] For the historian, he believes that temporal distance leads to a wider horizon of understanding and can help sort out the impact that prejudgment plays on the interpretation of a recent event. For example, historians writing thirty or forty years after World War I have a better grasp of the complex political situation in Europe that give rise to the war—an understanding that those who were close to the political conflict may not have been able to see because of the way their prejudgments shaped their horizon. (A century after the war began, historians are still wrestling with questions about what led to this global conflict.)[130]

Traditional formulations of Christ grew within the history of effects, a continuous chain of question and answers. The reception history of gospel traditions and christological doctrinal development traces back to a figure named Jesus, who, as expressed in the Christian doctrine of the incarnation, lived for a time within the confines of a limited historical horizon. Throughout the first five centuries of Christianity, the speech-acts and non-verbal performances of Jesus continued to have a ripple effect that resulted in the christological

---

129. Gadamer, *Truth and Method*, 298.

130. For a detailed analysis of the debates over the historiography of the First World War, see Annika Mombauer, *The Origins of the First World War: Controversies and Consensus* (New York: Routledge, 2013).

consensus of the ecumenical councils. Like the period in which the written gospels came to be, there was temporal distance and reflection—a widening of horizons—that gave rise to a more refined understanding of Jesus as the object of faith for the church.

Later questions about Christ's work provoked further developments. Anselm may have formulated his satisfaction theory of atonement in the socio-political context of feudalism, but he also sought to answer a question provoked by his exchange with the long-standing tradition of ransom theories: why was it necessary for God to become man (*Cur Deus Homo*)? Peter Abelard (1079–1142), dissatisfied with Anselm's answer and seeking to make sense of Rom. 3:19–26, posited what has come to be known as the "moral influence theory of atonement."[131] Luther and Calvin's penal substitutionary theory of atonement grew out of conversation with Anselm and Abelard and prompted responses with the respective theories of atonement from Fausto Sozzini (or Faustus Socinus, 1539–1604) and Hugo Grotius (1583–1645). These debates over atonement continue to the present day in traditions that grew out of these developments.

Luther's doctrine of justification by faith grew out of his uneasiness with the abuses of the papacy and questions he had about how to be faithful to Scripture. While Luther was clearly concerned with being faithful to Paul's ideas, the first-century apostle did not anticipate the particular concerns Luther had about the sales of indulgences and the Roman Catholic doctrine of merit. (Notably, even those uniquely Catholic developments also occurred in the dialectic of question and answer.) In order to discover how Paul might have responded to such issues, Luther needed to employ creative understanding, to fuse horizons, and to ask questions of the apostolic texts. Contemporary

---

131. See Peter Abelard, "Exposition of the Epistle to the Romans (An Excerpt from the Second Book," in *A Scholastic Miscellany: Anselm to Ockham*, The Library of Christian Classics 10, ed. and trans. Eugene R. Fairweather (Philadelphia: Westminster, 1956), 276–87.

debates over the so-called "New Perspective on Paul" are shaped by a new set of historical questions, in large part prompted by (1) the discovery of many Second Temple Jewish sources unknown to Luther and (2) ecumenical conversations in the twentieth century about the nature of justification. New trajectories, new developments, and new interpretations are inevitable in this ongoing chain of historical question and answer.

As illustrated in the previous chapter, even the so-called "problem" of development itself initially developed in a post-Enlightenment dialogue of question and answer between deeply held convictions about the authority of ecclesial tradition and the difficulties raised by historians of the new historical consciousness. These examples call attention to the way in which historical, social, and theological horizons, not theological abstraction done in isolation, give rise to the development of Christian doctrines. The development of doctrine is not just a formal, academic affair. It happens in pulpits and pews as well as in library carrels.

Concluding Remarks

Anthony Thiselton's hermeneutical description of doctrinal formation provides a helpful, big-picture way of thinking about the historical processes behind such development. His accomplishment is remarkable: he integrates insights from a number of key philosophical thinkers in the abstract and frequently cryptic Continental tradition to demonstrate the day-to-day practicality of Christian doctrine. His model also sets the stage for establishing continuity in the Christian tradition across developments. As I will argue in coming chapters, this descriptive hermeneutical model can also be a great aid in Christian apologetics.

Nonetheless, Thiselton's model does raise a few additional questions or concerns for evangelical theological method. First, Thiselton's descriptive account of doctrinal development raises additional unanswered questions about the *nature of heresy*. Does not "heresy" arise the same way doctrine does, from a historically contingent dialogue of question and answer? The so-called problem of heresy, the twin sister of the development question, gets little explicit attention in Thiselton's theological hermeneutics.[132] The criticism often given to the anti-methodical Gadamer—that he gives little by way of helpful criteria for distinguishing between good and bad interpretations—is equally applicable to Thiselton's model of development. He remains unclear about how to move from the Bible to doctrinal statements and confessions. He also neglects a question very important for the present concern: *How should the church distinguish heresy from genuine doctrinal development?* He stresses the importance of Scripture in giving stability to the tradition but without an explanation of its uniqueness or an explicit bibliology, it is unclear why The Gospel of Thomas, The Book of Mormon, or the Bhagavad Gītā are not also part of the ongoing discourse of the living God.

As Alister McGrath has shown, a descriptive model of the development of heresy is possible. McGrath identifies five cultural and intellectual motivations for heresy that are compatible with the hermeneutical dialectic of development offered by Thiselton.[133] First, he notes that every era presents Christian belief with cultural norms that are incongruous with traditional biblical and doctrinal ideas or beliefs. These norms, akin to the historically situated "questions"

132. The term "heresy" appears fewer than ten times in 581 pages of the body of *The Hermeneutics of Doctrine.*
133. Alister E. McGrath, *Heresy: A History of Defending Truth* (New York: HarperOne, 2009), 180–95.

posed by culture in Thiselton's model, perceive traditional Christian beliefs as fundamentally out-of-touch or outmoded concepts.[134] Second, McGrath identifies the expectation to "conform to the prevailing criteria of rationality" as a key factor in the development of heresy.[135] Many theologians ultimately deemed heretical within the Christian tradition began many of their projects with the basic hope of creating an apologetic that would satisfy the views of reason in their milieu. Third, some heresies emerge when groups make great efforts to establish a unique social identity.[136] Fourth, heresy can result from an unhealthy focus on religious accommodation, of establishing a concrete form of coexistence in a religiously plural setting.[137] Finally, heresy can develop as a response to perceptions of moral laxity or moral oppression within religious orthodoxy. Acetic cults and antinomian sexual activists alike can develop very different heresies for the same basic motivation: perceived moral inadequacies in the broader orthodox tradition.[138] All of these motivations go hand-in-hand with the hermeneutical dialogue of question and answer presented in this chapter.

A second problem with Thiselton's descriptive model is the openness of God presumably presupposed in Thiselton's hermeneutics of doctrine. In addition to the internal inconsistencies that openness theology creates for theology proper, it creates great difficulty for theories of doctrinal development as well. A full-orbed analysis of open theism is clearly well beyond the scope of this chapter, but this issue will likely be one of the more controversial elements of Thiselton's theological hermeneutics for evangelicals. In recent years, American evangelicals in particular have debated

134. Ibid., 181–83.
135. Ibid., 180.
136. Ibid., 187–88.
137. Ibid., 189–90.
138. Ibid., 180, 190–94.

whether this particular theological framework fits under the "big tent" of evangelicalism.[139] The confession of faith in my Southern Baptist tradition excludes the possibility of open theism: "God is all powerful and all knowing; and His perfect knowledge extends to all things, past, present, and future, including the future decisions of His free creatures."[140]

Whether it fits within the "boundaries" of evangelical theology or not, open theism appears to present more problems for doctrinal development than constructive solutions. By saying that believers should expect doctrines to "evolve" because they are dynamic and living just as *"God is the living, dynamic, ongoing God,"*[141] Thiselton seems to imply that (1) doctrine evolves because God is evolving and that (2) God is always providing a *de novo* revelation of the divine nature. The former inference would hinder a doctrine of God's constancy and fidelity (not necessarily the same as divine immutability in the stronger sense), while the latter would rob theology of a stable source. The latter point seems to imply that the inspiration and illumination of biblical texts are often tantamount events without any kind of qualitative difference. Neither of these inferences seems to resonate well with confessional evangelical theology.

139. Much of the debate over evangelical boundaries and open theism has been argued along traditional lines of Reformed theology and Arminian theology. See Bruce A. Ware, "Defining Evangelicalism's Boundaries Theologically: Is Open Theism Evangelical?" *Journal of the Evangelical Theological Society* 45/2 (June 2002): 193–212; idem, "Rejoinder to Replies by Clark H. Pinnock, John Sanders, andnd Gregory A. Boyd," *Journal of the Evangelical Theological Society* 45/2 (June 2002): 245–56; Clark H. Pinnock, "There Is Room for Us: A Reply To Bruce Ware," *Journal of the Evangelical Theological Society* 45/2 (June 2002): 213–19; John Sanders, "Be Wary of Ware: A Reply to Bruce Ware," *Journal of the Evangelical Theological Society* 45/2 (June 2002): 221–31; Gregory A. Boyd, "Christian Love and Academic Dialogue: A Reply to Bruce Ware," *Journal of the Evangelical Theological Society* 45/2 (June 2002) 233–43; Roger E. Olson, "Open Theism: A Test Case for Evangelicals," August 23, 2010, http://www.patheos.com/blogs/rogereolson/2010/08/open-theism-a-test-case-for-evangelicals/ (accessed December 9, 2012).

140. *Baptist Faith & Message 2000*, article 2.

141. Thiselton, *The Hermeneutics of Doctrine*, 63.

Nevertheless, Thiselton's pursuit of a doctrine of the "living God" grounded in biblical exegesis and not merely derived from philosophical theology is a truly commendable enterprise. It is reminiscent of Pascal's plea for the revealed God of Scripture over and against the god "of the philosophers and scholars" (*des Philosophes et des savants*).[142] As Thiselton rightly observes, many philosophical theologians too readily dismiss personal descriptions of God's actions and emotions in Old Testament narratives as merely anthropomorphic or anthropopathic language with no literal significance. Moreover, many classical theists often have affirmed philosophical categories alien to Scripture, such as the Aristotelian and Platonic ideal of divine impassibility.

Even so, Thiselton gives little convincing evidence that some of his own doctrinal affiliations are any more biblical in their orientation. The very same criticism that Thiselton makes of Helm's model of divine timelessness—that it fails to give serious attention to "careful exegesis of relevant passages"[143]—is equally applicable to Sallie McFague's privileged "hermeneutical" doctrine of divine immanence. One would be hard pressed to find much exegetical consideration in many of McFague's works in constructive theology, as she primarily views the Bible not as an "authoritative text" for doctrine but as a "case study," a "prototype," and a "model for how theology should be done" rather than "the authority dictating the terms in which it should be done."[144] Daniel J. Treier, another evangelical hermeneutics scholar, rightly wonders whether "Thiselton makes adequately clear why *these* theologians [particularly

---

142. Blaise Pascal, *Pensées*, ed. Jean-Frédéric Astié (Paris, 1857), 98; cf. idem, *Pensées and Other Writings*, ed. Anthony Levi, trans. Honor Levi (New York: Oxford University Press, 1995), 178.

143. Thiselton, *Life After Death*, 140.

144. See Sallie McFague, *The Body of God: An Ecological Theology* (Minneapolis: Fortress Press, 1993), 43; idem, *Models of God: Theology for an Ecological, Nuclear Age* (Philadelphia: Fortress Press, 1987).

Moltmann and Pannenberg] are distinctly excellent from a hermeneutical perspective."[145] My own suspicion is that Thiselton gravitates to these theologians because of their shared appreciation of Gadamer and the categories of his hermeneutic. If this suspicion is true, then Thiselton may be accused of exchanging the philosophical conception of God from one Western tradition (Plato, Aristotle, etc.) with another philosophical conception from a different Western tradition (Heidegger, Gadamer, etc.).

Finally, Thiselton's account of doctrinal development does not include an explicit missiological and ecclesiological dimension. In other words, he gives little or no explicit attention to the role of doctrinal development in the transcultural and transgenerational communication of the gospel. *Contextualization*, which plays some role in *New Horizons*, goes unmentioned in *The Hermeneutics of Doctrine*. This gap likely stems from his descriptive emphasis but even a descriptive account of development can for doctrine's missional significance. In the next chapter, we will explore a normative theological hermeneutics that addresses many of the questions related to development that are left unanswered in a purely descriptive model.

In summary, Thiselton provides a helpful and important reminder that "at the heart of hermeneutics stands a dialectical relation between particularity and universality, between contingency and coherence, and between a plurality of interpretations and a stable core of tradition."[146] The dialectical movements that permeate a remarkably consistent project spanning over fifty years and are vital to his interaction with the problem of doctrinal development. He is not interested in a conceptual theology removed from one's life setting

---

145. Daniel J. Treier, review of *The Hermeneutics of Doctrine*, by Anthony C. Thiselton, *International Journal of Systematic Theology* 11, no. 2 (April 2009): 225.
146. Thiselton, *Thiselton on Hermeneutics*, 40.

or historical situation, nor is he interested in a theology that consists of detached, timeless propositions. Doctrines are provisional, contingent, and action-guiding public commitments that develop in the context of Christian life, not in an isolated ivory tower.

4

Doctrinal Development in the Normative Theological Hermeneutics of Kevin J. Vanhoozer

Kevin J. Vanhoozer, one of the most creative and constructive evangelical theologians currently working, is best known for his work in theological prolegomena and the theological interpretation of Scripture.[1] Questions about the relationship between the Bible and systematic theology initially directed his work to hermeneutics, and interdisciplinary engagement with hermeneutical and literary theory has been a staple in his research ever since.[2] Much like Thiselton before him, Vanhoozer has endeavored to utilize the insights of non-theological resources like contemporary hermeneutical theory

---

1. More recently, Vanhoozer has turned his attention to specific Christian doctrines. For his exploration of the doctrine of God, see his *Remythologizing Theology: Divine Action, Passion, and Authorship* (Cambridge: Cambridge University Press, 2010).
2. See Kevin J. Vanhoozer, *Is There a Meaning in This Text? The Bible, the Reader, and the Morality of Literary Knowledge* (Grand Rapids, MI: Zondervan, 1998), 9.

in biblical interpretation and Christian theology. However, in contrast to Thiselton's descriptive approach, Vanhoozer's approach to theological hermeneutics is primarily normative in its orientation.

While Vanhoozer never attempts to give a one-size-fits-all, systematic procedure for doctrinal formulation, his theological hermeneutics is normative in the sense that he gives direction and purpose for the ongoing task of evangelical theology. For Vanhoozer, theology is more than the systematic, descriptive reordering of the propositional content of Scripture. It is not merely an attempt to discern "what the whole Bible teaches us today about a particular topic."[3] Theology is a discipline of critical contemplation on the larger narrative or "theo-drama" of Scripture with particular attention given to questions about how best to "perform" in this ongoing drama in ways that are fitting to what has gone before in the "canonical script" of Scripture. The theologian is not only concerned with re-telling the story of Scripture but also concerned with encouraging believers to take up a participatory role in the grand narrative Scripture invokes. Doctrine, according to Vanhoozer, is biblically based "practical wisdom" (*phronēsis*) for the Christian life, steering and shaping belief and practice. For Vanhoozer, there is an organic, yet distinguishable relationship between systematic theology and Christian ethics. His theological prolegomena, then, is a critical, second-order reflection on the performative nature of theology.

This emphasis on performance and narrative reflects a theme in *postliberal* and postmodern theologies, especially in the works of George Lindbeck. With Lindbeck, Vanhoozer shares discontent with the overly simplistic dichotomy between conservative and liberal theology. Whereas Lindbeck offers a postliberal approach to Christian doctrine, Vanhoozer uses the descriptor *postconservative* to

---

3. Wayne Grudem, *Systematic Theology* (Grand Rapids, MI: Zondervan, 2000), 25.

describe his own theological program.[4] While Vanhoozer has significant critiques of the methodologies of conservative theologies in the past, he agrees substantially with the consensus of evangelical theology in the Reformed tradition.[5] Vanhoozer stresses the need for a postconservative, performative theology, but he is primarily concerned with issues central to evangelical identity: faithfulness to Scripture as the written word of God, the nature of truth, and the centrality of the gospel proclamation.

Vanhoozer's extensive work in theological prolegomena and hermeneutical theory is not reducible to the issue of doctrinal development alone, but the issue plays an important role in his discussion of the nature and task of Christian doctrine. In his normative theological hermeneutics, postcanonical doctrinal development is more than an accident of history; it is a God-given calling for the church. This chapter is an exploration of that theme. We begin by tracing the development of Vanhoozer's normative theological hermeneutics, from his emphasis on a theologically informed general hermeneutics to a hermeneutically informed theology. Then we explore issues related to postcanonical doctrinal development in Vanhoozer's canonical-linguistic or theo-dramatic approach to Christian doctrine. This chapter closes with a case study used to examine Vanhoozer's normative model of development.

---

4. Kevin J. Vanhoozer, *The Drama of Doctrine* (Louisville: Westminster/John Knox, 2005), xiii. Vanhoozer's use of "postconservative" is distinct from other evangelical approaches under that same moniker, such as the program of the late Stanley Grenz (1950–2005). See also Kevin J. Vanhoozer, "On the Very Idea of a Theological System: An Essay in Aid of Triangulating Scripture, Church, and World," in *Always Reforming: Explorations in Systematic Theology*, ed. A. T. B. McGowan (Downers Grove, IL: InterVarsity, 2006), 143–47.

5. See Everett Berry, "Theological vs. Methodological Post-Conservatism: Stanley Grenz and Kevin Vanhoozer as Test Cases," *Westminster Theological Journal* 69 (2007): 105–26.

The Development of Vanhoozer's
Normative Theological Hermeneutics

Vanhoozer completed his 1985 doctoral dissertation on the hermeneutics of Paul Ricoeur at Cambridge University under the supervision of Nicholas Lash, a renowned Roman Catholic theologian who has been described as "exemplar of postmodern theology in the Anglo-American tradition."[6] (Notably, Lash also has done extensive work in the problem of doctrinal development but from a Catholic perspective, though his work in this area seems to bear little influence on Vanhoozer's approach to the topic.)[7] In many ways, Vanhoozer's dissertation did for Ricoeur what Thiselton's *The Two Horizons* did for Gadamer and Wittgenstein: showcase critical appropriation of his hermeneutical theory for evangelical biblical interpretation and Christian theology.[8]

By his own admission, Vanhoozer tends to highlight the normative dimensions of hermeneutics over against descriptive hermeneutical approaches such as Gadamer's.[9] This normative emphasis is due partly to the influence of Ricoeur, who rejects the dichotomy that Gadamer

6. Nancey C. Murphy and Brad J. Kallenberg, "Anglo-American Postmodernity: A Theology of Communal Practice," in *The Cambridge Companion to Postmodern Theology*, ed. Kevin J. Vanhoozer (Cambridge: Cambridge University Press, 2003), 26.

7. See Nicholas Lash, *Newman on Development: The Search for an Explanation in History* (Shepherdstown, WV: Patmos, 1975); idem, *Change in Focus: A Study of Doctrinal Change and Continuity* (London: Sheed and Ward, 1981). Vanhoozer shows no explicit interaction with either of these works in his discussion of the problem of development and credits his former student, Wheaton theologian Daniel Treier, for turning his attention to this issue. See Vanhoozer, *The Drama of Doctrine*, 346, n. 130.

8. See Kevin J. Vanhoozer, *Biblical Narrative in the Philosophy of Paul Ricoeur: A Study in Hermeneutics and Theology* (Cambridge: Cambridge University Press, 1990). It is worth noting that Ricoeur, who succeeded Paul Tillich as the John Nuveen Professor of Philosophical Theology at the University of Chicago, gives greater explicit attention in his writings to theology and biblical interpretation than many of his other continental contemporaries. See also Paul Ricoeur, *Essays on Biblical Interpretation*, ed. Lewis S. Mudge (Philadelphia: Fortress Press, 1980).

9. Kevin J. Vanhoozer, "Discourse on Matter: Hermeneutics and the 'Miracle' of Understanding," in *Hermeneutics at the Crossroads*, ed. Kevin J. Vanhoozer, James K. A. Smith, and Bruce Ellis Benson (Bloomington: Indiana University Press, 2006), 4.

presents between truth and method and attempts to reclaim method for hermeneutics.[10] Vanhoozer's notion of theological vocation plays an even larger role in this normative emphasis. The theologian plays an important advisory role in the church and to its pastoral leadership.[11] As a result, Vanhoozer's theological methodology is less of a descriptive analysis of the doctrinal task and more of a direct, prescriptive address to Christian believers.

Presently, Vanhoozer's most widely recognized contribution to hermeneutical theory is his 1998 volume, *Is There a Meaning in This Text? The Bible, the Reader, and the Morality of Literary Knowledge.* Using biblical interpretation as a model, Vanhoozer proposes an all-purpose ethic for reading that calls on readers to respect the communicative actions of authors. Tweaking the standard claim that general hermeneutics should direct special hermeneutics—Benjamin Jowett's (1817–1893) notion that the Bible should be read "like any other book"[12]—Vanhoozer boldly asserts that biblical interpretation should guide the interpretation of all other texts. He asserts that special hermeneutics has primacy over general hermeneutics: "I stake my claim that the Bible should be read like any other book, and that every other book should be read like the Bible, from within the Christian worldview."[13] Barth shapes the thinking of Vanhoozer on this point when he suggests that "it is from the word of man in

---

10. See Paul Ricoeur, *The Conflict in Interpretations: Essays in Hermeneutics*, ed. Don Ihde (Evanston, IL: Northwestern University Press, 1974), 11; cf. idem, *Hermeneutics and the Human Sciences: Essays on Language, Action, and Interpretation*, ed. and trans. John B. Thompson (Cambridge: Cambridge University Press, 1981), 59–62.

11. See Vanhoozer, *The Drama of Doctrine*, 244, 246–48. According to Vanhoozer, pastors also serve an important role as "public" theologians for their congregation and their local ministry contexts. See Kevin J. Vanhoozer and Owen Strachan, *The Pastor as Public Theologian: Reclaiming a Lost Vision* (Grand Rapids, MI: Brazos, 2014).

12. See Benjamin Jowett, *Essays and Reviews* (London: John W. Parker and Son, 1860), 377–78. Jowett writes, "*Interpret the Scripture like any other book.* . . . No other science of Hermeneutics is possible but an inductive one, that is to say, based on the language and thoughts and narrations of the sacred writers. And it would be well to carry the theory of interpretation no further than in the case of other works."

the Bible that we must learn what has to be learned concerning the word of man in general."[14] Questions about general hermeneutics are inherently theological, Vanhoozer observes, because (1) the relationship of the author to a text resembles the relationship of God to the world—as Derrida's rejection of the author is likewise a rejection of God—and because (2) so much of what goes on in the humanities mirrors of the concerns of theological anthropology.[15]

Naturally, Vanhoozer's earlier work in hermeneutical theory also sets the stage for his later work in theological method. In the introduction to *First Theology*, a 2002 collection of his early essays on theological method, he poses an important preliminary question that frames much of his project: What constitutes "first theology" or the starting point of theology?[16] Does theology begin with God or the Bible? That is, should theology begin with arguments from philosophy and natural theology or the insights of historical-critical biblical scholarship? As the history of natural theology demonstrates, approaches to theology totally detached from biblical interpretation often capitulate to current (and quickly outmoded) philosophical trends. On the other hand, many biblical scholars who put an excessive focus on the historical particularity of biblical texts—what the texts mean then—have great difficulty producing a theology in which the word of God can speak today.[17] Many in modern biblical scholarship have served systematic theology with divorce papers, citing the need for autonomy from theology in order to be truly

13. Kevin J. Vanhoozer, "The Spirit of Understanding: Special Revelation and General Hermeneutics," in *Disciplining Hermeneutics: Interpretation in Christian Perspective*, ed. Roger Lundin (Grand Rapids, MI: Eerdmans, 1997), 132.
14. Karl Barth, *Church Dogmatics*, vol. 1, pt. 1, *The Doctrine of the Word of God*, 466. See also Vanhoozer, "Discourse on Matter," 12.
15. Vanhoozer, *Is There a Meaning in This Text?*, 30.
16. Vanhoozer, *First Theology*, 15. "First theology," Vanhoozer's description of theological prolegomena in this volume, reflects Descartes' use of "first philosophy" to describe the starting point of philosophy.
17. Vanhoozer, *First Theology*, 27.

critical and free of questions or categories that distort the meaning of the text.[18]

Vanhoozer is dissatisfied with the false dichotomy often made between biblical interpretation and theological substance. For him, the theological interpretation of Scripture offers a much needed both-and approach: "We interpret Scripture as divine communicative action in order to know God; we let our knowledge of God affect our approach to Scripture."[19] We begin theology by *reading the Bible as Scripture*, as Trinitarian communicative discourse from the interpersonal God whose actions speak and whose speech is action.[20] Reading the Bible as Scripture entails theological interpretation, or reading the Bible in order to know and obey God, is the response that Scripture calls for, the intended purpose of its divine-human authorship.[21]

The interaction of hermeneutical theory and theological method is a critical theme in all of Vanhoozer's writings, but his 2005 monograph *The Drama of Doctrine* is the most comprehensive exploration of this relationship to date. Vanhoozer describes the approach put forward in this work as *canonical-linguistic* and *theo-dramatic*.[22] The moniker "canonical-linguistic" calls attention to the way in which his approach develops in critical, yet appreciative, engagement with George Lindbeck's postliberal, cultural-linguistic

---

18. Kevin J. Vanhoozer, "What Is Theological Interpretation of the Bible?" in *Dictionary for Theological Interpretation of the Bible*, ed. Kevin J. Vanhoozer (Grand Rapids, MI: Zondervan, 2005), 21.

19. Vanhoozer, *First Theology*, 38.

20. See Vanhoozer, *First Theology*, 28–30. This task of "reading as" suggests the need for an extrabiblical, "imaginative construal" in determining how the Bible functions authoritatively. Vanhoozer here relies on Wittgenstein's notion of "seeing as" and David Kelsey's (b. 1932) discussion of different "uses" of Scripture. See David H. Kelsey, *Proving Doctrine: The Uses of Scripture in Modern Theology* (Harrisburg, PA: Trinity, 1999).

21. Vanhoozer, *Is There a Meaning in This Text?*, 406. See also, Vanhoozer, *First Theology*, 28–30.

22. Vanhoozer, *The Drama of Doctrine*, 265–305; cf. idem, "The Voice and the Actor: A Dramatic Proposal about the Ministry and Minstrelsy of Theology," in *Evangelical Futures: A Conversation on Theological Method*, ed. John G. Stackhouse Jr. (Grand Rapids, MI: Baker, 2000), 75.

program. Vanhoozer, however, reframes the emphasis on performative theology for an evangelical context, envisioning a theological method that grounds doctrinal speech acts in the supreme authority of Scripture. For this reason, Vanhoozer substitutes *cultural* with *canonical* in his description of "canonical-linguistic" theology. (The term "theo-dramatic," which will be fleshed out in the following pages, is used interchangeably by Vanhoozer and myself to describe the same method.) The always-creative theologian gives his basic approach many other aliases, several of which are brought to you by the letter *P*: "postconservative," "postpropositionalist," "postfoundationalist," "pluralistic," "phronetic," "prosaic," and "prophetic."[23]

The theo-dramatic, canonical-linguistic approach represents a new period in Vanhoozer's program.[24] The slight redirection hardly constitutes a *Kehre* of Heideggerian proportions, but a few developments are worth noting. First, the focus moves from hermeneutical theory shaped by theology (theological hermeneutics) toward a theology shaped by hermeneutics (hermeneutical theology).[25] Second, this juncture represents a move away from general hermeneutics informed by special hermeneutics (what Vanhoozer calls a "*theological* general hermeneutic") toward "a *theological* special hermeneutic" that highlights the distinctive features of Christian biblical interpretation.[26] At this point, Vanhoozer wants to talk about ways in which "reading the Bible [is] *unlike* [reading] any other book."[27] This transition is important for the discussion

23. Vanhoozer, *The Drama of Doctrine*, xiii.
24. Treier, *Introducing Theological Interpretation of Scripture*, 144–45.
25. Vanhoozer, "The Voice and the Actor," 69.
26. Kevin J. Vanhoozer, "Imprisoned or Free? Text, Status, and Theological Interpretation in the Master/Slave Discourse of Philemon," in A. K. M. Adam, Stephen E. Fowl, Kevin J. Vanhoozer, and Francis Watson, *Reading Scripture with the Church: Toward a Hermeneutic for Theological Interpretation* (Grand Rapids, MI: Baker, 2006), 58–61.
27. Ibid., 75.

of doctrinal development because Vanhoozer suggests that general hermeneutics alone cannot give direction for how doctrine should develop or relate to contemporary issues.[28]

For Vanhoozer, the "theological interpretation of Scripture" is not an abandonment of authorial discourse as much as it is a return to practices modeled in Scripture: making *theological judgments* patterned after biblical texts.[29] The task of exegesis is a necessary but insufficient condition for the calling of Scripture.[30] That is, it is not enough simply to understand the grammar, background, and meaning of a text. Interpreters must strive to understand the authorial discourse, but they must *put Scripture into practice* as well. In order to respond accordingly to Scripture, the theological interpreter strives to understand God's ongoing activity in the world in terms of both the canonical context of Scripture and contemporary experience.

A theological interpretation of Scripture distinct from historical exegesis is possible because, as Vanhoozer notes, the Bible constitutes a "stratified semantic reality."[31] Here Vanhoozer echoes the critical realist philosophy of science of Roy Bhaskar, who, within the context of the natural sciences, observes that reality has many layers or "strata" that requires different methodologies and varying levels of engagement to understand.[32] Reality is complex, and every stratum is important for understanding the whole of a particular aspect of

---

28. Vanhoozer, *The Drama of Doctrine*, 152–53.

29. Ibid., 219.

30. Kevin J. Vanhoozer, "A Drama-of-Redemption Model: Always Performing?" in *Four Views on Moving Beyond the Bible to Theology*, ed. Gary T. Meadors (Grand Rapids, MI: Zondervan, 2009), 165.

31. Vanhoozer, "Imprisoned or Free?" 69–70.

32. See Roy Bhaskar, *The Possibility of Naturalism: A Philosophical Critique of the Contemporary Human Sciences*, 3d ed. (London: Routledge, 1998); idem, *A Realist Theory of Science*, 2nd ed. (London: Verso, 1997); and idem, *Scientific Realism and Human Emancipation* (New York: Routledge, 2009). Alister McGrath first applied Bhaskar's philosophy of science to theological method in his *Scientific Theology* trilogy. Alister McGrath explores the implications of Bhaskar's stratified reality for Christian theology in *A Scientific Theology*, vol. 2, *Reality* (Grand Rapids, MI: Eerdmans, 2002), 195–244.

reality. While the different strata affect each other in a vertical relationship, even in a causal relationship, the methodology used to explain one stratum would not explain all strata.[33] As Thomas F. Torrance observes, this stratified reality means "that we have to develop different languages appropriate to the distinctive kinds of reality we encounter, if we are to understand them adequately and coordinate them in our thought."[34] Not only do different strata of reality require different languages; they also require different "modes of rational order." Varying forms of reasoning are necessary for different aspects of reality. The tools of biological investigation are necessarily distinct from contemplating transcendent forms of Being like those described in Christian theology and philosophy.[35]

Biblical texts are also part of a complex, stratified reality, and no single discipline (e.g., biblical studies, theology, cosmology, etc.) can describe the content contained within exhaustively. Furthermore, no single sub-discipline within the broader field of biblical studies can address all the questions and issues that come up when we analyze a text. We may illustrate the complex, stratified reality of biblical texts with the following chart, which is intended to address the question, "What does God desire from contemporary readers of the narrative of the temptation of Jesus in Luke 4:1–13?" This chart takes into consideration some (but not all) of the various strata and methodologies required for addressing such a complex question, including an evaluation of the levels of human discourse and divine discourse.[36]

---

33. McGrath, *A Scientific Theology*, vol. 2, 219–24.
34. Thomas F. Torrance, *Christian Theology and Scientific Culture* (New York: Oxford University Press, 1981), 32–33.
35. Ibid., 34–37.
36. This chart is modeled after one developed by McGrath to describe the multiple strata required to describe what happens when sodium metal ($2Na$) meets with hydrochloric acid ($2HCl$) and produces hydrogen (H_2) and sodium chloride ($2NaCl$). McGrath, *A Scientific Theology*, vol. 2, *Reality*, 221.

Stratum	Object	Primary Method(s)
Stratum I▼	The text(s) of Luke 4:1–13 explained by	textual criticism
Stratum II▼	The grammar and syntax of Luke 4:1–13 explained by	grammar/linguistics
Stratum III▼	The literary background of Luke 4:1–13 explained by	source criticism; form criticism; intertextuality; etc.
Stratum IV▼	The historical background of Luke 4:1–13 explained by	social-science criticism; political history; religious history; rhetorical criticism; geography; cultural geography; archeology; etc.
Stratum V▼	The significance of Luke 4:1–13 in the Third Gospel explained by	redaction criticism; narrative criticism
Stratum VI▼	The relationship of Luke 4:1–13 to the canon explained by	theological interpretation
Stratum VII▼	The Christology of Luke 4:1–13 explained by	systematic theology; philosophical theology
Stratum VIII	The implications of the Christology in Luke 4:1–13 for Christian living	ethical analysis; homiletics; pastoral theology

We could probably go on listing a host of other disciplines outside of biblical studies and theology that could address additional strata described in the same text, such as anthropology, architecture, geography, Judaic studies, etc., but the point here is simple: the Bible—like all aspects of reality—is too multifaceted to be reduced to a single discipline. Neither grammatical-historical exegesis nor its more "enlightened" brother, historical criticism, can exhaust the rich resources of the crust, mantle, and core of the biblical texts. Other tools and disciplines, like theological interpretation (see Stratum VI above) and preaching can and should aid in extracting and relaying the real meaning of Scripture.

Theological interpretation is an attempt to allow Scripture to interpret Scripture for the dialogical voices of the canon to engage one another in testimony to Jesus Christ.[37] Theological interpretation is taking the subject matter of biblical authors seriously; it is reading the Bible as its divine-human authorship intended and responding appropriately. Theology, ultimately grounded in this canonical discourse, provides a means of facilitating participation in God's ongoing activity in the world.[38]

The Canonical-Linguistic Approach to Doctrinal Development

Quite frequently, Vanhoozer describes his canonical-linguistic or theo-dramatic theological method as a means of going beyond the written word of Scripture in a way that is faithful to the spirit and direction of Scripture.[39] This concern for bridging the horizon of the biblical text with a present horizon is at the heart of contemporary evangelical considerations of postcanonical doctrinal development. Unlike other recent evangelical approaches addressing the question of how to "move beyond" the ancient setting of Scripture, Vanhoozer does not desire to universalize contextual precepts, to abstract "timeless" principles from biblical contexts or to treat an evolving "extratextual trajectory" as authoritative.[40] Many of these approaches,

---

37. Vanhoozer, *The Drama of Doctrine*, 149.

38. Vanhoozer, "Imprisoned or Free?" 77.

39. See Kevin J. Vanhoozer, "'May We Go Beyond What is Written After All?' The Pattern of Theological Authority and the Problem of Doctrinal Development," in *"But My Words Will Never Pass Away": The Enduring Authority of the Christian Scriptures*, 2 vols., ed. D. A. Carson (Grand Rapids, MI: Eerdmans, forthcoming).

40. Vanhoozer distinguishes his own position from those of other recent evangelical accounts of how to "move beyond" the Bible to a contemporary setting, such as the "principlizing" models of biblical scholars I. Howard Marshall and Walter Kaiser Jr., the "second hermeneutic" put forth by Nicholas Wolterstorff, and the "trajectory" models of William J. Webb and Daniel M.

like the canonical-linguistic/theo-dramatic approach, are normative in their basic orientation; but according to Vanhoozer, they also tend to reduce Scripture to ahistorical, acultural generalizations and theology to ethics. Though theology and ethics share similar concerns, Vanhoozer insists that a directive theory of doctrine cannot be reduced to ethics because doctrine also is concerned with belief about the person and activity of God revealed in Scripture.[41]

Canonical-linguistic theology, by contrast, is an ongoing means of developing habitual, practical wisdom grounded in the canon of Scripture.[42] This notion of theology practical wisdom stems from the Augustinian distinction between *scientia* (knowledge) and *sapientia* (wisdom), between knowledge and wisdom.[43] For Vanhoozer, theology must be both *scientia* and *sapientia*, concerned first with biblical exegesis and the doctrinal content of Scripture (*scientia*) and then with cultivating practical judgment based on Scripture for

---

Doriani. See I. Howard Marshall, *Beyond the Bible: Moving from Scripture to Theology* (Grand Rapids, MI: Baker, 2004), 1–79; Walter C. Kaiser Jr., "A Principlizing Model," in *Four Views on Moving beyond the Bible to Theology*, ed. Gary T. Meadors (Grand Rapids, MI: Zondervan, 2009), 19–50; Nicholas Wolterstorff, *Divine Discourse: Philosophical Reflections on the Claim That God Speaks* (Cambridge: Cambridge University Press, 1995), 202–22; Daniel M. Doriani, *Putting the Truth to Work: The Theory and Practice of Biblical Application* (Phillipsburg, NJ: Presbyterian & Reformed, 2001); William J. Webb, *Slaves, Women & Homosexuals: Exploring the Hermeneutics of Cultural Analysis* (Downers Grove, IL: InterVarsity, 2001); idem, *Corporal Punishment in the Bible: A Redemptive-Movement Hermeneutic for Troubling Texts* (Downers Grove, IL: InterVarsity, 2011). For Vanhoozer's individual responses to these approaches, see Kevin J. Vanhoozer, "Into the Great 'Beyond': A Theologian's Response to the Marshall Plan," in *Beyond the Bible: Moving from Scripture to Theology*, ed. I. Howard Marshall (Grand Rapids, MI: Baker, 2004), 81–96, esp. 90–92, and *Four Views on Moving beyond the Bible to Theology*, 57–63, 126–32, 262–70.

41. Vanhoozer, *The Drama of Doctrine*, 311.

42. Vanhoozer, "Into the Great 'Beyond,'" 92, 93.

43. See Augustine *De Trinitate* 12.14.21–15.25; 13.19.24–20.25; 14.1.1–3. Daniel Treier offers a helpful historical overview of the wisdom/knowledge distinction in Christian theology from the second century to modernity in "Virtue and the Voice of God: Toward a Postcritical, Sapiential Understanding of Theology" (Ph.D. diss., Trinity Evangelical Divinity School, 2002), 6–14. For a discussion of the relationship between *scientia* and *sapientia* in contemporary evangelical theology, see David K. Clark, *To Know God and Love God: Method for Theology* (Wheaton, IL: Crossway, 2003), 208–19.

contemporary settings (*sapientia*).[44] The canon must guide the church's action, but in order to do so, the text must move from the past into the present. The canonical-linguistic approach, then, represents a new, favorable evangelical approach to doctrinal development.

Christian doctrine always serves to direct Christian speech and praxis in a manner that reflects the "eschatological ethos" of the kingdom of God. Every Christian believer in history may share the same already-not-yet "eschatological context," but because historical contexts are always changing, their doctrinal formulations and expressions often need recasting or re-visioning in order to retain their prophetic voice to their particular situation.[45] Vanhoozer credits Latin American liberation theology for reminding systematic theologians that "theology involves much more than theoretical reflection."[46]

Vanhoozer not only concedes to the idea of development; he embraces it as a vital dimension of *theology's central task* and the *church's mission in the world*. For this reason, Vanhoozer, echoing Ebeling and Newman, believes that the church cannot take the road of identical verbal repetition: "To repeat the same words in a new situation is in fact to say something different."[47] Once more, Ebeling's aphorism (ironically) is worth repeating: "The same word can be said to another time only by being said differently."[48] He essentially equates development with contextualization as a necessary and vital element in the church's missional practice. The prescriptive dimension of his model is clear: "The challenge is not to resist change

---

44. Vanhoozer, *The Drama of Doctrine*, 307–8.
45. Ibid., 111.
46. Vanhoozer, "On the Very Idea of a Theological System," 132.
47. Vanhoozer, *The Drama of Doctrine*, 125.
48. Gerhard Ebeling, "Time and Word," in *The Future of Our Religious Past: Essays in Honour of Rudolf Bultmann*, ed. James M. Robinson (London: SCM, 1971), 265.

so much as to change in a way that would be faithful to, even though different from, Christian beginnings."[49] The historical phenomenon of doctrinal development is the ongoing, much-needed hermeneutical practice of *theological method*.

The Impact of Bakhtinian *Dialogism*

The dialogical poetics of Russian literary theorist and philosopher Mikhail Mikhailovich Bakhtin (1895–1975) has a profound influence on Vanhoozer's hermeneutical theory and model of postcanonical doctrinal development.[50] Bakhtin was a later figure in the Russian Formalist tradition that emphasized the structure and form of literature over and against its content. In his influential analysis of the novels of Fyodor Dostoyevsky (1821–1881), *Problems of Dostoyevsky's Art* (1929; later re-titled *Problems of Dostoyevsky's Poetics*), Bakhtin introduces his readers to the concept of dialogism, a literary theory that recognizes the relational, conversational nature of reading and writing. Textual interpretation is a truly interpersonal exchange between persons within community—a plurality of voices participating in an ongoing, intersubjective conversation. Authors are in conversation with their readers and readers with their authors. In this conversation, there is mutual growth and development of ideas.

Bakhtin distinguishes his position on dialogue from the dialectical traditions of Plato, Hegel, and Marx that would see the development ideas merely as a synthesis of abstract concepts. Bakhtin charges

---

49. Vanhoozer, *The Drama of Doctrine*, 125.

50. "Poetics" is used here as a singular collective to describe the literary theory of Bakhtin. As Aristotle uses the term in his *Poetics*, it describes the theory and nature of poetry in its various forms. In modern literary theory, as in Bakhtin, the term also describes a study of a given literary genre, such as fiction or the novel. See also Ross Murfin and Supryia M. Ray, *The Bedford Glossary of Critical and Literary Terms* (Boston: Bedford/St. Martin's, 1998), 289.

these views with amalgamating differing voices into a synthesized "monologic" system.[51] The ideological monologism found in idealistic philosophy that reduces ideas to a "*single* consciousness"[52] or "*system* of thoughts"[53] but novels, particularly Dostoyevsky's, present a plurality of voices engaged in "dialogic *interaction.*"[54] As Susan M. Felch summarizes the difference between dialogism and dialectical theories, "Dialogism insists on the priority of two or more persons who remain distinct from one another. Thus, it is not words *that* communicate, but we *who* communicate in interactions that require, as a minimum, the irreducible community of two."[55]

For Vanhoozer, Bakhtin's dialogical approach to the history of interpretation plays a significant role in his understanding of the development of Christian tradition. The relationship between Scripture and tradition is not in dialectical synthesis between biblical texts and contemporary philosophical or cultural thought—as is often presumed in overly simplistic models that present doctrinal formulations like those in Nicaea merely as the synthesis of New Testament narrative and Greco-Roman metaphysics. Rather, doctrinal development grows out of an ongoing exchange occurring between new interpreters in new settings and the human-divine authorship of the Bible.[56]

Several of Bakhtin's dialogical terms aid Vanhoozer in structuring his model of doctrinal development. First, *polyphony* helps Vanhoozer define the relationship between the human and divine authors of

---

51. See Mikhail Mikhailovich Bakhtin, *Problems of Dostoevsky's Poetics*, ed. and trans. Caryl Emerson (Minneapolis: University of Minnesota Press, 1984), 78–100.

52. Ibid., 81.

53. Ibid., 93.

54. Ibid., 90.

55. Susan M. Felch, "Dialogism," in *Dictionary for Theological Interpretation of the Bible*, ed. Kevin J. Vanhoozer (Grand Rapids, MI: Baker, 2005), 174. For an evaluation of Bakhtin's relationship to the Christian tradition, see Susan M. Felch and Paul J. Contino, eds., *Bakhtin and Religion: A Feeling for Faith* (Evanston, IL: Northwestern University Press, 2001).

56. Vanhoozer, *The Drama of Doctrine*, 273.

Scripture. Bakhtin uses the term to describe the multiple unique voices at work in a single narrative, particularly within the novel. He claims that within Dostoyevsky's novels one finds a *"plurality of independent and unmerged voices and consciousnesses,"* that is, characters who are not "voiceless slaves" that reflect the ideology and consciousness of the author but rather distinct voices, personalities, and worldviews.[57] By contrast, Bakhtin believes authors like Leo Tolstoy (1828–1910) do not reflect this level of genius. Even as their novels contain multiple characters, each reflects the author's voice and consciousness. These novels are "monologic" rather than "dialogic."[58]

Bakhtin credits Dostoyevsky for creating the polyphonic novel, what he calls a "completely new type of artistic thinking."[59] Vanhoozer disagrees, suggesting that the divine author of Scripture created this genre with the biblical canon, as it contains a polyphony of human voices writing and speaking under the sovereign pen of God.[60] In so doing, Vanhoozer brilliantly couches an evangelical plenary-verbal theory of scriptural inspiration in the terminology and conceptual framework of Russian formalism. Rather than see the Bible merely as a collection of human texts—or even as a collection of records of divine encounters—Vanhoozer, with most evangelicals, recognizes that the verbal content of the Bible flows from the sovereign God who lorded over its production and collection. The idea of a divine playwright here is analogous to Bakhtin's use of Dostoyevsky—a single writer guiding the different characters of his novel. Having one sovereign author ultimately responsible for the biblical canon need not mean that the Bible is like the monologic novels of Tolstoy that only reflect a single author's consciousness,

---

57. Bakhtin, *Problems of Dostoevsky's Poetics*, 6.
58. Ibid., 69–70.
59. Ibid., 3.
60. Vanhoozer, *The Drama of Doctrine*, 272.

as is suggested in the fundamentalist theory of inspiration known as "dictation theory."[61] Instead, the Bible is a polyphonic collection of different voices and perspectives. The interpreter of the Bible encounters not one but many voices, perspectives, and horizons, all orchestrated by the God who inspires every illocutionary act in Scripture.

Second, Vanhoozer uses Bakhtin's term *chronotope* (literally, "time-place") to describe the way in which spatiotemporal conditions shape thinking and experience.[62] The term, first utilized in Einstein's theory of relativity, is a literary "intersection of axes" where "spatial and temporal indicators are fused into one carefully thought-out, concrete whole" and where "time . . . becomes artistically visible" as "space becomes charged and responsive to the movements of time."[63] This concept, much like the phenomenological horizon utilized by Gadamer and others, is a lens through which the interpreter sees the world. The most important difference, however, is that a chronotope also describes the time-place and genre of a given piece of literature, such as a Greek romance, an ancient biography, or a nineteenth-century Russian novel. As chronotopes, literary genres act as cognitive instruments that provide "new ways of thinking about or experiencing the world. . . . for saying and seeing things that could not be seen or said in other ways."[64]

---

61. American fundamentalists like John R. Rice (1895–1990), independent Baptist pastor and the founding publisher of *The Sword of the Lord* newspaper, helped popularize the "dictation theory" of inspiration. Rice not only affirmed the notion that human beings were merely secretaries for divine speech; he also explicitly denied stylistic differences between biblical books. See John R. Rice, *Verbal Inspiration of the Bible and Its Scientific Accuracy* (Wheaton, IL: Sword of the Lord, 1943); idem, *Earnestly Contending for the Faith* (Murfreesboro, TN: Sword of the Lord, 1965), 201–23; idem, *Our God-Breathed Book: The Bible* (Murfreesboro, TN: Sword of the Lord, 1969).

62. Vanhoozer, *The Drama of Doctrine*, 345.

63. Mikhail Mikhailovich Bakhtin, *The Dialogic Imagination*, ed. Michael Holquist, trans. Caryl Emerson and Michael Holquist (Austin: University of Texas Press, 1981), 84.

64. Kevin J. Vanhoozer, "From Speech Acts to Scripture Acts: The Covenant of Discourse and the Discourse of the Covenant," in *After Pentecost: Language & Biblical Interpretation*, ed. Craig

For Vanhoozer, chronotopes provide a means for discussing biblical authority in doctrinal development across time and space.[65] Despite a wide diversity of chronotopes within the canon, each one relates to the contemporaneity of Christ that Vanhoozer describes as the *Christotope*. In other words, Christ, who fills all time and space, is present to every particular chronotopic context. Vanhoozer frames the unity and the diversity of the canon in the relationship between these chronotopes and the communicative self-presentation of Christ.[66] The ever-present Christ continually gives significance to different time-spaces and genres within Scripture. Recognition of the christotopic context also speaks to the way in which Christ continues to give new significance to chronotopic contexts beyond the canon. The Christotope embedded concretely in every chronotopic context constitutes the "universal" dimension of the message of Scripture, not abstract, timeless principles. The church shares the same Christotopic context today that it did when the canon closed.[67]

Third, Vanhoozer adopts Bakhtin's term *great time* to explain the growth of doctrinal tradition over time. For Bakhtin, great time is a way of describing the way great literary works gain new significance through time.[68] "*Small time*," by contrast, is the present setting, a remote context awaiting new significances in great time. Welcoming something like Hans-Robert Jauss's (1921–1997) reader-reception theory, Bakhtin advocates a study of literature that goes beyond the

Bartholomew, Colin Greene, and Karl Möller (Grand Rapids, MI: Zondervan, 2001), 34–35. Vanhoozer also describes literary genres as "speech-acts of a higher order" with "both propositional matter and illocutionary energy" (*Drama of Doctrine*, 283).

65. Vanhoozer, *The Drama of Doctrine*, 345. In place of Bakhtin's chronotope, Vanhoozer offers a slightly modified term with *dramatope*, hoping to frame this terminology in his dramatic model, but then proceeds to use chronotope consistently, only returning to this neologism once more. For this reason, I opt to keep chronotope in place in the following discussion.

66. Vanhoozer, *The Drama of Doctrine*, 346.

67. Ibid., 347.

68. Mikhail Mikhailovich Bakhtin, *Speech Genres and Other Late Essays*, trans. Vern McGee, ed. Caryl Emerson and Michael Holquist (Austin: University of Texas Press, 1986), 5–7.

epoch of its initial composition: "Trying to understand and explain a work solely in terms of the conditions of its epoch alone, solely in terms of the conditions of its most immediate time, will never enable us to penetrate into its semantic depths."[69] Great literary works, made great by surpassing the boundaries of their own time, invite new developments in understanding with great time. Authors such as Shakespeare are often unaware of the new meanings and significance that their works will take on but, as Bakhtin reasons, this unawareness does not mean that the discovery of new meaning is a distortion of the text or the purpose of the author. Instead, "semantic phenomena can exist in concealed form, potentially, and be revealed only in semantic cultural contexts of subsequent epochs that are favorable for such disclosure."[70]

Perspective is particularly crucial for understanding great time. Bathkin illustrates this idea with interpersonal presence: "For one cannot even really see one's own exterior and comprehend it as a whole, and no mirrors or photographs can help; our real exterior can be seen and understood only by other people, because they are located outside us in time and space and because they are *others*."[71] *Distance* and *outsideness* grant perspective and create the occasion for dialogue.[72] Vanhoozer likewise suggests that the distance created by successive contexts provide new perspectives through which Scripture can be read. The canon gains new significance with the passing of great time. The Spirit aids in this process, directing the contextualization of Scripture in new settings.[73] Bakhtin's emphasis on dialogue between two persons in time makes it possible for Vanhoozer to forgo the either-or choice between leaving the

69. Ibid., 4.
70. Ibid., 5.
71. Ibid., 7.
72. Vanhoozer, *Is There a Meaning in This Text?*, 390.
73. Vanhoozer, *The Drama of Doctrine*, 349.

meaning of the text in the past or paying attention to the text's present significance.[74] For this reason, Vanhoozer calls on theologians to be familiar not only with Scripture in its "small time," but also with the history of the tradition in "great time."[75]

The final and most important import from Bakhtin's poetics is the notion of *creative understanding*, which provides the theoretical basis for Vanhoozer's model of doctrinal development. For Vanhoozer, creative understanding in theology is not the *ex nihilo* creation of theological ideas as is sometimes practiced in constructive theology but rather a utilization of Scripture in such a way that its ancient texts can speak to contemporary concerns.[76] For Bakhtin, understanding a text or a literary work is not simply about reproducing the author's perspective, but developing a productive dialogue between the author and the interpreter. The interpreter always should strive to be conscious of the otherness of the author because temporal and cultural distance often brings out new, *potential meaning* concealed within the communicative act of the text. In his recognition of potential meaning within the text, Bakhtin is not arguing for the radical indeterminacy of texts but rather potentiality of meaning determined by the author.[77]

Fuller, creative understanding is possible with the passing of "great time." Once more, distance or

outsideness is a most powerful factor in understanding. It is only in the eyes of *another* culture that foreign culture reveals itself fully and profoundly (but not maximally fully, because there will be cultures that see and understand even more.) A meaning only reveals its depths once it has encountered and come into contact with another, foreign meaning: they engage in a kind of dialogue, which surmounts the

---

74. Ibid., 350; cf. idem, *Is There a Meaning in This Text?*, 389.
75. Vanhoozer, *The Drama of Doctrine*, 349.
76. Ibid., 351.
77. Vanhoozer, *Is There a Meaning in This Text?*, 389.

closedness and one-sidedness of these particular meanings, these cultures. We raise new questions for a foreign culture, ones that it did not raise itself; we seek answers to our own questions in it; and foreign culture responds to us by revealing new semantic depths. Without one's own questions one cannot creatively understand anything other or foreign. . . . Such a dialogic encounter of two cultures does not result in merging or mixing. Each retains its own unity and open totality, but they are mutually enriched.[78]

Like Gadamer, Bakhtin notes that creative understanding is impossible without posing questions. Creative understanding occurs in the dialogic question-and-answer encounter between two cultures, yet these horizons do not "fuse" or mix but retain their own respective identities. Bakhtin sees creative understanding as a model for evaluating "the development of our literary scholarship."[79] Vanhoozer recognizes its value for the development of the Christian theological tradition: "*It is precisely the reader's distance from the text that creates the possibility of dialogue and the condition for discovering the full meaning potential of the text.*"[80]

Against biblicists and historical critics who would limit the reading of the Bible to the small time of a past epoch, Vanhoozer provocatively suggests that our readings of the Bible cannot be limited to their first-century significance.[81] Bakhtin's emphasis on consciousness of both the author and the reader in the interpretive process provides an account of the nature of understanding without losing the voice of the other, without the confusion of horizons.[82] In the case of biblical interpretation, the interpreter recognizes the uniqueness of his or her own context *and* the otherness of the biblical

---

78. Bakhtin, *Speech Genres*, 7
79. Ibid.
80. Vanhoozer, *Is There a Meaning in This Text?*, 390.
81. Vanhoozer, *The Drama of Doctrine*, 351; cf. idem, *Is There a Meaning in This Text?*, 390.
82. Vanhoozer, *Is There a Meaning in This Text?*, 389.

horizon. This recognition prevents conflating the present situation with the authority of the text.

Creative understanding does not entail free reign interpretation on the part of the reader, or some postmodern failure to distinguish between legitimate and illegitimate readings. Bakhtin refuses to grant such permission to readers of Shakespeare or Dostoevsky. No interpreter should recreate their works in a way contrary to the meaning these authors give their texts. The same is true for creative understanding in Christian theology. Theologians and biblical interpreters must strive for creatively understanding Scripture in a contemporary context in such a way that they recognize the authority of their inspired conversation partner. Creative understanding for evangelical interpretation thus becomes a matter of discovering the potential meanings for new contexts within the biblical canon.[83] This process often makes what is implicit in the text explicit when the right situation provokes its discovery—as is the case in formulations of Christian doctrines like the doctrine of the Trinity or ethical statements directed to contemporary issues. Other texts, left partially indeterminate in meaning by the choice of their authors, provide interpreters with opportunities to create entirely new meanings for their particular settings.[84]

"All the World's a Stage": Doctrinal Development and Theo-drama

The overarching theatrical metaphor of "theo-drama" (or alternatively, "theodrama") in Vanhoozer's canonical-linguistic approach first appears in the theo-dramatic, theo-pragmatic program of Roman Catholic theologian Hans Urs von Balthasar (1905–1988),

---

83. Ibid., 351.

84. Daniel J. Treier, "Bakhtin's Chronotopes for Doing Theology in Time: Or, We Never Metanarrative We Didn't Like" (paper presented at the annual meeting of the Evangelical Theological Society, Boston, MA, 17 November 1999), 9.

whose multivolume opus *Theodramatik* uses dramaturgical categories such as author, actor, director, role, and action to describe salvation history.[85] For Balthasar, the gospel of God's revelatory and saving action in Jesus Christ is intrinsically dramatic. Theo-drama, then, is a big-picture way of describing God's providential, dialogical action in the world. Vanhoozer acknowledges that describing the story of God as theo-drama bears certain family resemblances to "metanarrative" or "mega-narrative" but stresses that instead of merely being a first- or third-person monologic recital of a story (à la narrative), it is a drama performed by several actors in their words and deeds.[86] The *action* of God is central, as "Christianity is fundamentally neither a philosophy nor a system of morality but a theodrama, a *doing* in which God gets the most important speaking and acting part."[87] The gospel, with all its narrative features like plot, character, conflict, and resolution, is also more about the dramatic, dialogical interaction between God and humanity than static, timeless ideas.[88]

Taking a cue from Lindbeck's description of doctrine as grammar or rule, Vanhoozer distinguishes his own project from Balthasar's,

85. Hans Urs von Balthasar, *Theo-Drama: Theological Dramatic Theory*, 5 vols., trans. Graham Harrison (San Francisco: Ignatius, 1988). *Theo-Drama* is the second part of Balthasar's larger triptych, which also includes the seven-volume work *The Glory of the Lord: A Theological Aesthetics* (San Francisco: Ignatius, 1986–1990), and the *Theo-Logic* trilogy (San Francisco: Ignatius, 2001–2005). For another recent and more comprehensive exploration of Balthasar's project, see Ben Quash, *Theology and the Drama of History* (Cambridge: Cambridge University Press, 2005).

86. Vanhoozer, *The Drama of Doctrine*, 48–49. Vanhoozer acknowledges that describing the story of God as theo-drama bears certain family resemblances to "metanarrative" but notes that the theo-drama, contrary to monologic metanarrative, is polyphonic (49, n. 48). Michael Horton (b. 1964) reemphasizes this point in his discussion of the Christian faith as drama. See Horton, *The Christian Faith*, 14–19. For Horton, metanarratives are attempts to transcend story, to "demythologize" by replacing historical particularities with "higher" truths. Metanarratives also tend to "give rise to ideologies" that are monolithic and totalizing in nature (17). With Merold Westphal, Horton describes the biblical drama as a "*mega*narrative," not a "*meta*narrative" (16). See also Merold Westphal, *Overcoming Onto-Theology: Toward a Postmodern Christian Faith* (New York: Fordham University Press, 2001), xiii.

87. Vanhoozer, *Remythologizing Theology*, xiv.

88. Vanhoozer, *The Drama of Doctrine*, 44–46.

noting that while Balthasar focuses on the dramatic content of Christian doctrine, the focus of his canonical-linguistic approach is on the performative nature of doctrine itself.[89] In other words, doctrine is more than a description of and a reflection on the plot. It also provides normative *direction* for the Christian community theatre troupe as they perform the theo-drama of the gospel for the spectators of the world in new and varying contexts.[90] Doctrine is *dramaturgy*, a critical reflection on the drama and its performance used to train everyone involved in the production.[91] Doctrine helps cultivate "theodramatic vision," that is, a worldview that fosters Christian practice.[92] In the local church, the pastor acts as the *director* (or more precisely, the assistant director) that leads a congregation in ministry and service.[93] The theologian serves a role similar to the *dramaturge*, who, in European theatre, assists the director by researching the script and the history of its performances in order to help the theatre company stage a production that is both faithful to the essence of the script and relevant to contemporary audiences.[94]

Another dramatic metaphor important for canonical-linguistic theology enters at stage right: *performance*. This aspect of the theo-

89. Vanhoozer, *The Drama of Doctrine*, 18.
90. Vanhoozer, "A Drama-of-Redemption Model," 161–62.
91. Ibid., 173. Theology is not the first discipline to incorporate dramaturgical theory and dramatic metaphors to daily lives and interaction. Since the late 1950s, sociologists have incorporated the insights of dramatic theory and the dramatism of literary critic Kenneth Burke (1897–1993) into the social sciences. For a broad sampling of this application, see Dennis Brissett and Charles Edgley, eds., *Life as Theatre: A Dramaturgical Sourcebook* (Chicago: Aldine, 1975).
92. Vanhoozer, "A Drama-of-Redemption Model," 162–63. Vanhoozer modifies Wright's five worldview questions to fit his theo-dramatic metaphor: (1) "Where are we in the theodrama? What scene are we playing?" (2) "Who are we? In what kind of plot are our lives entangled?" (3) "What time is it? What act and what scene of the drama of redemption are we playing?" (4) "What is happening? What is God doing?" (5) "What should we say or do?" Doctrine is an attempt to answer these worldview questions using the canonical script. See also Wright, *The New Testament and the People of God*, 123; idem, *Jesus and the Victory of God* (Minneapolis: Fortress Press, 1997), 443–74.
93. Vanhoozer, *The Drama of Doctrine*, 244.
94. Ibid., 245.

dramatic model builds on the influential work of Nicholas Lash, Vanhoozer's doctoral mentor at Cambridge. Lash proposes that "different kinds of text call for different kinds of reading," with some texts calling for specific types of action.[95] He maintains that the New Testament calls for Christlike performance from the Christian community.[96] Other theologians have since taken up similar guiding analogies,[97] but Vanhoozer's notion of performance is specific to theatrical performances. Scripture is the *script* that calls for faithful, creative understanding and performance.[98] In the same sense that scripts that are not "complete" until they are performed—i.e., they have not met with intention for which their authors created them—Scripture is not complete until the believing community has appropriated it in Christian practice.[99] Vanhoozer here appeals to Mortimer J. Adler and Charles van Doren, who stress that "when you read a play, you are not reading a *complete* work."[100] The theoretical basis for this metaphor appears earlier in Vanhoozer's general hermeneutics: "Properly to attend the text requires more than a fascination with its locutions (*langue*). The responsible interpreter is answerable to illocutions and perlocutions, the matter and energy of the text, as well. Interpretations are . . . attempts *to describe* and *to respond* to communicative acts."[101] Genuine understanding not only entails intellectual apprehension but also "the kind of understanding that demonstrates itself in action."[102]

95. Nicholas Lash, *Theology on the Way to Emmaus* (London: SCM, 1986), 38.

96. Ibid., 44–46.

97. For a sampling of other performance analogies, see Frances Young, *The Art of Performance: Towards a Theology of Holy Scripture* (London: Darton, Longman, and Todd, 1990); and Stephen Barton, "New Testament Interpretation as Performance," *Scottish Journal of Theology* 52 (1999): 179–208.

98. Vanhoozer, *The Drama of Doctrine*, 22.

99. Ibid., 101.

100. See Mortimer J. Adler and Charles van Doren, *How to Read a Book*, rev. ed. (New York: Touchstone, 1972), 223.

101. Vanhoozer, *Is There a Meaning in This Text?*, 405.

The most important metaphor in the theo-dramatic approach for the issue of development is *improvisation*. For Vanhoozer, doctrinal development is improvisation with the biblical script in hand.[103] Theology's ongoing task is training minds to think about the world biblically and cultivating a gospel-oriented *phronēsis* that aids in "faithful improvisation" of the biblical theo-drama in new contexts.[104] The metaphor of improvisation has potentially problematic connotations that Vanhoozer wishes to avoid, so he offers important qualifications to its use. Improvisation may be spontaneous and unscripted, but it does require "training" and "discernment."[105] It is not the same thing as "ad-libbing"—the "theatrical equivalent of heresy."[106] The actor improvises by following the story, understanding characterization, and adapting appropriately when faces with new twists in the plot unfolding on the stage.[107] In Vanhoozer's theo-dramatic model, theological improvisation requires a thoroughgoing knowledge of the canonical script so that one can make the right theological judgments in new situations. It demands creative understanding.

Utilizing the terminology of drama theorists, Vanhoozer draws out further analogies from the art of improvisation relevant to this controlling metaphor for doctrinal development. An *offering* is any action performed within the improvisation to initiate or advance the narrative. Co-improvisers can *accept* the offer by building on the offering and advancing the narrative further, or they can *block* the

---

102. Vanhoozer, *The Drama of Doctrine*, 120. On this point, Vanhoozer evokes the Gadamerian idea that understanding necessarily entails application.

103. Vanhoozer, *The Drama of Doctrine*, 353. One of Vanhoozer's primary interlocutors is Christian ethicist Samuel Wells (b. 1965), who applies the metaphor of improvisation to ethical inquiries. See Samuel Wells, *Improvisation: The Drama of Christian Ethics* (Grand Rapids, MI: Brazos, 2004).

104. Vanhoozer, *The Drama of Doctrine*, 338.

105. Vanhoozer, *The Drama of Doctrine*, 336–37.

106. Ibid., 338.

107. Ibid., 128; cf. Wells, *Improvisation*, 65.

action by disregarding the offer and attempting to take the narrative in a completely different direction.[108] If the initial offering is a dramatic monologue about a character's fear of commitment in romantic relationships and a co-improviser tries to hijack the story by turning it into a action-adventure sequence, shouting "Somebody has a gun!," then the offer has been blocked, and the plot that has emerged is not the same story at all.[109] If, on the other hand, a co-improviser attempts to offer the first character consolation, advice, or discontent over his inability to make good on previous romantic promises, then the co-improviser has accepted the offer and improvised according to the nature of the given drama.

Good improvisers also practice the skill of *reincorporation*, or the working in of previously established narrative details in order to make the improvisation work as a coherent whole.[110] In the case of the drama about a character's fear of commitment, an improviser can bring into the narrative details about previous relationships wrecked by his fear to commit. A co-improviser could drudge up familial abandonment issues at the root of the problem. *Overaccepting* is a type of accepting offers that takes the task of reincorporation into consideration.[111] It is also "an active way [of accepting offers] that enables one to retain identity and relevance."[112] The improviser playing the commitment-phobe in the dramatic scene overaccepts by acting in a way that is both consistent with his character and fitting to the new offers given. He may choose to shrug off the friend's advice; he might make a promise to change his ways, only to change his mind a moment later; or he might take ownership of his situation by

---

108. Vanhoozer, *The Drama of Doctrine*, 338–39; cf. Wells, *Improvisation*, 103–13.
109. This instance of improvisation "blocking" was inspired by *The Office*, "E-Mail Surveillance," episode 15 (originally aired 22 November 2005).
110. Vanhoozer, *The Drama of Doctrine*, 339–40; cf. Wells, *Improvisation*, 147–50.
111. Vanhoozer, *The Drama of Doctrine*, 340.
112. Wells, *Improvisation*, 131.

determining to confront the father who abandoned him as a child. A number of improvisational options are available with reincorporation and overaccepting. Most importantly, actors need to be cognizant of their environment and the narrative that is developing around them.

For the theo-drama, this act of overacceptance means advancing the narrative by accepting one's role in relationship to the larger dramatic framework of Scripture and making good theological judgments when new offers come forward. Improvisation is the "task of discipleship: to find ways to be faithful to our script in the midst of constantly changing circumstances."[113] To make use of Tom Wright's analogy of a five-act Shakespearian play with only four extant acts, overaccepting would be a way of improvising the final act in such a way that incorporates the overarching narrative framework and established character patterns of the first four acts.[114] Wright makes a similar emphasis to Vanhoozer: "Faithful improvisation in the present time requires patient and careful puzzling over what has gone before, including the attempt to understand what the nature of the claims made [about Jesus] . . . really amount to."[115] Reincorporation, then, is the careful reflection on Scripture; overaccepting is responding creatively to new situations in a way that is consistent with the roles God has given. A failure to acknowledge God's covenantal advances blocks the action.[116]

---

113. Vanhoozer, "Imprisoned or Free?" 81.
114. For Wright's use of the five-act metaphor, see his *The New Testament and the People of God*, 139–43; "How Can the Bible Be Authoritative?" *Vox Evangelica* 21 (1991): 7–32; and *The Last Word*, 121–27. In the original metaphor Wright describes the biblical story in five acts: (1) Creation, (2) Fall, (3) Israel, (4) Jesus, and (5) the Church. In his theo-dramatic model, however, Vanhoozer adopts Wells's modification. See Vanhoozer, *The Drama of Doctrine*, 2; idem, "A Drama-of-Redemption Model," 174; cf. Wells, *Improvisation*, 51–57. Arguing that the fall is not an act of God but a "human misconstrual of God's created gift of freedom" and that Wright's original model neglects biblical eschatology, Wells provides this five-act alternative: (1) Creation, (2) Israel, (3) Jesus, (4) the Church, and (5) the eschaton (*Improvisation*, 53).
115. Wright, *The New Testament and the People of God*, 143.
116. Vanhoozer, *The Drama of Doctrine*, 341.

So, what does this metaphor mean for doctrinal development? The church in every epoch has the responsibility to address the moral and theological crises of their day, issues not explicitly addressed or anticipated by biblical authors.[117] Theological controversy can provoke doctrinal improvisation, which often requires extrabiblical formulations and terminology. New moral dilemmas unfamiliar to biblical authors require improvising that overaccepts offers by incorporating the theo-drama these authors establish. These moments require canon-directed theological judgment—what Vanhoozer has called *sapientia, phronēsis,* creative understanding, improvisation, or doctrinal development. For Vanhoozer, development or improvisation must be able to direct Christian belief and practice in relevant ways to new settings but do so in a way that is faithful to the authoritative, communicative acts of Scripture.[118]

Reviewing the Theo-Drama

Besides the holding the auspicious label of being "the leading academic theologian of the evangelical movement today,"[119] Vanhoozer is a master of metaphor whose literary prowess and clever wordplay put him in a category of theologians all his own. He practices the Ricoeurian gospel he preaches, often demonstrating that metaphor has an explanatory power lacking in straightforward, literal description. He is particularly adroit at developing complex, multi-layered metaphors that stimulate new ways of thinking about ideas, proving that imagination must play an important role in cognition.

---

117. Ibid., 309.
118. Ibid., 354.
119. Gregory Alan Thornbury, *Recovering Classic Evangelicalism: Applying the Wisdom and Vision of Carl F. H. Henry* (Wheaton, IL: Crossway, 2013), 105.

The most provocative metaphor Vanhoozer has employed to date is his use of theo-drama and performance in describing the Christian theological task. So, are the theo-dramatic metaphors helpful in addressing the problem of doctrinal development? In some ways, yes, and in some ways, no. This postcanonical metaphor is simply that and only one among many possible options for describing soteriological history creatively. While drama is by no means the only way of describing God's interaction with the world in salvation history, it is an adequate working metaphor, even if it is not an explicitly biblical one.

Other aspects of the performance metaphor prove more troubling. At certain points, Vanhoozer appears to exchange the historical significance of the Bible for contemporary relevance: "The canon is less textbook than playbook; it does not preserve a set of ideas so much as patterns of speech and action."[120] Using this analogy, one could make the case that the historicity of biblical narratives is inconsequential as long as one patterns his or her praxis after the characters of the biblical theo-drama. This analogy potentially raises additional problems that seem counterproductive to his argument for *sola scriptura*. Does this approach allow the word of God to speak for itself, or do the performers always need a dramaturge or director (i.e., a theologian or a pastor) on stage who can revise the script when necessary? If additional stage direction is in fact necessary, then it is somewhat difficult to distinguish between his evangelical position and a position that requires supplemental authorities in biblical interpretation, such as the Catholic or Orthodox positions.

Vanhoozer discourages performance of the script by rote memorization or "repeat[ing] the old lines over and over,"[121] but this analogy raises additional questions for discipleship and the doctrine

---

120. Vanhoozer, *The Drama of Doctrine*, 145.
121. Ibid., 340.

of Scripture. The locutionary acts of Scripture appear entirely inconsequential, its signs completely arbitrary: "The Bible *is the* Word of God (in the sense of its illocutionary acts) and . . . the Bible *becomes* the Word of God (in the sense of achieving its perlocutionary effects)."[122] Does this dismissal mean that Scripture memorization plays no role in a theology of practical wisdom? What, then, does the psalmist mean when he says he has hidden God's word in his heart so that he might not sin against him (Ps. 119:11)? Vanhoozer may be able to avoid some of these criticisms if he gives attention to another dramatic metaphor strangely absent in the theo-dramatic approach: *rehearsal*. How do believers rehearse for their participation in the theo-drama apart from acquainting themselves with the script by memorizing their lines?

Some of Vanhoozer's critics, like New Testament scholar Ben Witherington III, disapprove of his description of the Bible as theo-drama because a drama, "while it may mime or depict reality, is not reality."[123] As we shall see in chapter six, Vanhoozer consistently argues for the truthfulness of Christian doctrine (à la a nuanced version of the correspondence theory) within his theo-dramatic scheme. Other critics, like philosophical theologian Paul Helm, charge the move away from more traditional propositional theologies toward "dramatic" re-readings of the gospel as confusing and unnecessary steps that "fuzzy the distinctive cognitive character of God's revelation, its good news, and make our thinking about divine things less exact, less exacting."[124] Other critics, like Old Testament

---

122. Vanhoozer, "From Speech Acts to Scripture Acts," 38.
123. See Ben Witherington III, *The Indelible Image: The Theological and Ethical Thought World of the New Testament*, vol. 2, *The Collective Witness* (Downers Grove, IL: InterVarsity, 2010), 49. Furthermore, Witherington appears to misunderstand Vanhoozer when he describes the drama "as if it were a one-actor play" with "the one actor being God" (49). Vanhoozer emphasizes the many voices in the action and many roles in the theo-drama. Contrary to what Witherington and others may suspect, Vanhoozer never allows his Reformed theology to reduce the theo-drama to divine monologue.

scholar Walter C. Kaiser Jr. contend that the dramatic metaphor is just too confusing and impractical. Kaiser laments, "For the life of me I cannot explain to anyone else, much less myself, how the 'drama-of-redemption approach' works or really solves any of the crucial questions being put to the Bible in our day."[125]

The dramatic metaphor is not universal in its application. Other metaphors could work better in different settings or for different audiences, but this one metaphor is hard to rival in its explanatory power for doctrinal development. Its emphasis on action, performance, and different genres may make it a better analogy than a purely narrative approach. When qualified as creative performance faithful to both Christian character and the canonical script, improvisation is an appropriate metaphor for development. It speaks to the need of believers and theologians for creative, on-their-feet thinking and acting.

Some critics of Vanhoozer disapprove of the shift toward theological hermeneutics in his theo-dramatic approach. Thiselton, for instance, laments the smaller role of general hermeneutics in *The Drama of Doctrine*: "He gives us a few lines on the role of the Spirit, the role of apostolic tradition, the role of the church, the role of the canonical text, even on 'otherness,' but *none of this engages with the resources of hermeneutical theory and practice*."[126] Thiselton appears to offer this criticism because Vanhoozer engages *different* resources than he does or he would prefer. However, as we will have seen and will see, every aspect of Vanhoozer's model of development utilizes resources from philosophical hermeneutics and/or literary theory.

124. Paul Helm, "Analysis 2 – Propositions and Speech Acts," *Helm's Deep*, May 1 2007, http://paulhelmsdeep.blogspot.com/2007/05/analysis-2-propositions-and-speech-acts.html (accessed December 10, 2013); cf. Thornbury, *Recovering Classic Evangelicalism*, 111–12.

125. Walter C. Kaiser, "A Response to Kevin J. Vanhoozer," in *Four Views on Moving beyond the Bible to Theology*, ed. Gary T. Meadors (Grand Rapids, MI: Zondervan, 2009), 204.

126. Thiselton, *The Hermeneutics of Doctrine*, 80, italics mine.

He describes the process of development through Bakhtin's notion of creative understanding. In his answer to the question of biblical authority, he builds on previous work in general hermeneutics, arguing for the determinacy of meaning in canonical texts. Overall, Vanhoozer uses these resources effectively in building a case for the need for ongoing doctrinal development.

In some ways, Vanhoozer's theo-dramatic model of development constitutes a significant break with many evangelical theologies of the past. Yes, Vanhoozer affirms the biblical canon as inerrant, infallible, and the supreme authority of Christian doctrine and practice. He affirms the cognitivity and reality-depicting nature of biblical and doctrinal statements as well. Yet two crucial differences separate his program. First, he moves away from defining doctrine in mere conceptual terms, choosing rather to define it in terms of patterns of judgment—an important step for establishing continuity between different conceptual frameworks in theology. While this move clearly bears Lindbeck's influence, it does not go the way of the antirealist tendencies in Lindbeck's approach. (This will be addressed in detail in chapter 6.) Vanhoozer does not discount the need for concepts to express particular judgments, nor does he neglect the fact that judgments often depend on certain affairs actually being the case.

Vanhoozer encourages the ongoing development of the Christian tradition, largely by redefining what tradition means. One gets the impression from his depiction of some propositionalist theologies that, in these schemes, once one abstracts timeless, immutable doctrinal statements from Scripture, the theological task is once-and-for-all complete. The Bible thus becomes a monologic document that looks more like Wittgenstein's *Tractatus* than a variety of genres and voices. At this point, all one would need to do is pass along this complete set of propositions. Tradition is more than the transmission of static concepts. It constitutes the continuing practice of theological judgment in the life of the church. Vanhoozer's model is not the first to define tradition in terms of the church's continuing activity but appears to be the first model that links this ongoing activity with canonical patterns. With these redefinitions of doctrine and tradition in mind, Vanhoozer invites the further development of Christian doctrine in a way that is fitting to both the canon of Scripture and the contemporary context.

The true value of the theo-dramatic model is in its normative direction for doctrinal development. Vanhoozer provides helpful guidance for discriminating between *fitting* and inappropriate developments. He successfully addresses the hermeneutical and theological questions of authority by contending for textual determinacy and by framing *sola scriptura* as a practice whereby believers submit to Scripture as the supreme authority. The human-divine words of Scripture bear ultimate authority on development, not the lone interpreter, the interpretive community, or an interpretive ecclesial body.

5

Interpretive Authority and Doctrinal Development

By whose "authority" does the church develop doctrine? What guide can aid in differentiating between positive developments and doctrinal distortions? By whose rule can we draw the line between orthodoxy and heterodoxy? The construction of doctrine in the broader Christian tradition and in systematic theology is a complex operation that involves many people over a great span of time with many disciplinary specialties and pastoral concerns. Naturalist interpretations of religion chalk all of these processes up to socio-cultural or bio-cultural factors. These are undirected by external forces and products of a human culture, a building of gods in the images of the people that create them. Christians, by contrast, like to think that faithful doctrinal development happens under the purview of the sovereign God we seek to know and obey. We like to think that God is the ultimate authority over the process, guiding our direction and our tasks along the way.

But several practical questions remain. How does God exert his design over the process? Is there a normative or formal authority can Christians appeal to in order to justify these doctrinal developments or advancements? Is appealing to the Bible alone a sufficient approach, especially when many of the disagreements and developments have to do with the meaning and interpretation of biblical language? What guide can aid in differentiating between positive developments and doctrinal distortions? By whose rule can we draw the line between orthodoxy and heterodoxy? In the church's present postmodern context, do we even recognize such a line? Should we grant such authority to a person, group, or text?

Questions about authority in doctrinal development have *theological* and *hermeneutical* dimensions. Theologically, a model of doctrinal development must address the standards or channels by which doctrine is formed, modified, or amended. Theologians here distinguish between *norms* and *sources*. Sources are what John Macquarrie calls "formative factors," factors that shape the content of our religious beliefs, either consciously or non-consciously.[1] Throughout history, theologians have recognized several sources or formative factors: (1) Scripture, (2) tradition, (3) the ecclesial magisterium (in its doctors, councils, and popes), (4) reason, (5) religious experience, and (6) contemporary culture.[2] Non-conscious formative factors can include tradition, religious experience, or psychological factors. Scientific studies of religion have also shown that other, more personal influences such as family rearing and emotional well-being can play an important role in the formation of individual religious (or anti-religious) beliefs.[3]

---

1. John Macquarrie, *Principles of Christian Theology*, 2nd ed. (New York: Charles Scribner's Sons, 1977), 4.
2. For a brief but helpful analysis of these sources from an evangelical perspective, see James Leo Garrett, *Systematic Theology*, vol. 1, 3d ed. (North Richland Hills, TX: B.I.B.A.L., 2007), 193–209.

Norms are, according to Tillich, "the criterion to which the sources as well as the mediating experience must be subjected."[4] Norms color and arbitrate the use of formative factors or sources; they establish the standard by which sources are evaluated. In some traditions, such as Roman Catholic and Eastern Orthodox traditions, the norms are *formal* because "Christian doctrine is what the church declares it to be through its official authorities."[5] In other traditions, norms are *material*, such as creeds or confessions. Evangelicals contend that Scripture is the primary source and material norm of belief and practice.

The theological issue of authority is a central concern in most models of development, and, as George Lindbeck explains, the debate over legitimate authority in development is the cardinal difference between Catholic and Protestant approaches:

> The Protestant problematic is the reverse of the Catholic one. The Catholic starts with highly authoritative developments going far beyond what is explicitly in the bible, and must then explain how this is reconcilable with the primacy of Scripture (to which he also is committed in view of the principle that Scripture alone is inspired). The Protestant, beginning with the *sola scriptura*, needs to interpret the *sola* in such a way as not to exclude the development of doctrinal traditions possessing some degree of effective authority.[6]

For Roman Catholics since Trent, the theological "problem" of authority in doctrinal development has been about defending the

---

3. For a sampling of these studies in the field of psychoanalysis, see Ana-Maria Rizzuto *The Birth of the Living God: A Psychoanalytic Study* (Chicago: University of Chicago Press, 1979); idem, *Why Did Freud Reject God?: A Psychodynamic Interpretation* (New Haven: Yale, 1998); Paul C. Vitz, *The Faith of the Fatherless: The Psychology of Atheism*, 2nd ed. (San Francisco: Ignatius, 2013).

4. Paul Tillich, *Systematic Theology*, vol. 1. (Chicago: University of Chicago Press, 1951), 47.

5. Ibid.

6. George A. Lindbeck, "The Problem of Doctrinal Development and Contemporary Protestant Theology," in *Man as Man and Believer*, ed. Edward Schillebeeckx and Boniface Willems (New York: Paulist Press, 1967), 135.

living ecclesial tradition embodied in councils and the papacy as a necessary supplement to biblical revelation. By contrast, most Protestants and evangelicals addressing development usually seek to alleviate the tension between the principle of *sola scriptura* and the need for creeds, confessional statements, and contemporary or constructive expressions of Christian doctrine.

Protestants, evangelicals, and Catholics may share similar convictions about the nature of revelation and the primacy of the Bible in doctrinal development, but there are significant points of disagreement about *how biblical authority functions in the church* and over *the relationship between Scripture and tradition.* Many Catholics prior to the Reformation contended that Scripture is *materially insufficient* for the Christian faith and ascribed the same status of authority to some postcanonical oral and written traditions as they ascribed to the Bible. In this view, tradition functions as a type of supplemental revelation. Reformation historian Heiko A. Oberman dubs this "two-source theory" in late-medieval Catholicism "Tradition II."[7] Additional "sources" may include extra-biblical and unrecorded apostolic traditions, ecclesial histories or hagiographies, logical deductions from Scripture, or new and more recent revelations.[8] According to Oberman, this view of tradition was one of the central points of concern that Protestant reformers like Luther had with the Catholic Church of his era.[9]

Other Roman Catholics, Anglo-Catholic Protestants, and Eastern Orthodox Christians recognize Scripture as *materially sufficient* but *formally insufficient* for faith, practice, and development. In this view, which Oberman labels "Tradition I," no other extra-biblical source

---

7. Heiko Oberman, *Forerunners of the Reformation: The Shape of Late Medieval Thought* (New York: Holt, Rinehart, and Winston, 1966), 54–56, 58–60.
8. Ibid., 72–73.
9. Ibid., 54.

or revelation shapes the content of Christian belief, but because Scripture is not in and of itself clear enough to be interpreted on its own, Tradition I adherents argue for the necessity of an external aid like ecclesial tradition to help interpret the biblical texts. Scripture may constitute the only needed special revelation in Christian doctrine, but it is not a solitary guide or norm. For Oberman, Vincent of Lérins exemplifies Tradition I hermeneutics because he called upon the tradition of Christian belief "believed everywhere, always, and by all people" as a *necessary guide* for scriptural interpretation.[10] As we saw in chapter 2, Johann Sebastian Drey and John Henry Newman take up similar approaches in their respective models of doctrinal development.

Evangelicals committed to some form of biblicism typically make a concerted effort to describe the Bible as *materially and formally sufficient* for Christian praxis, but with some qualification.[11] That is to say, evangelicals like myself affirm that (1) Scripture alone provides the revelatory content needed to know and love God and (2) that no extracanonical tradition (written or oral) acts as a necessary, binding norm for the interpretation of Scripture. By asserting the sufficiency of Scripture, we do not mean to suggest that the Bible gives exhaustive knowledge of God or the created order or that there is no further need to develop contemporary expressions of biblical faith. For evangelicals, the sufficiency of Scripture simply "means that Scripture contained all the words of God which he intended his people to have at each stage of redemptive history, and that it now contains everything we need God to tell us for salvation, for trusting him perfectly, and for obeying him perfectly."[12]

10. Ibid., 57–58.
11. Anthony Lane provides a helpful critical qualification of the term *sola scriptura* and the sufficiency of Scripture in Anthony N. S. Lane, "*Sola Scriptura?* Making Sense of a Post-Reformation Slogan," in *A Pathway into the Holy Scripture*, ed. Philip E. Satterthwaite and David F. Wright (Grand Rapids, MI: Eerdmans, 1994), 297–327.

However, not all evangelical biblicists understand the nature of biblical authority or the relationship between the Bible and tradition in the same way. From the outset of this study we have recognized that some naïve biblicists, particularly in the framework of fundamentalism, suggest that one can read and interpret the Bible apart from any external influence whatsoever. Contemporary hermeneuticists, however, teach us that such attempts are impossible because we are waist deep in the rushing tide of history, drenched by history's effects. In addition to the failure to take into consideration non-conscious interpretive factors such as individual religious experience and socio-psychological development, this type of theologian typically shows little use for general revelation, reason, or experience in theology or apologetics. The critical biblicist, by contrast, may welcome the use of other sources in the interpretation of biblical texts (though not necessitating them) and simultaneously recognize Scripture as the only norm or standard by which these sources are evaluated. Baptist theologian James Leo Garrett offers the helpful term *suprema scriptura* to describe the view of biblical authority espoused by critical biblicists in the evangelical tradition.[13]

Since the late nineteenth century, conservative and evangelical scholars, particularly in North America have framed the issue of biblical authority in terms of a doctrine of scripture. Within this broader context, two traditions have emerged. B. B. Warfield and his intellectual heirs speak of biblical authority in ontological and epistemic terms of *inspiration* and *inerrancy* in order to defend the Bible from the threat of modernist distortions or disavowals of its truth content.[14] Theologians in the tradition of James Orr normally

12. Wayne Grudem, *Systematic Theology* (Grand Rapids, MI: Zondervan, 2000), 127.
13. Garrett, *Systematic Theology*, vol. 1, 206–9.
14. For a small sampling of this tradition, see Benjamin Breckenridge Warfield, *The Inspiration and Authority of the Bible*, ed. Samuel G. Craig (Philadelphia: Presbyterian and Reformed, 1948), and Harold Lindsell, *The Battle for the Bible* (Grand Rapids, MI: Zondervan, 1976).

define the authority of the Bible in terms of its *function* or *purpose*.[15] So, the question becomes, Is the Bible authoritative because it is divinely inspired and entirely trustworthy, or does the Bible become authoritative when it transforms the lives of its readers and hearers according to God's purpose? Evangelicals like myself take the former option, grounding the authority of Scripture in its nature and not merely in its use. Nevertheless, both sides of the so-called "Bible wars" are concerned that Scripture can "speak" authoritatively to the present.

As we shall see, the hermeneutical question of authority is broader in scope than this theological question. In contemporary hermeneutical theory, the term "authority" has come to represent the *person or object responsible for producing meaning in the interpretive process*. Do texts have meanings established by their authors that are "authoritative" over readers or do readers have ultimate say in what the text "means" to them? These questions about the nature of texts and the role of readers are crucial in addressing the problem of doctrinal development hermeneutically. How one understands the nature of interpreting all texts (general hermeneutics) has

---

The impact of the Warfield tradition on my own Southern Baptist context can be seen in Benajah Harvey Carroll, *The Inspiration of the Bible* (New York: Revell, 1930); Wallie Amos Criswell, *Why I Preach That the Bible Is Literally True* (Nashville: Broadman, 1969); David S. Dockery, *Christian Scripture: An Evangelical Perspective on Inspiration, Authority, and Interpretation* (Nashville: Broadman & Holman, 1995); and James T. Draper Jr. and Kenneth Keathley, *Biblical Authority: The Critical Issue for the Body of Christ* (Nashville: Broadman & Holman, 2001).

15. See Donald K. McKim, *What Christians Believe about the Bible* (Nashville: Thomas Nelson, 1985), 91. McKim speaks clearly for this tradition when he says that "the purpose of Scripture is to bring people to faith and salvation in Jesus Christ" and that the "function of Scripture . . . is of primary concern." Other works in the "functionalist" tradition include James Orr, *Revelation and Inspiration* (New York: Charles Scribner's and Sons, 1910); Jack B. Rogers and Donald K. McKim, *The Authority and Interpretation of the Bible* (San Francisco: Harper & Row, 1979); Jack B. Rogers, ed., *Biblical Authority* (Waco: Word, 1977); David L. Bartlett, *The Shape of Scriptural Authority* (Philadelphia: Fortress Press, 1983); and Clark H. Pinnock, *The Scripture Principle* (San Francisco: Harper & Row, 1984).

considerable consequence for the reading of specific texts like Christian Scripture (special hermeneutics).

The concern of the present chapter is expressly hermeneutical in nature: how does biblical interpretation contribute to the development of Christian doctrine? Specifically, how does contemporary hermeneutical theory contribute to the understanding of "authority" in doctrinal formulation? This chapter addresses the question by answering two very different challenges to religious authority: the modernist challenge that undermines external authorities in favor of autonomous reason and postmodern challenges that relativize the meaning in religious authoritative traditions or limit the scope of authority.

Reason, Tradition, and Authority

One way we might resolve the problems surrounding authority and theology is to *reject the notion of authority itself*, specifically, to reject any authority *external to ourselves* in the development of religious beliefs. We might, to use the informal vernacular of popular anti-authoritarianism, reject "the Man"—anyone or anything that would attempt to assert social, political, or religious influence over us. This type of intellectual rebellion against external authorities was a predominate feature in Enlightenment thought, especially the rebellion against religious dogmas not derived from rational argument or evidence. Figures in this period committed to a notion of autonomous reason posed a uniquely modernistic challenge to evangelical doctrinal development: the need to defend *revelation and doctrine as authorities for Christian knowledge.*

The trend of rejecting religious authorities in Western culture progressed in several stages. Across Europe, the rise of nationalism drew new lines of cultural identification and loyalty, often resulting in a choice between king and country or Rome and the papacy. The Protestant Reformation plainly was not a rejection of religious authority itself but certainly a *protest* (hence "Protest-ant") directed at some religious authorities (e.g., papal authority, ecumenical councils, and extracanonical traditions). In the centuries that followed, many Enlightenment thinkers simply took the next step. Instead of selectively rejecting some religious authorities (like churches or competing religious traditions), many of these Enlightenment thinkers rejected all religious authorities, including the Bible the Protestant reformers defended so enthusiastically. Some of these figures attempted to develop a rational religion divorced from every form of authoritative special revelation. Theologians in this rationalist or Deist tradition such as Hermann Samuel Reimarus (1694–1768) and Gotthold Lessing rejected all appeals to the historical testimony of the Bible for religious belief.[16] American rationalists such as Thomas Paine (1737–1809) popularized deist alternatives to traditional Christian notions of biblical authority.[17]

Other Enlightenment thinkers, like the French materialist Paul-Henri d'Holbach (1723–1789), advocated a naturalistic worldview entirely devoid of divine authority.[18] For those in this antireligious, anti-tradition stream, "God" posed the final line of defense in the battle for intellectual freedom. "Science" (as it is frequently

---

16. Gotthold Ephraim Lessing, *Lessing's Theological Writings*, trans. and ed. Henry Chadwick (London: Adam and Charles Black, 1956), 54–55.

17. Paine offers a heavy handed critique of traditional Christianity and an outline of his deist theology in *The Age of Reason; Being an Investigation of True and Fabulous Theology* (1794, 1795, 1807). For a fuller examination of the development of Paine's critiques of biblical authority and institutional religion, see Edward H. Davidson and William J. Scheick, *Paine, Scripture, and Authority:* The Age of Reason *as Political and Religious Idea* (Cranbury, NJ: Associated University Press, 1994).

18. See Paul-Henri d'Holbach, *Le christianisme devoile, ou examination of principes et des effets de la religion chrétienne* (Paris, 1766); idem, *Christianity Unveiled: Being an Examination of the Principles and Effects of the Christian Religion*, trans. W. M. Johnson (New York, 1835).

personified by materialists) put the final nail in the proverbial coffin.[19] This kind of revolt against tradition still occurs in contemporary atheistic arguments. Many of the so-called New Atheists in America and Great Britain have helped popularize this radical dichotomy between faith grounded in an inherited religious tradition and reason independent of tradition and external religious authorities.[20] For those in this atheistic Enlightenment tradition, the rational person rejects authority—particularly religious authority—because they believe it is adverse to individual reason and science. Contrasted with the religious person who affirms other intellectual authorities outside of her own reason, the rationalist is a "freethinker" or a "Bright." This perceivably condescending view of religious authority is characteristic of the modernist assault on tradition.

While not particularly religious himself,[21] Gadamer charged this kind of modernist, anti-authoritarian thinking with a serious crime: "prejudice against prejudice itself, which denies tradition its power."[22] In other words, Gadamer criticizes the Enlightenment rebellion against all forms of intellectual authority—the refusal to grant

---

19. Naturalists credit figures like Galileo Galilei (1564–1642) for beginning the charge against religious tradition and establishing individualism. See Manfred Weidhorn, *The Person of the Millennium: The Unique Impact of Galileo on World History* (Lincoln, NE: iUniverse, 2005), 77–86.

20. Popular new atheist works include Richard Dawkins, *The God Delusion* (New York: Houghton Mifflin, 1996); Daniel C. Dennett, *Breaking the Spell: Religion as Natural Phenomenon* (New York: Penguin, 2006); Christopher Hitchens, *God is Not Great: How Religion Poisons Everything* (New York: Twelve, 2007); Sam Harris, *The End of Faith: Religion, Terror, and the Future of Faith* (New York: W. W. Norton, 2005); and Victor J. Stenger, *God: The Failed Hypothesis—How Science Shows That God Does Not Exist* (Amherst, NY: Prometheus, 2007).

21. Jean Grondin, *Hans-Georg Gadamer: A Biography*, trans. Joel Weinsheimer (New Haven: Yale University Press, 2003), 335–36. When journalists asked Gadamer whether he believed in God or life after death, he answered in the negative, but added "I often think how nice it must be to be able to believe in God." For a more optimistic reading of Gadamer's views on transcendence, see Jens Zimmermann, "Ignoramus: Gadamer's 'Religious Turn,'" in *Gadamer's Hermeneutics and the Art of Conversation*, International Studies in Hermeneutics and Phenomenology 2, ed. Andrzej Wierciński (London: Transaction, 2011), 209–222.

22. Hans-Georg Gadamer, *Truth and Method*, 2nd rev. ed., trans. Joel Weinsheimer and Donald G. Marshall (New York: Continuum, 2004), 273.

epistemic worth to cultural traditions and institutions including, but not limited to, religious authorities. Such a bias is a bias against bias itself, a presupposition against presuppositions. Even those casting doubt on our ability to obtain knowledge by means of tradition are part of a tradition that shapes their concerns! Against Enlightenment notions to the contrary, Gadamer asserts that authoritative traditions are not only helpful in acquiring knowledge and understanding but are necessary as well. Enquirers cannot even learn how to ask questions without a tradition that shapes their search for knowledge.

Hermeneuticists challenge what they perceive to be individualism run amok in the Western philosophy—an individualism that shortchanges or denies the epistemic value of "tradition." Anthony Thiselton traces this individualist impulse back to Socrates and Plato, who distinguish a "true opinion" or "true belief" (*alēthēi doxa*) from second-hand information and genuine "knowledge" (*epistēme*) that is apprehended first hand. In his dialogue with Meno, Socrates explains the difference between true knowledge and true opinion with the illustration of a young man who has received a "right opinion" about how to get to Larissa but who does not "know" the way to Larissa because he has not made the journey himself.[23] In so doing, Socrates suggests that the reception of true beliefs by means of credible testimony or tradition does not necessarily constitute genuine knowledge because such accounts or traditions cannot provide the justification or warrant necessary for knowledge.[24] Right opinion or belief may be useful for an individual, especially in cases like taking directions that actually get one to a desired location, but accepting true accounts or testimonies does not constitute knowledge.[25]

---

23. Thiselton, "Knowledge, Myth and Corporate Memory," 45; Plato, *Meno* 96b–98d.
24. Plato, *Theaetetus* 201d–210a.
25. Plato, *Meno* 97c.

The emphasis on reason isolated from authoritative tradition that began with Socrates and Plato reached new heights during the Renaissance and the Enlightenment. René Descartes (1596–1650) bears much of the blame for this resurgence of individualism, especially in his endeavor to establish epistemic certainty by doubting everything he learned in an authoritative tradition, to build knowledge only what is indubitably true and drawn from reason.[26] Of Descartes, Thiselton echoes the hyperbolic lamentation of William Temple (1881–1944), who writes, "If I were asked what was the most disastrous moment in the history of Europe I should be strongly tempted to answer that it was that period of leisure when René Descartes, having no claims to meet, remained for a whole day 'shut up alone in a stove.'"[27] Even with considerable methodological differences in their respective rationalist and empiricist programs, Descartes and Hume both emphasize the "thinking self" as the primary arena of inquiry. For Descartes and Hume, inquirers attempt to gain knowledge *apart from the communal traditions that shape them.* Thus the idea of "corporate knowledge," or "knowledge grasped, transmitted, and tested by the community," appears incompatible with "true knowledge" acquired through individual, critical thought.[28]

This hermeneutical criticism of aspects of Western epistemology need not result in a rejection of the discipline or in a rejection of all forms of "foundationalism."[29] While they bear certain family

---

26. René Descartes, *Discourse on Method* 1.15–22; cf. idem, *Meditations on First Philosophy* 1.18–22.

27. William Temple, *Nature, God, and Man* (Edinburgh: R&R Clark, 1934), 57.

28. Thiselton, "Knowledge, Myth and Corporate Memory," 45–47; cf. idem., *Hermeneutics: An Introduction* (Grand Rapids, MI: Eerdmans, 2009), 12, 17–20.

29. Thiselton does however criticize a "postmodern" tendency to conflate epistemology with "foundationalism" and objects vociferously to the clumsy, uncritical use of the latter term that he sees in North American theological scholarship. See Anthony C. Thiselton, *The Hermeneutics of Doctrine* (Grand Rapids, MI: Eerdmans, 2007), 126–34. Here he is responding directly to Richard Heyduck, whom he accuses of conflating epistemology as whole with foundationalist presuppositions (126). See also Richard Heyduck, *The Recovery of Doctrine in the Contemporary*

resemblances, epistemology and hermeneutics have different aims and spheres of operation. The central concerns of epistemology are questions about what constitutes knowledge and how one may attain such knowledge. These concerns more frequently manifest themselves in questions about how one may know things in the external world. Hermeneutics, by contrast, is more concerned with understanding of texts and interpersonal communication.[30] Hermeneutics specialists simply stress that critical thought cannot and must not begin in *de novo* intellectual isolation. Whether persons are born with a blank slate (*tabula rasa*), as John Locke (1632–1704) had suggested,[31] is not the concern of hermeneutics. Hermeneuticists simply demonstrate that critical inquiry cannot begin with a Cartesian "reboot." There is no reset button on human knowledge and no way to *unlearn everything taught by authoritative tradition*. Tradition is an inevitable—if not necessary—component of knowledge and interpretation.

Church: An Essay in Philosophical Ecclesiology (Waco, TX: Baylor University Press, 2002). Thiselton also makes note of the indiscriminate and ill-informed use of the term *foundationalist* in the work of Stanley Grenz and John R. Franke. See Stanley J. Grenz and John R. Franke, *Beyond Foundationalism: Shaping Theology in a Postmodern Context* (Louisville: Westminster/ John Knox, 2001). Notwithstanding his own criticism of Cartesian "hard" or "classical" foundationalism, Thiselton commends the "softer" or "modest" forms of foundationalism he finds in Alvin Carl Plantinga (b. 1932), Nicholas Wolterstorff, and W. Jay Wood (b. 1954). See also Alvin C. Plantinga and Nicholas Wolterstorff, *Faith and Rationality* (Notre Dame, IN: University of Notre Dame Press, 1983); W. Jay Wood, *Epistemology: Becoming Intellectually Virtuous* (Downers Grove, IL: InterVarsity, 1998), 77–104.

30. See Thiselton, *Hermeneutics*, 10–11. Thiselton identifies three crucial distinctions between traditional epistemology and hermeneutics or between *understanding* as described by hermeneuticists and *knowledge* as described by epistemologists in the analytic tradition. First, reversing what James M. Robinson (b. 1924) the "'traditional flow' of epistemology," the task of hermeneutics is listening to or *understanding* (*Verstehen*) interpersonal communication rather than *explaining* (*Erklärung*) an object. One stance implies an attempt at objectivity, describing an object or phenomenon as a neutral observer; the other implies the more subjective experience of being a conversation partner with those who are speaking. Second, Thiselton contrasts abstract problems in philosophy with the "questions that arise" in hermeneutics. Third, hermeneutics and philosophy in the Enlightenment tradition have radically different starting points for inquiry.

31. See John Locke, *An Essay Concerning Human Understanding* (1690), Book I.

The Inevitability and Necessity of Authoritative Tradition

Hermeneutics, in contrast to the legacy of Descartes, "does not place the individual human self at the center of the stage in heroic or illusory self isolation."[32] Whereas philosophers after Descartes (rationalists, empiricists, and idealists alike) often attempt to "clear the slate" with doubt as the starting point for inquiry, hermeneuticists such as Schleiermacher, the early Heidegger, and Gadamer recognize investigation must begin with preliminary, provisional pre-understandings shaped by tradition and culture.[33] Dilthey and the historicists sought to propose a method that would bring the interpreter out of the hermeneutical circle, to escape the presuppositions that shaped their understanding, but Heidegger and Gadamer recognized the inevitability of the hermeneutical circle, prejudgments, and presuppositions. As Heidegger aptly conceived the hermeneutical circle, it is not imperative "to get out of the circle but to come into it in the right way."[34]

Gadamer saw this way in through authoritative tradition, through conscious reflection on the reality of our "belonging" (*gehören*). The root of this word, *hören*, is the German word meaning "to hear" or "to obey." We belong to tradition and participate in it. We celebrate the tradition that shapes us. The inquirer is, in Gadamer's terms, the "historically-effected consciousness," who, according to Thiselton, belongs to an intersubjective, "shared public world" that not only frames the content of his thought "but also shapes the terms on

---

32. Anthony C. Thiselton, "Communicative Action and Promise in Interdisciplinary, Biblical, and Theological Hermeneutics," in *The Promise of Hermeneutics*, ed. Roger Lundin, Clarence Walhout, and Anthony C. Thiselton (Grand Rapids, MI: Eerdmans, 1999), 133.

33. See Gadamer, *Truth and Method*, 268–78; cf. Martin Heidegger, *Being and Time*, trans. John Macquarrie and Edward Robinson (New York: Harper & Row, 1962), 188–95. In his earlier works, Thiselton appeals to the sociology of knowledge to buttress this claim (see Thiselton, "Knowledge, Myth and Corporate Memory," 49–54), but his later works place less emphasis on this area.

34. Heidegger, *Being and Time*, 195.

which he examines and tests that knowledge."[35] Rationality is not, as Descartes suggests, an ahistorical or transcendental axiom.[36] Rather, as Gadamer observes, rationality is shaped by one's time and place in history. It does not operate in a realm transcendent of historical particularity.[37] Even the notion of "common sense" (*sensus communis*) is indicative of corporate knowledge, things learned acquired through accounts of information.[38]

The most striking blow against Descartes' program comes with Gadamer's recognition that acquired language is necessary for meaning and thought.[39] The vehicle of cultural transmission in language takes out much of global, methodological epistemic skepticism's gusto as it forces the inquirer to acknowledge that a "human being is never dependent merely on his own experience for information or knowledge."[40] Descartes may have desired to doubt everything he learned in communal formation, but he never could escape *language*. After all, *language rooted in tradition and history* is what makes Descartes' methodological skepticism possible. Language is a necessary condition for acquiring and critiquing knowledge. He may as well have said, "I think, therefore I am dependent upon the communal tradition of language!" Thiselton, with Gadamer,

---

35. Thiselton, "Knowledge, Myth and Corporate Memory," 47.
36. Descartes advocated a trans-historical rationalism universal in all ages and civilizations: "Good sense is the most evenly distributed commodity in the world, for each of us considers himself to be so well endowed therewith that even those who are the most difficult to please in all matters are not wont to desire more of it than they have. . . . [This fact] provides evidence that the power of judging rightly and distinguishing the true from the false (which, properly speaking, is what people call good sense or reason) is naturally equal in all men" (Descartes, *Discourse on Method* 1).
37. Gadamer, *Truth and Method*, 277.
38. Ibid., 16–27. In his discussion of the historical shaping of "common sense," Gadamer appeals to Giambattista Battista Vico's (1668–1774) apologetic for the humanist tradition over and against its Cartesian and Jansenist critics. See also Giambattista B. Vico, *New Science*, trans. David Marsh (New York: Penguin, 2000).
39. See Gadamer, *Truth and Method*, 397–436. Gadamer employs a metaphor from the Christian doctrine of the incarnation of the Word to illustrate the embodiment of language.
40. Thiselton, "Knowledge, Myth and Corporate Memory," 51.

concedes that language "shapes the frame of reference through which knowledge is *grasped*, and within which it is *criticized*."[41] As Wittgenstein rightly observes, "Doubt comes *after* belief."[42] Language *rooted in tradition and history* is what makes Descartes' methodological skepticism possible.

Merold Westphal makes three points about Gadamer's use of tradition here. First, tradition simultaneously enables and limits understanding. The hermeneutical circle tells us that there can be no understanding apart from tradition, but our place in tradition also limits our perspective. Second, tradition is not a monolithic concept. We are products of innumerable streams of tradition—economic, ethnic, familial, geographical, philosophical, religious, and socio-political. Third, tradition provides us with the prejudgments required to interpret.[43]

Others, like Thiselton, have found in Gadamer's notion of authoritative tradition a parallel to the later Wittgenstein's notion of "language games" (*Sprachspiel*) and their related "forms of life" (*Lebensformen*). These language games or forms of life constitute the corporate, inherited "scaffolding" of knowledge from which we think and operate.[44] The corporate context gives shape to these language

41. Thiselton, "Knowledge, Myth and Corporate Memory," 52. While Thiselton recognizes the dependence of thought and rationality on inherited language, he rejects the linguistic determinism of Benjamin Lee Whorf (1897–1941), who contends that language is the primary determinant of worldview. See Anthony C. Thiselton, *The Two Horizons: New Testament Hermeneutics and Philosophical Description with Special Reference to Heidegger, Bultmann, Gadamer, and Wittgenstein* (Carlisle: Paternoster, 1980), 137. Whorf, along with anthropologist Edward Sapir (1884–1939), put forward this linguistic determinism in a theory now known as the "Sapir-Whorf hypothesis." Though Whorf never published a single volume, he was a frequent contributor to several anthropology and linguistics journals. The primary collection of his articles, published posthumously, is *Language, Thought, and Reality: Selected Writings of Benjamin Lee Whorf*, ed. John B. Carroll (Cambridge: MIT Press, 1956).

42. Ludwig Wittgenstein, *On Certainty*, trans. and ed. G. E. M. Anscombe and George Hendrik von Wright (New York: Harper Perennial, 1972), §160.

43. Merold Westphal, *Whose Community? Which Interpretation? Philosophical Hermeneutics for the Church* (Grand Rapids, MI: Baker, 2009), 71.

games: "When language-games change, then there is a change in concepts, and with the concepts the meanings of words [and understandings of these words] change."[45]

So what does Gadamer's defense of tradition and authority mean for an evangelical, hermeneutical model of doctrinal development? If authority, tradition, or communal memories can be a legitimate means to knowledge and understanding, then it is possible that the apostolic testimony of the New Testament can be a vital means to knowing God and developing Christian knowledge and belief. This transmission of tradition gives Christian believers access to the past that shapes their collective identity. As Alister McGrath observes, "Information concerning Jesus of Nazareth is not scattered throughout the universe" as empirical data that can be evaluated by an objective observer "but is transmitted through certain definite social and literary channels. . . . Our knowledge of Jesus and his perceived significance for the first Christian communities are transmitted to us by tradition."[46] *It is only through the transmission of tradition in Scripture that we have access to the historical narratives that shape our worldview.*

Contrary to Plato and the Western epistemic tradition that followed, Christians have long recognized the value of authoritative tradition for belief formation. Even within the New Testament, we can find a distinction between *firsthand knowledge* and *truthful authoritative testimony*. John tells his readers that on the evening of his resurrection, Jesus appeared to the disciples from within a locked room (John 20:19). He blessed them and gave them the Holy Spirit (John 20:21–22). Yet the evangelist also notes that one of the

---

44. Ludwig Wittgenstein, *On Certainty*, trans. and ed. G. E. M. Anscombe and George Hendrik von Wright (New York: Harper Perennial, 1972), §211. See also Patrick Sherry, "Is Religion a 'Form of Life'?" *American Philosophical Quarterly* 9 (1972): 159–67.

45. Wittgenstein, *On Certainty*, §65.

46. Alister E. McGrath, *The Genesis of Doctrine: A Study in the Foundation of Doctrinal Criticism* (Grand Rapids, MI: Eerdmans, 1990), 185.

disciples, the one nicknamed "the Twin," was absent when these events occurred (John 20:24). When the other disciples informed him that they had been in the presence of Jesus, he rejected their claim, asserting that he would only believe their testimony if he had a first-hand experience with the risen Lord. The warrant or justification he demanded for such knowledge was sight and physical touch (John 20:25). This doubting Thomas was fortunate enough to have such an encounter eight days later, and after acquiring this knowledge first hand, relented his doubts (John 20:28). While Jesus acknowledges Thomas's *first-hand accrual of belief,* he also confers a special blessing on those *who believe the apostolic testimony without first-hand epistemic confirmation* (John 20:29). Jesus and the evangelist also pose a challenge to the rejection of authoritative testimony prevalent in the Greco-Roman philosophical tradition.

This critique of Western individualism becomes decisive for the question of doctrinal development as Thiselton highlights not only the synchronic social transmission of knowledge across geographical space but also the diachronic transmission through what he calls corporate memory or tradition. Individual biography is important in the way the thinking individual contributes to the stream of intellectual development, but it is only part of the wider course. Isolated thinkers do not control the course of the development of ideas. Echoing Collingwood and Gadamer's logic of question and answer, Thiselton makes the point that "even the way that people *raise questions* and the terms in which they examine and *test* knowledge builds on the thought and experience of others."[47]

In the development of doctrine, tradition (again, in the broadest sense) provides a framework of shared experience and common biography for the faith community and "provides access to an

47. Thiselton, "Knowledge, Myth and Corporate Memory," 52.

understanding and knowledge of realities which transcend individual experience."[48] Authorities such as Scripture and postcanonical doctrine "anchor the community's present both in the founding events of its past and within the overall framework of ongoing life in a way which transcends individual experience and provides a control against undue novelty or individual innovation."[49] The communal, multi-voiced nature of doctrine helps guard against the corruption of the depository.

Thiselton uses the term "corporate memory" to describe this transmission of *communal tradition* and *shared worldview* of a particular community. Corporate memory is more than a "source" of knowledge; it is a praxis-shaping worldview or framework.[50] It serves to create a "framework . . . into which . . . the individual slots his own perceptions and experiences in such a way that they acquire *significance* or meaning."[51] In light of these developments from Gadamer and Wittgenstein, Thiselton defines corporate memory as "the frame of reference which gives meaning to the present" and that which "guides present action."[52] This corporate memory is akin to *worldview*, a shared common communal vision from which individuals see the world. Corporate memory or tradition is a vehicle for transmitting worldviews cross-generationally and provides a frame of reference to develop new knowledge and understandings.

Using terminology and concepts from the sociology of knowledge, Thiselton notes that corporate memory is preserved, transmitted, and institutionalized through various instruments such as creeds, laws, proverbs, maxims, myths, songs, and stories.[53]

---

48. Thiselton, "Knowledge, Myth and Corporate Memory," 64.
49. Ibid., 63.
50. Ibid., 66.
51. Ibid., 55.
52. Ibid., 66.
53. Ibid. 53. Sociologists of knowledge Peter Berger and Thomas Luckmann describe this social or communal transmission of knowledge as a three-way dialectic between *institutionalization*

Statements of belief are not merely individual statements but *communal utterances of belief* passed from one generation to the next.[54] The deuteronomic tradition provides scriptural witness to this activity. While renewing the covenant YHWH gave Israel the command to "listen to" or "obey" (*shema*) the creed ("YHWH our God, YHWH is one"; Deut. 6:4) and the greatest commandment (Deut. 6:5). (The semantic domain of *shema* notably resembles Gadamer's use of *gehören* or "belonging.") God instructed Israel to *hear* and *obey* these words and gave another commandment: to maintain the corporate memory of YHWH in Israel by passing these things to their children (Deut. 6:7–9). Specifically, YHWH commanded Israel to retain her identity by *remembering* and *re-telling their shared narrative* of the covenants, the exodus, and the defeat of their enemies (Deut. 6:10–19). This instruction calls for ongoing *participation* in Israel's corporate memory.[55]

The primary instruments of "maintaining and preserving the stable background against which the faith could spread" in Christian corporate memory include the Bible as well as creeds, liturgies, and pastoral oversight.[56] These instruments provide "access to an understanding and knowledge of realities which transcend individual experience."[57] Doctrinal confessions and statements of belief are a means of transmitting the corporate memory of apostolic testimony in the Christian community from generation to generation. These

---

(or *externalization*), *legitimation*, and *internalization through socialization*. See Peter L. Berger and Thomas Luckmann, *The Social Construction of Reality* (New York: Anchor, 1966). Berger more recently has disassociated himself from the stronger, postmodern constructivist perspectives that appeal to his early work, insisting that social "constructions" are not created apart from some reference to extra-systemic realities. Rather, these social constructions are "socially derived interpretations" of reality. See Peter L. Berger and Anton Zijderveld, *In Praise of Doubt: How to Have Convictions without Becoming a Fanatic* (New York: HarperOne, 2009), 66.

54. Thiselton, *The Hermeneutics of Doctrine*, 43–44.
55. Ibid., 45.
56. Thiselton, "Knowledge, Myth and Corporate Memory," 63.
57. Ibid., 64.

statements or testimonies provide grounds for doctrinal reflection and development.[58] These statements likewise provide a means for transmitting interpretations of the biblical texts in a faith community.

The hermeneutical inquirer must not neglect the communal dimensions of knowledge in shared life-worlds, corporate memory, and language. The theologian cannot work in isolation from the living tradition passed along through apostolic testimony and confessions. The most important aspect of corporate memory for evangelical Christians is the revelation of God in inspired Scripture, which provides a stable anchor for the tradition in its various forms and developments.[59] The whole of Christian corporate memory, which includes Scripture and postcanonical doctrine, provides a valuable frame of reference for interpreting experience but is not beyond the scope of "public criteria" or universal tools by which it can be evaluated. This is particularly true when assessing postcanonical doctrine. While the Enlightenment thinkers drew too sharp a distinction between the thinking individual and the tradition of knowledge, they rightly stressed the need for critical evaluation of the tradition.[60]

Tradition and Critique

In his assessment of corporate memory's impact on Christian belief, Thiselton raises two concerns that could be problematic for a hermeneutical model of doctrinal development: (1) neglect of the larger stream of Christian tradition or "corporate memory" and (2) an overestimation of a corporate memory's role in shaping knowledge that results in historical relativism. Gadamer's mission to revitalize

58. Thiselton, *The Hermeneutics of Doctrine*, 43.
59. Thiselton, *New Horizons in Hermeneutics*, 63.
60. McGrath, *The Genesis of Doctrine*, 185.

tradition as a valuable source for knowledge motivates the former concern, while the latter concern, which reflects one of Jürgen Habermas's initial criticisms of Gadamer's program, is an attempt to protect the rehabilitation of tradition from charges of incommensurability, relativism, and fideism.[61]

Relativistic interpreters of Gadamer and Wittgenstein tend to overemphasize the pole of corporate memory and tradition in their works, often to the neglect of their emphasis on the critical appropriation of tradition in reason. Thiselton charges Richard Rorty with an imbalanced approach to Gadamer that recognizes his emphasis on *the role of tradition* but neglects his use of *critical appropriation*.[62] Gadamer himself refuses to allow a dichotomy between authority and reason.[63] Wittgenstein, too, offers criteria of meaning by which language games and forms of life can be criticized, despite some of his interpreters attributing a form of fideism to his program.[64] Thiselton treads a similar path. On the one hand, he is critical of the individualistic Western tradition, but on the other, he is critical of the *relativistic tendency to neglect reason and critique.*

The philosophy of science is instructive for hermeneutics in striking this balance. Hermeneutics and philosophy of science are both concerned with the nature of interpretation but with very different "objects" of study. Philosopher of science Thomas Kuhn contested the notion of scientific rationality as a trans-historical,

---

61. Anthony C. Thiselton, *New Horizons in Hermeneutics: The Theory and Practice of Transforming Biblical Reading* (Grand Rapids, MI: Zondervan, 1992), 329. See also Grondin, *Introduction to Philosophical Hermeneutics*, 129–35. Werner Jeanrond (b. 1955) adds that Gadamer's theory of phenomenological description is "overly optimistic" and lacking any sufficient criteria that would prevent "ideological distortions" (*Theological Hermeneutics*, 68–69). See also Jack Mendelson, "The Habermas-Gadamer Debate," *New German Critique* 18 (1979): 44–73.

62. See Thiselton, *New Horizons in Hermeneutics*, 394.

63. Thiselton, "Knowledge, Myth and Corporate Memory," 55; cf. Gadamer, *Truth and Method*, 282.

64. Thiselton, *New Horizons in Hermeneutics*, 395; cf. idem, *The Two Horizons*, 379–85. See also Kai Nielsen, "Wittgensteinian Fideism," *Philosophy* 42 (1967): 191–209.

universal trait[65] and suggested that "rationality"—even in science—is an interpretive framework established by local, historically situated communities of knowledge for the purpose of theorization. Kuhn contended that revolutions in scientific thinking were not merely part of a process of escalation, progress, and discovery wherein a neutral observer builds on or discredits the work of another objective scientist. Rather, he argued that scientists—and members of all other disciplines—operate out of frameworks or paradigms that shape their thinking. These frameworks, which may encompass an entire field for a significant period, color the researcher's methodology, observation, and conclusions, but when these frameworks shift, so does the whole perception of the work that has gone before the reallocation of ideals. A science does not gradually move from one paradigm to another through the process of discovery but rather there are, on occasion, revolutionary paradigm shifts wherein one new framework of knowledge seizes another. Kuhn demonstrates that science—like any other discipline—operates within interpretive communities who view their discipline through certain paradigms that dramatically shift on occasion, resulting in changed commitments and radically new understandings in the field.[66] Evangelical theologian Vern S. Poythress (b. 1946) demonstrates that the same sorts of paradigm shifts occur in biblical interpretation and theological disciplines, such as the revolution of the "historical-critical method" following the rise of the historical consciousness in the nineteenth century.[67]

---

65. See René Descartes, *Discourse* 1, AT 6:2. Descartes writes, "Good sense is the most evenly distributed commodity in the world, for each of us considers himself to be so well endowed therewith that even those who are the most difficult to please in all matters are not wont to desire more of it than they have. . . . [This fact] provides evidence that the power of judging rightly and distinguishing the true from the false (which, properly speaking, is what people call good sense or reason) is *naturally equal in all men.*"

66. See Thomas S. Kuhn, *The Structure in Scientific Revolutions*, 3d. ed. (Chicago: University of Chicago Press, 1996).

Arguing for what he calls an "incommensurability of paradigms," Kuhn maintains that scientists working in different paradigms or conceptual frameworks cannot integrate their insights without one of the competing parties "converting" to the paradigm of the opposition. One may change conceptual frameworks entirely when a new, paradigm-shifting theory arrives on the scene, but the new worldview emerging in the transformative process cannot be measured either by the rational criteria of a previously held paradigm or an appeal to rational criteria outside the paradigm.[68] The result of this incommensurability is a kind of relativism that contends that "no supraparadigmatic criteria exist" and "it is not possible to establish objectively whether one paradigm necessarily provides a more rational, true, or reliable perspective on matters than an earlier one."[69]

The acknowledgment of corporate memory and tradition in doctrinal development need not result in the tired accusation of "paradigmatic incommensurability." As fellow philosopher of science Karl R. Popper (1900–1994) noted in his balanced critique of Kuhn, a paradigm might provide a framework for knowledge, but it is not beyond criticism and comparison with other paradigms.[70] Furthermore, recognition of the framework of corporate memory does not mean uncritical allegiance to transmitted knowledge.[71] Thomas F. Torrance makes the same observation in his engagement with scientific theology:

It is important that we realize that the logical structure of human

---

67. Vern S. Poythress, *Science and Hermeneutics* (Grand Rapids, MI: Zondervan, 1988), 58–63.

68. Kuhn, 103, 112, 148–50, 198–99.

69. J. Wentzel van Huyssteen, *Theology and the Justification of Faith: Constructing Theories in Systematic Theology*, trans. H. F. Snijders (Grand Rapids, MI: Eerdmans, 1989), 58.

70. See Karl R. Popper, "Normal Science and Its Dangers," in *Criticism and the Growth of Knowledge: Proceedings of the International Colloquium in the Philosophy of Science, London, 1965, Vol. 4*, ed. Imre Lakatos and Alan Musgrave (Cambridge: Cambridge University Press, 1970), 51–58; Thiselton, "Knowledge, Myth and Corporate Memory," 58–59.

71. Thiselton, "Knowledge, Myth and Corporate Memory," 76.

thought grows out of the way in which the inner ordering of our consciousness interacts with the external ordering inhering in the world around us, and is not unaffected by the psychological and social structures of our history and culture, but this means that the logical reconstruction which scientific theories require in every forward advance must involve reconstruction also in the social and psychological patterns of the community in which we live, and indeed change and reconstruction in ourselves as those who are engaged in scientific inquiry and who have to be questioned and changed along with the revision of our questions.[72]

Conscious awareness of corporate memory does not entail that the "frame of reference may not itself undergo conscious criticism and a measure of revision. If this were not possible, we should be imprisoned in the inevitability of being determined solely by contingency."[73]

As Thiselton understands the growth of knowledge in general, and by extension, doctrinal development, it occurs between the poles of an authoritative corporate memory and its critical appropriation or analysis. The development of ideas requires a dialogue between *individuals* and an *authoritative* tradition. The theologian wrestles with these two poles anytime she works through an aspect of Christian belief. Her initial approach to biblical texts, to postcanonical historical doctrine, and toward the specific issues posed by her contemporary setting would be shaped by her participation within a particular Christian tradition. Distinctives of her theological tradition inevitably color her process. Yet she recognizes when she engages in theological dialogue that her position is only one of many. Critical appropriation of her tradition means assessing her point of view in light of this dialogue and in light of the limitations and/or advantages posed by her own view of a doctrinal topic. Sometimes this means that the

---

72. Thomas F. Torrance, *Theological Science* (Oxford: Oxford University Press, 1967), 221.
73. Thiselton, "Knowledge, Myth and Corporate Memory," 54; idem, *The Hermeneutics of Doctrine*, 128.

tradition or paradigm from which we work must change as well in light of new evidence.

The call for the critical, hermeneutical development of biblical interpretation and doctrine is not a pretext for transforming the message and content of the Bible. For evangelicals, Scripture is the supreme instrument of corporate memory that shapes the Christian community. For us, critical appropriation means weighing our opinions and putting our hermeneutical approaches to biblical texts under careful scrutiny. All the while, we maintain habits of mind that put us under authority of the text. In hermeneutics as in life, we must emulate the practice of our Lord in Gethsemane. In critical appropriation of corporate memory under the authority of Scripture, we must place our beliefs, desires, and preconceptions before God and say, "Not our will or interpretation or theological preference, but yours be done."

Answering the Postmodern Challenges to Religious Authority

One temptation characteristic of modernist thought is to reject all external authorities and traditions because they pose a threat to autonomous reason, to locate "authority" in the individual. The consequence for religion is either a religion devoid of authority or a rejection of religion altogether. The postmodern is far less optimistic about the objectivity and autonomy of individual reason than the modernist but poses a similar threat to religious authority. Rather than rejecting all authority, the distinctively postmodern temptation is to *ghettoize tradition*, to relocate authority to the local community.

Textuality, Meaning, and Authority

The most basic and most far-reaching issue for the authority problem in contemporary hermeneutics is the question of textuality: *What is a text?* Implicit in a theory of textuality are answers to questions about (1) the role of the author, (2) the role of the reader, and (3) the location of meaning.[74] For the last half century, two broad approaches to textuality have dominated discussions in hermeneutics: *author-centered* approaches that locate the meaning of the text in the intention of the author and *reader-centered* approaches that highlight a plurality of meanings either within an autonomous text or in the reading activity of a local community.[75] A theory of textuality has tremendous consequence for evangelicals concerned about faithfulness to Scripture in the development of doctrine. Is the meaning of Scripture in the design of its divine–human authorship, its internal sign-system now independent of its authorship, or in a local community of its readers? Rightful "authority" in doctrinal development resides with meaning.

Many evangelical scholars have appropriated the earlier author-oriented approach of literary critic E. D. Hirsch, Jr. in their defense of grammatical-historical exegesis.[76] In *Validity in Interpretation* (1967), Hirsch introduced many of the hermeneutical concepts of Italian jurist Emilio Betti (1890–1968) to American audiences, particularly in Betti's criticism of Gadamer's hermeneutics. In his earlier writings,

---

74. Kevin J. Vanhoozer, *Is There a Meaning in This Text? The Bible, the Reader, and the Morality of Literary Knowledge* (Grand Rapids, MI: Zondervan, 1998), 103.

75. Thiselton, *New Horizons in Hermeneutics*, 55.

76. See Walter C. Kaiser, "Issues in Contemporary Hermeneutics," in *Rightly Divided: Readings in Biblical Hermeneutics*, ed. Roy B. Zuck (Grand Rapids, MI: Kregel, 1996), 47–52; Walter C. Kaiser and Moisés Silva, *An Introduction to Biblical Hermeneutics: The Search for Meaning* (Grand Rapids, MI: Zondervan, 1994), 30ff; John P. Newport, "Contemporary Philosophical, Literary, and Sociological Hermeneutics," in *Biblical Hermeneutics: A Comprehensive Introduction to Interpreting Scripture*, 2nd ed., ed. Bruce Corley, Steve W. Lemke, and Grant I. Lovejoy (Nashville: Broadman & Holman, 2002), 171–73.

Hirsch separates the meaning of the text ("meaning-in") given by an author from the significance or application of the text ("meaning-to") discovered by a reader. Readers might apply the meaning of texts in new ways, but they never create the meaning in the text because it is *determinate* or fixed by the author. Any alteration of meaning-in is a departure from authorial intent.[77]

If meaning is, as Hirsch suggests, determined entirely by the author and is inextricable from his or her own historical situation, then the authors of Scripture hold complete primacy over the process. If, on the other hand, individual readers or the reading community as a whole creates meaning, then every local community has the final word on how best to formulate doctrine for themselves. Thiselton finds neither of these mirroring alternatives entirely satisfactory for biblical hermeneutics and, by extension, doctrinal development. He aspires to formulate a multi-tiered or *three-dimensional model of biblical authority*.[78] This model plays a critical role in understanding the nature of biblical and traditional authorities in Thiselton's hermeneutical description of doctrinal development.

The mirroring theories of textuality in traditional reader-oriented approaches and author-oriented approaches threaten the balance between the poles of corporate memory and critical appropriation by overemphasizing one against the other. Some interpreters affirm that authors have complete determinative control over the meaning of a text. Evangelicals frequently make this assertion, especially in the particular case of Scripture. As the framers of the Chicago Statement on Biblical Hermeneutics (1982) affirm, "The meaning expressed

---

77. See E. D. Hirsch Jr., *Validity in Interpretation* (New Haven: Yale University Press, 1967), 44–67, esp. 61. In later writings, he shows openness to the possibility of authors leaving some texts partially indeterminate in meaning.; cf. idem, "Meaning and Significance Reinterpreted," *Critical Inquiry* 11 (1984): 202–24.

78. Anthony C. Thiselton, *Thiselton on Hermeneutics: Collected Works with New Essays* (Grand Rapids, MI: Eerdmans, 2006), 106.

in each biblical text is single, definite and fixed." Heeding Hirsch's earlier distinction between meaning in the text and significance produced by the text, the Council denies that the "recognition of this single meaning eliminates the variety of its application."[79] J. I. Packer, one of the framers and signatories of this statement, draws a clear dividing line between meaning and significance in the pneumatological terms of *illumination* and *inspiration*:

> Different people in different situations find the same Scripture passages bringing them illumination from God in different ways with different specific messages. (Think, for instance, of the many different human contexts in which down the centuries Psalm 23 will have brought reassurance from God.) But it has yet to be shown that the historico-theological meaning of each text that is applied for reassurance and guidance today does not continue to be identical.[80]

Thiselton finds this sort of assumption reductionistic: "The authority of the Bible does not depend upon a supposed wooden literalism, which assigns a single, sharply bounded meaning to every word and every sentence. . . . Conservative theologians who veer towards this view have actually *absorbed* the very Enlightenment rationalism that they often attack, even if they imagine that they protest against it."[81] Thiselton recommends that this approach "tends to demote the importance of non-referential, non-representational, language" by "suggesting that [Hirsch's] grossly over-simple, over-general, exhausted distinction between meaning and significance could serve as a panacea for all hermeneutical headaches."[82] The methodical

---

79. The International Council on Biblical Inerrancy, "The Chicago Statement on Biblical Hermeneutics" (1982), Article VII. The council likewise denies "that the 'horizons' of the biblical writer and the interpreter may rightly 'fuse' in such a way that what the text communicates to the interpreter is not ultimately controlled by the *expressed meaning* of Scripture" (Article IX, italics mine).

80. J. I. Packer, "Infallible Scripture and the Role of Hermeneutics," in *Scripture and Truth*, ed. D. A. Carson and John D. Woodbridge (Grand Rapids, MI: Baker, 1992), 329.

81. Thiselton, *Thiselton on Hermeneutics*, 639.

search for a single, determinate meaning in every biblical text thus impairs the more "open" genres such as parable, poetry, psalms, wisdom literature, and apocalypse from their fuller meaning.[83]

Thiselton is no less concerned with the "radical indeterminacy" of postmodern theories of textuality that denies the biblical text any stable meaning.[84] Those in the neopragmatic tradition of Rorty desire to create meaning in biblical texts only according to their "local" usefulness.[85] Not surprisingly, Thiselton finds little more that is profitable for biblical interpretation in deconstructionist theories of textuality. Derrida's appeal to an endless series of signifiers relating only through *différance* fares no better as it "fails to do justice to the nature of language, as well as to the force of biblical authority."[86] "The biblical texts," he insists,

> teach, but they also invite us to celebrate with joy the deeds and reign of God. They make truth-claims about the world and reality; but they also make us uncomfortable recipients of judgment and comfortable recipients of grace. They subvert our idols, but they also address us, heal us, build us, and transform us. Any theory of textuality which cannot make room for these textual functions cannot be given a paradigmatic place in biblical interpretation.[87]

82. Anthony C. Thiselton, "'Behind' and 'in Front of' the Text: Language, Reference and Indeterminacy," in *After Pentecost: Language & Biblical Interpretation*, ed. Craig Bartholomew, Colin Greene, and Karl Möller (Grand Rapids, MI: Zondervan, 2001), 103; cf. idem, *New Horizons in Hermeneutics*, 36. Thiselton believes Vanhoozer to be a representative of this approach but seems a little premature in passing this judgment on Vanhoozer's work. Contrary to Thiselton, Vanhoozer does seem open to a degree of indeterminacy of meaning when indeterminacy is "intended" or a "definite feature of the meaning of the text." See Vanhoozer, *Is There a Meaning in This Text?*, 313–14.

83. Thiselton, "'Behind' and 'in Front of' the Text," 104. See also Anthony C. Thiselton, "The Varied Hermeneutical Dynamics of Parables and Reader-Response Theory," in Roger Lundin, Anthony C. Thiselton, and Clarence Walhout, *The Responsibility of Hermeneutics* (Grand Rapids, MI: Eerdmans, 1985), 83–106.

84. Thiselton, "'Behind' and 'in Front of' the Text," 106; cf, Thiselton, *New Horizons in Hermeneutics*, 55–79.

85. Thiselton, *New Horizons in Hermeneutics*, 393–405.

86. Thiselton, *Thiselton on Hermeneutics*, 639.

87. Thiselton, *New Horizons in Hermeneutics*, 131–32.

While biblical interpretation and doctrinal development may allow for a degree of openness in creating meaning or applications, a degree of stability found in the corporate memory is essential for maintaining identity and continuity with the tradition.

Consequently, Thiselton attempts to forge a middle path for biblical interpretation that maintains the "stable" authority of the Bible but that does not neglect the "open" and partially indeterminate nature of certain genres within Scripture.[88] The use of Ricoeur's metaphor of worlds "behind the text," "within the text," and "in front of the text" in W. Randolph Tate's "integrated hermeneutics" offers Thiselton a helpful model that can be adopted in constructing a multi-tiered, "three-dimensional" approach to biblical authority that recognizes various degrees of determinacy.[89] "Author-centered" approaches to meaning that focus on the world "behind the text" typically highlight authorial intent, the world of the author, and the circumstances behind the development of the text.[90] The world "within the text" describes the "text-centered" approaches to meaning celebrated by Russian formalism, the New Criticism, and linguistic structuralism.[91] The world "in front of the text" is the reader's world, wherein the text has *a variety of effects* on its interpreters.[92] These three

---

88. Thiselton, *Thiselton on Hermeneutics*, 638, italics mine.
89. W. Randolph Tate, *Biblical Interpretation: An Integrated Approach* (Peabody, MA: Hendrickson, 1991). See also Thiselton, "'Behind' and 'in Front of' the Text," 105; idem, *Thiselton on Hermeneutics*, 637; idem, "Authority and Hermeneutics: Some Proposals for a More Creative Agenda," in *Pathway into the Holy Scripture*, ed. Phillip E. Satterthwaite and David F. Wright (Grand Rapids, MI: Eerdmans, 1994), 123. Ricoeur's metaphor appears in his "World of the Text, World of the Reader," in *A Ricoeur Reader: Reflection and Imagination*, ed. Mario J. Valdés (Toronto: University of Toronto Press, 1991), 491–98.
90. Tate, *Biblical Interpretation*, xvi–xvii, 1–57. Historical-critical approaches such as source, form, and redaction criticisms focus on the world behind the text (xvii, 176–85).
91. For examples of these "text-oriented" approaches, see Roman Jakobson, "Closing Statement: Linguistics and Poetics," in *Style in Language*, ed. Thomas A. Sebeok (New York: Wiley, 1960), 350–77; John Crowe Ransom, *The New Criticism* (Westport, CT: Greenwood, 1979); William K. Wimsatt and Monroe C. Beardsley, "The Intentional Fallacy," *The Sewanee Review* 4 (1946): 468–88; and Stephen Bann and John E. Bowlt, eds., *Russian Formalism: A Collection of Articles and Texts in Translation* (Edinburgh: Scottish Academic Press, 1973).

"worlds" are not mutually exclusive, as Tate and Thiselton rightly discern, because all the worlds behind the text, within the text, and in front of the text are simultaneously present and at work.[93] Notably, these three worlds are somewhat analogous to the threefold nature of every speech act. The world "behind the text" is like the illocutionary act (i.e., what the author intends to do with the text). The world "within the text" is akin to the locutionary act (i.e., the signs utilized in communication). With its emphasis on the effects of the text on readers, the world "in front of the text" is like the perlocutionary act (i.e., the effect the text has on its readers or hearers). As all three acts constitute every speech act, the simultaneous presence of the three worlds may apply to every interpretive act.

A multi-tiered, three-dimensional model of biblical authority then can find varying degrees of authority and meaning in all three worlds. First, the divine and human authors of Scripture stand behind the text as an "ontological *source* of authority."[94] This level, Thiselton observes, evokes Nicholas Wolterstorff's description of the Bible as God's "deputized discourse," that is, human illocutionary acts (i.e., the meaning or intention of a human author in writing a biblical text) that serve as divine illocutionary acts (i.e., God's intention in inspiring a text).[95] Second, the "*text* itself embodies a word 'within' it, just as the incarnate Christ embodies the word 'lived' and enfleshed."[96] Third, the word of God (in Ricoeur's terminology) "sets going" a world "in front of text" wherein it forms and transforms its

92. Thiselton, "'Behind' and 'in Front of' the Text," 99–100.
93. Ibid., 108.
94. Thiselton, *Thiselton on Hermeneutics*, 637.
95. See Nicholas Wolterstorff, *Divine Discourse: Philosophical Reflections on the Claim that God Speaks* (Cambridge: Cambridge University Press, 1995), 37–57, 114–23. See also Anthony C. Thiselton, "Speech-Act Theory and the Claim that God Speaks: Nicholas Wolterstorff's *Divine Discourse.*" *Scottish Journal of Theology* 50 (1997): 97–110.
96. Thiselton, *Thiselton on Hermeneutics*, 637. Thiselton notes that this analogy is not perfect. The manifestation of the word within the text should is a "prophetic utterance . . . to be tested," while the manifestation of the word in Christ "is to be worshipped."

readers through its "life-changing and thought-shaping . . . effects."[97] Doctrinal development occurs in this world beyond the text.

Thiselton is favorable to some "reader-centered" programs that draw attention to the world in front of the text. Rather than insisting on a single, determinate meaning or total indeterminacy in every biblical text, he suggests that biblical interpreters follow the more "constructive" application of reader-response theory in the works of semioticians Jurij Lotman and Umberto Eco in seeking to "enquire about the *degree* of determinacy exhibited within a wide spectrum of language, and show how this relates to whether we are reading 'open' texts . . . or 'closed' texts."[98] He suggests that certain biblical texts have a degree of openness by design, inviting the reader to create meaning or co-participate in the narrative world that the text is projecting. Rather than generalizing about the nature of reader-response in all texts, these scholars call readers to examine particular cases.[99]

Thiselton believes that the reception theory of Hans-Robert Jauss can be valuable in determining which genres invite readers to produce meaning or in evaluating the effects of specific texts on their readers.[100] With reception theory, Jauss, a former pupil of Gadamer, attempts to incorporate the "history of effects" or the "history of influences" (*Wirkungsgeschichte*) into the analysis of specific texts by analyzing their interpretations throughout history.[101] For Thiselton, the significance of the history of influences and the "historically-effected consciousness" for reception theory is evident in the way that

---

97. Thiselton, *Thiselton on Hermeneutics*, 637.
98. Ibid., 638; cf. idem, *New Horizons in Hermeneutics*, 524–29. The primary works Thiselton utilizes in discussion of Lotman and Eco are Jurij Lotman, *The Structure of the Artistic Text* (Ann Arbor: University of Michigan Press, 1977) and Umberto Eco, *The Role of the Reader: Explorations in the Semiotics of Texts* (Bloomington: Indiana University Press, 1979).
99. Thiselton, *New Horizons in Hermeneutics*, 66.
100. Thiselton, "'Behind' and 'in Front of' the Text," 104–5.
101. See Hans Robert Jauss, *Toward an Aesthetic of Reception*, trans. Timothy Bahti (Minneapolis: University of Minneapolis Press, 1982). This area of inquiry is to some extent adverse to Gadamer's original notion of the "history of effects." See Gadamer, *Truth and Method*, 299.

these terms highlight "both the influence of readers on texts and the influence of text on readers."[102] Thiselton also finds in this theory a balanced approach that features stability and a relative degree of determinacy:

> On the one side, he [Jauss] accepts the importance of a given tradition of continuity of interpretation which suggests constraints beyond which interpretation becomes idiosyncratic or irresponsible. Nevertheless, hermeneutical agenda are not simply replicated from era to era. Meaning is not grossly indeterminate and unbounded. Nevertheless, hermeneutical agenda are not simply replicated from era to era. New questions and new thought-forms arise in relation to which paradigms exhibit both continuity and discontinuity as traditions of interpretation expand.[103]

In its analysis of the effects of texts on readers throughout history, reception theory does much to "expose the fallacy of 'objectivism.'"[104]

Reception theory is more than the history of an interpretation of a text. It offers a critique of potentially *"threatening"* readings which distort the stable meaning of a text, and it calls attention to the way in which a *"text can change our horizons,"* such as the Bible's formative effect on its readers.[105] Jauss also invites readers to think critically about their own "horizon of expectation" and to discover the various ways they could read a text. When this critical analysis occurs, the reader discovers new horizons of expectation. Perhaps most importantly for analyzing doctrinal development, the historical analysis of reception theory focuses on specific periods of interpretive history and highlights the impact of those texts on those particular time-horizons.[106] The real value of this approach for a descriptive

102. Thiselton, *Hermeneutics*, 316. See Joel Weinsheimer and Donald G. Marshall, "Translator's Preference," in Gadamer, *Truth and Method*, 2nd rev. ed. (New York: Continuum, 2004), xv.
103. Thiselton, "'Behind' and 'in Front of' the Text," 105.
104. Thiselton, *Hermeneutics*, 317.
105. Ibid., 318; cf. idem, *The Hermeneutics of Doctrine*, 99.

hermeneutical model of doctrinal development is the way in which it demonstrates that "'rereadings' of a tradition become necessary" in certain circumstances. These "rereadings" serve to *form* new horizons and reassess previously held positions. These new horizons shape current and future readings.[107] The recurrent theme of doctrinal development as a "question and answer" dialectic is also implicit here.

Even with the degrees of indeterminacy allotted in certain genres and in the history of interpretation, Thiselton reminds readers of the importance of biblical authority in doctrinal formulation and development. The meaning of Scripture remains the plumb line by which interpretations and formulations are measured. Christian experience, for example, is only valuable as a hermeneutical "starting point" for construing doctrine: "'Experience,' then offers a reliable hermeneutical starting point if it is regarded as a *provisional* way into the subject, in effect more strictly to yield to *pre-understanding* or *preliminary* understanding rather than understanding itself (*Vorverständis* rather than *Verstehen*)."[108] This experience, however,

---

106. Thiselton, *Hermeneutics*, 318–19. The application of reception theory to biblical texts is relatively new. Thiselton applies reception theory to his own exegetical work in numerous places, as does the Swiss theologian and New Testament scholar Ulrich Luz (b. 1938). See Anthony C. Thiselton, "The Hermeneutical Dynamics of 'Reading Luke' as Interpretation, Reflection, and Formation," in *Reading Luke: Interpretation, Reflection, Formation*, ed. Craig G. Bartholomew, Joel B. Green, and Anthony C. Thiselton (Grand Rapids, MI: Zondervan, 2005), 3–52, esp. 41–52; idem, *The First Epistle to the Corinthians: A Commentary on the Greek Text*, The New International Greek New Testament Commentary (Grand Rapids, MI: Eerdmans, 2000), xvii; idem, *1 & 2 Thessalonians through the Centuries*, Blackwell Bible Commentaries (Oxford: Wiley-Blackwell, 2010); Ulrich Luz, *Matthew in History: Interpretation, Influence, and Effects* (Minneapolis: Fortress Press, 1994), 17. For a fuller commentary exploration along the lines of Luz's thesis here, see *Matthew 1-7: A Continental Commentary*, trans. W. C. Linss (Minneapolis: Fortress Press, 1992); *Matthew 8-20: A Commentary*, trans. W. C. Linss (Minneapolis: Fortress Press, 2001); and *Matthew 21-28: A Commentary*, trans. J. E. Crouch. (Minneapolis: Fortress Press, 2005). Catholic theologian Ormund Rush (b. 1950) applies Jauss' theory to the history of Christian doctrine. See Ormond Rush, *The Reception of Doctrine: An Appropriation of Hans Robert Jauss' Reception Aesthetics and Literary Hermeneutics*, Tesi Gregoriana, Serie Teologia 19 (Rome: Pontifical Gregorian University, 1997).

107. Thiselton, *The Hermeneutics of Doctrine*, 102–4.

108. Ibid., 453.

cannot have the final word. Revelation must serve a more sizable role. For example, Schleiermacher's experience-driven theological method is testimony to the insufficiency of experience for deriving the doctrine of the Trinity.[109] Doctrinal development needs an authority capable of providing stability in the tradition: "'Experience' offers a hermeneutical bridge, but if it is abstracted from Scripture, tradition, and reason, it is notoriously capable of *unstable or diverse interpretation.*"[110]

There is a stability of meaning in the communicative acts of divine and human authors but a degree of relative indeterminacy in certain texts and the various ways some texts are read in different time-horizons. Certain biblical genres, such as psalms and wisdom literature, invite numerous forms of participation. Prophetic texts, like the "messianic" suffering servant passages of Isaiah, took on new interpretations for New Testament authors in light of the Christ-event. This kind of stable, yet not completely determinate meaning makes possible the formulation and development of doctrine at later periods in time without succumbing to hermeneutical anarchy.

Authority and Performance Metaphors

Once it has been established that there is a possibility for meaning in biblical texts—even with some varying degrees of determinacy dependent upon the text in question—we must address the role of the reader or reading community. How do reading communities orient themselves in relationship to Scripture? The role of the reading

---

109. See Friedrich D. E. Schleiermacher, *The Christian Faith*, ed. and trans. H. R. Mackintosh and J. S. Stewart (Edinburgh: T&T Clark, 1928), §§170–72. Thiselton quips, "In spite of his comments about the importance of the doctrine of the Trinity, Schleiermacher leaves this to some dozen or so pages at the end of his 750-page treatise, to which it forms hardly more than a postscript or tailpiece" (Thiselton, *The Hermeneutics of Doctrine*, 453).

110. Thiselton, *The Hermeneutics of Doctrine*, 453.

community is central point of difference between evangelical and postliberal theological hermeneutics.

These differences have considerable consequence for how both approach the ongoing task of doctrinal development as well. Whereas cultural-linguistic advocates like Lindbeck, Frei, and Kelsey ultimately locate doctrinal authority in the church's use of Scripture, evangelical hermeneuticists like Thiselton and Vanhoozer ultimately locate authority in the divine-human authorship of Scripture.[111] The former group practices a kind of postmodern hermeneutical skepticism, whereas the latter expresses greater confidence (though not absolute certainty) in the ability of readers to discern the "meaning" of a biblical text.

Both Thiselton and Vanhoozer use metaphors of "performance" to describe what the critical appropriation of Scripture does for the growing Christian tradition. The first metaphor, drawn from the performance of a musical composition, accentuates the self-preserving qualities of Christian corporate memory. Drawn from dramatic performance, the second metaphor contrasts different approaches to biblical texts in development.

Using a metaphor akin to one Gadamer employs in *Truth and Method*,[112] Thiselton likens contemporary biblical interpretation to the *performance of a musical work*. A score has within it controlling mechanisms, such as structures, melodies, and notes, which allow it to retain its identity throughout various performances and interpretations. Even with these components, each new audience experiences new performances of the same work, sometimes with

---

111. Kevin J. Vanhoozer, *The Drama of Doctrine* (Louisville: Westminster/John Knox, 2005), 7–12. Vanhoozer observes that the cultural-linguistic emphasis is a later development in Frei's project. See Frei, *The Eclipse of Biblical Narrative*; idem, *The Identity of Jesus Christ* (Philadelphia: Fortress Press, 1975); idem, *Types of Christian Theology* (New Haven: Yale University Press, 1992), 15. See also David H. Kelsey, *Proving Doctrine: The Uses of Scripture in Modern Theology* (Harrisburg, PA: Trinity, 1999).

112. Gadamer, *Truth and Method*, 106–10.

different tempos, additional improvisation, different performers, or slightly modified arrangements. Thiselton concludes that the performance does not need to be a wooden, uncreative duplication. Nevertheless, if it is to be a performance of the same work, the performer must play within the *established boundaries of the work*.[113]

So what established boundaries direct the performance of the tradition in the ongoing development of doctrine? In order to answer this question, Thiselton appeals to the work of sociologists of knowledge Peter Berger and Thomas Luckmann, who observe that "institutionalization," or the process of making worldviews plausible and maintainable, contains internal "standards of role-performance" which keep traditions and social institutions functioning.[114] Cultural traditions are preserved over time by building in certain roles or mechanisms for maintaining continuity within the tradition. In the biblical narrative of Israel, YHWH's instruction to teach children the narrative of Israel is a role built into the tradition that sustains this worldview cross-generationally.

In the Christian tradition, belief is a "role" that comes with certain standards of performance. The Christian believer learns her role through institutionalization, through the communal practices of repeating and habituating belief and conduct. These practices give stability to the tradition as it develops and provide a safeguard against heresy. Doctrinal corruption results from abandoning corporate memory for individual innovation and failing to heed these standard roles. With this rehearsal of the authoritative tradition, "when deviation or eccentricities occur, they are identified as *deviation or eccentricities*."[115] Furthermore, attention to the standard role performances of corporate memory in doctrinal development is an

---

113. Thiselton, "Knowledge, Myth and Corporate Memory," 74.
114. Berger and Luckmann, *The Social Construction of Reality*, 74.
115. Thiselton, "Knowledge, Myth and Corporate Memory," 67.

essential component of establishing continuity within the tradition. If Christian believers universally deviate from the standard role performances within a given tradition, it would be difficult to ascribe them as belonging to the same tradition afterwards. Even more troublesome, if the pole of corporate memory and its standards of performance within the Christian tradition are ignored, "language about *God* . . . would also lose its grounding and stability."[116]

Returning to a theatrical metaphor of performance fleshed out in his theodramatic hermeneutics, Vanhoozer draws two ways of understanding the Scripture-tradition relationship. Loosely alluding to Oberman's differentiation between "Tradition I" and "Tradition II," he calls these two approaches "Performance I" and "Performance II."[117] Vanhoozer's notion of Performance II builds on Nicholas Wolterstorff's criticism of the practice he labels *performance interpretation*. For Wolterstorff, performance interpretation is an alternative to authorial-discourse interpretation that begins with the mistaken assumption that texts have a "sense" that is discernibly different from the discourse of authors, either in an autonomous text or an interpretative community.[118] An interpreter may perform the text by playing the role of the author, describing what he or she would have meant by using the same words or arrangements. The interpreter constructs meaning, and the text subsequently becomes little more than a vehicle for expressing his or her own tradition or convictions.[119] This manner of Performance II interpretation appears in several strands of postmodernism, including Derridean deconstruction and Fish's social pragmatism.[120] For instance, Fish

---

116. Ibid.
117. Vanhoozer, *The Drama of Doctrine*, 167.
118. Nicholas Wolterstorff, "The Importance of Hermeneutics for a Christian Worldview," in *Disciplining Hermeneutics: Interpretation in Christian Perspective*, ed. Roger Lundin (Grand Rapids, MI: Eerdmans, 1997), 42–44.
119. Wolterstorff, *Divine Discourse*, 171–82. The rejection of the "sense of a text" is a direct challenge to Ricoeur's claim of textual autonomy. See Vanhoozer, *Is There a Meaning in This Text?*, 108–9.

describes interpretation as a performance wherein interpreters "make sense" of texts or "manufacture" meaning.[121] Interpretive strategies, not texts or authors, "give texts their shape."[122] Interpretive communities "produce meanings and are responsible for the emergence of formal features."[123]

Wolterstorff classifies the later Frei a representative of performance interpretation (the approach Vanhoozer calls Performance II) because he claims that the "literal sense" (*sensus literalis*) by which the church interprets Scripture is determined by traditional consensus.[124] For the later Frei, the literal sense of Scripture is the "literal *reading*" of the text.[125] Vanhoozer concurs with Wolterstorff and extends the same designation to Lindbeck, Frei's postliberal protégé.[126] The type of performance interpretation employed in the cultural-linguistic approach is somewhat more difficult to identify because, Vanhoozer notes, Lindbeck tends to equivocate between an "intratextual theology" that recognizes the text and a communal grammar that dictates the text's meaning.[127] The community's interpretation of the text is more authoritative than the text itself because the community's performance—not the canonical script—ultimately determines the

---

120. Vanhoozer, *The Drama of Doctrine*, 168–69; cf. idem, *Is There a Meaning in This Text?*, 48–57.

121. Stanley Fish, *Is There a Text in This Class? The Authority of Interpretive Communities* (Cambridge, MA: Harvard University Press, 1980), 29.

122. Ibid. 13.

123. Ibid. 14.

124. Wolterstorff, *Divine Discourse*, 179. Wolterstorff finds this development of Frei's thought in George A. Lindbeck, "The 'Literal Reading' of Biblical Narrative in the Christian Tradition: Does It Stretch or Will It Break?" in *The Bible and the Narrative Tradition*, ed. Frank McConnell (New York: Oxford University Press, 1986), 37–77.

125. Kevin J. Vanhoozer, "The Spirit of Understanding: Special Revelation and General Hermeneutics," in *Disciplining Hermeneutics: Interpretation in Christian Perspective*, ed. Roger Lundin (Grand Rapids, MI: Eerdmans, 1997), 144, n. 47, italics mine.

126. Vanhoozer, *The Drama of Doctrine*, 166; cf. idem, "Scripture and Tradition," in *The Cambridge Companion to Postmodern Theology*, ed. Kevin J. Vanhoozer (Cambridge: Cambridge University Press, 2003), 160–61.

127. Vanhoozer, *The Drama of Doctrine*, 171–72. In his earlier work, Vanhoozer credits Lindbeck for finding "a way to escape the relativity of interpretive communities" with his clarion call for intratextual theology. See Vanhoozer, *Is There a Meaning in This Text?*, 174.

248

meaning and belief of the community.[128] In this performance model, authority belongs to the *world in front of the text* rather than the *world of the text* itself.[129] Vanhoozer rightly asks whether performing the text is even possible with this sort of approach: "If there is no hard and fast distinction between what is in the text and what is in the reader, how can different readers of the same text get the same meaning out of it? Can we even say that two readers have read the same text?"[130]

The Performance II interpretation represented in the postliberal models of doctrinal authority present a number of major problems for the present concern for doctrinal development. First, this approach veers toward antirealism. God-talk does not describe the reality of God as much as it describes communal beliefs about God.[131] The postliberal approach faintly resembles Feuerbach's description of religious belief: "Religion is a dream, in which our own conceptions and emotions appear to us as separate existences, beings out of ourselves. The religious mind does not distinguish between the subjective and the objective—it has no doubts; it has the faculty, not of discerning things other than itself, but of seeing its own conceptions out of itself as distinct beings."[132] Theology reduced to communal self-description is *de facto* a form of Feuerbachian self-referentiality. Whereas Feuerbach reduces religious belief to anthropology, Lindbeck teeters on limiting the formulation of doctrine to anthropological discourse.

A second, related concern is that Performance II interpretation offers no clear criteria for distinguishing appropriate developments

---

128. Vanhoozer, *The Drama of Doctrine*, 172.

129. Kevin J. Vanhoozer, "A Drama-of-Redemption Model: Always Performing?" in *Four Views on Moving Beyond the Bible to Theology*, ed. Gary T. Meadors (Grand Rapids, MI: Zondervan, 2009), 168.

130. Vanhoozer, *Is There a Meaning in This Text?*, 384.

131. Vanhoozer, *The Drama of Doctrine*, 6–7; cf. 174–75.

132. Ludwig Feuerbach, *The Essence of Christianity*, 2nd ed., trans. George Elliot [Marian Evans] (London: Trübner & Company, 1881), 204–5.

from non-appropriate developments.[133] Lindbeck may want to affirm the creed of Nicaea as grammar for regulating Christian belief but offers no good reason for believing that the development of Arianism was not also a suitable performance of the biblical text. Why didn't the Council at Nicaea practice the kind of ecumenism Lindbeck proposes in the cultural-linguistic model of doctrine? Could not the Arians and Homoousians experience the kind of "reconciliation without capitulation" of which Lindbeck speaks had they only acknowledged their differing local grammars and authorities?[134]

Most importantly, the postliberal model, like other postmodern hermeneutical theories, offers no protection from ideological control. For that reason, every community can read texts in a way that seems right in their own eyes. Neither the conservative nor the progressive, the Catholic nor the Protestant, the militant nor the pacifist is in a place to make judgments of the legitimacy of other readings. Without the possibility of textual determinacy and interpreting authorial discourse, all ideologies and community readings are incommensurable. It is here that the intersection between the theological and hermeneutical dimensions of the question of authority become most evident. Interpretive authority placed ultimately in the hands of the community essentially means that the reading community becomes the primary "source" of doctrinal formulation, a notion contrary to traditional and evangelical understandings of Scripture's supreme authority.

In contrast to the postliberal version of performance, Vanhoozer's Performance I interpretation is an effort to describe the Scripture-tradition relationship in a way that is faithful to the divine and human authorial intentionality of scripture. Much like Vanhoozer's

133. Vanhoozer, *The Drama of Doctrine*, 175.
134. See George A. Lindbeck, *The Nature of Doctrine: Religion and Theology in a Postliberal Age* (Louisville: Westminster John Knox, 1984), 15–16.

earlier work in general hermeneutics, the guiding hermeneutical assumption of this approach is the interpreter's need to attend to the communicative acts of a text. In theo-dramatic terms, the play belongs to God, not the local theatre troupe.[135] What stands apart, however, is the new emphasis on distinctively Christian practices of reading: "If God is the ultimate communicative agent, and if divine illocutions have been canonically inscribed, then it is incumbent on the Christian interpreter to read for the divinely appropriated prophetic and apostolic discourse."[136] God is a necessarily communicative agent of speech who also acts freely through a number of communicative speech acts, particularly in the canonical discourse of Scripture. In Vanhoozer's more recent foray into the doctrine of God, he describes God's being not in traditional terms of causal relations but in communicative action. God is "being-in-communicative-act," and as triune communicative being, he is "constrained by no greater metaphysical principle than himself to be self-communicative."[137]

The metaphor of performance takes a markedly different turn in Performance I. Vanhoozer distances himself from Wolterstorff, whom he believes to force a false dichotomy between authorial discourse interpretation and performance interpretation. As the divinely authored script for the theo-drama, Scripture constitutes triune communication that elicits a response from the people of God in the church.[138] Speech-act theory and the construal of God as a communicative agent thus provide a way around the personal/propositional impasse forged in twentieth-century debates about the nature of revelation. As divine communicative action not limited

---

135. Vanhoozer, *The Drama of Doctrine*, 183.
136. Ibid., 180.
137. Kevin J. Vanhoozer, *Remythologizing Theology: Divine Action, Passion, and Authorship* (Cambridge: Cambridge University Press, 2010), 226.
138. Vanhoozer, *The Drama of Doctrine*, 184.

to the act of revealing,[139] divine speech is simultaneously reality depicting and moving toward a purpose. Fidelity to Scripture does not end with the abstraction of doctrinal propositions from the biblical text because the illocutionary acts of Scripture call for continuing participation. As the "script" of the theo-drama, the Bible is the authority that directs the church's continuing performance, for "action and embodiment."[140] To use Thiselton's terminology, Scripture often transforms the world of the readers by a *"world-to-word fit."* Texts not only picture the world but also *transform the world* of the readers.[141] Scripture plays the single most important role in shaping the worldview of or "forms of life" in the church. If defined as responding to the illocutionary acts of Scripture in a contemporary setting, authority in doctrinal development ultimately belongs to God alone.

If doctrine is going to succeed in directing Christian discipleship in contemporary settings, theologians must also attend to worlds in front of the text, past and present. The theologian fluent in the history of doctrine is able to evaluate how the church, under the illumination of the Holy Spirit, has interpreted and performed Scripture in its various settings.[142] As Barth explains, "With regard to theology, we cannot be in the Church without taking as much responsibility for the theology of the past as for the theology of our present. Augustine, Thomas Aquinas, Luther, Schleiermacher and all the rest are not dead but living. They still speak and demand a hearing as living voices, as surely as we know that they and we belong together in the Church."[143] The voices of the past act as

---

139. See Wolterstorff, *Divine Discourse*, 19–36.
140. Vanhoozer, *The Drama of Doctrine*, 115.
141. See Thiselton, *New Horizons*, 291–307.
142. Vanhoozer, "A Drama-of-Redemption Model," 181.
143. Karl Barth, *Protestant Theology in the Nineteenth Century*, trans. Brian Cozens and John Bowden (Grand Rapids, MI: Eerdmans, 2002), 3.

living sages for the present. However, performance of the script must yield to the final authority of the "world of the text," or the biblical author's illocutionary acts.[144] It is improvisation patterned by the script and mindful of the playwright's communicative acts. This performance means neither reenacting biblical scenes nor rewriting them but rather relating the situation in front of the text to the theo-drama within the text. Fittingness to both the script and the present situation, not novelty for novelty's sake, is the end goal of improvisation.

Concluding Remarks

One of the crucial questions models of doctrinal development must address is the question of authority in development. Traditional models treat the question theologically by attempting to determine *what source* has say-so in genuine development. Catholic scholars such as Drey, Newman, and Möhler appeal to infallible ecclesial authority that retains continuity with the apostolic tradition. Later Catholics granted the same status of infallible authority to the pope in developing doctrines, as illustrated in the development of the dogmas of the Immaculate Conception and the Assumption of Mary. Protestants and evangelicals traditionally assert a particular doctrine of the Bible, describing its authority either in ontological and/or functional terms.

The present chapter has addressed this question hermeneutically. In light of postmodern hermeneutical theory, the question is now about who determines meaning in the interpretive process. One modernist temptation is to exchange all authorities with autonomous reason. This move reduces doctrine to natural theology or leads

---

144. Vanhoozer, "A Drama-of-Redemption Model," 167–68.

to the abandonment of the theological task altogether. Making use of insights from the hermeneutical and philosophical programs of Gadamer and Wittgenstein, Thiselton advances an apologetic for authority in which he argues that reason and tradition share in a mutually beneficial symbiotic relationship. Tradition plays a vital role in shaping rationality, and reason provides checks and balances that keep the tradition from relativistic fideism. This balanced approach demonstrates that the Christian tradition can remain authoritative even when it is appropriated critically in new contexts.

Postmodernists tend to show more appreciation for tradition but also tend to localize it by reducing it to controlled communal frameworks. As seen in the neopragmatism of Richard Rorty and the reader-response theory of Stanley Fish, interpreters who reject textual determinacy see the interpretive community as the decisive authority in interpretation. The notion of textual indeterminacy in Lindbeck's cultural-linguistic approach gives ultimate doctrinal authority to the local faith community, which results in hermeneutical anarchy and theological antirealism. Speech-act theory, as utilized by Vanhoozer and Thiselton, supplies a decisive correction to this postmodern maneuver. Defining texts as the communicative acts of their authors, Vanhoozer and Thiselton contend for their general stability of meaning. These literary speech acts may be *relatively indeterminate* in meaning if *so determined* by their authors.

Perhaps the most significant implication of speech-act theory for models of doctrinal development is the way that it calls attention to the illocutionary acts of Scripture. Scripture has meaning, yes. Nevertheless, its human-divine authorship also has purpose. The authors of Scripture call for *response*. Rather than relegating the biblical text to the dustbin of history, a doctrine of Scripture shaped by speech-act theory calls attention to the way biblical authors expect perlocutionary action from their readers. For Thiselton, the world of the text continues to transform the world in front of the text. The perlocutionary acts of Scripture on the believers throughout history constitute the tradition of the church. Vanhoozer offers a uniquely Protestant view of tradition as the Spirit-directed practice of *sola scriptura* in the church. This practice, under the supreme authority of God's communicative acts in Scripture, leads to the development and enactment of doctrine.

6

Religious Language, Reality, and Doctrinal Development

Evangelicals, eponymously named for their fervor for *evangel* or gospel, are concerned about truth, particularly the truth content of the good news of Jesus Christ. We are committed to the universal proclamation of the gospel because we operate with the conviction that God has entrusted Christian believers with the only "message of reconciliation" (2 Cor. 5:19) and that it is our duty as "ambassadors for Christ" to implore every man, woman, and child to be reconciled to God (2 Cor. 5:20). We likewise operate with the deeply held conviction that the proclamation that "Christ died for our sins in accordance with the Scriptures, that he was buried, and that he was raised on the third day" (1 Cor. 15:3b–4) is, to use a popular expression, "gospel truth." New Testament writers called this gospel proclamation "the word of truth" (Eph. 1:13; Col. 1:5; 2 Tim. 2:15; Jas. 1:18). We are concerned about the *reality-depicting nature* of this apostolic kerygma because if it does not correspond to the historical reality of space-time events, "our preaching and our faith are completely useless" (1 Cor. 15:14) and we are guilty of falsely testifying about the things of God (1 Cor. 15:15).

With these convictions and concerns, most evangelicals instinctively commit to some form of *ontological truth* and the *cognitivity of religious language*. By "ontological truth," I mean a belief in a real, external world that can be known and real space-time events distinct from our perceptions of them. By the "cognitivity of religious language," I mean the ability of religious language to represent realities external to the mind. This cognitivity does not mean that all postcanonical theological statements depict divine realities accurately or truthfully. It means that doctrinal language, whatever its other uses or functions may be, also reflects the speaker's beliefs about divine ontology and God's acts in history. Furthermore, by defining all religious language as "cognitively meaningful," I do not mean that all religious language is propositional because a sentence can be cognitively meaningful without being a propositional statement. As Aristotle observes, "every sentence has meaning . . . [but] not all [meaningful sentences] can be called propositions."[1] By definition, *propositions* are statements of fact that have truth-value. They are binary statements in the sense that they are either true (^{T}) or false ($\perp$); there is no third choice. Propositions are cognitively meaningful statements, but they are not alone in this category. Some sentences such as prayers, requests, commands, and promises are also dependent upon truth-value because they are dependent on certain states of affairs actually being the case. Perhaps to the surprise of some overly sheltered evangelical readers, appeals to the cognitivity or reality depicting nature of religious language are not universal among contemporary theologians. When Yale

1. Aristotle, *On Interpretation* 4.

theologian George A. Lindbeck published *The Nature of Doctrine* in 1984, a firestorm in American and British theology ensued, particularly among Lindbeck's conservative and evangelical critics. This slender volume in theological method, which Lindbeck initially intended to serve as prolegomena to a larger work in historical theology, addressed a very important and often neglected question in theological prolegomena: What are doctrines and what purpose do they serve in the church? Lindbeck's own "cultural-linguistic" exploration of this question, shaped by his own involvement in the Protestant side of the ecumenical movement and insights from the contemporary philosophy of language, posed significant challenges to conservative and liberal theology alike. Lindbeck forced evangelicals to answer second-order questions about the nature of doctrine that many had never considered before. Most importantly for our present concern, he challenged many assumptions common to evangelicals about the nature of religious language and its role in doctrinal development.

As previously noted in chapter 2, Lindbeck describes three basic ways theologians conceive of the nature of doctrine: doctrine as *reality-depicting propositions* (what he calls the "cognitive-propositional" approach), doctrine as *expressions of religious sentiment or affection* (the "experiential-expressivist" approach), or his own postliberal, "cultural-linguistic" approach that treats doctrine like *grammatical rules that guide the local faith community*. Dissatisfied with the problems he perceives in propositional theology and the notion held by the liberal theologians of modernity that religious language is primarily therapeutic or emotive, Lindbeck proposes what he believes to be a middle way between these extremes in the cultural-linguistic approach. In the same way that a middle school English grammar textbook is designed to teach adolescents Standard English and none of the gory plot details from *Macbeth*, Lindbeck believes that doctrines, as grammatical rules, are "second-order" statements that say nothing about the content of Christian belief and "affirm nothing about extra-linguistic or extra-human reality."[2] In other words, doctrine really says more about *how to believe* than *what we believe.* For many of Lindbeck's conservative critics, his cultural-linguistic approach teeters on postmodern antirealism or, even worse, a kind of theological solipsism that reduces all theological statements to the fictions of religious communities.

Lindbeck is certainly not the first theologian to question the value of reducing religious doctrines to propositions, and in fairness to his project, he never explicitly or unequivocally embraces the ontological antirealism so often charged to him by some of his critics.[3] He simply contends that his cultural-linguistic or "rule theory" approach to doctrinal statements better serves ecumenism and the ongoing task of doctrinal development. Regarding ecumenism, Lindbeck believes that propositional doctrinal commitments lead to unnecessary conflict because one tradition might say "A" while another says "not-A," which in propositional terms, would be a violation of the law of non-contradiction. He wonders whether interfaith dialogue can genuinely happen when differences are expressed in such binary terms.

More pressing for the problem of development, Lindbeck states that *theologians committed to the cognitivity of doctrinal language have difficulty envisioning any kind of genuine development or growth in doctrine.* He suggests that propositionalists, whether Roman Catholic or Protestant, "tend to take a particular formulation of a doctrine

---

2. George A. Lindbeck, *The Nature of Doctrine* (Louisville: Westminster/John Knox, 1984), 80.

3. As Bruce D. Marshall observes, Lindbeck assumes some notion of "ontological" truth akin to the correspondence theory, even if he stresses "categorical" truth and "intrasystematic truth" in *The Nature of Doctrine*. See Bruce D. Marshall, "Introduction: *The Nature of Doctrine* After 25 Years," in George A. Lindbeck, *The Nature of Doctrine: Religion and Theology in a Postliberal Age*, rev. ed. (Louisville: Westminster/John Knox, 2009), xvii.

. . . as a truth claim with objective or ontological import, and thus have difficulty envisioning the possibility of markedly different formulations of the same doctrine."[4] They believe that "if a doctrine is once true, it is always true, and if it is once false, it is always false."[5] As a result, theologians in the cognitive-propositionalist tradition strive "to preserve identity by reproducing as literalistically as possible the words and actions of the past."[6] Consequently, Lindbeck argues, doctrinal development is not only improbable for the propositionalist, it is logically impossible:

1. If doctrines are timeless propositions with truth-values, they cannot not grow or develop.
2. According to cognitive-propositional theology, doctrines are timeless propositions with truth-values.
3. Therefore, according to cognitive-propositional theology, doctrines cannot not grow or develop.

Lindbeck concludes that genuine development is an unfeasible concept for evangelicals committed to a cognitive-propositional understanding of religious language any real change in doctrine would constitute either a change in God or a change in the truth-value of the statement, both of which are impossible.[7]

This chapter is an exploration of the relationship between this issue of reality depiction in religious language and the problem of doctrinal development. It begins with a brief history of twentieth-century debates over the nature of religious language, many of which grew out of the philosophical contributions of Ludwig Wittgenstein, J. L. Austin, and ordinary language philosophy. Their influence extends

---

4. Lindbeck, *The Nature of Doctrine*, 80; cf. 89, n. 11. Lindbeck looks to the narrative described in Chadwick's *From Bossuet to Newman* for anecdotal evidence of this suggestion.
5. Lindbeck, *The Nature of Doctrine*, 16.
6. Lindbeck, Ibid., 79.
7. Ibid., 80.

to both Lindbeck and his evangelical critics on the issue of religious language. What follows is a discussion of the promises and pitfalls of propositional or reality depicting language in Christian theology, the role of genres and metaphors in doctrinal development, and the promises and pitfalls of hermeneutical provisionality in doctrinal development. In contrast to Lindbeck, I will argue that evangelicals can adopt a positive stance toward doctrinal development and affirm the cognitivity of religious and doctrinal language but also suggest that no completely propositional approach to doctrinal language will suffice in explaining this historical phenomenon.

Doctrinal Language and the "Linguistic Turn"

Debates in Christian theology over the nature of religious language did not begin with modernism or postmodernism. The nature of religious or doctrinal language has been a hot-button topic since medieval Christianity, beginning in the works of Augustine.[8] Later medieval theologians would debate whether doctrinal language was *univocal*, *equivocal*, or *analogical*.[9] The univocal tradition, best represented by John Duns Scotus (1264–1308), argues for a one-to-one correspondence in the application of human expressions to the divine. For Scotus and those in his tradition, religious language always features some literal correspondence between terms that makes it cognitively meaningful, even in the figurative language of scripture.[10] The equivocal tradition rejects the cognitivity of religious language altogether and, in a way akin to the experiential-expressivist approach, tends to reduce religious language to emotive expressions

---

8. See Augustine *On Christian Doctrine* Books 1–3.
9. Dan R. Stiver, *The Philosophy of Religious Language: Sign, Symbol and Story* (Malden, MA: Blackwell, 1996), 15–29.
10. Ibid., 20–22.

of religious experiences. Christian mystics like Meister Eckhart (1260–1327), as well as most in Eastern religious traditions, view religious language this way.[11]

Thomas Aquinas rejected the dichotomy between univocal and equivocal views of religious language, preferring to describe religious language as analogical. In one sense, he views all theological language as equivocal, since God does not have any attributes in the same manner as his creatures.[12] But he rejects a completely equivocal view of religious language in another sense, fearing such a view leads to the "fallacy of equivocation" in which "nothing could be known or demonstrated about God at all."[13] Thomas believes all names given to God (e.g., "Father," "Lion," "Fortress," etc.) to be metaphorical descriptors that, while normally applied to creatures or created things, bear some similarities to God in his essence.[14] These metaphorical descriptors used in religious language are, for Thomas, only temporal. When human beings have a full knowledge of God in eternity, these metaphors will no longer be of value, not because of any change in God but because of a change in the reason and eternal situations of creatures.[15]

Throughout the Reformation and the Enlightenment, the nature of religious language went largely unaddressed. Many theologians who implicitly held certain views of religious language simply took the question for granted. All this would change in the twentieth century under the influence of Austrian-born Cambridge philosopher Ludwig Wittgenstein. With his declaration that all philosophy is the "criticism of speech" (*Sprachkritik*),[16] Wittgenstein

---

11. Stiver, *The Philosophy of Religious Language*, 15–16.
12. Thomas Aquinas *Summa Theologica* I, q. 13, a. 5.
13. Thomas Aquinas *Summa Theologica* I, q. 13, a. 5.
14. Thomas Aquinas *Summa Theologica* I, q. 13, a. 6.
15. Thomas Aquinas *Summa Theologica* I, q. 13, a. 7.
16. See Ludwig Wittgenstein, *Tractatus Logico-Philosophicus*, trans. C. K. Ogden (New York: Barnes and Noble, 2003), §4.0031; cf. §4.112.

ushered in the so-called "linguistic turn" of twentieth-century philosophy. In this "turn," many philosophers shifted their focus away from traditional problems in philosophy (e.g., metaphysics, epistemology, axiology, etc.) to the analysis or philosophy of language.[17]

Two stages of Wittgenstein's work influenced two radically divergent movements in the philosophy of language: (1) logical positivism (or logical empiricism) and (2) the so-called "ordinary language school." These two stages also had very different implications for religious language, as the first stage provided a basis for a criticism of religious language and belief and the second stage a basis for an apologetic of sorts for religious language. Along with Austin's speech-act theory, Wittgenstein's philosophy of language has had a wide-ranging impact on theological conversation—even across traditional and denominational lines.[18] These developments are of great importance for how Christian theologians describe the cognitivity of religious language in doctrinal development.

The Early Wittgenstein, Logical Positivism, and Religious Language

The first stage of Wittgenstein's philosophy of language is detailed in his *Tractatus Logico-Philosophicus* (1921), most of which was written while the young philosopher was serving as an officer in the Austro-

---

17. Wittgenstein himself never used the phrase "linguistic turn." Vienna Circle member Gustav Bergmann coined the phrase, but Richard Rorty popularized it with a collection of essays bearing the phrase as a title. See also Richard Rorty, ed., *The Linguistic Turn: Essays in Philosophical Method* (Chicago: University of Chicago Press, 1967), esp. 1–40. Rorty describes philosophy's linguistic turn "as a reaction against the notion of philosophy as a discipline which attempts the solution of certain traditional problems—problems (apparently) generated by certain commonsense beliefs" (23).

18. Fergus Kerr first explored this issue in his *Theology after Wittgenstein*, 2nd. ed. (London: SPCK, 1997). For an evangelical assessment, see Bruce R. Ashford, "Wittgenstein's Theologians? A Survey of Ludwig Wittgenstein's Impact on Theology," *Journal of the Evangelical Theological Society* 50/2 (June 2007): 357–75.

Hungarian Army and later as a prisoner of war in Italian prison camps during the first World War. In this very concise work, the only monograph he published in his lifetime, Wittgenstein ambitiously attempts to explain the relationship between language and reality with seven logical axioms or propositions, six of which he qualifies with a descending hierarchy of additional propositions. He puts forward a "picture theory" of language, wherein he argues that for a sentence to have meaning, it must have a logical, propositional structure that represents a state of affairs in the world.[19] The early Wittgenstein's logical positivist interpreters in the Vienna Circle and in British analytical philosophy advocated a "verification principle" of meaning, contending that synthetic statements (i.e., *a posteriori* statements based on observation of the world) are meaningful if and only if their content is susceptible to the tools of the scientific method. These statements are true if and only if they could successfully pass the stringent tests of regularity and empirical verification.[20]

While it was certainly was not by design, Wittgenstein's *Tractatus* had an immense impact on the understanding of religious language in the early twentieth century. His logical positivist interpreters, such as such as Bertrand Russell (1872–1970), attempted to apply principles from the *Tractatus* to a unitary, reductionistic science that would govern all philosophical language. They considered many conventional philosophical questions in metaphysics, ethics, aesthetics, or the philosophy of religion meaningless because these inquiries do not meet criteria like the verification principle. Trying to ascribe truth-value to metaphysical sentences is like ascribing truth-

19. Wittgenstein, *Tractatus*, §§3–4.53, esp. §§3, 4, 4.001, 4.021, 4.032.
20. Bernard Hodgson, "Logical Positivism and the Vienna Circle," in *Columbia Companion to Twentieth-Century Philosophers*, ed. Contantin V. Boundas (New York: Columbia University Press, 2007), 97–101.

value to a dog's bark or cat's meow or logical axioms to a Baroque sonata; it is a nonsensical notion. As Vienna Circle member Rudolf Carnap famously quipped, "Metaphysicians are musicians without musical ability."[21]

British logical positivist A. J. Ayer contends that religious statements such as "God exists" are not "true" or "false" but meaningless sentences because one can never empirically test, observe, or verify the existence of a transcendent being that is, by definition, beyond the bounds of the observable material universe.[22] Historian of philosophy Bernard Hodgson notes that the logical positivist is fully aware that some synthetic statements will never be verified, like the assertion that there could be life on one of the moons of Jupiter. Yet despite the inability of the observer to verify the reality depiction of such an assertion, "such a statement remains a cognitively meaningful one as long as we can conceive what sorts of observation would verify/falsify the statement if we could undertake them."[23]

For logical positivists, doctrinal development is an exercise in linguistic futility. Logical positivists view the description of God as a transcendent being, fundamentally beyond the bounds of this world as beyond a conceivable means of verification. Without such means, Ayer insists, no creed or religious statement purporting to God or spiritual beings can possess any "literal significance" and "all utterances about the nature of God are nonsensical."[24] In asserting the inconceivability of religious language ever meeting the stringent standards of empirical observation, it seems that Ayer and other logical positivists had an *a priori* assumption that other forms of

21. Rudolf Carnap, "The Elimination of Metaphysics through Logical Analysis of Language," trans. Arthur Pap, in *Logical Positivism*, ed. A. J. Ayer (New York: Free Press, 1959), 80.

22. A. J. Ayer, *Language, Truth, and Logic* (New York: Dover, 1992), 114–15.

23. Hodgson, 99.

24. Ayer, 115.

religious language verification, such as eschatological verification (i.e., the notion that the faith of believers will become sight in the eschaton) are also logically impossible. This death "sentence" issued to metaphysical statements and religious language by logical positivists ultimately proved premature and impossible to sustain, as their own chief tenet failed its own test of verifiability. Philosophers quickly realized that the maxim "Only sentences that can undergo empirical verification are meaningful" is self-refuting.[25]

To the chagrin of his logical positivist interpreters, Wittgenstein himself never explicitly denies mystical, ethical, or poetic truth, even in the early stages of his work. He only questions the ability of words to picture it, ultimately rendering language incapable of speaking it. In the perplexing, uniquely unqualified final proposition of the *Tractatus*, Wittgenstein writes of some truths that must operate beyond the bounds of world-depicting language: "Whereof one cannot speak, thereof one must be silent."[26] As many of his later interpreters have observed, Wittgenstein's final proposition may be an indication that the logical positivists fundamentally misunderstood the *Tractatus*.[27]

25. Philosopher of science and contemporary of the Vienna Circle Karl Popper offered a most creative critique of the logical positivist program. Instead of a verification criterion of meaning, Popper offered a criterion of falsifiability. See Karl Popper, *The Logic of Scientific Discovery* (New York: Routledge, 1992), 57–73. The criterion of falsifiability distinguishes between scientific and non-scientific statements not based on verifiability—as some scientific assertions can never be verified universally or consistently—but rather based on an assertion's ability to be falsified by contradictory instances.
26. Wittgenstein, *Tractatus*, §7.
27. Anthony C. Thiselton, *The Two Horizons: New Testament Hermeneutics and Philosophical Description with Special Reference to Heidegger, Bultmann, Gadamer, and Wittgenstein* (Carlisle: Paternoster, 1980), 369.

The Later Wittgenstein on the Many Uses of Language

In the years following the *Tractatus*, Wittgenstein's work at Cambridge began to parallel the "ordinary language philosophy" movement that swept the philosophy department at Oxford in the 1940s and 1950s under the leadership of figures like J. L. Austin and Gilbert Ryle. This later, more mature Wittgenstein shows more concern for the "everyday use" of language than analysis of propositions.[28] The most systematic presentation of this phase of his philosophy is in the posthumously published *Philosophical Investigations* (1953), in which abandons his earlier "picture theory" of language and argues that the meaningfulness of language is not contingent upon pictures of the world but rather in *how speakers use language* in particular life settings or "language games" (*Sprachspiel*).[29] Language works like "tools in a tool-box" and the "functions of words . . . as diverse as the functions of these objects."[30] Like his Oxford counterparts, the later Wittgenstein is primarily concerned with how words function, not what they signify.[31]

After observing different athletic matches at Cambridge, Wittgenstein noticed that different games with superficial linguistic similarities play by very different rules, and he came to believe that language operates in a similar fashion—having one function in one "language game" and another function in different game. He notes, "The term 'language-*game*' is meant to bring into prominence the fact that the *speaking* of a language is part of an activity, or a form of life."[32] Words neither have meaning independent of a particular

---

28. Ludwig Wittgenstein, *Philosophical Investigations*, 4th ed., trans. G. E. M. Anscombe, P. M. S. Hacker, and Joachim Schulte (Oxford: Blackwell, 2009), I, §116.

29. Ibid., I, §65.

30. Ibid., I, §11.

31. For an analysis of Wittgenstein's relation to the ordinary language school, see Oswald Hanfling, *Philosophy and Ordinary Language: The Bent and Genius of Our Tongue* (New York: Routledge, 2000), 38–52.

language game, nor does their meaning remain the same between different games. Wittgenstein likewise said that language only has meaning in the various "forms of life." That is, language only has meaning within a particular activity such as command performances, reporting an event, commentating on an event, praying, proclaiming, play-acting, and joke telling.[33] Just as the rules of basketball carry no influence in football or hockey, the rules of scientific language have no application or means of censure in the language game of Christian theology. The promise of the later Wittgenstein's work for religious or doctrinal language was in its less rigid definition of meaningful language and its greater tolerance for religious traditions, but with such newfound enthusiasm, there was also the looming threat of non-cognitive interpretations of religious language.

Some interpreters of the later Wittgenstein have used his work to justify this kind of linguistic anti-realism. The "Wittgensteinian fideists"[34] started applying his views of language's usefulness to their discussion of religious language.[35] Proponents of Wittgensteinian fideism suggest that every mode of discourse or language game has its own internal rules of logic, and as a result, these language-games are beyond criticism and external evaluation.[36] In this scheme, religious language has "no need for explanatory support and in the end can hardly be seen as more than a groundless language game."[37] The only

32. Wittgenstein, *Philosophical Investigations*, I, §11.
33. Stiver, *The Philosophy of Religious Language*, 62.
34. Kai Nielsen, "Wittgensteinian Fideism," *Philosophy* 42 (1967): 192–93.
35. A short list of proponents of this noncognitivist perspective includes Richard B. Brainwaithe, *An Empiricist's View of the Nature of Religious Belief* (Cambridge: Cambridge University Press, 1955); D. Z. Phillips, *Belief, Change, and the Forms of Life* (Atlantic Highlands, NJ: Humanities Press International, 1986); J. H. Randall Jr., *The Role of Knowledge in Western Religion* (Boston: Beacon Press, 1958); and despite his claims of holding a critical realist position in contrast to Phillips's position, John Hick, *An Interpretation of Religion* (New Haven, CT: Yale, 1989), 343–61.
36. Stiver, *The Philosophy of Religious Language*, 69.

meaning religious discourse takes in this non-cognitive view is in its particular function within the language-game. Wittgensteinian fideist John H. Randall Jr. writes, "What is important to recognize is that religious symbols belong with social and artistic symbols, in the group of symbols that are both *nonrepresentative* and *noncognitive*. Such noncognitive symbols can be said to symbolize not some external thing that can be indicated apart from their operation, but rather what they themselves *do*, their particular functions."[38] Thiselton and other evangelical critics have challenged the Wittgensteinian fideists for misrepresenting Wittgenstein's view of language here, because language for Wittgenstein is dependent on its "surroundings" and "public domain."[39] Language, even religious language, can attempt to make external reference.

Most importantly for our present discussion about the cognitivity of doctrinal statements, Wittgenstein also makes "a radical break with the idea that language always functions in one way, always serves the same purpose: to convey thoughts."[40] Language does other things besides *picturing* the world. It has many uses or functions besides reference. Furthermore, language can do more than one thing at a time. A sentence may *refer* to something and command something. An interrogative sentence can also express the beliefs of the speaker. This observation presents a much-needed correction to the dichotomous and trichotomous models of language that suggested that language only functions one way or another.[41]

37. J. Wentzel van Huyssteen, *Essays in Postfoundationalist Theology* (Grand Rapids: Eerdmans, 1997), 186.
38. Randall, 114.
39. Anthony C. Thiselton, *Interpreting God and the Postmodern Self: On Meaning, Manipulation, and Promise* (Grand Rapids, MI: Eerdmans, 1995), 38–39; cf. idem, *The Two Horizons*, 379–385.
40. Wittgenstein, *Philosophical Investigations*, I, §304.
41. Anthony C. Thiselton, *The Two Horizons: New Testament Hermeneutics and Philosophical Description with Special Reference to Heidegger, Bultmann, Gadamer, and Wittgenstein* (Carlisle: Paternoster, 1980), 196; cf. Luis Alonso Schökel, *The Inspired Word: Scripture in the Light of Language and Literature*, trans. Francis Martin (New York: Herder and Herder, 1965), 134–35.

Doctrinal language can serve many functions and depict reality simultaneously. The insistence that doctrinal language either depicts reality or performs a particular function (e.g., guiding the community or expressing belief) is a false dichotomy. Wittgenstein and the ordinary language philosophers demonstrate that language is not limited to a singular function (as it simultaneously can explain, express, direct, promise, curse, etc.).[42] Wittgenstein has made it perfectly clear that "functions of language repeatedly overlap, and they occur frequently in more than one mode simultaneously."[43] Doctrinal language is no different. Because doctrinal language can be multifunctional, it can be used in any number of ways and still be reality depicting.

Throughout his career, Thiselton has used Wittgenstein's insights here to correct dichotomous views of language in biblical hermeneutics. He spills much ink in his early writings addressing the propensity of many early twentieth-century biblical scholars, including Gerhard von Rad and Rudolf Bultmann, to view language as an *either-or* (e.g., either existential expression or a propositional truth claim) rather than a *both-and* with regard to function and

---

For example, the German linguist Karl Bühler offers his trichotomous "organon model" of language that limited language to one of three basic functions. According to Bühler, language is either a neutral representation (*Darstellung*) of states of affairs, an expression (*Ausdruck*) of the speaker's feelings, or an appeal (*Appell*) directed toward the recipients of language. See Karl Bühler, *Sprachtheorie: Die Darstellungsfunktion der Sprache* (Stuttgart: Verlag von Gustav Fischer, 1965), esp. 24–33. Bühler, too, describes language as a "tool," though he defines it very differently than Wittgenstein. Bühler borrows from Plato the notion that language is an "organon" (*organum*) or tool "used to say something to another about things" (24). Communication occurs between the sender and the receiver (*Empfänger*) regarding objects and states of affairs (*Gegenstände und Sachverhalte*). According to Bühler, the three functions in the act of communication can be determined by the direction of the linguistic sign. Language directed to states of affairs is neutral representation. Signs focusing on the feelings of the sender function as expression, and signs directed toward the receiver function as *appeal* (*Appell*). Jesuit biblical scholar Luis Alonso Schökel (1920–1998) argues that language hardly ever serves only one of these three functions.

42. Thiselton, *The Two Horizons*, 370–79.
43. Anthony C. Thiselton, *Thiselton on Hermeneutics: Collected Works with New Essays* (Grand Rapids, MI: Eerdmans, 2006), 630; cf. Wittgenstein, *Philosophical Investigations* I, §304.

content.[44] These scholars tend to create a false dichotomy between "the two supposed *alternatives* of factual, descriptive functions of language, and value-laden, proclamatory, and transforming functions of language, as if the latter could or should operate independently of the former."[45]

The same criticism applies to Lindbeck's model of doctrinal language. For Thiselton, Lindbeck's three models of doctrine (i.e., cognitive-propositional, experiential-expressive, and cultural-linguistic) are artificial categorizations that neglect Wittgenstein's concerns about generalizing models of language and the need to examine particular cases.[46] While the positive contribution of existentialist hermeneutics in biblical studies and the cultural-linguistic approach in theology is the recognition that biblical and theological language is not merely descriptive or propositional speech, both Bultmann and Lindbeck are guilty of overcompensating in their critiques of traditional language. Biblical and theological language may be more than propositional in its use and function, but it is no less than propositional or reality depicting.

Though Vanhoozer shares Lindbeck's concerns about limiting doctrine or revelation to propositions, he likewise refuses the dichotomy Lindbeck makes between first-order propositions and second-order rules. The language of doctrine and revelation can be ontologically truthful and regulative.[47] Doctrine, as Alister McGrath

---

44. Anthony C. Thiselton, "The Supposed Power of Words in the Biblical Writings," *Journal of Theological Studies* 25 (1974): 282–99; idem, *The Two Horizons*, 205–92; idem, *New Horizons in Hermeneutics: The Theory and Practice of Transforming Biblical Reading* (Grand Rapids, MI: Zondervan, 1992), 272–82. See also Gerhard von Rad, *Old Testament Theology*, vol. 2, trans. D. M. G. Stalker (Edinburgh: Oliver and Boyd, 1965), 82–87; Rudolf Bultmann, "New Testament and Mythology," in *Kerygma and Myth: A Theological Debate*, ed. Hans Werner Bartsch, trans. Reginald H. Fuller (London: SPCK, 1953), 1–44.

45. Thiselton, *New Horizons in Hermeneutics*, 272.

46. Anthony C. Thiselton, *The Hermeneutics of Doctrine* (Grand Rapids, MI: Eerdmans, 2007), 79; cf. idem, *The Two Horizons*, 430–31.

47. Ibid., 276.

has shown, can have multiple dimensions with different concurrent functions.[48] Doctrine can simultaneously direct the faith community (like in Lindbeck's own cultural-linguistic model), express religious sentiments (like the experiential-expressivist model), and depict extra-linguistic theological realities (like the cognitive-propositional model). A multifaceted understanding of religious language shaped by Wittgenstein's theory shows these categories are not mutually exclusive.

Lindbeck, who himself utilizes insights from the philosophy of language, seems to acknowledge this at points. He offers this point of clarification to his critics: "To say that doctrines are rules is not to deny that they involve propositions."[49] However, with his insistence that doctrines are either first-order truth claims (i.e., propositions about the content of theology) or second-order rules (i.e., instructions that guide the faith community), Thiselton and Vanhoozer's concerns that Lindbeck is offering a false dichotomy between speech acts or rules and cognitive truth appear to be justified. This dichotomy is particularly evident in Lindbeck's designation of the cultural-linguistic model as an "alternative" to a cognitive-propositional model, which is a crucial point of contention with Lindbeck's critics.[50] Despite this claim, doctrines can be both first-order truth claims and second-order rules.

---

48. Alister E. McGrath, *The Genesis of Doctrine: A Study in the Foundation of Doctrinal Criticism* (Grand Rapids, MI: Eerdmans, 1997), 37.

49. Lindbeck, *The Nature of Doctrine*, 80.

50. Ibid., 32–41; Thiselton, *The Hermeneutics of Doctrine*, 79–80; cf. 8–9. For a similar critique, see Richard S. Briggs, *Words in Action: Speech-Act Theory and Biblical Interpretation, Toward a Hermeneutic of Self-Involvement* (New York: T&T Clark, 2001), 214–15.

Austin, Searle, and Religious Speech Acts

The later Wittgenstein of *Philosophical Investigations* was not the last significant contributor in the ordinary language school who would argue along these lines. J. L. Austin, the progenitor of *speech-act theory*, would also argue for (1) multiple uses of language in a given statement and (2) the potential of truth-value in speech acts. With his notion of "speech acts" or "performatives," Austin, like Wittgenstein before him, showed that language entails more than but no less than reference. In so doing, he adapted for the philosophy of language what grammarians have always instinctively known: speakers can use language to do different things.[51] Speech is a kind of action on the part of the speaker.[52] Contra logical positivism, Austin showed that a number of different types of sentences, including religious and theological statements, could be cognitively meaningful.

Austin assigned every speech-act—every written or spoken use of language—three distinct components: the *locutionary act*, the *illocutionary act*, and the *perlocutionary act*. The locutionary act is the set of signs and syntactical meaning that make up a sentence. The illocutionary act is what the speaker and/or author intends to do with her words (e.g., "informing, ordering, warning, undertaking," etc.). The perlocutionary act is the "what we bring about or achieve *by* saying something, such as convincing, persuading, deterring."[53] According to Austin, whenever someone speaks or writes, at least three things are happening:

---

51. J. L. Austin, *Philosophical Papers*, 3d ed., ed. J. O. Urmson and G. J. Warnock (Oxford: Oxford University Press, 1979), 233–34.
52. For this reason, many philosophers believe speech-act theory to be a subset of action theory.
53. J. L. Austin, *How To Do Things with Words*, 2nd. ed., ed. J. O. Urmson and Marina Sbisà (Cambridge: Harvard University Press, 1962), 109.

a) the speaker/writer is expressing a series of utterances with meaning (i.e., the locutionary act),

b) the speaker is trying to do something to her hearers with her words (i.e., the illocutionary act),

c) and the speaker is eliciting some kind response of some kind from her hearers or readers (i.e., the perlocutionary act).

John Searle advanced the work of Austin and Wittgenstein by creating a comprehensive taxonomy for speech acts and by modifying Austin's categories.[54] Whereas Austin put the basic syntactical meaning of a sentence in with the utterance of the sentence in the locutionary act, Searle divided this locutionary act into two categories: *utterance acts* and *propositional acts*. The utterance act contains the words, morphemes, sentences assembled in communication. For Searle, the utterance act consists of the signs or sounds used in communication. The propositional act contains the "referring and predicating" elements of every speech act; it is the syntactical meaning of a sentence.[55] The illocutionary act serves the same function in Searle's taxonomy as it does in Austin's; it is what the author or speaker is trying accomplish with her words.

Many Christian academicians have taken to the contributions of the later Wittgenstein, Austin, and Searle like a duck to water, finding several ways that their descriptions of language correlate with other Christian ideas like belief, textual interpretation, and doctrinal statements. Among the first was James Wm. McClendon Jr., who,

---

54. See John R. Searle, *Speech Acts: An Essay in the Philosophy of Language* (New York: Cambridge University Press, 1969); idem, *Expression and Meaning: Studies in the Theory of Speech Acts* (New York: Cambridge University Press, 1979). See also Kevin J. Vanhoozer, *Is There a Meaning in This Text?* (Grand Rapids, MI: Zondervan, 1998), 209. Vanhoozer dubs Searle the "systematic theologian" of speech-act theory, the "Melanchthon" to Austin's "Luther."

55. Searle, *Speech Acts*, 24–25.

writing with atheist philosopher James M. Smith, incorporated Austin's speech-act theory into discussions about religious beliefs and relativism.[56] McClendon's former student, Roman Catholic theologian Terrence W. Tilley, appropriated it in a very innovative criticism of the discourse of theodicy.[57] Philosopher of religion Nicholas Wolterstorff offers a very helpful application of speech-act theory in his philosophical examination of divine speech.[58] As we saw in the previous chapter, Thiselton has appropriated elements of Austin and Searle's respective approaches speech-act theory to hermeneutics, and Vanhoozer has attempted to frame a doctrine of Scripture in the language of speech-act theory.

Yet not all evangelical theologians are convinced that speech-act theory is a helpful way forward in discussing religious language. In his defense of the theological method of Carl F. H. Henry, Gregory Thornbury expresses concern about the propriety of speech-act theory in evangelical biblical interpretation. He remains unconvinced that speech-act theory provides a sufficient epistemic basis for theological method because it is "epistemologically modest."[59] Second, Thornbury stresses that Austin, who like Searle after him, probably never intended for speech-act theory to be used in Christian theology, particularly discussion about the nature of Scripture. Thornbury finds irony in the attempts of evangelical theologians to

---

56. James Wm. McClendon Jr. and James M. Smith, *Understanding Religious Convictions* (Notre Dame: University of Notre Dame Press, 1975), 49–84; idem, *Convictions: Defusing Religious Pluralism* (Valley Forge, PA: Trinity Press International, 1994), 19–80. The latter book, an overhaul of the former, is even dedicated to J. L. Austin. McClendon and Smith attempt to address the problem of relativism using something elements from Austin and the later Wittgenstein, but ultimately offer an unsatisfying non-foundationalist account of religious beliefs that can never be defended on apologetic grounds.

57. Terrence W. Tilley, *The Evils of Theodicy* (Washington, DC: Georgetown University Press, 1991).

58. Nicholas Wolterstorff, *Divine Discourse: Philosophical Reflections on the Claim that God Speaks* (Cambridge: Cambridge University Press, 1995).

59. Gregory Alan Thornbury, *Recovering Classical Evangelicalism: Applying the Wisdom and Vision of Carl F. H. Henry* (Wheaton, IL: Crossway, 2013), 113.

use speech-act theory in order to talk about divine intentionality in the text, especially considering the materialist worldview of its progenitor and earliest proponents. He writes, "I think it is fair to enquire, on the basis of authorial intent . . . whether Searle would be horrified to learn that his iteration of speech-act theory was being put into service theorizing about divine revelation."[60]

Before addressing the usefulness of speech-act theory in addressing the cognitivity of religious language, it seems necessary to address some of the apprehensions about speech-act theory held by some evangelicals like Thornbury. Firstly, the metaphysical or religious beliefs of Austin and Searle are of little or no consequence to how theologians like Vanhoozer, Thiselton, Erickson, and myself use their theories about language. Talking about speech-acts, after all, is a *second-order* exercise in talking about the way language *functions*, not *first-order* theories about the origins of language, meaning, etc. Austin and Searle offer these tools to analyze *all language*—religious or non-religious—because they believe all language functions this way. These tools are now *res nullius*; they belong to no particular worldview in the same way that the laws of mathematics are not bound to the ancient Egyptians and Greeks who discovered them.

To say that we should not use Searle's insights about language because he has a materialist view of the mind is like saying, "Because Jonas Salk was an atheist we shouldn't vaccinate our children with the polio vaccine." While there may be more than a few mommy bloggers out there who hold this tenet religiously, it is faulty logic and a potentially dangerous practice. Using the vocabulary and acumen of speech-act theory is, in principle, no different from Christians using the philosophical tools of Aristotle to describe the nature of the proposition. No, Austin and Searle probably did not

60. Ibid., 114.

anticipate the use of speech-act theory to describe divine illocutionary acts, but neither did ancient pagan philosophers foresee Christian theologians using their terminology to talk about biblical inspiration and inerrancy.

The more substantial and relevant concern Thornbury raises about the use of speech-act theory is about its alethic and epistemic expediency. He contends that Austin's version of "speech-act theory simply underdetermines its own promise as a device for talking about theological truth."[61] Here it is important to stress that speech-act theory proper does not belong in the category of metaphysics (i.e., the study of reality) or epistemology (i.e., the study of how we know what we know). It belongs, properly, in the philosophy of language—a branch of philosophy, like hermeneutics, that can have *descriptive* or *normative* dimensions.

Austin's primary purpose in developing speech act theory was not, like the logical positivists before him, to create a normative or standard philosophy of language. He was more or less interested with *describing* the way language usually works or functions. Like with other philosophers of language in the twentieth century, *epistemology was only a secondary concern* for Austin. He does not put the cognitivity of language squarely in the court of whether it corresponds to reality or not, whether language is true or false. What is of greater interest to Austin is the overall effectiveness of human communication, whether speech acts are *felicitous* or *infelicitous*, whether they are "happy" or not. The "happiness" of a speech act has nothing to do with its truthfulness or relationship to the world but everything to do with whether the speaker accomplishes what she sets out to do—that her intention is understood—with her hearers.

---

61. Ibid., 112.

The primary purpose of speech-act theory is not epistemological; it is a description of how language works. I recently asked a postmodern New Testament scholar who has published extensively in reader-response hermeneutics what he thought about Austin's speech-act theory. He told me that he basically agreed with me about the *elements* of Austin's description of language—the locutionary act, the illocutionary act, and the perlocutionary act—but expressing his own postmodern skepticism, told me that illocutionary acts are nearly impossible to re-discover once they have left the mouth or the pen of a speaker. I say all this to illustrate that our fundamental differences were not in understanding the building blocks of the language or how the language is used but in our varying degrees of epistemic certainty about whether illocutionary acts can be recovered. To call attention to speech-act theory is *not* to call attention to any particular epistemology or hermeneutic; it is to call attention to a tool set useful in the second-order analysis of discourse.

Speech-Act Theory and Reality Depiction

Though the original framers of speech-act theory did not set out to create a new tool for epistemology, they worked with certain assumptions about how language does correspond to reality. Austin remarks, "For a certain performative utterance to be happy," or for a speech act to be felicitous or successful, "certain statements have *to be true*"[62]—true in a sense akin to the correspondence theory of truth.[63] In order for me to tell my wife, "That's not the way my mother makes it" and get an appropriate response, there's a needed

---

62. Austin, *How to Do Things with Words*, 45.
63. Anthony C. Thiselton, "Truth (*Alēthia*)," in *The New International Dictionary of New Testament Theology*, vol. 3, ed. Colin Brown (Grand Rapids, MI: Zondervan, 1978), 900; cf. idem, *Thiselton on Hermeneutics*, 895–96; cf. idem, *New Horizons in Hermeneutics*, 275.

assumption on my part (1) that mothers exist and (2) that mothers do things in certain ways. Apart from these ontological assumptions, these speech acts can never succeed.

Searle's modification of speech act theory to include locutionary acts, propositional acts, and illocutionary acts makes explicit an idea already implicit in Austin's description: multiple functions of language are dependent upon "propositional content." Every speech act carries with it some propositional baggage, because in every illocutionary act, there is both an "indicator of illocutionary force" (F) and an "indicator of propositional content" (p).[64] Simply having propositional content does not make every speech-act a propositional assertion, but all speech acts posit certain states of affairs for the consideration of the hearer.[65]

Every illocutionary act looks something like this: $F(p)$. The illocutionary force (F) is what the speaker or author means her reader to do or take away from the sentence. The illocutionary force (F) may be a simple assertion or a promise, a pledge, a warning, a direction, or an address.[66] The propositional content (p) is the state of affairs assumed in the speech act. For instance, the imperative statement "Sit in the chair" is not a propositional sentence, but it can be cognitively meaningful if and only if the speaker believes a hearer and a chair exists. Words and syntax are located in the locutionary

---

64. Searle, *Speech Acts*, 30.

65. Kevin J. Vanhoozer, *The Drama of Doctrine* (Louisville: Westminster/John Knox, 2005), 279; cf. 90. This observation builds upon John Searle's division of speech acts into propositional content and illocutionary force. See also Kevin J. Vanhoozer, "The Semantics of Biblical Literature: Truth and Scripture's Diverse Literary Forms," in *Hermeneutics, Authority, and Canon*, ed. D. A. Carson and John Woodbridge (Grand Rapids, MI: Zondervan, 1986), 87–91; cf. Searle, *Speech Acts*, 24–31.

66. Searle, *Speech Acts*, 31–33. Searle also makes the important distinction between the negation of the proposition and the negation of illocutionary force indicators, as illustrated in $F(-p)$ and $-F(p)$. This distinction also serves to evaluate the force of similar belief statements. For example, it may help distinguish between *harder* and *softer forms of atheism* linguistically. To say "I assert there is no god" or "⊢ (-p)"is different in its illocutionary force from saying "I do not assert that there is a god" or "- ⊢ (p)."

act, but the illocutionary act or speaker's intention can vary greatly with context. The illocutionary force (*F*) may be a command to a toddler standing in his chair, a gentle request to an elderly patient in a doctor's waiting room, or of a way of offering rest to a weary traveler. The propositional content of the sentence (*p*)—the state of affairs assumed by the speaker—is that chairs exist, as does the person to which she speaks. The speech act would fall flat in a world without chairs, as would the hearer looking to sit in a chair that does not exist.

The *F*(*p*) relationship has great explanatory power for biblical passages as well, as Thiselton has shown in great detail.[67] The command to love "the Lord your God with all your heart and with all your soul and with all your might" (Deut. 6:5) is clearly *more* than a proposition affirming the existence and uniqueness of God, although it is certainly not *less* (cf. Deut. 6:4). The illocutionary force (*F*) is *directive*, as the imperative syntax indicates, but the illocutionary force of the sentence is contingent on the reality (*p*) of the God who is Lord and the human person that is capable of giving her entire being over to divine rule. The most common illocutionary acts in the Psalter are *expressives* or *behabitives* that give expression to religious sentiments of the psalmists (e.g., feelings of joy, anger, or confusion), but even these emotive expressions are contingent on propositional content. The psalmist expresses "shouts for joy" because he believes the truth-claim that YHWH has redeemed him (Ps. 71:23). Complaints directed against God also carry with them propositional content: belief in a God who can do something about their situation. The promises of prophetic literature are of little or no value if their illocutionary force does not correspond to propositional content that describes either a current state of affairs or a future state of affairs. This important distinction between *F* and *p* helps prevent

---

67. Thiselton, *New Horizons*, 298–307.

unnecessary dualistic tendencies in the interpretation of biblical texts, but the same is true for doctrinal confessions.[68]

A postcanonical creed or confession is also a complex speech act or performative. It is more than a reality depicting statement, but not less. With a creed an individual, community or council can *assert* a reality, *commit to* reality, *promise* reality, or even *enforce* belief in reality; but in every case, the illocutionary force behind a creed hinges on a truth claim. The first line of the Chalcedonian Creed (451) demonstrates the relationship between the illocutionary force (*F*) of a command and reality-depicting content (*p*) regarding Jesus Christ: "We . . . *teach* men [*F*] to confess one and the same Son [*p*], our Lord Jesus Christ." The Nicene Creed (325) may be an even clearer illustration of the relationship between the propositional content (*p*) and illocutionary force (*F*):

> We believe [*F1*] in one God [*p1*] . . . and in one Lord [*p2*] . . . and in the Holy Spirit [*p3*]. . . . But those who say: "There was a time when he was not;" and "He was not before he was made;" and "He was made out of nothing," or "He is of another substance" or "essence," or "The Son of God is created," or "changeable," or "alterable"—they are condemned [*F2*] by the holy catholic and apostolic Church.

The propositional content of the creed (*p1*, *p2*, *p3*) asserts the reality of one God, one Lord, and the Holy Spirit. The illocutionary force (*F*) of the creed establishes the parameters of the community by *defining* or *enforcing* the beliefs of the group (*F1*) and explicitly *excludes* (*F2*) the parties affiliated with Arius of Alexandria who

---

68. Thiselton, *The Hermeneutics of Doctrine*, 8–18. Stephen E. Fowl (b. 1960) and Richard S. Briggs, both former students of Thiselton, as well as Vernon H. Neufeld (1920–2008) have written extensively on the confessional statements of Scripture with attention to these themes. See Steven E. Fowl, *The Story of Christ in the Ethics of Paul: An Analysis of the Function of the Hymnic Material in the Pauline Corpus* (Sheffield: Sheffield Academic Press, 1990); Briggs, *Words in Action*; Vernon H. Neufeld, *The Earliest Christian Confessions* (Grand Rapids, MI: Eerdmans, 1963).

would deny the propositional content of the creed (especially *p2*) by asserting that there was a time when the Son of God came into being. With both of these creedal statements, the councils who frame them are simultaneously attempting to depict reality and performing speech acts of self-commitment, teaching, or exclusion.

A faith community would not enforce or require a belief that its adherents did not believe depicted reality. The individual who gives expression to her religious experience believes something in something beyond her imaginative constructs. The performance of religious activities like prayer, worship, and proclamation is void of utility if the speaker does not believe her doctrinal language has reality depicting power. The efficacy of the various functions of doctrinal language is dependent upon the belief of the speakers that their language corresponds to reality.

Propositionalism, Reality Depiction, and Development

The insights of Wittgenstein, Austin, and ordinary language philosophy help us address the challenge posed by Lindbeck to the cognitivity of theological language. Is he correct in assuming that cognitive-propositional views of truth are contrary to the possibility of doctrinal development? In short, it depends on what one means by "cognitive-propositional."

If by "cognitive-propositional," one simply means the ability to state the doctrinal truth propositionally, then no, commitment to the proposition does not necessarily create a problem for development. We can call this position "soft propositionalism." But if by "cognitive-propositional," one means that the only task of Christian theology is to express timeless and transcontextual truth-claims in the form of propositional sentences, then yes, development is not ideal. We will call this use of the term "hard propositional." In this hard propositionalist understanding of the theological task, any bona fide advance in or revision of doctrine is either a correction of mistaken formulations of the past or a distortion of a timeless truth.

Despite its often-unfair association with a particular brand of conservative or evangelical theology, hard propositionalism may be theologically conservative or theologically liberal. In other words, propositionalist theologians may disagree about first-order issues in theology (i.e., the "content" of theology or religious belief) and still share general agreement about second-order issues (i.e., the nature of doctrinal statements). Whatever her theological point of view, the hard propositionalist theologian tends to reduce theology to "facts" or "statements." Hard propositionalists who are more theologically conservative tend to reduce biblical and theological language to univocal statements picturing extra-linguistic states of affairs.[69]

Fairly or unfairly, Charles Hodge, the orthodox rationalist of nineteenth-century Princeton Theology, is exemplary to critics of hard propositionalism in conservative theology. He once described the Bible as a divinely inspired "store-house of facts." For Hodge, systematic theology is the deductive and scientific harmonization of those divinely revealed facts.[70] The charge often brought to Hodge and his intellectual heirs is that they ignore the various genres of Scripture by reducing interpretation to a propositional scavenger hunt. Interestingly enough, he actually affirms some notion of doctrinal development and carefully distinguishes it from the emergence of Roman Catholic tradition: "All the facts, truths, doctrines, and principles, which enter into Christian theology, are in the Bible. . . . No addition has been afforded to their nature or relations."[71] Hodge fundamentally sees development simply as

---

69. Vanhoozer, *The Drama of Doctrine*, 87; cf. idem, "The Semantics of Biblical Literature," 66.
70. See Charles Hodge, *Systematic Theology*, vol. 1 (Peabody, MA: Hendrickson, 2003), 9–12.
71. Ibid., 116.

unpacking the boxes that the divine Mover has already brought into the house. There may be more boxes to break open, but they are already housed in divine revelation.

Hard propositionalist theologies in the liberal theological tradition, such as the existentialist theology of Paul Tillich, are clearly are not dependent upon biblical exegesis in the same manner as their conservative counterparts, but they are no less prone to this kind of propositional reductionism. Tillich, for instance, reduces the usefulness of poetry and music in theology to their ability to help give expression to questions of ultimate concern.[72] Tillich desires to translate the metaphorical and the poetic aspects of religion into propositional language that describes the existential concerns of the culture. Theologians like Hodge and Tillich may be as different as night and day in their conceptual systems and conclusions, but they share a tendency to purport an Archimedean vista from which they can espouse absolutist, universal truths.

Soft propositionalists are those theologians and hermeneutics specialists who have built on twentieth-century developments in the philosophy of language and who have come to reject what they perceive to be an overly simplified view of propositional truth in some sectors of evangelical theology. First, these evangelical theologians hold to the cognitivity of doctrinal language, but they also oppose a false dichotomy between non-cognitive approaches to doctrine and propositionalist theologies. Second, against Lindbeck's charge that cognitive-propositionalists conceive of doctrines as exhaustive, univocal, and timelessly true propositions with one-to-one correspondence to divine realities, soft propositionalists patently reject having definitive and exhaustive knowledge of God.[73] Even

---

72. Paul Tillich, *Systematic Theology*, vol. 1 (Chicago: University of Chicago Press, 1951), 10–13. See also, Stiver, *The Philosophy of Religious Language*, 21–22. Stiver (b. 1954) describes some of what Tillich writes as being a univocal view of theological language, univocal in a way that is strangely akin to one of his conservative counterparts like Carl F. H. Henry.

Carl F. H. Henry, who is a frequent target of these kinds of criticisms stressed the limitations of human knowledge and the provisionality of religious truth claims.

Soft propositionalists also reject Lindbeck's claim that the reality-depicting nature of doctrines makes verbal reformulation impossible.[74] To assume verbal repetition is necessary for propositional meaning to hold is, as Colin Gunton observes, "to confuse a sentence with a proposition."[75] Aristotle affirms that propositional statements, as "symbols or signs of affections or impressions of the soul," can vary with "all races of men," but "mental affections" (i.e., the objects of meaning) are "the same for all of mankind."[76] Development often demands new verbal expression, but this recognition does not mean that theological language is non-cognitive.

Despite his misgivings about hard propositionalist theologies, Vanhoozer aims to *"rehabilitate the cognitive-propositional approach to theology by expanding what we mean by 'cognitive' and by dramatizing what we mean by 'proposition.'"*[77] Thiselton, by contrast, prefers to drop the descriptors "proposition" or "propositional" altogether because

---

73. Vanhoozer, *The Drama of Doctrine*, 88; cf. McGrath, *The Genesis of Doctrine*, 16–17; cf. idem, *A Scientific Theology*, vol. 2, *Reality*, 43–46.

74. Vanhoozer, *The Drama of Doctrine*, 88.

75. Colin E. Gunton, *A Brief Theology of Revelation: The 1993 Warfield Lectures* (Edinburgh: T&T Clark, 1995), 8.

76. Aristotle, *On Interpretation* 1.

77. Vanhoozer, *The Drama of Doctrine*, 88. While Thiselton is appreciative of Vanhoozer's endeavor to *"rehabilitate the cognitive-propositional approach"* by means of clarifying and articulating the issues in the "propositionalist" debate, he warns that "we cannot generalize about the role of propositions, metaphors, or poetry in the biblical writings as a whole." See Thiselton, *The Hermeneutics of Doctrine*, 78. Thiselton's judgment of Vanhoozer on this point is somewhat premature as Vanhoozer, taking up Ricoeur's suggestion that "Scripture's subject matter requires attention to the diverse literary forms in which it is presented," conceives of biblical and theological language as multifaceted dramatic discourse—not as a collection of systematized propositions. See Vanhoozer, "The Apostolic Discourse and Its Developments," 192–93; cf. Paul Ricoeur, *Figuring the Sacred: Religion, Narrative, and Imagination*, ed. M. I. Wallace, trans. D. Pellauer (Minneapolis: Fortress Press, 1995), 144–66.

he believes that these often carelessly used terms create unnecessary diversions. He prefers the discussion move forward with the terms "reality depicting" and "ontological."[78] This basic intuition seems right, as most theologians do not show concern for the syntactical structure of the proposition itself (i.e., what makes a propositional sentence function) as much as a concern for the ability of religious and doctrinal language to describe things outside of the mind.

A rejection of hard propositionalism need not result in a non-cognitive or antirealist view of doctrinal statements, nor should evangelicals who observe problems in harder forms of propositionalism abandon the proposition altogether. The ontological baby need not be tossed out with the hard propositionalist bathwater! What's more, confessional evangelicals can affirm biblical inerrancy and acknowledge that biblical expressions of truth are more than but not less than propositional statements. While it is true that ontological truth can always be restated in the form of a proposition and that biblical expressions of truth are no less than propositional truths, the Bible depicts this reality through numerous speech acts and genres. Through the inspired texts of Scripture, God speaks, but not every speech act is a revelation in the sense that it discloses something previously unknown. Scripture utilizes many other speech acts, like commanding, inviting, praising, promising, and warning.[79]

Whereas hard propositionalist theologians conceive of the doctrinal enterprise as constructing comprehensive systems that displace the various genres and voices of scripture with a closed, absolute structure, evangelical theologians like Thiselton and Vanhoozer see the need for a more open approach to Christian

---

78. Thiselton, *Thiselton on Hermeneutics*, 631; idem, *The Hermeneutics of Doctrine*, 78; idem., "Authority and Hermeneutics: Some Proposals for a More Creative Agenda," in *Pathway into the Holy Scripture*, ed. Phillip E. Satterthwaite and David F. Wright (Grand Rapids, MI: Eerdmans, 1994), 109.

79. Wolterstorff makes this point abundantly clear in his *Divine Discourse*, 19–57.

doctrine that recognizes ongoing participation, performance, and practical wisdom. With Lindbeck, they recognize that hard propositionalism can create unnecessary problems from doctrinal development, as many theologians within this category believe their doctrinal formulations to be timeless appeals to universal reason, without need of contextualization or reformulation.[80] For the hard propositionalist, one may simply "transplant" doctrinal propositions from one place and time to another, provided enough explanation is given.[81] The soft propositionalist, by contrast, recognizes the need for "translating" the revelatory content of Scripture in new ways for new settings.

Doctrine and Self-Involvement

Even the doctrinal proposition itself can be a more complex speech act than it first appears. Professing a doctrinal tenet, for example, involves more than an objective restatement of a propositional truth. Sometimes profession is the act of drawing the line in the sand, creating a boundary between groups, as is the case in orthodoxy's response to heresy. Sometimes this subscription to a doctrinal statement is an act of open defiance to authority, as was the case of the Protestant princes at the 1530 Diet of Augsburg. The confirmation of a statement of faith can also be a way of abating external religious or social pressures. Something that takes the form and syntax of a propositional statement can have many illocutionary acts associated with it.

Even when the illocutionary act is profession of a said proposition, it is a complex speech act dependent upon the ability of said speech act to depict theological realities. Thiselton illustrates the relationship

---

80. Vanhoozer, *The Drama of Doctrine*, 85–86.
81. Millard J. Erickson, *Christian Theology*, 3rd ed. (Grand Rapids, MI: Baker, 2013), 73–75.

between the various functions of speech acts and their dependence on reality depiction with his model of doctrine as *self-involving speech acts*.[82] The term "self-involving" comes from Austin's student, Donald D. Evans, who observes that speakers are, in varying degrees, personally involved in the truth claims that they make. When a speaker makes a statement about certain states of affairs, she involves herself in relation to the statement by the stance taken.[83] She makes a commitment to the responsibilities asserting that proposition entails.[84]

Evans illustrates his argument for the self-involving nature of the *performative* (the term he prefers to Austin's "speech act") with the statement "God is *my* creator." As Thiselton notes, the "self-involving speech-act often depends for its efficacy on certain states of affairs being the case, or certain statements being true."[85] Correspondence to a state of affairs—in this case, the notion that God is the first cause in creation—is a necessary condition for these self-involving performatives, but simple ontological description is insufficient in describing these manifold speech acts. This statement is not merely recognition of the states of affairs regarding the source of creation—though it is no less than this—it is a recognition of one's "status as God's obedient servant and possession" and an acknowledgment of one's "role as God's steward and worshipper" and of "God's self-commitment" to the speaker.[86]

The Pauline confession "Jesus is Lord" (Rom. 10:9; 1 Cor. 12:3) is an example of a self-involving speech act in Scripture. By declaring

---

82. Thiselton, *The Hermeneutics of Doctrine*, 9.
83. Donald D. Evans, *The Logic of Self-Involvement: A Philosophy Study of Everyday Language with Special Reference to the Christian Use of Language about God as Creator* (London: SCM Press, 1963).
84. Thiselton, *New Horizons in Hermeneutics*, 617.
85. Thiselton, *The Hermeneutics of Doctrine*, 12. For a similar discussion on doctrinal beliefs as self-involving speech acts, see Terrence W. Tilley, *The Evils of Theodicy* (Washington, DC: Georgetown University Press, 1991), 10–81.
86. Evans, *The Logic of Self-Involvement*, 158.

Jesus as Lord, the speaker recognizes that Jesus, not Caesar or empire, is ultimately deserving of her allegiance.[87] In noting that it is only through the agency of the Holy Spirit that one can say, "Jesus is Lord" (1 Cor. 12:3), Paul implies that this confession involves more than a mere repetition of a verbal formula, as anyone can employ these locutionary acts without self-involvement or genuine belief. I can likewise repeat or echo the words "Jesus be accursed" (1 Cor. 12:3) in a sermon or exposition of this text without actually performing the illocutionary act of cursing the Lord. Though he does not have such philosophical terminology at his disposal, Paul indicates that one cannot perform the illocutionary act of affirming Jesus' lordship (i.e., affirm those words with meaning) apart from the activity of the Holy Spirit in her life. Paul also stresses that no one who speaks with the active presence of the Spirit in her life will ever truly curse the Lord.

This "Jesus is Lord" formula also attests to the multifunctional nature of language that can be simultaneously self-involving and reality depicting. Bultmann, as noted above, is prone to forcing false hermeneutical choices. He reduces the meaning of the "Jesus is Lord" formula to "Christ *pro me*," what Christ *means for me*.[88] That is to say, Christ is only Lord in a *subjective, experiential sense* when one encounters him in the kerygmatic proclamation. For Bultmann, this statement carries no objective or historical meaning.

Against Bultmann Thiselton contends that with this formula Paul simultaneously affirms (1) *belief* about Jesus' objective identity as the sovereign Lord of history and (2) a subjective statement about one's "*heart orientation of stance and will.*"[89] In other words, for Paul, Jesus is not only the Lord of all—an objective statement that is true

---

87. For a recent exploration of this theme from biblical scholarship, see Scot McKnight and Joseph B. Modica, eds., *Jesus Is Lord, Caesar Is Not: Evaluating Empire in New Testament Studies* (Downers Grove, IL: InterVarsity, 2013).
88. Rudolf Bultmann, *New Testament and Mythology and Other Basic Writings*, ed. and trans. Schubert M. Ogden (Philadelphia: Fortress Press, 1984), 120.

whether or not one affirms it—Jesus is *his* Lord, the one to whom he entrusts his whole being. Without the ability to depict the theological realities of Christ's Lordship that ground Christian experience, these formulas cannot be genuinely *self-involving*.[90] Thiselton warns that this dichotomous reading of the formula can result in a violation of the first and greatest commandment: "To ascribe 'lordship' to someone who cannot rightfully exercise it is, from the linguistic viewpoint, *empty* or logically arbitrary and from the theological viewpoint *idolatrous*."[91] If someone thinks of Christ only as a subjective lord or guide and not as the objective Lord of all reality, then that person not only makes meaningless statements and holds logically incoherent beliefs but also is in danger of fashioning a god that is profitable for nothing (Isa. 44:10).

Postcanonical doctrinal confessions, creeds, and even hymnody can function in the same fashion as the "Jesus is Lord" formula. In these statements and songs, speakers are not merely declaring value-free truth claims; they are making personal and public declarations of commitment and trust.[92] Trust and commitment do not exclude truth-claims because these actions are contingent upon certain beliefs about the way the world is.

This point calls to mind the Reformers' distinction of *notitia*, *assensus*, and *fiducia*. *Notitia* is synonymous with *cognitio* or factual knowledge; it refers to propositional content of a particular belief. Mere *notitia* does not constitute saving faith, as James observes that even demons acknowledge the existence of one God and "shudder" (Jas. 2:19). *Assensus* or assent is agreement or approval of

89. Anthony C. Thiselton, *The First Epistle to the Corinthians: A Commentary on the Greek Text*, The New International Greek New Testament Commentary (Grand Rapids, MI: Eerdmans, 2000), 924.

90. Thiselton, *New Horizons in Hermeneutics*, 282.

91. Ibid., 284.

92. Thiselton, *The Hermeneutics of Doctrine*, 13.

propositional content. Mere *assensus* may describe the belief of "nominal" Christian who "approves" of Christian beliefs (e.g., "Jesus is just alright with me") but refuses to rearrange their lives accordingly. By contrast, *fiducia* is "trust" or "faithful apprehension" (*apprehensio fiducialis*), which, in the case of Christian belief, "appropriates savingly, by an act of the will, the true knowledge and promises of God."[93]

While the Reformers contended that *notitia* and *assensus* are not sufficient for genuine faith (*fiducia*), but they are, nevertheless, necessary conditions for it. Barth makes this point clear:

> The possibility of excluding the element of *notitia* or *assensus*, i.e., the element of knowledge from faith, of making faith a trust either devoid of intellectual form or indifferent to it . . . was one of which we can say with complete certainty . . . that even in the early days of the Reformation none of the responsible leaders ever considered it seriously even for a single moment. . . . To be sure, faith becomes faith only when it is *fiducia*. *Notitia* and *assensus* alone would not be faith, but only the *opinio historica* that the ungodly can have too. Nevertheless, how can faith be *fiducia* without also being, even as *fiducia*, *notitia* and *assensus*, *fiducia promissionis*, trust in the mercy of God, which encounters us . . . in the objectivity of the Word?[94]

Without truth content (or *notitia* and *assensus*), trusting or saving faith not only loses its meaning; it is dangerously close to disobedience. Statements of Christian faith can (and must) entail propositional content and volitional or existential participation.

Rather than shunning development, theological realism anticipates it and even invites it. Advocates of the theological interpretation of Scripture instinctively know this. In contrast to purely historical-critical approaches to Scripture, a theological interpretation of

---

93. See "fides," in Richard A. Muller, *Dictionary of Latin and Greek Theological Terms: Drawn Principally from Protestant Scholastic Theology* (Grand Rapids, MI: Baker, 1985), 115–16.

94. Barth, *Church Dogmatics*, vol. 1, pt. 1, *The Doctrine of the Word of God*, 234–35.

Scripture seeks to go beyond the "world of the text" to the "world behind the text." More important than describing the beliefs of biblical authors like intellectual artifacts of the past is the call placed on readers of the Bible by its authors to partake in its ongoing story. As Thomas Torrance explains,

> The basic lesson which we must surely learn today in biblical scholarship, in the light of a realist relation between language and things, is that real understanding arises when biblical statements refer us to what is true independently of them, so that in a profound sense genuine understanding begins where biblical statements leave off. This requires from us a basically *theological* exegesis and interpretation of the Bible, in which we learn to understand what it says through its function in mediating to us knowledge of divine truths which are what they are independently of the Bible.[95]

Without an attempt on our parts to understand theological realities external to text, we have fallen short of what biblical authors desire from their readers. If biblical language conveys more than the existential considerations of its authorship—if it points to a divine reality external to the text itself—then an appropriate way to speak of and respond to those realities is to address their continued significance for readers today. Given the realism of the text, doctrinal development and theological interpretation are necessary and related ongoing tasks of biblical interpreters.

Doctrine and Canonical Diversity

Neither Thiselton nor Vanhoozer reduce systematic theology to the explanation of biblical texts by means of constructing a system of propositions (à la hard propositionalism). Both cling to the ability

---

95. Thomas F. Torrance, *Reality and Evangelical Theology: The Realism of Christian Revelation*, 2nd ed. (Downers Grove, IL: InterVarsity Press, 1999), 68–69.

of doctrinal language to depict biblical and theological realities, but both see doctrine as something more—something *formative* and *directive* for Christian life and practice. Neither of these figures wants to reduce biblical interpretation or developing doctrine to one strategy or method. For Thiselton, Wittgenstein is an important voice who reminds his readers to pay more attention to specific uses of language than generalizing rules or schemes that tend to neglect the uniqueness of some texts, speech-acts, or genres.[96] While he stresses the diversity of biblical texts, Thiselton is careful to say that these texts are not so conflicting that the task of developing biblically faithful systematic theologies is insurmountable.[97]

The hermeneutics of Paul Ricoeur is instrumental in shaping Vanhoozer's appreciation of biblical and hermeneutical diversity.[98] Because of their frequent inattentiveness to the various forms of biblical discourse, Ricoeur has little appreciation for systematic theologians.[99] He laments, "Theology itself, when it strives to be biblical theology, is too often content with extracting from all these texts a conception of God and man and of their relations from which the specific traits that pertain to the forms of discourse have been removed."[100] For Ricoeur, theologians may desire to be biblical, but they tend to read the Bible only for propositions. Ironically, many conservative interpreters committed to biblical inspiration and uniqueness often seem to exchange the diverse literary genres of the canon with a list of authoritative propositions abstracted from it.

96. See Ludwig Wittgenstein, *The Brown and the Blue Books: Preliminary Studies for the 'Philosophical Investigations'* (New York: Harper & Row, 1965), 18. See also Thiselton, *The Two Horizons*, 430;
97. Thiselton, *The Hermeneutics of Doctrine*, 144.
98. Kevin J. Vanhoozer, "The Apostolic Discourse and Its Developments," in *Scripture's Doctrine and Theology's Bible*, ed. Markus Bockmuehl and Alan J. Torrance (Grand Rapids, MI: Baker, 2008), 192–94.
99. Kevin J. Vanhoozer, *Biblical Narrative in the Philosophy of Paul Ricoeur: A Study in Hermeneutics and Theology* (Cambridge: Cambridge University Press, 1990), 123–24.
100. Ricoeur, *The Conflict of Interpretations* (Evanson, IL: Northwestern University Press, 1974), 482.

Vanhoozer charges this practice, all too common in contemporary evangelical theology, with reducing the multiple genres and speech acts in scripture to *"dedramatized"* propositions.[101]

Taking a cue from Bakhtin's analysis of Dostoyevsky's novels, Vanhoozer and Thiselton describe the speech acts of scripture as *polyphonic* and *pluriform*. Instead of a totalizing, monologic voice that exhausts the knowledge of God in propositions, Scripture "takes many voices, literary forms, and conceptual schemes to articulate the reality of God and the truth of the gospel."[102] The variety of genres, voices, and perspectives of the Bible are valuable in addressing the greatness of its subject matter.[103] A variety of chronotopes (i.e., Bakhtin's term for places and times represented in a given work of literature) and *speech genres* can provide better understanding than one, monologic voice. "Speech genre" is a term Bakhtin uses that is roughly equivalent to a speech act, but the term specifically calls attention to the way language utterances work differently in various social situations.[104] The Bible, as a polyphonic canon, is

not a book but a library. Each canonical voice represents a distinct point of view in time, space, and culture. Indeed, even within a single book, such as the Psalter, there are multiple authorial voices. And just as authors speak through the voices of their characters, *so God speaks through the voices of the biblical authors when they are read together in canonical context* as the unified work of the divine playwright.[105]

No single, controlling "integrative motif" or theological scheme for reading the Bible (e.g., dispensationalism, covenantalism, etc.) will suffice in exploring the many speech acts and voices of Scripture.[106]

---

101. Vanhoozer, *The Drama of Doctrine*, 269.
102. Vanhoozer, *Remythologizing Theology*, 30; cf. Thiselton, *The Hermeneutics of Doctrine*, 134–144.
103. Vanhoozer, *The Drama of Doctrine*, 270.
104. Vanhoozer, "From Speech Acts to Scripture Acts," 34; cf. idem, "God's Mighty Speech Acts," 173.
105. Vanhoozer, *The Drama of Doctrine*, 272.

No single *Mitte* or theological "center" abstracted from the Bible (e.g., the glory of God, the *missio Dei*) can exhaust the theological richness of the canon.[107] No one hermeneutical approach, whether historical, literary, propositionalist, existentialist, or narrativist, is sufficient for canonical interpretation. Scripture is more than, but not less than, propositional revelation; it is a collection of divine speech acts whereby God speaks *and* acts.[108]

Genres, like illocutionary acts, perform a number of different functions as communicative discourse. In the same way that the success of illocutionary acts is in some way predicated on the correspondence to real world objects and ideas, every genre—a "text act"—must *do something* "'about' something."[109] Both traditional propositionalist and non-cognitive accounts of doctrine neglect this important correlation between genre and propositional content. Traditional propositionalists tend to sift complex speech-acts for their propositional content often to the neglect of genre and illocutionary force, but the non-cognitive tends to ignore the cognitive components of language altogether, reducing language to the symbolic or metaphorical.[110]

With his postpropositionalist approach to evangelical theological method (or what may be better called a "soft propositionalist" approach), Vanhoozer does not desire to replace the proposition but

---

106. For an exploration of the "integrative motif," see Stanley J. Grenz, *Revisioning Evangelical Theology: A Fresh Agenda for the Twenty-First Century* (Downers Grove, IL: InterVarsity, 1993), 137–63.

107. Vanhoozer, *The Drama of Doctrine*, 272–73. For surveys of different "centers" in twentieth-century biblical theology, see Rudolf Smend, *Die Mitte des Alten Testaments: Exegetische Aufsätze* (Tübingen: Mohr Siebeck, 2002); Gerhard Hasel, *Old Testament Theology: Basic Issues in the Current Debate*, 4th ed. (Grand Rapids, MI: Eerdmans, 1991), 139–72; idem, *New Testament Theology: Basic Issues in the Current Debate* (Grand Rapids, MI: Eerdmans, 1978), 140–70; and Ben C. Ollenburger, ed. *Old Testament Theology: Flowering and Future* (Winona Lake, IN: Eisenbrauns, 2004), 33–241.

108. Vanhoozer, *The Drama of Doctrine*, 276–77.

109. Vanhoozer, "The Semantics of Biblical Literature," 91–92.

110. Vanhoozer, *The Drama of Doctrine*, 279.

to supplement it in a way that is respectful to these diverse genres of Scripture. Doctrine must retain informative components because, as Vanhoozer notes, "without this propositional core, the church would be evacuated of its raison d'être, leaving only programs and potlucks."[111] At the same time, limiting theology or revelation to propositions is reductionistic and falls short of the telos of Christian biblical exegesis and doctrine: transformation into the likeness of Christ. In affirming the truthfulness of Scripture, one should not neglect its illocutionary acts. Like scripture, doctrine entails *scientia* and *sapentia*; it is both the informative substance and practical wisdom of the Christian life.[112]

Doctrine is more than simply describing what the Bible says about a topic. Following the pedagogical pattern of inerrant scripture, it can do more than state "what is the case." Perhaps in the future evangelical systematic theologies will heed the advice of the soft propositionalists and take the distinct genres of Scripture more seriously. In addition to describing the God revealed in Scripture, theology can direct believers, encourage doxology, and employ creative new metaphors to depict theological realities. Good preachers instinctively know this. They not only explain the text in its ancient context but also offer fresh applications and rich sermon illustrations that help their hearers understand and apply the meaning of the text.

Doctrine and Metaphor

With his moderate or "well-versed realism," Vanhoozer strives for a via media between the absolutism of hard propositionalism and the perspectivalism of the cultural-linguistic approach. This middle

111. Ibid., 91.
112. Ibid., 268.

way is simply an extension of the path he forged between "absolute . . . interpretation" and an "agnostic abandonment of the quest for meaning" in his earlier work in general hermeneutics.[113] He defines the reality-depicting nature of doctrinal truth as *adaequatio intellectus et rei* ("conformity of the intellect to things") but with the caveat that *adaequatio* should be rendered as "adequate" or "sufficient" rather than Aristotle's notion of perfect equivalence or "conformity."[114] This is clearly a little bit of playful equivocation on Vanhoozer's part. He shares William Alston's basic sentiment that "even though we are unable to speak and think about truth with perfect precision, we are not thereby prevented from saying useful and true things about it."[115]

Doctrinal language does not mirror reality with perfect equivalence but renders it through various modes, voices, and literary tools. Adequate representation means taking into account the need for diverse forms of representation, including imagination, in rendering different aspects of reality. Language and texts may render reality but can never exhaust it. Yet the inexhaustibility of language does not entail its indeterminacy.[116] Canonical discourse serves as testimony and confession to the reality of God's saving action in Jesus Christ, yet it does so through a plurality of voices and varying kinds of communicative acts or genres. Diverse genres in Scripture describe the varying strata of reality.[117] Because singular events require

---

113. Vanhoozer, *Is There a Meaning in This Text?*, 139.
114. Vanhoozer, *The Drama of Doctrine*, 286. Thomas Aquinas, following Aristotle, also defines truth as *veritas et adaequatio rei et intellectus* (*Summa Theologia* 1 Q. 16, 1).
115. William P. Alston, *A Realist Conception of Truth* (Ithaca, NY: Cornell University Press, 1996), 64; cf. Vanhoozer, *First Theology*, 339.
116. Vanhoozer, *Is There a Meaning in This Text?*, 139.
117. Vanhoozer, *The Drama of Doctrine*, 289; cf. idem, "Imprisoned or Free?" 69. In dialogue with the works of the late Roy Bhaskar, McGrath writes extensively on the stratification of reality. See Alister E. McGrath, *A Scientific Theology*, vol. 2, *Reality* (Grand Rapids, MI: Eerdmans, 2002), 195–244. In contrast with the Enlightenment project to collapse all disciplines into some sort of universal method, McGrath suggests that both natural science and theology can engage with reality each according to its own distinct nature.

different explanatory mechanisms and methodologies (determined largely by the ontology in question), interpreters and theologians should strive to avoid reductionism.[118] Diverse genres, descriptions, and metaphors are valuable in different aspects of reality. Convinced that the cognitivity of religious language entails more than experience and reason, Vanhoozer reintroduces *imagination* as a vital tool for doctrinal understanding.[119] The polarity between imagination and descriptive scientific language has been overstated.[120] The imagination is "a cognitive instrument," and Scripture addresses human imagination by appealing to "minds, wills, and emotions alike."[121] C. S. Lewis provides valuable guidance for Vanhoozer in his insistence that God uses various literary forms, not a systematized series of propositions, to stir a response from the whole person.[122] In Lewis's words, Jesus "will always prove to be the most elusive of teachers" for the "literalist" because no system, "no net less wide than the whole heart . . . will hold the sacred Fish."[123]

Contrary to popular understanding, the imagination is not limited to the fantastic, nor does it conjure up images ex nihilo. (Even the most fanciful human imagination cannot create from nothing.) Rather, the imagination allows the mind to arrange seemingly unrelated ideas in creative coherence.[124] The most fantastic ideas and

---

118. For example, no one account can exhaust the complex levels of reality at work in the single event of Jesus' crucifixion. The biblical scholar might raise literary questions about why the evangelists told the story in the particular ways that they did. The theologian, on the other hand, might concern herself with the implications of the event for a theology of the atonement. A historian may raise "big picture" questions about the political circumstances that led to Jesus' death or even ask microcosmic questions about the physical construction of the cross itself. Concerned with the relationship between crucifixion and asphyxiation, biologists and medical professionals might describe the event in an entirely different way. Sociologists, anthropologists, linguists, philosophers, astronomers, and physicists could all make a unique contribution in describing the event. No one discipline or method can plumb its depths fully.

119. Vanhoozer, *The Drama of Doctrine*, 280.

120. Vanhoozer, "The Semantics of Biblical Literature," 54.

121. Vanhoozer, *The Drama of Doctrine*, 12.

122. Vanhoozer, "The Semantics of Biblical Literature," 77–78.

123. C. S. Lewis, *Reflections on the Psalms* (New York: Hartcourt, 1986), 119.

mental worlds that humans in their God-given creativity can produce are arrangements or compilations of concepts, themes, and objects from the world. Paul testifies of this limitation in human imagination in his paraphrase of the prophet Isaiah: "No eye has seen; no ear has heard; and no human heart has imagined what God has prepared for those who love him" (1 Cor. 2:9; cf. Isa. 52:15; 64:4). Human beings cannot even conceive of a way to do what God did in creating the world from nothing.

Imagination is a God-given capability that enables us to think about and depict the world in creative ways that reflect his glory. Theology and Christian discipleship require imagination as well. This cognitive faculty gives followers of Jesus the gospel narratives to their individual lives. We can imagine or project ourselves as characters in the heavenly drama that has unfolded in Christ's redemptive action.[125] Vanhoozer appears to be invoking the idea of "emplotment" in Ricoeur's "narrative arc" on this point.[126] For

---

124. Vanhoozer, *The Drama of Doctrine*, 281.

125. Ibid., 15.

126. See Vanhoozer, *Biblical Narrative in the Philosophy of Paul Ricoeur*, 90–92; cf. Dan R. Stiver, *Theology after Ricoeur: New Directions in Hermeneutical Theology* (Louisville: Westminster/John Knox, 2001), 66–70. Narrative emplotment is an important tool in Ricoeur's later philosophical anthropology. The focus on narrative is a move away from Ricoeur's earlier focus on *symbol* and *metaphor*, but his focus on philosophical anthropology begins with his earliest influences in French reflective and existentialist philosophy. For a brief, helpful overview of the "periods" in the thought of Ricoeur, see Anthony C. Thiselton, *Hermeneutics*, 228–54. In his earlier works, Ricoeur's philosophical anthropology, shaped by existentialist and phenomenological concerns, dealt with philosophy of the will, suffering and human limitation. See Paul Ricoeur, *Fallible Man*, trans. Charles Kelbley (Chicago: Henry Regnery, 1967); idem, *The Symbolism of Evil* (Boston: Beacon, 1969). In his "middle period," Ricoeur turns from phenomenology toward language and hermeneutics. He exposes the hermeneutical issues of Sigmund Freud's psychoanalytic project in the 1961–1962 Terry Lectures. See Paul Ricoeur, *Freud and Philosophy: An Essay on Interpretation*, trans. Denis Savage (New Haven: Yale University Press, 1970). In this text, he introduces his "postcritical" concept of the "second naïveté" (28–29). Also during this middle period, Ricoeur moves his focus from "symbol" to "metaphor. See Paul Ricoeur, *The Rule of Metaphor: Multi-disciplinary Studies of the Creation of Meaning in Language*, trans. Robert Czerny, Kathleen McLaughlin, and John Costello (Toronto: University of Toronto Press, 1975. The Ricoeur of *Time and Narrative* (3 vols., trans. Kathleen McLaughlin and David Pellauer [Chicago: University of Chicago Press, 1984, 1985, 1988]) and *Oneself as*

Ricoeur, interpretation begins with *prefiguration* (what Ricoeur also calls "mimesis[1]" or "preunderstanding," the world of the reader before the encounter with the text.[127] Historians use imagination to *configure* ("mimesis[2]") the past by organizing its events, determining its key players, and attempting to discern patterns of meaning. Vanhoozer compares mimesis[2] with metaphor: "Like the master of metaphor, the historian does not make copies but invents in order to discover."[128] *Refiguration* ("mimesis[3]") is the recasting or remaking of reality in narrative or fiction, which in turn has the ability to offer insight into human existence beyond literal reference or description.[129] Fiction does not *refer to reality* but recasts reality. It ultimately refigures "the world by enabling us to see it, and ourselves in new ways."[130] Utilizing imagination, followers of Jesus can "configure" or "refigure" their history so that it is seen in relationship to the theo-drama of God's saving action.

The use of imagination in theology need not lead to the conclusion that theology is imaginary or fictive. Imagination also enables interpreters to discover the cognitive value of metaphor, something often ignored by the cognitive-propositionalist. Again, this is where Thiselton's distinction between propositional and reality depicting is so helpful. Creative metaphors, not just propositional statements, can depict extralinguistic realities. For example, some biblical metaphors and symbols may not be propositional in the same sense as literal historical statements but nonetheless can be reality depicting in nature. Descriptions of God as "Father" (Isa. 63:16; Gal. 4:1–7),

---

Another (trans. Kathleen Blamey [Chicago: University of Chicago Press, 1992]) is in view in the discussion here.

127. Ricoeur, *Time and Narrative*, vol. 1, 53–64; cf. Stiver, *Theology after Ricoeur*, 66–67. Stiver notes the similarity between prefiguration and Gadamer's notion of "prejudices."

128. Vanhoozer, *Biblical Narrative in the Philosophy of Paul Ricoeur*, 96, cf. 92–95.

129. Stiver, *Theology after Ricoeur*, 69–70.

130. Vanhoozer, *Biblical Narrative in the Philosophy of Paul Ricoeur*, 98.

"Shepherd" (Ps. 23:1), and "Rock" (Deut. 32:4, 15, 18; Ps. 18:2, 31, 46) may be metaphorical, but they are reality depicting in the sense that they are referential and in the sense that they depict the characteristics of God analogously.

Furthermore, not every biblical metaphor is easily explained in propositional language, and not simply because the metaphors themselves are difficult to interpret. The temptation of the propositionalist is to replace the metaphorical language of Scripture with literal, scientific language or to replace the diverse genres of Scripture with propositions about their content. In this view, which might be called a *verbal-substitutionary theory of analogy*, metaphors are merely hood ornaments on scientific language, replacing the non-metaphorical with excessive embellishment.[131] Ricoeur is critical of the idea that metaphors are simply superfluous, non-cognitive embellishments for ordinary vocabulary. As he insists, "Real metaphors are not translatable."[132] Sometimes metaphors are irreducible in the sense that they cannot and should not be broken down into smaller units of meaning. Instead, they act like verbal ginseng, as cognitive stimulants for creating meaning and enabling deeper understanding of reality. As Ricoeur explains, "Metaphor is living not only to the extent that it vivifies a constituted language. Metaphor is living by virtue of the fact that it introduces the spark of imagination into a 'thinking more' at the conceptual level. This struggle to 'think more'. . . is the soul of interpretation."[133]

The teaching ministry of the Lord epitomizes Ricoeur's understanding of the function of metaphors. The disciples questioned Jesus about his insistence of speaking in parables (Matt. 13:10),

---

131. Stiver, *The Philosophy of Religious Language*, 113–14.
132. Paul Ricoeur, *Interpretation Theory: Discourse and the Surplus of Meaning* (Fort Worth: Texas Christian University Press, 1976), 52. Bakhtin and the dialogists make a similar claim. See Felch, "Dialogism," 174.
133. Ricoeur, *The Rule of Metaphor*, 303.

perhaps because they were hoping, as many of us, for him to speak more like a systematic theologian with propositional statements. But even his own explanation of his pedagogy was a metaphorical riddle: "because seeing they do not see, and hearing they do not hear, nor do they understand" (Matt. 13:13). The definition of "parable" in the New Testament Gospels is a demanding issue far beyond the scope of this chapter,[134] but it is clear that many different kinds of metaphorical figures of speech were a staple in Jesus' teaching, especially in his discussion of certain concepts that would not have benefited as much from non-poetic speech. In describing the kingdom of God in terms of simile (Matt. 13:24, 31, 33, 44, 45, 47, 52), Jesus described reality in non-literal but cognitively stimulating ways.

His teaching on hell highlights his use of metaphor to stimulate understanding that literal language cannot express. In describing hell both as a "hell of fire" (Matt. 5:22; 18:9) where the "worm does not die and the fire is never extinguished" (Mark 9:48) and as a place of "outer darkness" where "there will be weeping and gnashing of teeth" (Matt. 8:12; 22:13; 25:30), he creates difficulties for those who interpret hellfire literally. Hellfire cannot univocally be what human beings know and experience of fire *and* be a place of darkness. Jesus must be using one or both of the concepts analogously. Rather than describing hell in scientific language, his use of metaphor creates imaginative understanding that goes deeper than literal depiction could produce. To describe Jesus' imagery of hell as metaphorical is not, as John Walvoord suggests, a move made to coax contemporary concerns one might have about the abhorrence of this imagery.[135] Instead, noting the metaphorical nature of biblical language can mean that a literal description of fire does not and cannot go far

134. Thiselton explores this question in Anthony C. Thiselton, *Hermeneutics: An Introduction* (Grand Rapids, MI: Eerdmans, 2009), 35–39.
135. See John F. Walvoord, "A Response to William V. Crockett," in *Four Views on Hell*, ed. William Crockett (Grand Rapids, MI: Zondervan, 1996), 77–81

enough in describing the tortuous, grueling realities of an (everlasting) eternity without Christ.

The cognitive, meaning-creating value of metaphor is not limited to literary or theological understanding. Science, too, is dependent upon the explanatory power of analogy and the non-literal. For example, science employs numerous models that help describe physical realities in non-literal, representative manners. For instance, scientists may represent DNA as a double helix or explain molecules through two- and three-dimensional models that illustrate bonds and the arrangement of atoms (e.g., electron density plots, CPK models, ball and stick models, etc.). These models are illustrative devices that help the human mind comprehend deeper realities.[136] Operative metaphors in doctrine, like those in science, may change with the passing of time, but this type of change does not mean that scientists or theologians do not pursue understanding of reality.

The development of trinitarian doctrine Christianity involved the utilization of new metaphors to give expression to Christian belief. These new metaphors aided in understanding God's self-revelation in Scripture at a deeper level, taking Christians from an incipient understanding of the economic Trinity to a more nuanced and refined understanding of the immanent Trinity.[137] For example, John of Damascus (c. 675–749) utilized *perichoresis* as a way of describing the way in which the Father, the Son, and the Spirit relate to one another in the Godhead—inseparable yet distinct, never confused yet moving with "one impulse and one motion."[138] This metaphor helps address one of the most significant problems facing reflection on the immanent Trinity: how three distinct subsistences or persons

---

136. See J. Wentzel van Huyssteen, *Theology and the Justification of Faith: Constructing Theories in Systematic Theology*, trans. H. F. Snijders (Grand Rapids, MI: Eerdmans, 1989), 138.

137. Thomas F. Torrance, *The Christian Doctrine of God, One Being Three Persons* (Edinburgh: T&T Clark, 1996), 110.

138. John of Damascus, *Exposition of the Orthodox Faith*, 1.14.

who share in the same divine essence can be one God. *Perichoresis* has numerous other metaphorical applications in ecclesiology, theological anthropology, and soteriology. All metaphors are limited in their ability to express God, and, as Torrance explains, those that we use properly should provoke humility:

> To speak like this of God's inner Being, we cannot but feel to be a sacrilegious intrusion into the inner holy of holies of God's incomprehensible Mystery, before which we ought rather to cover our faces and clap our hands upon our mouths, for God is utterly ineffable in the transcendence and majesty of his eternal Being. . . . All true theological concepts and statements inevitably fall short of the God to whom they refer, so that, . . . their fragility and their inadequacy, as concepts and as human statements about God must be regarded as part of the correctness and truthfulness of their reference to God.[139]

Postcanonical metaphors should point us to God's self-revelation in Scripture and stir within us "committed rational worship and praise through godly ways of thought and speech that are *worthy* of God."[140]

Not all theological metaphor making is beneficial in this way. Some postcanonical theological metaphors fail to depict divine reality adequately or in ways that cohere with the historical particularities of the Christian tradition. New metaphors need to be *faithful* to Scripture and *fitting* to context. Because of our commitment to the material and formal sufficiency of Scripture, evangelicals will always approach theological metaphor making cautiously. In contrast with other postmodern approaches to metaphorical theology that reduce the Bible's role in doctrinal formation to the way it "models" metaphor-making in the Christian experience,[141] evangelicals will ask whether new metaphors utilized in theology are ways of

---

139. Torrance, *The Christian Doctrine of God*, 110–11.
140. Ibid., 111.
141. See Sallie McFague, *Models of God: Theology for an Ecological, Nuclear Age* (Philadelphia: Fortress Press, 1987), 40–57.

contemporizing biblical judgments or concepts or ways of introducing notions and concepts alien or contrary to Scripture. The ultimate norm in these creative metaphors is neither experience nor utility, but God's self-revelation in the Bible.

Realism, Provisionality, and Development

Doctrinal development occurs in the dialectic of received Christian tradition and critical engagement, in the conversation between the theological heritage of the church and a contemporary setting. In some sense, doctrinal development is not unlike the development of ideas in the natural sciences. While scientific researchers may work from within a common framework or paradigm of scientific knowledge, this does not mean that the framework itself is beyond revision or correction. Cognizance of working within a paradigm need not lead to despair in the scientific enterprise, nor should such awareness lead to an instrumentalist denial of reality that would limit scientific theory making to its usefulness.

Both science and Christian theology both work within frameworks of belief and both typically strive for what Wentzel van Huyssteen calls "intelligibility as an understanding at the deepest possible level."[142] As McGrath demonstrates, in doctrinal development, like in scientific inquiry, inquirers work with a guiding assumption that while models or theories may grow, change, or be discarded, they are nevertheless *attempting* to articulate or describe theological realities.[143] Doctrinal statements, like scientific theories, may strive for reality depiction but also like scientific theories, they are corrigible or open to revision and correction if deemed necessary.

---

142. Van Huyssteen, *Essays in Postfoundationalist Theology*, 164.
143. Alister E. McGrath, *A Scientific Theology*, vol. 3, *Theory* (Grand Rapids, MI: Eerdmans, 2003), 214.

So, how can hermeneutical theory address the tension between the desire to depict reality in Christian doctrine and the corrigibility of doctrinal statements (i.e., the occasional need to correct or develop doctrines)? Thiselton notices the way in which provisionality in scientific theorizing (and by extension, doctrinal theorizing) parallels Schleiermacher's hermeneutical observation that all interpretations are to some degree provisional and open to re-interpretation or correction.[144] Schleiermacher's hermeneutical circle exposes the provisionality of understanding in interpretation. In the "circle," interpreters are trying to make sense of a larger written text by its individual components or smaller units, but smaller units only make sense in the larger whole. To operate in the hermeneutical circle, albeit in the interpretation of a written text or in the observation of natural phenomena, is to come to an object of interpretation with the necessary prerequisites or pre-understandings about the whole that make said interpretation possible, and to operate with the awareness that such pre-understandings can change.

Thiselton considers this tension in his discussion of the corrigibility of biblical interpretation and the need for provisional judgments. However, does the corrigibility in biblical hermeneutics extend to Christian doctrine? Thiselton asks, "Is doctrine less fallible than hermeneutical judgments, especially when much Protestant doctrine depends precisely on judgments about the meaning and application of biblical texts as foundations for doctrinal construction?" Contrary to notions of static dogma or timeless propositions, Thiselton insists, "Christian doctrine arises from the *provisionality* and *corrigibility* of judgments in hermeneutics."[145] Because doctrines are interpretations of scripture and because interpretations of scripture can be fallible, they can have a provisional or tentative quality. The evangelical

144. Thiselton, "Authority and Hermeneutics," 135.
145. Thiselton, *The Hermeneutics of Doctrine*, 122.

interpreter devoted to the supreme authority of Scripture recognizes that her theological beliefs should change if, through reading and weighing arguments about interpretation, she convinces herself that her previous interpretation of biblical texts was incorrect.[146] Such a doctrinal change does not entail a denial of reality or a change in the meaning of scripture but rather a change in the orientation and stance of the one who interprets scripture.

Hermeneutical Realism and Interpretive Diversity

This recognition of provisionality in biblical interpretation imagination need not result in the "epistemic fallacy"—the postmodern (and borderline solipsist) presumption that without an objective epistemology there can be no objective ontological reality.[147] Postmodernists who are skeptical about the ability of interpreters to discern authorial meanings from texts are not *anti-modern* as much as they are *hyper-modern* in their epistemologies. As R. Albert Mohler Jr. has apply described the postmodern mindset, it "is nothing more than the logical extension of modernism in a new mood."[148] There is an irony in the postmodern and antirealist demand for an unachievable ontological objectivity, which makes their position "much more akin to positivism than its proponents allow."[149]

By contrast, realist interpreters recognize that (1) there is a reality external to the knower (in the case of texts, a real meaning that authors establish) and (2) that the knower can know this external

---

146. Thiselton, "Authority and Hermeneutics," 134.
147. Margaret S. Archer, Andrew Collier, and Douglas V. Porpora, *Transcendence: Critical Realism and God* (New York: Routledge, 2004), 2.
148. R. Albert Mohler Jr. "What Is Truth? Truth and Contemporary Culture," *Journal of the Evangelical Theological Society* 48/1 (March 2005): 65.
149. Archer, Collier, and Porpora, 1.

reality through a process of interpretive dialogue, dialogue that sometimes entails models or metaphors to explain that reality.[150] This realist hermeneutic recognizes a meaning in the text but also recognizes provisionality and room for interpretive difference. This is no different when interpreting the Bible. The literary and theological diversity of the canon, coupled with the fallibility of all knowledge, makes multiple theological traditions and development within those traditions an inevitable reality. On this side of the eschaton, Christian believers struggling to interpret biblical texts will disagree about their meaning. Paul himself recognizes that Christian believers have not yet—but should strive for—"unity in the faith" (Eph. 4:13). For Vanhoozer, this difference between theo-drama (what God really does in history) and interpretation of the theo-drama (how Christian believers interpret God's acts in history) invites "an equivalent plurality on the level of interpretive traditions."[151]

Hermeneutical interpretation, Vanhoozer proposes, is no different. Earlier, in his general hermeneutics, he describes his own position as critical hermeneutical realism. In the same way that critical realists contrast ontology and epistemology, he distinguishes the reality of a "single correct interpretation" of a text from having full possession of it. Textual determinacy (i.e., a notion of meaning determined by authors) does provide a standard for correcting interpretations, but the critical hermeneutical realist anticipates "conflicts in interpretations" because of the provisional nature of interpretation.[152] Biblical interpretation (and by extension, the development of doctrine) requires "careful (and humble) exegetical work" which must be held tentatively as its "outcome remains provisional."[153] The provisionality and finitude of interpretation extend to postcanonical

---

150. N. T. Wright, *The New Testament and the People of God* (Minneapolis: Fortress Press, 1992), 35.
151. Vanhoozer, *The Drama of Doctrine*, 275.
152. Vanhoozer, *Is There a Meaning in This Text?*, 300.
153. Vanhoozer, "God's Mighty Speech-Acts," 175.

doctrinal development as well: "Church tradition grows as a result of the community's attempt to preserve the message of the text and to develop its implications. The development of doctrine . . . can be seen as a *growth* in biblical understanding."[154]

Vanhoozer welcomes theological diversity, and again by extension, the possibilities for new doctrinal development: "I for one would be sorry if everyone thought just like me. I would deeply regret if there were no Mennonite, or Lutheran, or Greek Orthodox voices in the world."[155] He advocates a "'Pentecostal' plurality" that recognizes the unity of meaning (or reality) and the diversity of interpretations:

> To the extent that it fosters humility in the biblical interpreter, theological diversity is surely to be welcomed. By contrast, when an emphasis on diversity becomes so radical that one denies the possibility of a biblical view on anything, it can become an excuse for avoiding the concrete claims of particular texts. If those who exaggerate the canon's unity are susceptible to interpretative pride, those who exaggerate the canon's diversity must be aware of interpretative sloth.[156]

This plurality does not mean that "the meaning of a text changes at the behest of the reader, at the influence of an interpretive community, or as a result of the Spirit's leading."[157] Rather, this plurality means that multiple traditions, voices, and methods provide the best opportunity for determining the meaning of the text. Vanhoozer's call for theological diversity closely resembles a similar move by Vern Poythress, who under the influence of the presuppositionalism of Cornelius Van Til and John M. Frame and the linguistic theory of Kenneth Lee Pike, argues for a *symphonic*

---

154. Vanhoozer, *Is There a Meaning in This Text?*, 420.
155. Vanhoozer, "The Voice and the Actor," 80.
156. Vanhoozer, *The Drama of Doctrine*, 274–75.
157. Vanhoozer, *Is There a Meaning in This Text?*, 419.

theology that shows appreciation for alternative interpretations of biblical texts.[158]

This form of critical hermeneutical realism is valuable in addressing the question of reality depiction throughout development. The attempt to depict reality, like the attempt to interpret texts, is a mediated, conversational experience. While interpreters can have a varying degree of confidence in their understanding, conclusions are provisional and tentative. Regardless of disagreements and changes in interpretation, a "Pentecostal plurality" can be valuable in assessing truth claims based on text. Concerning conflicts and provisionality in interpretation, Vanhoozer asks a provocative rhetorical question for the critical hermeneutical realist: "Would we be better off without, say, Rudolf Bultmann's reading of the Fourth Gospel, or Raymond Brown's, [Brooke] F. Westcott's, Augustine's, or for that matter, Origen's allegorical fancies?"[159] On some level, Vanhoozer is right in suggesting that the answer is no, we would not be better off without a variety of readings. As seen in the history of the relationship between heresy and developing doctrine, even bad interpretations can force the production or exposure of better interpretations.

On another level, the answer is *yes*, we can live without some interpretations. For Paul, some misunderstandings are more than epistemic mistakes. They are the products of demonic deception or sinful self-deception. The serpent deceives by his cunning (2 Cor. 11:3), and that deception leads to transgression (1 Tim. 2:14) that ultimately worsens the situation (2 Tim. 3:13). With this biblical concern in mind, the world would seem to be a better place without Joseph Smith Jr.'s explanation of 1 Cor. 15:29[160] or Richard Dawkins's

---

158. See Vern Poythress, *Symphonic Theology: The Validity of Multiple Perspectives in Theology* (Grand Rapids, MI: Zondervan, 1987).

159. Vanhoozer, *Is There a Meaning in This Text?*, 420; cf. idem, *The Drama of Doctrine*, 453.

160. See Joseph Smith Jr., "An Epistle of the Prophet to the Twelve," in *History of the Church of Jesus Christ of Latter-day Saints*, vol. 4, ed. B. H. Roberts (Salt Lake City: Deseret, 1978), 231.

reading of Old Testament narratives.[161] Sometimes these readings result in apologetic responses and positive developments, but at what cost? As Poythress rightly observes, not all interpretative perspectives are equal, nor are they "equally useful."[162] Vanhoozer might qualify his call for theological diversity and Pentecostal plurality with a doctrinal taxonomy to distinguish bad readings, good readings, better readings, and best readings, much like other recent attempts to stratify Christian doctrine by levels of importance.[163]

Provisionality and Indecision

Yet for some, this recognition of provisionality might result in a kind of existential indifference, hesitation, or skepticism about the believer's ability to understand and respond to scripture. Concerning the need for provisional interpretation—for framing a belief for the moment—Thiselton appeals to the influential study of Pauline theology from Johan Christiaan Beker, who proposes that the any evaluation of Pauline thought must account for the two poles of *contingency* and *coherence*.[164] "Contingency" is acknowledgment of the historical and contextual situation in hermeneutics. Contingency accounts for the particular situations in churches or among individual

---

161. See Richard Dawkins, *The God Delusion* (New York: Houghton Mifflin, 2006), 237–50.

162. Poythress, *Symphonic Theology*, 44.

163. For examples of doctrinal taxonomy, see M. James Sawyer, *The Survivor's Guide to Theology: Investigation of the Critical Issues, Survey of Key Traditions, Biography of Major Theologians, Glossary of Terms* (Grand Rapids, MI: Zondervan, 2006), 143–76; R. Albert Mohler Jr., "Confession Evangelicalism," in *Four Views on the Spectrum of Evangelicalism*, ed. Andrew David Naselli and Collin Hansen (Grand Rapids, MI: Zondervan, 2011), 77–80. Mohler offers a "doctrinal triage" that organizes doctrines according to their "theological urgency" (78). He distinguishes between first-, second-, and third-order doctrines. Baptist theologians Stanley Grenz and Roger E. Olson make a similar stratification with *dogma*, *doctrine*, and *belief*. See Stanley J. Grenz and Roger E. Olson, *Who Needs Theology? An Invitation to the Study of God* (Downers Grove, IL: InterVarsity, 1996), 70–77.

164. Beker, *Paul the Apostle*, esp. 11–19; cf. Thiselton, *New Horizons in Hermeneutics*, 239–47; idem, *The Hermeneutics of Doctrine*, 124–27.

believers that Paul addressed in his letters. "Coherence," in contrast, is recognition that persons operate from a general framework of thought, which is neither a specific theory nor a web of immutable ideas.[165] The ad hoc or occasional nature of Pauline theology bears witness to both of these poles.

Never at any point does Paul lay out a systematic theology in the contemporary sense, as he writes each of his letters to contingent theological or pastoral crises going on in the churches he leads or advises. Yet it is safe to assume that Paul operates from some sort of coherent theological framework, a system of beliefs that guides his interaction with these churches. In the dialectic of historical development, doctrinal formulations are largely dependent upon the kinds of questions being asked at the time. Paul responds to particular issues going on in the churches (e.g., antagonism toward Gentile believers, debates over food offered to idols, the loss of believers before Parousia, etc.). Were Paul pressed or asked to ask the kind of questions systematic theologians typically address (e.g., "Who is God?," "Who is Christ?," "What is salvation?," etc.), Paul would have answered them from the pole of coherence that contained his thought-world.

Contingency and coherence are interrelated in the way that coherence guides contingent response and contingency directs the coherent framework of ideas. Beker believes that in order to understand the "contingent," that is, the particular historical situation in which a letter was written, one must have at least a provisional

---

165. See also Johann Sebastian Drey, *Brief Introduction to the Study of Theology with Reference to the Scientific Standpoint and the Catholic System*, Notre Dame Studies in Theology, vol. 1, trans. Michael J. Himes (Notre Dame: University of Notre Dame Press, 1994), §117. Drey makes a similar observation in his prolegomena. In his discussion of biblical theology's relationship to dogmatics, he writes, "For even if ideas and doctrines are not systematically arranged within the Bible, *there is a system inherent in the ideas and doctrines themselves*, a system which is all the more reliable because those ideas and doctrines have been revealed and are in continuity with a revelation handed down from the beginning."

grasp of Paul's coherent framework of thought, which can be constructed only with a view to the contingent and particular. As Thiselton observes, Beker's dialectic of contingency and coherence clearly reflects Schleiermacher's circle.[166] For Thiselton there is peril in over-systematizing the diversity and historically contingent elements of Paul's letters, but conversely there is also danger in failing to make provisional judgments about the coherence of his thought—never taking that necessary interpretive step of attempting to discern Paul's beliefs and worldview.[167] The former action results in a "fixed, static, and closed system" irrelevant to the contingencies of Christian life and doctrine; the latter results in a "quasi-positivist approach" that is incapable of making truth claims that inform the present situation.[168]

For Thiselton, Luther is a model of the critical hermeneutical practice that balances contingency and coherence in evaluating the truth assertions of Scripture.[169] He revered tradition but despised traditionalism. He believed that tradition provides a helpful voice in the interpretation of Scripture but that it is also clearly open to the critical assessment.[170] Desiderius Erasmus (1466–1536) undoubtedly held the same critical spirit, but, Thiselton suggests, with one discernible difference: a belief in the "insufficient coherence and clarity" of Scripture.[171] While Luther argues for the clarity of Scripture (*claritas scripturae*) and the ability to initiate biblically

---

166. Thiselton, *New Horizons in Hermeneutics*, 240.
167. Ibid., 238.
168. Thiselton, *The Hermeneutics of Doctrine*, 125.
169. Thiselton, *New Horizons in Hermeneutics*, 182.
170. See Jaroslav Pelikan, *The Vindication of Tradition: The 1983 Jefferson Lecture in the Humanities* (New Haven: Yale University Press, 1986), 65. In his famous aphorism, Pelikan makes the distinction between "tradition . . . the living faith of the dead" and "traditionalism . . . the dead faith of the living." He explores the theme of Luther's critical reverence for tradition in his *Obedient Rebels: Catholic Substance and Protestant Principle in Luther's Reformation* (New York: Harper & Row, 1964).
171. Thiselton, *New Horizons in Hermeneutics*, 23.

directed Christian action, Erasmus deems that the contingencies and difficulties of biblical texts almost make decision making futile. By rejecting the clarity of Scripture, the Dutch humanist anticipates a manner of postmodern skepticism about the ability of interpreters to discern authorial meaning and intent. This rejection of biblical perspicuity results in decisional paralysis. The biblical interpreter has no way of construing a coherent thought world for living in the present.[172] According to Thiselton, Luther is particularly concerned about any reading of the Bible that would prevent one from making doctrinal assertions, which would ultimately forestall "faith and action."[173] Luther recognizes the need for criticism but rejects the epistemic skepticism of Erasmus.

Noncommittal Erasmuses still abound in the twenty-first century. McGrath criticizes postmodern philosopher Hilary Lawson for his insistence that "closure" or a state of rational commitment is never an option for open-minded intellectuals. Nothing is permanent for Lawson, save for the possibility of having his beliefs and theories about reality changed once more. McGrath concedes that Christian believers should give constant consideration and examination to their theological positions and doctrinal formulas, in order to confirm and vindicate them.[174] He also admits that orthodox belief has a tentative, "unfinished" quality

> in that it represents the mid of the church as to the best manner of formulation of its living faith at any given time. Conflicts and tensions past and present may help the crystallization of fresh insights and the development of new ways of thinking about traditional ideas, or they may bring about the realization that a certain way of speaking and thinking, once thought to be adequate, must now be regarded as problematic.[175]

172. Ibid., 179–85.
173. Ibid., 182.
174. Alister E. McGrath, *Heresy: A History of Defending Truth* (New York: HarperOne, 2009), 220; cf. Hilary Lawson, *Closure: A Story of Everything* (New York: Routledge, 2001).

But McGrath also maintains that "Christian orthodoxy is as much an ongoing process as a fixed set of outcomes."[176] While many of its interpreted elements remain provisional on this side of eternity, the Christian tradition is stable and established, enough so that Christian believers can commit and act on what they know.

Provisional Theological Judgments and the Eschatological Horizon

Can one have confidence in the truth-value of doctrinal statements when the hermeneutical circle between contingency and coherence seems inescapable? Thiselton appeals to Wolfhart Pannenberg's notion of "*Truth as coherence*"—a modified version of the coherence theory of truth—for direction in addressing this question.[177] In contrast to a correspondence theory of truth that posits a proposition to be true if and only if it corresponds to the way things really are, advocates of coherence theories of truth generally describe a statement as true if it is internally consistent with all other true statements in a web of beliefs.

It is important to note that Thiselton is critical of, but does not reject entirely, the correspondence theory of truth. He is critical of what he perceives to be a stronger form of the correspondence theory that hinges on some sort of empirical observation for epistemic justification, like the view of truth propagated by the early Wittgenstein and in his logical positivist fan base. Furthermore, he does not seem to see a conflict between his criticism of some versions of the correspondence theory of truth and with his claim that language can be both reality depicting and self-involving. In his lexicographical survey of the biblical usage of "truth" (*alēthia*),

---

175. McGrath, *Heresy*, 221.
176. Ibid.
177. Thiselton, *The Hermeneutics of Doctrine*, 125.

Thiselton concludes, "The biblical writings are clearly not committed to a formal 'correspondence theory' of truth as a *general* theory, but biblical writers regularly use 'truth' in the non-technical everyday sense of *what corresponds with facts of the case.* Such uses are indispensable to ensure a semantic exclusion of deception, lies, and ignorance."[178]

Thiselton rightly acknowledges that many systematic theologians traditionally test their truth claims by a coherence theory of truth. After all, they are interested in creating a coherent system of belief. Yet Thiselton also suggests that the Christian theologian's general dependence on historical claims (i.e., claims about Israel, Jesus, etc.) depend upon coherence rather than correspondence:[179]

> When we speak of a "true" report in the press, we usually mean that it corresponds to the facts of the matter, as may be confirmed by the eye-witnesses of the event. When a historical statement is described as "true," this generally also means "corresponding to the facts," but in this case contemporary eye-witnesses (as opposed to the reports of other past eye-witnesses) can no longer corroborate the event. Indeed in this case the usual way of testing the truth may be with reference to the internal coherence of a variety of historical traditions and reconstructions.[180]

By contrast, the correspondence theory of truth "places virtually all of its weight on the status of propositions rather than the testimonies of persons."[181] By arguing that historical accounts are not true strictly in the sense of correspondence because they are not repeatable, observable phenomena but rather dependent upon eyewitness reports, Thiselton seems to suggest that a statement's truth-value is itself contingent upon how one is justified in holding a belief—an unfortunate misstep in Thiselton's approach.

---

178. Thiselton, *Thiselton on Hermeneutics*, 284.
179. Thiselton, "Truth (*Alēthia*)," 896.
180. Ibid., 894.
181. Thiselton, *A Concise Encyclopedia*, 312.

Thiselton recognizes that coherence theories leave the possibility open for a number of different systems in which all propositions cohere as truth. He thus qualifies his position to speak about the coherence of all truth in history: "Only if the whole of truth, embracing all human history and the whole of reality, can be expressed as single comprehensive system, can the coherence theory retain its fullest value as a criterion of truth."[182] So how can truth as coherence demonstrate its embrace of all of history? Enter Pannenberg, whose work offers Thiselton a modified version of the coherence theory of truth which is (1) open rather than closed, (2) which remains *provisional upon the realization of the eschaton,*" and (3) which "must prove itself anew in the future."[183]

Thiselton believes that by introducing an eschatological horizon that looks to the future, Pannenberg has provided an important theological corrective to Gadamer's metacritical hermeneutics. Gadamer essentially only envisioned two horizons in the interpretive process: the present horizon of the reader and the ever distancing past horizon of the text. The present interpreter strives to make sense of the past horizon by bringing the text of the past into her own present situation, by attempting to "fuse horizons" by applying the text to her own situation.[184] Because the fusion of horizons is an ongoing process, the interpreter never reaches an omega point; she never crosses the finish line. She never can call the interpretive process complete. Rather than an endless fusion of horizons, Pannenberg offers a future horizon wherein the whole picture can be seen.[185] The future plays an important role in interpreting the present, as

182. Thiselton, "Truth (*Alēthia*)," 896.
183. Thiselton, *The Hermeneutics of Doctrine*, 125.
184. Hans-Georg Gadamer, *Truth and Method*, 2nd rev. ed., trans. Joel Weinsheimer and Donald G. Marshall (New York: Continuum, 2004), 304–05
185. Thiselton, *New Horizons in Hermeneutics*, 331–38. See also James Clark McHann Jr., *The Three Horizons: A Study in Biblical Hermeneutics with Special Reference to Wolfhart Pannenberg* (Ph.D. diss., University of Aberdeen, 1987).

the resurrection of Jesus makes possible a proleptic claim for the eschatological horizon by which all history should be interpreted.[186]

The provisionality of truth perception has some value in explaining the phenomenon of developing Christian belief, and if the Christian story is in fact true, the eschaton should provide confirmation of present truth claims, as John Hick argues in his earlier work.[187] But to limit one's notion of truth to its internal coherence is to substitute the sufficient condition for truth with a necessary condition. In other words, having consistency across one's framework of beliefs is an important, even necessary component of understanding the whole truth, but internal consistency alone is not itself sufficient for knowledge of reality. Readers of elaborate science fiction and fantasy are well aware of this notion. Stories like *The Lord of the Rings* may take place in brilliantly conceived fictional worlds and feature complex, internally consistent mythologies, but internal consistency alone does not make a world like Tolkien's Middle-earth legendarium a real world outside of texts.[188]

Interpreters of reality instinctively and intuitively rely on something like a correspondence theory of truth to distinguish between the world in which they live and the worlds about which they read. Christian believers usually operate with the conviction that the claims made about Jesus are true because they correspond to the way things really were, are, or will be, not simply that claims about Christ are internally consistent with other Christian claims in a web of doctrinal beliefs. God truly raised Jesus from the dead. Jesus truly has been exalted to the right hand of the Father, whatever that biblical metaphor may mean. In the eschaton, Christ really will

---

186. Pannenberg, *Theology and the Philosophy of Science*, 296.
187. See John Hick, *Faith and Knowledge*, 2nd ed. (Ithaca, NY: Cornell University Press, 1966), 176–99.
188. David K. Clark, *To Know and Love God: Method for Theology* (Wheaton, IL: Crossway, 2003), 366.

come again to judge the quick and the dead. Furthermore, while the interpreter's epistemic perceptions or understandings of truth are clearly provisional in nature in that they can be corrected or modified, this does not mean that truth itself (in the ontological sense) is provisional. Realism acknowledges that truth and statements about truth are not mind dependent.

For Thiselton, theories about language, the nature of texts, and truth call for attention to different types of statements and texts. Thiselton repeatedly rejects "either-or" approaches to language in favor of multiform or polymorphous concepts.[189] In addition, individual texts help determine the value of theories of textuality, not overarching "rules" or "method" of engagement.[190] Likewise, Thiselton argues that "truth is multiform," and that different types of statements are true in different senses, whether by correspondence, coherence, poetic, or personal standards of truth:[191] "Each theory of truth offers criteria relevant to different contexts in life, thought, history and experience. None is to be rejected on the ground that it fails to offer a comprehensive theory of truth."[192] With language, truth, and texts, no "one-size-fits-all" approach typically suffices.

Thiselton makes a helpful correlation between biblical authority and corrigible interpretation with the relationship between justification by faith and sanctification. Trust in biblical authority is, like justification by faith, faith in God's accomplished action that awaits final confirmation in the eschaton. Interpretation, like sanctification, is an ongoing process in which the fallible believer comes to understand more fully the implications of this faith. Thiselton's comments about the provisionality of the corporate

---

189. Thiselton, *The Two Horizons*, 407–15.
190. Thiselton, "'Behind' and 'in Front of' the Text," 103.
191. Thiselton, "Truth (*Alēthia*)," 894.
192. Thiselton, *A Concise Encyclopedia*, 314.

interpretation of Scripture are relevant for the present concern in doctrinal development:

> For interpretation serves to advance the reading community towards those verdicts and corroboration of promises and pledges which will become public and revealed as definitive at the last judgement. In this corporate and historical process, we need not regard conflicts of interpretation with dismay. For they belong to a broad process of testing, correcting, and initiating readiness for fresh advance, even if from time to time they also enter blind alleys. But such is the nature of appropriating the gifts and grace of God which is both fallible and bold, touched by sin, yet empowered and directed by the Holy Spirit. 'Now we know in part. . . . Then shall I know, even as I am known' (1 Cor. 13:9, 10).[193]

Recognition of the corrigibility of interpretation and doctrinal development need not result in hermeneutical skepticism, nor should the admission that theological judgments are provisional result in inaction. Interpretation may be fallible and revisable, but it should be an attempt to depict reality as it anticipates future authentication. Doctrinal statements may be provisional and contingent in their character, but they are also statements that concern real states of affairs and public declarations of first-person testimony and Christian commitment.

Conclusion

The question about the reality or cognitivity of doctrinal statements has existential implications. Often when the question "Is this truly the case?" is asked, there is another implicit question behind it: "Can I really live my life according to this belief?" or "Can I *commit* to this belief?" One need not assume this observation is a retreat into

---

193. Thiselton, "Authority and Hermeneutics," 137.

neopragmatic relativism or, in the case of the present discussion, some sort of theological instrumentalism that reduces the truth-value of theological claims to their "usefulness" in the Christian life and practice.[194] Recent developments in the philosophy of language show that reality-depicting language is rarely value neutral. Even reality-depicting propositions involve a degree of "self-involvement" on the part of the speaker. If doctrinal development is inevitable and new formulations are needed on occasion, how are such formulations described as reality depicting? The real concern in doctrinal development is whether one can maintain Christian commitment when these doctrines clearly develop over time.

The Protestant or evangelical who adheres to the material and formal sufficiency of Scripture is in a better position to answer affirmatively. The supreme authority in faith and practice has remained constant throughout time.[195] The author-given meaning of the inspired text may not change with time or context, but its interpretations certainly do. The biblical text may be inerrant and infallible, but its interpreters are not. Herein lies the value of a critical hermeneutical realism for development theory. Recognition of the finitude and fallibility of interpreters need not undermine the fact that authors establish meaning in texts. Authors do things with words, even if their readers misunderstand what it is they are doing. While recognizing authorial intention, the critical realist interpreter

194. Anthony C. Thiselton, "'Behind' and 'in Front of' the Text: Language, Reference and Indeterminacy," in *After Pentecost: Language & Biblical Interpretation*, ed. Craig Bartholomew, Colin Greene, and Karl Möller (Grand Rapids, MI: Zondervan, 2001), 103. According to Thiselton, Rorty's neopragmatic brand of relativism disregards any and "all referential or representational theory under the pretence of arguing on the basis of local contextual criteria from community to community."

195. This chapter is not the place to take up any extended discussion of textual criticism or the textual reliability of the New Testament. Changes within the manuscript tradition are relatively minor and do not appear to impact any major doctrines of the Christian faith. For a brief overview of the current debate from evangelical and non-evangelical perspectives, see Robert B. Stewart, ed., *The Reliability of the New Testament: Bart Ehrman and Daniel Wallace in Dialogue* (Minneapolis: Fortress Press, 2011).

recognizes that the interpretation of texts is open to revision. The task of interpretation is an ongoing critical investigation; it is, as N. T. Wright describes it, an *"appropriate dialogue or conversation between the knower and the thing known."*[196] In science, biblical interpretation, and theology alike, one can affirm her attempts to construe reality while simultaneously maintaining that her conclusions are provisional and open to correction.

To affirm provisionality and openness to correction need not result in an existential crisis or postmodern despair, especially if the possibility of correction may result in a deeper understanding of reality. Because biblical interpretation is imperfect, it also remains provisional and may require reevaluation of the text. Fidelity to the text provides protection from doctrinal and ethical corruption. This idea is consistent with the appeal of the Renaissance humanists for *ad fontes* ("back to the sources")[197] and the battle cry of the second-generation Reformers for a church that is *semper reformanda* ("always being reformed") according to the written word of God.[198] The allegiance of theologians and biblical interpreters is to the biblical text, not previously established theological constructs. Developments in doctrine, at least for those based on a return to communicative acts of the biblical text, may be welcomed without necessarily assuming a rejection of realism.

Furthermore, as Thiselton and Vanhoozer demonstrate, speech-act theory provides an important correction to dichotomous approaches to doctrinal language that would reduce doctrines to propositions or rules. By the same measure, doctrinal statements can be both reality depicting and regulative. As statements, they have truth-value. As

---

196. Wright, *The New Testament and the People of God*, 35.
197. See Alister E. McGrath, *Reformation Thought: An Introduction*, 3d ed. (Malden, MA: Blackwell, 1999), 44–45.
198. The seventeenth-century Dutch reformer Jodocus van Lodenstein (1620–1677) introduced this phrase in his *Beschouwinge van Zion* (Amsterdam, 1674).

speech acts, statements also function as self-involving commitments. The call to *witness* makes little sense without witnessing to something or someone the speaker perceives to be real. The practice of Christian testimony loses all meaning if the speaker does not act with belief that what she is saying is in fact true. In fact, she bears false witness.

In summary, doctrinal development and reality depiction are not conflicting ideas. The theologian should not reduce the reality-depicting nature of biblical texts to propositional statements but should recognize the literary diversity of the canon. Non-propositional literary devices such as metaphor have cognitive value in formulating doctrine and understanding texts. Theologians can develop new doctrinal metaphors as long as they are faithful to the *pattern and content* of Scripture. The diversity of theological content and voices in the canon means that interpreters should also be wary of totalizing schemes. Most importantly, a commonsense hermeneutical realism that acknowledges that texts do in fact have meanings given by authors but nevertheless recognizes the fallibility of the interpreter and welcomes the possibility of a conflict of interpretations and new developments in understanding.

7

Development and Continuity

Hermeneutical Approaches to the Problem

The most critical issue for any model of doctrinal development is the question of doctrinal continuity. Can doctrines *develop, grow,* or *progress* without compromising their fidelity to "the faith once delivered unto the saints" (Jude 3)? Can there be maintained identity between New Testament teachings and later doctrinal formulations that utilize very different conceptual frameworks? Most importantly, if doctrines do in fact develop over time through expansion, contextualization, and critical correction, how can the faith communities that develop and reformulate doctrines claim to be part of the same broad Christian tradition?

Since the nineteenth-century turn toward historical criticism, many liberal and skeptical scholars have argued for significant discontinuity between the beliefs of first-century faith communities and the apologetic works and creeds put forward by patristic and medieval theologians. Historians such as Baur, Harnack, Bousset, and

Bauer popularized this discontinuity thesis in their respective milieus, and contemporary critics of traditional Christianity still make similar claims.[1] This is not the place to rehearse or refute their particular historical arguments.[2] Rather, I am concerned here with a more theoretical question. If we take the evidence of history seriously—that explicit formulations of essential tenets of the Christian faith do not appear on the historical record until later—is it possible for contemporary evangelicals to establish continuity with the earliest forms of the faith? To what degree is sameness of expression and conceptual frameworks necessary for establishing such continuity? Is it logically possible to have the "same" doctrine if the language and concepts surrounding the doctrine change over time? My concern in this chapter is apologetic in nature, both (1) in defense of the ongoing theological task and (2) in defense of the established claims of orthodoxy.

As we have seen, theologians throughout history have taken different approaches to the question of identity throughout doctrinal development. Few theologians prior to modern historical criticism addressed the issue of development. Those who did, however, did not recognize the need for new doctrines or developments as much as the need to unpack ideas or concepts necessarily entailed in revelation. Vincent of Lérins popularized organic models for the growing Christian tradition along these lines. Many late medieval theologians and reformers rejected the possibility of development altogether. By the nineteenth century, Roman Catholic theologians such as

---

1. New Testament scholar Bart Ehrman has recently written a popular book along these lines, arguing that neither Jesus nor his earliest followers envisioned him as the exalted God of later Christian worship. See Bart D. Ehrman, *How Jesus Became God: The Exaltation of a Jewish Preacher from Galilee* (San Francisco: HarperOne, 2014).
2. Evangelical New Testament scholars have responded in kind to Ehrman's most recent attack on the development of orthodox Christology with Michael F. Bird, Craig A. Evans, Simon Gathercole, Charles E. Hill, and Chris Tilling, *How God Became Jesus: The Real Origins of Belief in Jesus' Divine Nature—A Response to Bart D. Ehrman* (Grand Rapids, MI: Zondervan, 2014).

Johann Sebastian von Drey, Johann Adam Möhler, and John Henry Newman were conceding changes in the tradition but making apologetic cases for the authority of the Church to develop doctrine. For these theologians, new and developing doctrines can retain continuity with the divinely posited revelation of the past if they grow in the living apostolic tradition of the Church. None of these options is particularly appealing to contemporary evangelicals like myself (1) who recognize the frequent need for new, constructive theologies in ever-changing cultural contexts and (2) who are committed the material and formal sufficiency of Scripture. I do not believe that these dual commitments are in conflict. One may yield to the unique authority of God in Scripture and develop new doctrinal or ethical solutions for contemporary problems in a way that is faithful to the Bible's supreme authority.

Evangelicals can commit to the task of constructive theology and maintain continuity with the revealed teachings of Scripture, and hermeneutical theory provides a way to make a case for this continuity. In this chapter, I will explore explicitly hermeneutical approaches to the problem of continuity and development, particularly in the works of evangelical theologians. Again, Anthony Thiselton and Kevin Vanhoozer are important dialogue partners. Once more, Thiselton provides a more descriptive hermeneutical approach to the problem at hand, while Vanhoozer's approach is more normative in nature. Thiselton's "dispositional" account of Christian belief, developed in large part through his interaction with twentieth-century philosophy of belief, is of great value to theological method and Christian apologetics, particularly in response to historical critics who challenge continuity between the New Testament and later christological creeds. Vanhoozer's approach, utilizing conceptual tools from Paul Ricoeur, cultural theory, and New Testament studies provides an apologetic for the ongoing task of developing doctrine and even offers valuable direction for the task.

A Descriptive, Dispositional Account for Continuity

Thiselton addresses many of the issues related to the problem of doctrinal continuity with his dispositional account of communal Christian belief.[3] Invoking insights about the nature of beliefs from Wittgenstein and Henry Habberley Price, Thiselton offers a dispositional and intersubjective model of Christian beliefs.[4] First, he hopes to show the way in which confessional statements and doctrines relate to action, to one's situation, and to particular states of affairs being the case. Second, and more importantly for our present concern, Thiselton suggests that a dispositional account of belief can help establish continuity between the New Testament and later confessions of faith.[5]

While metaphysicians use the term "disposition" to describe the properties of objects and their causal relations (e.g., such as the characteristic or disposition of a rubber ball to bounce on a hard surface when dropped),[6] Price and Thiselton use the term to describe the *dispositional nature of human beliefs*. In this model for understanding belief, beliefs are "the reservoir of knowledge,

---

3. Anthony C. Thiselton, *The Hermeneutics of Doctrine* (Grand Rapids, MI: Eerdmans, 2007), esp. 19–42.

4. H. H. Price, *Belief* (New York: Humanities Press, 1969); Anthony C. Thiselton, *The Two Horizons: New Testament Hermeneutics and Philosophical Description with Special Reference to Heidegger, Bultmann, Gadamer, and Wittgenstein* (Carlisle: Paternoster, 1980), 422–27; idem, *New Horizons in Hermeneutics: The Theory and Practice of Transforming Biblical Reading* (Grand Rapids, MI: Zondervan, 1992), 244; idem, *The Hermeneutics of Doctrine*, 19–42.

5. Thiselton, *The Hermeneutics of Doctrine*, 37.

6. For a variety of metaphysical evaluations of dispositions, see David Malet Armstrong, Charles Burton Martin, and Ullin Thomas Place, *Dispositions: A Debate*, ed. Tim Crane (London: Routledge, 1966); J. L. Mackie, *Truth, Probability, and Paradox: Studies in Philosophical Logic* (Oxford: Oxford University Press, 1973), 120–52; Stephen Mumford, *Dispositions* (Oxford: Oxford University Press, 2003).

understanding, or conviction upon which the believer draws to perform appropriate belief-utterances or action."[7] Dispositions are a complex web of interrelated beliefs or convictions that guide praxis or action. Dispositions function like worldviews in that they entail "*intellectual* belief, *emotional* depth, *volitional* commitment, and *total* stance."[8] Price elaborates further:

> When we say of someone 'he believes the proposition *p*' it is held that we are making a dispositional statement about him, and that this is equivalent to a series of conditional statements describing what he *would* likely say or do or feel if such circumstances were to arise. For example, he would assert the proposition (aloud, or privately to himself) if he heard someone else denying it or expressing doubt of it. He would use it, when relevant, as a premiss in his inferences. If circumstances were to arise in which it made a practical difference whether *p* was true or false, he would act as if it were true. If *p* were falsified he would feel surprised, and would feel no surprise if it were verified.[9]

Price maintains that "believing a proposition consists just in being disposed to act as if the proposition were true, where the proposition is one which is *actually entertained sometimes* by the person who is disposed to act on it."[10] Cultural, political, and religious beliefs all function as dispositions from which we operate in our environments.

Advocates of dispositional belief challenge the notion of some epistemologists that we only believe through conscious and temporal states of the mind.[11] As Wittgenstein observes, if belief in a proposition is only a temporal mental occurrence or event, the person

---

7. Thiselton, *The Hermeneutics of Doctrine*, 30.
8. Anthony C. Thiselton, *The First Epistle to the Corinthians: A Commentary on the Greek Text*, The New International Greek New Testament Commentary (Grand Rapids, MI: Eerdmans, 2000), 599.
9. Price, *Belief*, 20.
10. Ibid., 252.
11. Anthony C. Thiselton, "Knowledge, Myth and Corporate Memory," in *Believing in the Church: The Corporate Nature of Faith, A Report by the Doctrine Commission of the Church of England* (London: SPCK, 1981), 74.

who believes a proposition *p* ceases to believe *p* every time he or she thinks about something else or falls asleep. Wittgenstein notes that "one hardly ever says that one has believed, understood or intended something 'uninterruptedly' since yesterday" because an "interruption of belief would be a period of unbelief, not e.g. the withdrawal of attention from what one believes—e.g. sleep."[12] Likewise, if Christian belief is merely a conscious mental state—an active fixation on faith propositions—then I cease to be a Christian whenever I occupy my mind with anything other than religious beliefs and, worse still, become an atheist every time I go to bed.

Dispositions as Embodied Beliefs

The dispositional account of belief shows that beliefs are not isolated propositions we can disengage from intellectually, emotionally, or volitionally. We cannot believe something to be true without connecting to that belief or integrating it into our life on some existential or emotional level. Drawing upon Wittgenstein, Thiselton highlights the logical asymmetry between first-person utterances of belief (for example, "I believe," "we believe") and third-person utterances ("he believes," "she believes"), which serve to indicate the self-involving nature of belief.[13] For instance, to say "He believes *p* to be the case" is not the same act as saying "I believe *p* to be the case." Wittgenstein illustrates this with the apparent absurdity in the paradox of G. E. Moore, also known as a "Moorean sentence," which states, "*P*, and I do not believe that *p*."[14] While it is patently absurd to say, "It is raining and *I* don't believe it," it is not absurd

---

12. Ludwig Wittgenstein, *Zettel* (English and German Edition), ed. and trans. G. E. M. Anscombe and G. H. von Wright (Berkeley: University of California Press, 1967), §85.
13. Thiselton, *The Hermeneutics of Doctrine*, 20; cf. Price, *Belief*, 29. Price also believes that "the difference between first-person and third-person belief-sentences is of considerable philosophical importance."

to say, "It is raining and *she* doesn't believe it," especially if "she" is extremely skeptical of her sense data, in a windowless building on what she believed to be a clear day, or particularly distrusting of television meteorologists.[15] As Wittgenstein notes, the "expression 'I believe that this is the case' is used like the assertion 'This is the case'; and yet the *hypothesis* that I believe this is the case is not used like the hypothesis that this is the case." Likewise, the statement "I believe it's going to rain" is the same as "It's going to rain," while the past tense "I believed it was going to rain" is not the same as saying "It did rain then." As Wittgenstein concludes, "If there were a verb meaning 'to believe falsely', it would not have any significant first person indicative."[16] Belief is "embedded" in life situations.[17]

This logical asymmetry, Thiselton asserts, is compatible with Price's dispositional account of belief, as the utterance of belief "is inextricably *embodied* in patterns of *habit, commitment, and action,* which constitute endorsement, 'backing,' or 'surroundings' for the utterance."[18] These first-person belief utterances have what Austin dubs a "performatory character," as a first-person belief utterance is a speech-act that constitutes more than a proposition concerning third-person belief. As Price notes, "Ordinarily when someone says 'I believe that *p*' he is not giving us a piece of information about himself. He is expressing an attitude, rather than telling us he has it. And sometimes, in the act of expressing it, he is doing something more as well. Sometimes he is taking a stand in the face of a hostile or sceptical audience. 'This is what I believe. Call me a fool or an idiot

---

14. See G. E. Moore, "Moore's Paradox," in *G. E. Moore: Selected Writings,* ed. Thomas Baldwin (London: Routledge, 1993), 207–12.
15. The paradoxical description of the Moorean sentence would lose some of its force if I were to replace the third-person "he" with a third-person self-reference: "It is raining and *Rhyne* does not believe it."
16. Wittgenstein, *Philosophical Investigations* II, x, §162e; cf. Moore, "Moore's Paradox," 208–9.
17. Thiselton, *The Two Horizons,* 375.
18. Thiselton, *The Hermeneutics of Doctrine,* 20.

if you like.' It is a public act of self-commitment."[19] For Thiselton, public declarations of Christian belief have this same performative character: "If a Christian believer nails his or her colors to the mast in situations of persecution, hostile criticism, pledging oneself in baptism, liturgical doxology and declaration, kerygmatic proclamation, or the need to correct error, these are precisely the moments when the disposition becomes *explicit, active, and public.*"[20]

To describe Christian belief as dispositional belief means more than an affirmation of truth claims about the nature of God or biblical history. Christian belief, if dispositional, also entails commitment, volition, and praxis. In some situations, it calls for new responses and taking a stand for its truth claims.

Dispositions as Implicit Beliefs

The dispositional account of belief offers great explanatory power in addressing the relationship between dormant or implicit belief and explicit expressions in doctrines and confessions. With it, it is possible to defend the chronological priority of orthodox belief theoretically, even if orthodox statements of faith appear later on the historical record than their heretical counterparts. Even conservative critics of historical critics like Harnack tend to agree that Gnostics may have been among the first systematic theologians but disagree that Gnostics were the original keepers of "doctrine." As Harold O. J. Brown observes, "In order to have heresy, to be a heretic, it is necessary that there be an orthodoxy against which to react."[21]

---

19. Price, *Belief*, 29–30.
20. Thiselton, *The Hermeneutics of Doctrine*, 21.
21. Harold O. J. Brown, *Heresies: The Image of Christ in the Mirror of Heresy and Orthodoxy* (Grand Rapids, MI: Baker, 1988), 2.

Brown adds that the very notion of "heresy . . . presupposes orthodoxy."[22]

Nevertheless, considerable difficulty remains. How can one account for the intervening period when there is no explicit doctrinal formulation of belief? Is implicit propositional belief even possible? With Price, Thiselton answers in the affirmative: "A belief may be dormant or buried in the subconscious until a new set of circumstances confronts us that brings it out, to self-awareness."[23] Such development makes sense in a dispositional account of belief because *"circumstances of challenge and denial draw forth belief that had remained latent and implicit."*[24] Furthermore, "If a believer remains silent in situations that do *not* necessarily call for explicit expressions of belief in the public domain, this would not necessarily imply unbelief."[25]

Price explains how this dispositional response might work with the notion of "propositional extensibility," an idea that, surprisingly, is not mentioned explicitly in Thiselton's analysis of dispositional beliefs. In his discussion of inference and dormant belief, Price appeals to Cambridge mathematician and economist Frank P. Ramsey, who gives him the idea that propositions accumulate into a "stock" of premises from which the believer can draw inferences and act accordingly when certain situations call for response.[26] This property of belief is its "extensibility." Price illustrates this property by a counterexample to genuine belief: "If a person claims to believe a proposition, but fails to believe even its most obvious consequences (e.g., shows no surprise at all when one of them is falsified) we

---

22. Ibid., 4.
23. Thiselton, *The Hermeneutics of Doctrine*, 28.
24. Ibid., 29–30.
25. Thiselton, *The Hermeneutics of Doctrine*, 21.
26. Price, *Belief*, 254, 290–301; cf. F. P. Ramsey, "General Propositions and Causality," in *F. P. Ramsey: Philosophical Papers*, ed. D. H. Mellor (Cambridge: Cambridge University Press, 1990), 145–63.

are inclined to doubt whether he does believe the proposition."[27] Genuine belief in a proposition does "extend itself to at least some of the consequences of the proposition."[28]

In a conscious act of inference, belief can spread from one proposition (p) to another to its probable consequence (q). All the same, as Price notes, "sometimes we just find ourselves feeling confident of the conclusion . . . though we did not actually experience any process of inferring."[29] When proposition p is the major premise and q is the conclusion, this extensibility produces results akin to drawing inferences in a categorical syllogism:

All A is C
All B is A
∴ All B is C

While this process sometimes happens unconsciously, Price wants to assert the autonomy of rational persons in their ability to slow or halt this extension of belief until they are "satisfied . . . about the strength of the logical connection between" p and q.[30] Whether this propositional extensibility comes through conscious deliberation or non-conscious processes, the believer—depending on the degree of his or her belief that p— ultimately will show little surprise that q is a consequence of the belief that p or will most likely be astonished if not q. According to Price, the degree of extensibility of proposition p to a consequence q is contingent upon two factors: (1) the degree of belief that p and (2) the degree to which the believer believes q is a consequence of the belief that p.[31] The degree of belief can vary in

27. Ibid., 290.
28. Ibid., 291.
29. Ibid., 293.
30. Ibid.
31. Ibid., 292.

certainty, ranging from disbelief or doubt to hesitant belief and on to confident belief.[32]

A historical case study is helpful here. Could early Christians hold implicit belief in the divinity and personhood of the Holy Spirit without explicit expression or are such affirmations only fourth-century constructs? Propositional extensibility in doctrinal development is clear in the fourth-century formulations of the Holy Spirit made between Nicaea and Constantinople. The original Nicene Creed of 325, drafted in response to the Arian controversy, was more explicitly christological than pneumatological in its focus. While the creed is clearly Trinitarian, the third proposition related to the Holy Spirit lacks qualification: "we believe . . . also in the Holy Spirit." When confronted with the challenge of the semi-Arian

---

32. Ibid., 306. A dispositional account of belief aids in distinguishing between authentic belief and inauthentic belief. Price calls reluctant belief "half-belief." He describes half-belief as the tension one holds between a belief and unbelief. Half-belief is incoherent and inconsistent practice and belief, to be sure. According to Price, it is not the same thing as hypocrisy. He illustrates this distinction with the example of a man who acts very kindly at Church on Sundays but does not act the same way throughout the week: "It would not be fair to describe this man as a hypocrite, someone who pretends or professes to believe what he actually disbelieves or doubts. Nor would it be fair to say that his religion is just a matter of outward conformity. He resembles a hypocritical conformer in some ways, but not in others. For he really does assent to these theological propositions on some occasions; and then he not only behaves outwardly, but also thinks and feels inwardly, as a genuinely religious person would. His religious attitude is not just a pretended one. But it is, so to speak, a part-time one. It is operative only in some parts of his life but not in others. He is seldom in it except on Sundays" (306). Thiselton cites Jonah as an example of what Price calls a "half-believer" who acts according to his belief only when it suits his purposes (Thiselton, *The Two Horizons*, 426). What is key is that Jonah "has *beliefs that operate in some circumstances but not in others*" (Thiselton, *The Hermeneutics of Doctrine*, 31). For Thiselton, the Book of Jonah is "a virtually self-contained satire on *incoherent* self-centered *theoretical theistic belief*" (Thiselton, "'Behind' and 'in Front of' the Text," 100). "Half-belief" in Price resembles what psychologists call "cognitive dissonance," the sort of emotional stress induced by a person who holds two contradictory beliefs. Leon Festinger (1919–1989) was a pioneer in this area, describing this tension in *A Theory of Cognitive Dissonance* (Evanston, IL: Row, Peterson, and Co., 1957). For example, a religious believer may have cognitive convictions about the normative sexual ethics of the Bible—that Jesus condemns extramarital lust as adultery (Matt. 5:27–28)—and nevertheless struggle with an addiction to pornography or masturbation fantasies. This kind of cognitive dissonance or half-belief creates additional emotional stress for the believer who wants to be obedient to Christ and who cannot seem to shake her addiction.

pneumatomachi (or "Spirit-fighters"), who argued that the Holy Spirit was merely a creature, Basil of Caesarea (330–379) and Gregory of Nyssa (c. 335–c. 394)[33] responded with explicit affirmations of the Holy Spirit's deity and personhood that went beyond the Nicene Creed's (325) bare statement on the Spirit. Again, the extensibility of this proposition can be stated as a categorical syllogism:

(1) God is personal and not a creature.

(2) The Holy Spirit is God.

(3) Therefore, the Holy Spirit is personal and not a creature.

If believers affirmed (1) God is a person and not a creature and that (2) the Holy Spirit is counted in the divine triad with God the Father and God the Son (as stated in the 325 Nicene Creed) then (3) one can infer the explicit Constantinopolitan conclusion that the Holy Spirit is personal God as "the Lord" and "the Savior" without a drastic shift in belief. Whether the consequent proposition (i.e., the Holy Spirit is Lord and the Giver of Life) resulting from its antecedent belief (i.e., the Holy Spirit is counted as the same substance with God the Father and God the Son) is the result of conscious deliberation or non-conscious processes, those who held the antecedent belief have little or no difficulty with accepting this consequential proposition This development resulted in the more symmetrical, balanced trinitarian statement in the Niceno-Constantinopolitan Creed (381),

With his discussion of implicit beliefs, Thiselton's dispositional account of Christian doctrine shares qualities with theories of development that Jan Walgrave places in the category of "logical theories."[34] Thiselton, however, does not describe doctrine as a closed

---

33. See Basil, *On the Holy Spirit*; Gregory of Nyssa, *Against Eunomius*; idem, *On the Holy Trinity, and of the Godhead of the Holy Spirit*; idem, *On the Holy Spirit, Against Macedonius*.

series of interconnected, timeless propositions but rather as products of life and situation-related dispositional responses. His approach is also reminiscent of some of Newman's comments on the nature of belief: "But what is remarkable at first sight is this, that there is good reason for saying that the impression made upon the mind need not even be recognized by the parties possessing it. It is no proof that persons are not possessed, because they are not conscious of an idea."[35] Thiselton's work here builds on the works of Price and Wittgenstein, but it is not a carbon copy of either. Thiselton derives his understanding of the "extensibility" of beliefs and the degrees of belief from Price and the communal, teachable nature of beliefs from Wittgenstein.

Dispositions as Communal Beliefs

Price does not extend the application of "disposition" beyond individual belief. Thiselton, however, contends for an "*inextricable logical grammar that connects Christian doctrine or communal belief with dispositional responses and the habits of mind to live and act in a correlative way in the public domain.*"[36] At this point, the study of dispositional belief takes on hermeneutical qualities. As discussed earlier, Thiselton rejects the idea that individuals form beliefs independently of the stream of history and tradition. *Corporate memory provides the framework for individual belief.* Again, he deduces that dispositional beliefs have an "intersubjective" character. Thiselton invokes Wittgenstein's notion of "logical grammar" at this point, particularly in his argument against "private language"—an idea Wittgenstein

---

34. See Jan Hendrik Walgrave, *Unfolding Revelation: The Nature of Doctrinal Development* (Philadelphia: Westminster, 1972), 164–78.
35. Newman, *Fifteen Sermons*, 321.
36. Thiselton, *The Hermeneutics of Doctrine*, 46.

infers from the Cartesian tradition.[37] Private language is a language that is, in the words of Wittgenstein scholar David Pears, an "unteachable" language.[38] What makes language teachable, Thiselton writes, "is *its connection with observable regularities in human behavior.*"[39] Private language lacks "'currency' in the public, intersubjective world."[40] Dispositions are not "private" in the sense that they are unlearned and without continuity to an intersubjective world. Dispositional belief, Thiselton argues, is possible only in a world in which concepts are communicated through shared, conceptual grammar.

Christian dispositional belief is no different. Self-involving Christian belief in particular depends upon a "shared world of interpersonal relations."[41] Thiselton argues, "Christian beliefs are thus, by definition, shared beliefs."[42] As he observes in one of his earlier arguments against Bultmann, "Concepts like 'being redeemed,' 'being spoken to by God,' and so on are made intelligible and 'teachable' *not on the basis of private existential experience but on the basis of a public tradition of certain patterns of behavior.*"[43] A believer not only accepts certain theoretical statements but also "commits . . . to certain ways of understanding and acting towards God and others which transcend the limits of a strictly 'private' or individual

---

37. See Wittgenstein, *Philosophical Investigations* I §§243–315. Wittgenstein asks, "Could we also imagine a language in which a person could write down or give vocal expression to his inner experiences—his feelings, moods, and the rest—for his private use?" (§243)

38. David Pears, *Ludwig Wittgenstein* (New York: Viking Press, 1970), 150–52. See also Hans-Johann Glock, *A Wittgensteinan Dictionary* (Oxford: Blackwell, 1996), 309–15. Glock (b. 1960) adds that a private language is "not a language which is unshared as a matter of fact, but one which is unsharable and unteachable in principle, because its words refer to what can only be known to the speaker, namely his immediate private experiences."

39. Thiselton, *The Two Horizons*, 381.

40. Thiselton, *The Hermeneutics of Doctrine*, 23; cf. idem, *Interpreting God and the Postmodern Self: On Meaning, Manipulation, and Promise* (Grand Rapids, MI: Eerdmans, 1995), 38–39.

41. Thiselton, "Knowledge, Myth and Corporate Memory," 74.

42. Ibid., 75.

43. Thiselton, *The Two Horizons*, 382.

world."[44] Self-involving belief stands not only in relation to the belief that doctrinal statements reflect a real state of affairs but also places one in relation to the believing community; such belief is *"closely embedded in life-situations and actions."*[45] Doctrinal statements develop in a context of shared grammar, experience, and narrative. Confession is, after all, *homologion,* or a common word between two or more parties. Accounting for dispositional belief is a hermeneutical concern because such "belief . . . is *action-oriented, situation-related,* and embedded in the *particularities and contingencies* of everyday living" and because "hermeneutics is concerned with particularity and embodied life, as well as a distinct dimension of coherence and with expanding horizons of understanding."[46]

As noted from the outset, hermeneutics for Thiselton involves "formation" in the same sense of Gadamer. Even if Thiselton shies away from the use of *worldview* to describe the process of communal formation, his notion of doctrinal formulation as a means of transforming horizons and cultivating habits and practices resonates with the idea of shaping and transforming worldviews through Christian discipleship. Like practical wisdom, dispositions are the result of training and habit—training that provokes appropriate reactions when occasion calls for them.[47] His description of dispositional belief no doubt resonates with the idea that worldviews are not merely cognitive, but that they involve *theory* and *practice.*[48] Narrative also plays a sizable role in this process of formation: "These communities, even if separated in time or place, perceive themselves

44. Thiselton, "Knowledge, Myth and Corporate Memory," 74–75.
45. Thiselton, *The Hermeneutics of Doctrine,* 43, 58. This statement is reminiscent of Wittgenstein's observation that language games are embedded in forms of life.
46. Thiselton, *The Hermeneutics of Doctrine,* 21.
47. Thiselton, *The First Epistle to the Corinthians,* 943.
48. See N. T. Wright, *The New Testament and the People of God,* Christian Origins and the Question of God, vol. 1 (Minneapolis: Fortress Press, 1992), 124–25, 133.

as taking their stand and as staking their identity through *sharing in the same narrative*, and through the recital and retelling of the same founding events."[49]

Dispositions and Doctrinal Continuity

The dispositional model of identity appears to have great value for Christian apologetics. Often unacknowledged in discussions of the problem of doctrinal development are the adverse conditions which normally accompany fundamental changes in belief. Just as a dispositional account of belief explains the rise of explicit doctrine congruent with dispositional belief, the recognition that a belief is a "multiform disposition . . . manifested or actualized in many different ways"[50] should account also for noticeable changes in belief. For instance, if subapostolic Christianity transformed the thought world of the first-century Christian teaching into a Hellenistic dogma unrecognizable to Jesus and Paul, as Baur, Harnack, and the *religionsgeschichtliche Schule* believed to be the case, considerable conflict marking this drastic change likely would surface in the historical record. If Walter Bauer and Bart Ehrman are right in supposing that orthodoxy began as one of many options in a cafeteria of competing geographical Christianities rather than the original faith from which they all stem, one would expect evidence of Ebionite and gnostic "apologists" explicitly challenging the claims of a rival orthodox party that corrupted their depositories of belief. A dispositional account of belief acknowledges that such dramatic changes hardly would go unnoticed. Price brings home the far-reaching consequences of changes in belief:

---

49. Thiselton, *The Hermeneutics of Doctrine*, 43.
50. Price, *Belief*, 294.

Our beliefs are like posts which we plant in the shifting sands of doubt and ignorance. They are fixed points or stable landmarks; and once they are there, we are able to make short journeys into the surrounding wastes, planting another post or two as we go. That is why the *loss of a belief can be such a serious matter for us*. We have lost something which we have been using to find our way about a wilderness. We are in a state of "bewilderment."[51]

James Wm. McClendon Jr. and James M. Smith echo this dispositional account of belief in their discussion of *convictions*, or "the beliefs that make people what they are."[52] They observe that the loss of a deeply held conviction is of no small consequence for the individual or community that holds it: "A conviction . . . means a persistent belief such that if X (a person or a community) has a conviction, *it will not easily be relinquished and cannot be relinquished without making X a significantly different person (or community) than before*."[53] Dispositions, whether they are individual beliefs or communally held worldviews, do not shake easily.

A Normative Model for Doctrinal Continuity

Whereas Thiselton's dispositional model of Christian belief showed how doctrine *can* develop and maintain continuity with the past, Vanhoozer's theo-dramatic theological method shows that doctrine *should* develop in order to be faithful to the past. The prescriptive nature of Vanhoozer's approach to doctrinal development is clearest in his answer to the question of doctrinal continuity. He maintains that doctrines must develop and grow in order to maintain their identity as a living tradition, a notion redolent of Nicholas Lash's

---

51. Ibid., 293, italics mine.
52. James Wm. McClendon Jr. and James M. Smith, *Convictions: Defusing Religious Relativism*, rev. ed. (Valley Forge, PA: Trinity Press, 1994), 7.
53. McClendon and Smith, *Convictions*, 5, italics mine.

influence.[54] Doctrinal continuity is not primarily in cognitive content, expressions of piety, or ecclesial praxis. The central criterion of identity in Vanhoozer's theo-dramatic theological method is not propositional, emotive, or practical but *missiological*. Doctrines may grow or develop in ways that are not exact duplications of past formulations, but they may retain continuity or identity in a shared mission found the in gospel of the triune God. We do not face the same historical situation as first-century or sixteenth-century Christians, but we do share in the same task: to reach every man, woman, and child with the good news of Jesus Christ.[55] The challenge of doctrinal development is being faithful to the mission—and the authority of God revealed in Scripture—in new settings and scenes.[56]

Cultural theory also helps Vanhoozer frame the question of doctrinal continuity. In order to understand how doctrine can maintain identity throughout changing conceptual forms, it is helpful to understand how cultures maintain their identity across time and space. Lest anyone accuse Vanhoozer of equivocation, he is clear that it would be impossible to identify a single Christian *culture*.[57] After all, Christianity takes different shapes in different cultures. Yet the idea of culture provides a helpful analogy for thinking about Christian stability and identity.

54. See Nicholas Lash, *Theology on the Way to Emmaus* (London: SCM, 1986), 44. On the performance of Scripture, Lash writes, "To put it very simply: as the history of the meaning of the text continues, we can and must tell the story differently. But we do so under constraint: what we may *not* do, if it is *this* text which we are to continue to perform, is to tell a different story."
55. Kevin J. Vanhoozer, *The Drama of Doctrine* (Louisville: Westminster/John Knox, 2005), 125.
56. Ibid., 126.
57. The most exhaustive treatment of cultural analysis in Vanhoozer's corpus is his 2007 article "What is Everyday Theology? How and Why Christians Should Read Culture," in *Everyday Theology: How to Read Cultural Texts and Interpret Trends*, ed. Kevin J. Vanhoozer, Charles A. Anderson, and Michael J. Sleasman (Grand Rapids, MI: Baker, 2007), 15–60.

Vanhoozer is equally concerned about the modern description of cultures as closed, immutable, and insular structures and the postmodern view of culture that offers no stable, unifying centers by which a culture can maintain its identity. Postmodern theologians like Lindbeck rightly challenge the modern conception of a hermetically sealed culture, but the postmodern alternative of no stable unifying principle does not help Lindbeck's case for a cultural-linguistic model of doctrine. On this point, Vanhoozer appeals to Kathryn Tanner, who demonstrates that one cannot appeal to the practices of a culture as a norm if, as many postmodernists claim, cultures or communities have no stable or unifying center.[58] But if cultural identity relates to a stable norm such as the rule of law, then a culture has an anchor for continuity throughout historical change. The question of identity then closely relates to the question of authority, as authority provides a means for stabilizing the tradition throughout its varying historical and cultural forms. While authority does not constitute the primary criterion for doctrinal continuity in Vanhoozer's model, it is an integral component.

Identity and the Task of Development

The problem of identity falls under four topical headings in *The Drama of Doctrine*, all of which are hermeneutical in nature. First, Vanhoozer addresses how identity relates to tradition. As the ongoing life of the Christian faith, tradition bridges the past to the present and serves Christian identity with an anchor that preserves its essence in changing historical and geographical settings. Tradition is *transmission*. Its function is mediation of the past, but the church must take careful measures in order to ensure its faithful interpretation.

58. Vanhoozer, *The Drama of Doctrine*, 121; cf. Kathryn Tanner, *Theories of Culture: A New Agenda for Theology* (Minneapolis: Fortress Press, 1997), 141–42.

Christian believers have the responsibility of taking up the mantle of this living tradition without losing sight of the hermeneutical otherness of the past.[59] Those who define tradition merely as a historical collection of conceptual content find the question of identity extremely difficult to address. For this reason, Vanhoozer recognizes the need for a model of doctrinal identity that leaves room for both continuity and discontinuity with the past.[60]

Second, Vanhoozer analyzes the relationship between *identity* and *otherness*. How can identity remain intact across verbal and conceptual change? Vanhoozer finds an analogy for identity preservation throughout change in Ricoeur's study of *personal identity*. For Ricoeur, hermeneutics is but a tool of the larger and more significant project of philosophical anthropology—an area of philosophy concerned with questions about human nature.[61] The question of self-identity is critical to Ricoeur's narratival, philosophical anthropology.[62] In *Oneself as Another* and *Time and Narrative*, he makes a distinction between what he calls "*idem*-sameness" and "*ipse*-selfhood," between "substantial or formal identity and narrative identity."[63] *Idem*-sameness is synonymous with substantial definitions of sameness, either in terms of *numerical*

---

59. Ibid., 125. Vanhoozer here utilizes the definition of tradition from John E. Thiel, who describes it as "the handing down of the Bible, and more specifically, its interpretation, throughout the Christian centuries." See John E. Thiel, *Senses of Tradition: Continuity and Development in Catholic Faith* (Oxford: Oxford University Press, 2000), 13.

60. Vanhoozer, *The Drama of Doctrine*, 126.

61. See Kevin J. Vanhoozer, *Biblical Narrative in the Philosophy of Paul Ricoeur: A Study in Hermeneutics and Theology* (Cambridge: Cambridge University Press, 1990), 7. As Vanhoozer summarizes Ricoeur's hermeneutics, "the final destination is still understanding of human being, but the route now passes by symbols, myths, metaphors, and texts—all of which attest to the meaning of human existence. . . . Human existence is only reached via these works which *mediate* it."

62. Ricoeur calls this kind of identity "narrative identity." See Ricoeur, *Time and Narrative*, vol. 3, 244–49; cf. idem, *Oneself as Another*, 17–18.

63. Ricoeur, *Time and Narrative*, vol. 3, 246; cf. idem, *Oneself as Another*, 113–39. The Latin term *idem* means "same," while the term *ipse* means "self." The related French term *ipséité* also means "self."

identity ("one and the same" object or person) or in terms of *qualitative*, material identity (such as the Nicene identification of *homoousios*).[64] In *ipse*-selfhood, continuity or constancy through time expresses itself in *character* and *fidelity to one's promises*.[65] These qualities are two distinct aspects of *ipse*-identity: "The perseverance of character is one thing; the perseverance of faithfulness to a word that has been given is something else again. The continuity of character is one thing, the constancy of friendship quite another."[66] Yet neither constancy nor promise keeping resembles "sameness" in the sense of *idem*-identity.

Vanhoozer employs this *ipse/idem* comparison to differentiate "hard" and "soft" forms of identity in doctrinal development. He equates *idem*-identity with "hard" or "uncritical, uninformative, and unimaginative repetition of the past."[67] Mere repetition of biblical phraseology does not necessarily constitute faithfulness to canonical

---

64. Ricoeur, *Oneself as Another*, 116–17. Aristotle describes substance-identity in a similar fashion. He primarily defines substance or essence as "that which is neither predicable of a subject nor present in a subject" and secondarily the general quality shared by a genus that makes each individual belonging to a species a member of that group (*Categories* 2a 11–18). Substances retain their identity even as their accidental properties change and they remain self-identical in every moment of their existence. This primary substance (*prōtē ousia*) is the concrete individual with a unique identity. The secondary substance (*deutera ousia*) of which Aristotle speaks is that essence which makes an individual substance part of a genus of like beings. The former substance is particular and the latter more general. For an application of this to the Nicene distinction between *ousia* and *hypostases*, see William P. Alston, "Substance and the Trinity," in *The Trinity: An Interdisciplinary Symposium on the Trinity*, ed. Stephen T. Davis, Daniel Kendall, and Gerald O'Collins (Oxford: Oxford University Press, 1999), 181–82.
65. Ricoeur, *Oneself as Another*, 118–19. Ricoeur defines character as "the set of distinctive marks which permit the reidentification of a human individual as being the same."
66. Ricoeur, *Oneself as Another*, 123.
67. Vanhoozer, *The Drama of Doctrine*, 127. The *ipse/idem* distinction appears in several of Vanhoozer's analogies. In *The Drama of Doctrine*, he uses it to talk about doctrinal development. He applies the analogy to translation theory in *Is There a Meaning in This Text?* (Grand Rapids, MI: Zondervan, 1998), 390–92. He also describes the identity and constancy of God in terms of *ipse*-selfhood. See Kevin J. Vanhoozer, "Does the Trinity Belong in a Theology of Religions? On Angling in the Rubicon and the 'Identity' of God," in *The Trinity in a Pluralistic Age*, ed. Kevin Vanhoozer (Grand Rapids, MI: Eerdmans, 1997), 41–71; cf. idem, *Remythologizing Theology*, 455–57.

script. Sometimes in doctrinal development, non-biblical language is necessary to communicate the ideas of Scripture faithfully, as the Arian controversy illustrates.[68] With his use of Scripture, Arius (c. 250–336) may well fit the description of a naïve biblicist.[69] By contrast, *ipse* or "soft" identity "allows for development, growth, and perhaps even a certain degree of change in the way that *idem*, or 'hard' identity ('self-same'), does not."[70] Vanhoozer thus links the identity of the tradition with *ipse*-identity because of its emphasis on character. While the Christian tradition does not show signs of *idem*-sameness throughout history, it can maintain continuity with the past through *ipse*-identity, personal continuity despite growth and change over time.[71] The canon is itself a witness to *ipse*-identity in development—not *idem*-sameness—in the relationship between the Old and New Testaments. The New Testament retains the character and plot of the covenant with Israel while simultaneously taking the story in fresh new directions that are faithful to previously established patterns.[72]

---

68. Vanhoozer, *The Drama of Doctrine*, 127; cf. Alister E. McGrath, *The Genesis of Doctrine: A Study in the Foundation of Doctrinal Criticism* (Grand Rapids, MI: Eerdmans, 1990), 6.

69. Arius's extant writings reveal his frequent use of Scripture. Copies of the letters to Eusebius of Nicomedia (c. 318), Alexander (c. 320), and Constantine (c. 327, c. 333) are available in Hans-Georg Opitz, *Urkunde zur Geschichte des arianischen Streits* (Berlin: Leizpig, 1934). Quotations from his *Thalia* are in Athanasius *Orationes contra Arianos* 1.5–6 and *De Synodis* 15. See also Maurice Wiles, *Archetypal Heresy: Arianism through the Centuries* (Oxford: Clarendon, 1996), 10–17. In his "sympathetic reconstruction" of Arius's thought, Wiles shows the presbyter's commitment to the authority of the Scripture in doctrinal formation. See also Robert C. Gregg and Dennis Groh, *Early Arianism: A View of Salvation* (Fortress: Philadelphia, 1981), 2. Gregg and Groh add, "So firmly entrenched in all of our minds has been the picture of Arius as a logician and a dialectician that our tendency has been to overlook his concern for biblical exactitude."

70. Vanhoozer, *The Drama of Doctrine*, 127.

71. Ibid., 128. By "disposition," Vanhoozer does not (explicitly) refer the kind of dispositional belief employed in Thiselton's answer to the identity question. Rather, following Ricoeur, he defines dispositions as "habits" or practices "*to see, judge, and act according to*" (376). See also Ricoeur, *Oneself as Another*, 121–22.

72. Vanhoozer, *The Drama of Doctrine*, 128.

The *ipse/idem* relationship prepares the reader for Vanhoozer's third concern: the connection between canon and its cultural contextualization. The Christian tradition displays *ipse*-identity in its commitment to Christian mission throughout the ages, a mission exercised through contextualization and development. As noted above, he uses the dramaturgical metaphor of *improvisation* to describe the act of faithful development. Vanhoozer prefers improvisation to the metaphor of memorizing the lines because merely reciting the script "does not quite address the problem of having to speak and act in ways that fit *new* situations and address *new* problems."[73] Seemingly channeling Gadamer's notion of understanding as application, Vanhoozer asserts that regurgitation of the script's dialogue does not necessarily constitute understanding of the script's meaning.[74] Many actors can memorize lines without understanding the intentions or design of the playwright. In development and contextualization, understanding the character of the canon is more important than transplanting its locutions. Once more, the metaphor of improvisation means that *idem*-sameness repetition will not suffice in contextualization.

Returning to the example of the Arian controversy, Vanhoozer praises Athanasius as an exemplary improviser who, directed by the canonical script, offered *homoousios* as an "improvised" answer to questions about Jesus' sonship.[75] Athanasius himself defends the Nicene use of the word despite the fact that it does not appear in the canon: "Even if the expressions are not in so many words in the Scriptures, yet, as was said before, they contain the *sense of the Scriptures*, and expressing it, they convey it to those who have their hearing unimpaired for religious doctrine."[76]

73. Ibid., 335.
74. Ibid., 128; cf. 63.
75. Ibid., 343.

Theological improvisation is also a never-ending task because the cultural backdrop against which the church witnesses to Christ is always changing. For Vanhoozer, culture provides the backdrop and stage props for the dramatic theological task, but this task is not Tillich's method of correlation. Culture does not *direct* theology by asking the questions it needs to address. Culture only provides the *scenery* and the *props*, not the script or the role performances. Scripture gives normative direction to contextualization and keeps the Christian tradition faithful to its *ipse*-identity, even if continually changing settings force the tradition and community beyond *idem*-sameness.[77]

Fourth, Vanhoozer relates identity in the development of doctrine to *translation*. The metaphor has a twofold purpose. First, it connotes the need for *fidelity* to the gospel and Scripture. Second, the metaphor addresses the need for *creative* performances of the canonical script in different ways to different contexts. Ultimately, the task of doctrinal development is like translation in the sense that it is an attempt to understand and communicate the illocutionary acts of Scripture in new cultural settings and to invite appropriate responses to Scripture in these new settings.[78] A parallel analogy appears in Vanhoozer's general hermeneutics, wherein he relates translation to development: "Faithful interpretation is . . . more like apostolic tradition; it is a matter not of betraying but continuing the communicative act, of passing it on. . . . *Like tradition, then, translation does not simply repeat the past but rather develops it.*"[79]

---

76. Athanasius *De Decretis* 21, italics mine.

77. Vanhoozer, *The Drama of Doctrine*, 129, italics mine; cf. Vanhoozer, *Is There a Meaning in This Text?*, 388–90. See also Paul Tillich, *Systematic Theology*, vol. 1 (Chicago: University of Chicago Press, 1951), 3–68.

78. Vanhoozer, *The Drama of Doctrine*, 131.

79. Vanhoozer, *Is There a Meaning in This Text?*, 392.

With literary critic George Steiner, Vanhoozer renders translation a type of interpretation, perhaps even the model for all interpretation: "Every reading is a translation, every reader a translator, someone who takes something (viz., meaning) from the text (the source language) and moves it somewhere else (the receptor language)."[80] Contra Derrida, who suspects that all translation is a recreation of meaning, Vanhoozer affirms the possibility of preserving *semantic identity* ("sameness of meaning") in the translation process. Even if meaning is stable in successful translation, interpreters should not aim for *idem*-sameness or material similarity. For example, a formal equivalence translation is an attempt to reproduce a text by reproducing the locutionary acts of a text as closely as possible.[81] The goal of one-to-one correspondence in translation is, however, unfeasible given the "realities of interpretation."[82]

In contrast, advocates of dynamic equivalence endeavor to reproduce the communicative acts of texts rather than mimicking phraseology and syntax. Vanhoozer affirms this basic intuition: "The notion that only word-for-word translations are faithful rests on a faulty view of semantics that sees words, rather than speech-acts, as the fundamental unit of meaning. Faithful translation, however, is not a matter of matching *locutions* so much as finding equivalent *illocutions*."[83] Nevertheless, he is not content with the implicit assumption in dynamic equivalence shared with its formal sister that translation occurs through "reproduction." Perfect reproduction is impossible because of the "bias principle"—the reality that interpreters live in different horizons than authors.[84]

---

80. Vanhoozer, *Is There a Meaning in This Text?*, 386. See also George Steiner, *After Babel: Aspects of Language and Translation*, 3d ed. (Oxford: Oxford University Press, 1998), 18–31.
81. Vanhoozer, *Is There a Meaning in This Text?*, 387.
82. Ibid., 391.
83. Ibid., 388.

Rather than construing translation as reproduction, Vanhoozer understands translation (and by extension, interpretation) as *productive* understanding. Translation and interpretation demand both faithfulness to the text and creativity. With a Ricoeurian twist, Vanhoozer submits that interpretation and translation function like creative metaphors that enable understanding,[85] what Mikhail Bakhtin calls "creative understanding."[86] Literary scholar Michael Edwards underscores the theological dimension of this approach to translation for Vanhoozer when he describes translation as a "re-creative possibility."[87]

Translation, too, can improve with new semantic discoveries within the text. As Bakhtin observes, texts frequently have meaning potential unknown to their original audiences. New questions bring forward undiscovered meanings.[88] Vanhoozer does not find that this possibility poses any real threat to the identity of interpretation or meaning. In his discussion of potentialities of meaning, he looks to literary theorist Wayne C. Booth, who argues for the essential identity of meaning using an organic metaphor. Understandings of *King Lear* may develop as interpreters discover new depths within it;

---

84. Vanhoozer, *Is There a Meaning in This Text?*, 389. See also Richard Lints, *The Fabric of Theology: A Prolegomenon to Evangelical Theology* (Grand Rapids, MI: Eerdmans, 1993), 20–21. Lints defines the "bias principle" as the recognition that "individuals never know the world apart from the biases that influence their view of what really is the case." He also affirms the "realism principle," the idea that "individuals normally know the world pretty much as it really is."

85. Vanhoozer, *Is There a Meaning in This Text?*, 389; cf. idem, *Biblical Narrative in the Philosophy of Paul Ricoeur*, 56–85.

86. Bakhtin, *Speech Genres*, 7.

87. Vanhoozer, *Is There a Meaning in This Text?*, 389. See also Michael Edwards, *Towards a Christian Poetics* (Grand Rapids, MI: Eerdmans, 1984), 169–70. Vanhoozer follows the argument of Edwards faithfully. Edwards writes, "If translation encroaches on the literature and language of the translator, so it can encroach on the work being translated. Instead of accounting the work untouchable, out of fidelity, or modesty, it may disturb it or even disrupt it. Once again, the translator joins the writer, within a theory of language, and particularly of writing, as re-creative possibility. Just as language, rather than duplicating the world, operates upon it, so translation, rather duplicating a work, may operate on the work and on the world of the work."

88. Bakhtin, *Speech Genres*, 7.

but in the same way a developing human fetus does not transform into a pig, the tragic *King Lear* does not transform into a comedy.[89] Recognition of undiscovered potentialities in the text does not change the nature of the text, nor need the discovery of new meanings disrupt its semantic identity.

An evangelical doctrine of Scripture that recognizes both its divine and human authorship is able to claim both authorial intent and undiscovered meanings in original contexts because evangelicals recognize that the human authors of Scripture may have been on occasion unaware of the full meaning of the revelation that they voiced. Intracanonical development illustrates the potential for discovering these deeper meanings. New Testament authors were able to retrieve layers of divine meaning in Old Testament texts that their human authors could not perceive. By the same measure, some christological and typological readings of Old Testament texts—as modeled by patristic and medieval interpreters—may be an apropos evangelical hermeneutical practice. This observation is not an open invitation to make Scripture a wax nose but simply to demonstrate that it is possible that there are meanings embedded in the text by the divine author that, with the aid of the Holy Spirit, can be unlocked in new settings and situations when needed.

Identity and Theological Judgments

The implications of translation for doctrinal development become clearer in Vanhoozer's interaction with David Kelsey, who offers a critique of translation metaphors for understanding the Scripture/

---

89. See Vanhoozer, *Is There a Meaning in This Text?*, 390; cf. Wayne C. Booth, *The Company We Keep: An Ethics of Fiction* (Berkeley: University of California Press, 1989), 86–90. This metaphor clearly resembles other organic metaphors used in discussions of doctrinal development, such as the seed model of Johann Möhler. See Thiel, *Senses of Tradition*, 63–67.

doctrine relation.[90] Kelsey maintains that translation is incapable of explaining the *"conceptual discontinuity"* between the Bible and theological formulations: "By definition the move from one conceptuality to another is to *change* the concepts. The move from one conceptuality to another is not 'translation' but a 'redescription.'"[91] Kelsey rightly concludes that translation is a poor metaphor, if translation means transporting an identical concept from one setting to another. Clearly, many traditional doctrinal terms are absent from Scripture. Many important concepts are similarly absent. *Homoousios*, for example, is not an explicit New Testament concept, nor for that matter does it seem to be an implicit idea in the minds of the apostles, as Newman and others who hold to a noetic model of development would suggest. The conceptual framework behind *homoousios*, shaped by third- and fourth-century metaphysics, likely would be alien to Paul's hearing.

The first problem with Kelsey's argument, Vanhoozer notes, is that Kelsey has a fundamentally insufficient understanding of translation. For Vanhoozer, translation is more like *ipse*-identity *idem*-sameness.[92] Semantic identity, like personal identity, is dependent upon self-constancy rather than self-sameness: "Interpretations that are creative *and* faithful demonstrate not identity but *constancy* with regard to the text." If meaning relates to *illocutionary* and *perlocutionary* constancy rather than *locutionary* sameness, then a translation or interpretation of a text that creatively reflects the illocutionary force, matter, and direction of the original communicative act preserves this kind of *ipse*-identity.[93]

---

90. See David H. Kelsey, *Proving Doctrine: The Uses of Scripture in Modern Theology* (Harrisburg, PA: Trinity, 1999), 185.

91. Ibid., 188.

92. Vanhoozer, *The Drama of Doctrine*, 130.

93. Vanhoozer, *Is There a Meaning in This Text?*, 391.

Vanhoozer's second rejoinder to Kelsey is crucial for understanding his answer to the identity question. With Kelsey, he concedes conceptual discontinuity between the New Testament and later doctrinal formulations. Yet the metaphor of improvisatory translation is not about the cross-cultural relocation of concepts. Vanhoozer appeals to Lutheran theologian David Yeago's differentiation between theological *judgments* and *concepts* to explicate why. As Yeago explains,

> We cannot concretely perform an act of judgement without employing some particular, contingent verbal and conceptual resources; judgement-making *is* an operation performed with words and concepts. At the same time, however, the same judgement can be rendered in a variety of conceptual terms, all of which may be informative about a particular judgement's force and implications. The possibility of valid alternative verbal/conceptual renderings of the identical judgement accounts for the fact that we ourselves often do not realize the full implications of the judgements we pass: only *some* of their implications are ever unpacked in the particular renderings we have given them.[94]

Continuity between the New Testament and later doctrinal formulations must be established on fidelity to biblical judgments, not in the recasting of biblical concepts.[95] Vanhoozer follows suit and describes theological judgment making as "a matter of deciding between right and wrong—right and wrong beliefs, right and wrong interpretations, right and wrong actions."[96] Heresy grows not by the incorporation of new conceptual frameworks but by making judgments that are contrary to the pattern of Scripture.[97] This

94. David S. Yeago, "The New Testament and Nicene Dogma: A Contribution to the Recovery of Theological Exegesis," in *Theological Interpretation of Scripture: Classic and Contemporary Readings*, ed. Stephen E. Fowl (Cambridge, MA: Blackwell, 1997), 93.
95. Ibid., 95.
96. Kevin J. Vanhoozer, "The Voice and the Actor: A Dramatic Proposal about the Ministry and Minstrelsy of Theology," in *Evangelical Futures: A Conversation on Theological Method*, ed. John G. Stackhouse Jr. (Grand Rapids, MI: Baker, 2000), 83.
97. Vanhoozer, *The Drama of Doctrine*, 424.

emphasis on judgments rather than concepts also coheres with his emphasis on doctrine as *phronēsis* or practical wisdom.

Yeago offers three steps for comparing judgments with different contexts and conceptual frameworks. Vanhoozer applies this threefold pattern to his own model of doctrinal development as improvisation and translation, calling it "theo-dramatic equivalence."[98] First, one must ask about "the logical subjects of which predicates are affirmed and denied."[99] To return to Vanhoozer's theo-dramatic metaphor, who are the *dramatis personæ* of the particular canonical judgment? Whose story is it? What is the story about? For Vanhoozer, identifying the correct divine *dramatis personæ* is the most important step in making good theological judgments and avoiding heresy. Instead of performing or improvising with a script, Arius and Marcion (c. 85–160) *rewrite* the theo-dramatic plot because they misidentify divine *dramatis personæ*, the triune God at work in the story. Marcion could not apprehend the covenantal theo-drama at work in both biblical testaments because he would not identify the God of Israel with the God of Christ.[100] By refusing to relate Christ to God, Arius undermines the soteriological scheme of the theo-drama.[101] Modalists confuse the *dramatis personæ* by conflating the persons of the triune God into a single voice, one actor playing multiple roles.[102]

Second, one must inquire about the "logical type of the particular predicates affirmed or denied within the conceptual idioms they employ." What do the concepts mean within their given conceptual framework and how do they predicate the given subject? [103]

---

98. Ibid., 320; cf. 343–45.
99. Yeago, "The New Testament and Nicene Dogma," 94.
100. Vanhoozer, *The Drama of Doctrine*, 82.
101. Ibid., 83.
102. See Fred Sanders, *The Deep Things of God: How the Trinity Changes Everything* (Wheaton, IL: Crossway, 2010), 32.

According to Vanhoozer, another mistake of the heretic is to mistake "*the action*" or the plot of the story.[104] Docetics and Apollinarians may recognize Jesus as an important character without grasping his role in the plot: "that Jesus Christ *has come in the flesh*" (1 John 4:2). Latter-day Saints misunderstand the saving action attributed to the divine *dramatis personæ* in the canonical script when they claim that the divine auteur himself was once a minor player who upstaged the theo-drama by making the correct hand gestures, using the right props, and wearing the proper costumes.

Third, one must ask about the purpose of the affirmations and denials in their respective contexts.[105] What illocutionary act is the author performing, and what perlocutionary act does he or she expect? When biblical interpreters miss these speech-acts, they give bad direction that is neither faithful to the script nor relevant to the ongoing theo-drama. Cults like Jehovah's Witnesses not only misidentify the divine *dramatis personæ* and misunderstand the plot; they likewise give faulty direction that can have disastrous consequences for the performers.

So, how do faithful theological improvisations relate to biblical texts? The christological hymn in Philippians 2:6–11 and the Nicene Creed provide Yeago (and in turn, Vanhoozer) with a test case for this three-step approach. First, both texts share the same logical subject: Jesus Christ. The Creed utilizes narrative descriptions of Christ as the one who "suffered" and "rose again" to ensure his identity with the Jesus of Nazareth described in the Gospels and the risen Lord described in Pauline literature.[106]

---

103. Yeago, "The New Testament and Nicene Dogma," 94.
104. Vanhoozer, *The Drama of Doctrine*, 424.
105. Yeago, "The New Testament and Nicene Dogma," 94.
106. Ibid., 94. The Niceno-Constantinopolitan Creed (381) adds additional narrative qualifications. The incarnation was accomplished "by the Holy Ghost through the Virgin Mary," and Jesus was "crucified for us under Pontius Pilate."

Second, "each text predicates of these two subjects the most intimate possible bond, using the strongest terms available within the conceptual idiom of each."[107] In other words, both texts use the best available language at their disposal to express the same predication of the logical subject. To claim that Christ "existed in the form of God" (Phil. 2:6) is to make the same basic judgment that Christ is "one and the same substance with God," even if these judgments utilize term terms and conceptual frameworks. Despite their uses of very different philosophical concepts, Paul and the Nicene Council come to roughly the same conclusion: Jesus is equal with God in every way and deserving of the same response given to God.

Third, both the Pauline hymn and the Nicene Creed make the same basic point in their respective affirmations about Jesus.[108] They perform similar illocutionary acts in calling attention to Jesus and demanding a certain response of his followers.[109] The Nicene Council, then, successfully followed the canonical pattern in developing doctrine, not with *idem*-sameness repetition but with *ipse*-identity constancy: "Nicaea neither imposed *homoousios* onto Philippians nor deduced it from Paul's text; instead, it discerned a pattern of judgments that were intrinsic to the text—canonical judgments—and articulated them in terms of the language and

---

107. Yeago, "The New Testament and Nicene Dogma," 94.
108. Ibid., 95.
109. In the case of Phil. 2:5–11, the performance Paul expects is Christlike humility (2:5). Philippians 2:9–11 (cf. Isa. 45:21) is a reminder that all persons ultimately answer to Christ's lordship because of his equality with God. The Nicene Council gives similar stage directions in calling for belief and trust in the one who shares the same substance with God. Lindbeck, too, distinguishes doctrine and concept, calling attention to the regulative dimension of the Nicene Creed. However, he also suggests that it is "easier to [restate the doctrine] if doctrines are taken as expressing second-order guidelines for Christian discourse rather than first-order affirmations about the inner being of God or of Jesus Christ" (*The Nature of Doctrine*, 94). Yet without the conviction that Jesus truly is equal in authority and power to God, a conviction made possible only by reality-depicting language, the direction to submit one's life to his lordship in both Phil. 2:9–11 and the Nicene Creed loses its principal grounding. Without grounding in the reality of God, ascribing lordship to Christ is idolatrous.

conceptuality of the day."[110] The conceptual resources of Paul and Nicaea may be worlds apart, but both make remarkably constant judgments about Christ.

In summary, improvisation and translation ultimately serve Christian mission, which provides continuity throughout the living Christian tradition. The identity of doctrine is not found in immutable concepts but in improvised judgments patterned after the Christian canon. Believers in the first-century biblical setting, Christians throughout history, and present-day Christians all share the same Lord and calling (i.e., the life situation Vanhoozer calls the "Christotope").[111] Translation makes transmission of values, norms, and judgments between specific places in time, space, and culture possible, and improvisation provides a means for creative responses to the challenges posed in every successive context. As improvisation and translation of the theo-drama in a variety of chronotopic contexts, doctrinal development, rather than threatening Christian identity, establishes it and maintains it.

The Doctrine of Scripture: Inerrancy

Doctrines of Scripture provide an interesting test case for doctrinal continuity, particularly the evangelical doctrine of biblical inerrancy. Many, if not most, evangelicals cherish the idea that Christian Scripture is completely trustworthy and true in all that it affirms.[112] Those within confessional evangelicalism define the doctrine as a theological boundary marker for distinguishing evangelicals from other Christian traditions.[113] Some within the broadly evangelical

---

110. Vanhoozer, *The Drama of Doctrine*, 344.
111. Ibid., 140.
112. Here, I use the "negative" term *inerrancy* interchangeably with biblical *veracity* or the *trustworthiness* and *truthfulness* of Scripture. The debate between American and non-American evangelicals about terminology is beyond the scope of this chapter.

fold minimize its historic significance for all evangelicals, while others who self identify as evangelical reject the doctrine altogether or revise it beyond recognition.

Since the 1970s, scholars on every side of the issue have had substantial debates in theological historiography about its significance for broader historical Christian tradition. On one side of the debate, confessional and neo-evangelicals contend that inerrancy is consistent with the doctrines of Scripture held throughout history. Those on the other side label the doctrine a nineteenth-century innovation, married to modernity and largely inconsequential for a global and postmodern context. For many on both sides, there is an implicitly negative attitude toward all postcanonical developments, whether they are making the case that inerrancy is not such a development or they are arguing that it is.

Though the term *inerrant* is itself a modern novelty, the *judgment* that the Scriptures should be trusted has been held by Christians throughout the history of the church, beginning with the patristic period.[114] Scripture was, for Irenaeus (d. 202), "perfect," for Hippolytus (170–235), "truth," and for Augustine, "infallible."[115] Patristic belief in the truthfulness of Scripture was an outflow of belief in its divine inspiration.[116] As Gregg R. Allison notes, the church fathers expressed their belief in truthfulness of Scriptures in both its correspondence to reality and in its internal consistent witness.[117]

---

113. For a recent argument along these lines, see R. Albert Mohler, "When the Bible Speaks, God Speaks: The Classic Doctrine of Biblical Inerrancy," in *Five Views on Biblical Inerrancy*, ed. J. Merrick and Stephen M. Garrett (Grand Rapids, MI: Zondervan, 2013), 29–58; idem, "Confessional Evangelicalism," in *Four Views on the Spectrum of Evangelicalism*, ed. Andrew David Naselli and Collin Hansen (Grand Rapids, MI: Zondervan, 2011), 89–91.

114. For a brief and helpful diachronic survey of the doctrine of inerrancy, see Gregg R. Allison, *Historical Theology: An Introduction to Christian Doctrine* (Grand Rapids, MI: Zondervan, 2011), 99–119. Historical references in this section follow Allison's timeline and structure.

115. Allison, 102, 104; cf. Irenaeus, *Against Heresies* 2.28.2; Hippolytus *Fragments from Commentaries* 2.27; Augustine, *The City of God* 21. 23; idem. *Letter* 28.

116. Allison, 101; cf. Irenaeus, *Against Heresies* 2.28.2; Athanasius *Easter Letter* 19.3

117. Allison, 100; cf. Tertullian, *A Treatise on the Soul* 21; Theophilus *To Autolycus* 3.17.

Later on in the Reformation, Luther and Calvin likewise insisted that the Bible did not and could not err.[118] In nineteenth- and twentieth-century engagement with modernism, this doctrine provided evangelicals a crucial defense against many of the charges against the Bible proffered by historical critical and liberal theological scholarship.

Those who affirm inerrancy continue to define and refine it for contemporary hearers. The Chicago Statement on Biblical Inerrancy (1978) is presently the most robust and carefully nuanced articulation of the doctrine. The statement is the closest thing to a modern ecumenical creed that American evangelicals have, albeit one drafted less ceremoniously in a Hyatt Regency ballroom. Having established a long history of the belief of Scripture's complete truthfulness in the history of the church, we can ask the more pressing question for evangelicals committed to biblical authority. Is such a doctrine consistent with Scripture itself?

Trying to sketch doctrines of Scripture from biblical exegesis alone, the method of biblical theology, proves a daunting, if not impossible task. First, no single text offers a comprehensive explanation of the doctrine of Scripture; the doctrine of Scripture must be inferred from several passages in a systematic fashion. Millard Erickson acknowledges the difficulty of formulating such a doctrine through biblical interpretation alone: "Belief in the inerrancy of the Scriptures is not an inductive conclusion arrived at by examining all the passages of the Bible. By its very nature, such a conclusion would only be probable at best. Nor is the doctrine of biblical inerrancy explicitly taught or affirmed in the Bible."[119]

---

118. Allison, 105–07; Robert D. Preus, "Luther and Biblical Infallibility," in *Inerrancy and the Church*, ed. John Hannah (Chicago: Moody, 1984), 99–142; J. I. Packer, "John Calvin and the Inerrancy of Scripture," in *Inerrancy and the Church*, ed. John Hannah (Chicago: Moody, 1984), 143–88.
119. Erickson, *Christian Theology*, 198.

Second, as Ben Witherington III and others have argued, many of the references to the "word of God" in the Old and New Testaments speak specifically to the oral proclamation of God and not specifically the written words in Scripture.[120] This is an issue for many of the common prooftexts appealed to in defense of inerrancy such as Psalm 12:6 ("the words of the LORD are flawless"), Psalm 33:4 ("the word of the LORD is right and true"), John 17:17 ("your word is truth"), and Revelation 21:5 ("these words are trustworthy and true"). While no single biblical text offers a clear-cut explanation of biblical inerrancy, Scripture repeatedly testifies to its divine inspiration in every part (2 Tim. 3:16; 2 Pet. 1:20–21) and the infallibility of God's spoken word (Isa. 55:11). The Bible also repeatedly testifies about the truthfulness of God himself (Num. 23:19; 1 Sam. 15:29; Prov. 12:22; John 1:14, 17; 3:33; Rom. 3:4, 7; Titus 1:2; Heb. 6:18).

The development of inerrancy can be described as a consistent development with the Scripture by means of Thiselton's dispositional account of Christian doctrine. Erickson argues that a belief in the truthfulness of Scripture appears to be held implicitly by biblical authorship: "The view of the Bible held and taught by the writers of Scripture implies the full truthfulness of the Bible. But this does not spell out for us the nature of biblical inerrancy."[121] The truthfulness of God's word (whether written or spoken) is a probable disposition of biblical authors.

In the dispositional account of doctrine, inferences occur when conscious thought about one proposition leads to a probable consequence. The dispositional belief in biblical inerrancy is an inference from a belief in biblical inspiration. We may illustrate

---

120. See Ben Witherington III, *The Living Word of God: Rethinking the Theology of the Bible* (Waco, TX: Baylor University Press, 2007), 1–14; cf. John H. Walton and D. Brent Sandy, *The Lost World of Scripture: Ancient Literary Culture and Biblical Authority* (Downers Grove, IL: InterVarsity, 2013), 121–42.

121. Millard J. Erickson, *Christian Theology*, 3d ed. (Grand Rapids, MI: Baker, 2013), 198.

what we believe biblical authors dispositionally believed about the truthfulness and trustworthiness of Scripture in this categorical syllogism:

> Every *Word of God* (A) is *Trustworthy and True* (C)
> Every *Scripture* (B) is *the Word of God* (A).
> ∴ Every *Scripture* (B) is *Trustworthy and True* (C)

The first premise (All *A* is *C*) can be deduced from passages like those cited above: Psalm 12:6, 33:4; John 17:17; and Revelation 21:5. Regardless of whether biblical authors are referring to the written or oral word of God, they believe the word of God to be trustworthy and true. The second premise (All *B* is *A*) is explicitly stated in places like 2 Timothy 3:16–17 or 2 Peter 1:20–21. Whether or not the biblical writers in these texts possessed a canonical consciousness of their own writing is, for the moment, inconsequential. They simply model their belief that Scripture, whether in the Old Covenant or in the New (2 Pet. 3:15–17), is, in fact, tantamount to the word of God. The concluding inference (All *B* is *C*) is that biblical authors likely affirmed the total trustworthiness of Scripture as God's word, or would have had they been asked the question.

Strictly speaking, biblical inerrancy is a doctrine *about* Scripture and not a doctrine explicitly taught *by* Scripture. Like theories of inspiration, it is a postcanonical doctrinal development based on a particular interpretation of Scripture. The doctrine is, however, consistent with the judgments and dispositions of biblical authors who assert the truthfulness of God and his spoken word. Inerrancy is not a significant issue for those who do not equate the written word of God with the whole of Scripture. If Scripture is merely a human witness to revelation and not a medium of revelation itself, then error is inevitable. On the other hand, if one construes Scripture to be God's written word, some notion of inerrancy is more likely.

Inerrancy may be a probable implication for those who affirm a dynamic theory of inspiration, but it is a logically necessary implication or consequent of plenary-verbal or dictation theories of inspiration, as argued in the syllogism above.[122]

The Practice of the Church: Baptism

Another interesting test case for doctrinal continuity is the practice of paedobaptism (i.e., the baptism of infants). This is not the place to rehearse traditional arguments for or against paedobaptism, which have been explored with detail and skill elsewhere.[123] Those within my own Baptist tradition characteristically reject paedobaptism (i.e., the baptism of infants) in favor of credobaptism (i.e., the baptism of adult believers or converts) because the former practice lacks explicit mention in the New Testament. However, is such an argument from silence convincing? As we have seen, doctrine often develops by making explicit that which is implicit in the text, by faithfully practicing the illocutionary acts of Scripture in new settings and situations. So, can paedobaptism represent appropriate development faithful to the judgments of Scripture, or does this practice model an appeal to ecclesial tradition as additional material authority in development? Further analysis of the issue is required.

---

122. Mohler, "When the Bible Speaks, God Speaks," 37.
123. Well-informed arguments from the Reformed tradition for padeobaptism include John Murray, *Christian Baptism* (Nutley, NJ: Presbyterian and Reformed, 1970); Pierre Marcel, *The Biblical Doctrine of Infant Baptism*, trans. Philip Edcumbe Hughes (London: James Clarke, 1959); Gregg Strawbridge, ed. *The Case for Covenantal Baptism* (Philipsburg, NJ: Presbyterian and Reformed, 2003); Michael F. Bird, *Evangelical Theology: A Biblical and Systematic Introduction* (Grand Rapids, MI: Zondervan, 2013), 761–71. Robust counterproposals from the credobaptist tradition include Fred A. Malone, *The Baptism of Disciples Alone: A Covenantal Argument for Credobaptism Versus Paedobaptism*, rev. ed. (Cape Coral, FL: Founders Press, 2007); G. R. Beasley-Murray, *Baptism in the New Testament* (Grand Rapids, MI: Eerdmans, 1962); Thomas R. Schreiner and Shawn D. Wright, eds., *Believer's Baptism: Sign of the New Covenant in Christ* (Nashville: Broadman and Holman, 2006); T. E. Watson, *Should Infants Be Baptized?* (Grand Rapids, MI: Guardian, 1976).

Thiselton briefly addresses the debate between Joachim Jeremias and Kurt Aland on the nature of "household" baptism formulae in the New Testament but withholds his own opinion on the matter, implying that the significance of the baptism is more important than its mode or proper subjects. Jeremias argues that paedobaptism was a practice in the New Testament and in the early church. Aland, on the other hand, argues that credobaptism is normative in the New Testament and standard practice for the first two centuries of Christianity.[124] Following the pattern of his treatment of other doctrines, Thiselton does not offer a conclusive statement about the meaning of baptism.[125]

On the other hand, Vanhoozer considers baptism an important participatory act in the theo-drama but is ambiguous regarding its mode, administration, and proper subjects:

> Baptism and the Lord's Supper . . . are communicative actions, less speech-acts than acts that speak. . . . Baptism marks our entry into the church, our regeneration, and purification from sin. . . . Baptism enacts our solidarity with Jesus' own death and resurrection; in baptism we participate in being buried with Jesus (united in death) and in being raised with Jesus (united in life). . . . [The sacraments] are able to draw us into the pattern of Jesus' own communicative action.[126]

Vanhoozer makes no clear-cut case for paedobaptism or credobaptism, but it is likely that the Presbyterian theologian would seem to favor paedobaptism and make a case for it within the covenantal framework he sketches in his theo-dramatic model of doctrine. Neither Thiselton nor Vanhoozer shows plainly, or for that

---

124. See Joachim Jeremias, *Infant Baptism in the First Four Centuries*, trans. David Cairns (Eugene, OR: Wipf & Stock, 2004); idem, *The Origins of Infant Baptism: A Further Study in Reply to Kurt Aland*, trans. D. M. Burton (Eugene, OR: Wipf & Stock, 2004); and Kurt Aland, *Did the Early Church Baptize Infants?* trans. George Raymond Beasley-Murray (Eugene, OR: Wipf & Stock, 2004).

125. Thiselton, *The Hermeneutics of Doctrine*, 512–14; cf. 536–38.

126. Vanhoozer, *The Drama of Doctrine*, 75, italics mine.

matter, attempts to show, how the practice of paedobaptism in their respective faith traditions is an appropriate development grounded in the unique authority of Scripture.

Notably, one using Yeago and Vanhoozer's normative model of discerning the pattern of judgments in Scripture and enacting their practice in new settings probably could make arguments for both positions. Advocates of traditional arguments for paedobaptism seem to rely on making canonical judgments consistent with (*ipse*-identity) but not the same as (*idem*-sameness) the covenantal practice of circumcision.[127] The first two steps of Yeago and Vanhoozer's approach are addressed successfully here. These arguments for paedobaptism (1) rightly identify the divine *dramatis personæ* of canonical judgments regarding baptism, and (2) rightly identify the plot or canonical significance of baptism: unity with Christ in his death and resurrection (Rom. 6:5–11).

The question remains: Is the practice of paedobaptism a fitting response to biblical illocutionary acts regarding baptism? In other words, what response (or perlocutionary act) to their description of baptism do biblical writers expect their readers to make? John the Baptist asks Jesus about the propriety of his request to baptize him. Only Matthew tells his readers of Jesus' response and motive in baptism: to "fulfill all righteousness" (Matt. 3:15). Jesus did not *need* baptism because he was a sinner needing forgiveness but allowed John to baptize him in order that he might demonstrate *obedience* and show public *solidarity* with Israel and the people of God.[128] Paul seems to stress continuity between the public performance of baptism and an ongoing, *volitional* reckoning of oneself as dead to

---

127. See Louis Berkhof, *Systematic Theology*, 2nd ed. (Grand Rapids, MI: Eerdmans, 1974), 631–42; cf. Horton, *The Christian Faith*, 794–98.

128. Donald A. Hagner, *Matthew 1-13*, Word Biblical Commentary 33a (Nashville: Thomas Nelson, 2000), 57.

sin (Rom. 6:11). In both cases, baptism appears to be a public act of *self-commitment*, something impossible for a non-cognizant infant to do. Credobaptism appears a better fit with the description of baptism as communicative action that enacts solidarity with Christ. Baptism is a public performance of declaring allegiance, an enacted, enfleshed confession. In brief, the development of paedobaptist doctrine appears to focus on the wrong set of canonical judgments, or misconstrue them all together. This doctrine also may have developed in order to justify the practices of later Christian tradition, in which case the focus of authority has shifted.

The Ethical Dilemma: Overpopulation

Many of the issues associated with the doctrinal continuity problem also aid in addressing contemporary ethical issues that biblical writers did not address or could not have anticipated. The overpopulation issue was not on the horizon when God told Adam to "fill the earth and subdue it" (Gen. 1:28) or when he made his covenant with Abram (Gen. 12:5)! But overpopulation appears to be an issue for many today, including when the United Nations Population Fund symbolically marked the world's population reaching seven billion.[129] The occasion was bittersweet for a number of researchers and doomsayers who have asked whether there are enough resources to sustain exponentially growing populations. The controversy over overpopulation presents an interesting test case because the solution proposed by population control advocates seems to contradict what appears to be a biblical mandate—the first "Great Commission"—to "be fruitful and multiply" (Gen. 1:22, 28; 8:17; 9:1, 7; 35:11; 48:4).

---

129. Jasmine Coleman, "World's 'seven billionth baby' is born," *The Guardian*, October 30, 2011, http://www.guardian.co.uk/world/2011/oct/31/seven-billionth-baby-born-philippines (accessed February 12, 2012).

Concern about global overpopulation is not new to the twenty-first century. Plato (c. 428–347 BC) and Aristotle (384–322 BC) advocated population control and land distribution in order "to support a given number of people in modest comfort."[130] Tertullian (c. 160–220) bemoaned that the earth "scarcely can provide for our needs" when such a vast population places such a "burden" on it.[131] During the population boom of the late eighteenth and early nineteenth centuries, Anglican clergyman and economist Thomas Robert Malthus (1766–1834) argued that overpopulation was an ethical problem because it brought unnecessary suffering on the poor and destitute. He suggested that wars and pestilence were divine gifts given to limit the population and that sometimes more proactive measures like abortion, birth control, and celibacy are necessary for restraining population growth.[132]

The suggestion that overpopulation might be a Christian concern is obvious given the moral implications of overpopulation and population control. Vanhoozer's normative model of doctrinal continuity may be helpful for developing ethical statements. So, practically speaking, how would one using theo-dramatic hermeneutics address "be fruitful and multiply" texts in the Genesis narratives? How do we improvise with a canonical script? First, one must ask *who* is speaking and *what* is the nature of the canonical judgment? To return to Vanhoozer's theo-dramatic metaphor, who are the *dramatis personæ* of the particular canonical judgment? Whose story is it? What is the speaker *doing* with his words?[133] Clearly, God is the primary actor (or speaking subject) in most of the significant texts in question.

130. Plato, *Laws* 737d; see also Aristotle, *Politics* 1326.
131. Tertullian, *On the Soul* 30.
132. Joseph Johnson [Thomas Robert Malthus], *An Essay on the Principle of Population* (1798).
133. Vanhoozer, "A Drama-of-Redemption Model," 179; cf. idem, *The Drama of Doctrine*, 343. See also Yeago, "The New Testament and Nicene Dogma," 94.

The question remains, what illocutionary act is he performing with the locutionary act of "Be fruitful and multiply"? Perhaps he is simply describing a state of affairs, namely the role of the human race in reproducing itself throughout consecutive ages. He also may be issuing a stern command like, "You will procreate or there will be hell to pay!" Yet in most instances where God issues this imperative, the narrator offers a remarkable detail: "And God *blessed* them" or, in the other narratives, God blesses Noah or Jacob (Gen. 1:22, 27; cf. Gen. 9:1; 35:9; 48:3). God does not *enforce* or *dictate* reproduction like Hitler infamously did with his German youth camps in the 1930s; rather, he *blesses* the world with the gift of life.

Blessing is a directive illocutionary act that, depending on the authority and institutional status of the speaker, can actually change a state of affairs or create a state of affairs simply by its utterance.[134] In the case of this creation ordinance, God *gives enthusiastic approval* and *reproductive functionality* to the living creatures of the air and sea (Gen. 1:22) and humankind made in his image (Gen. 1:28) to populate the world he has created. In the flood and restoration narrative, God renews this blessing to Noah and his sons, encouraging them to "swarm," "teem," or "populate [the earth] abundantly" (Gen. 9:7). God's blessing of Jacob came with a promise: "A nation and a company of nations shall come from you, and kings shall come from your own body" (Gen. 35:11b; cf. 48:4b). In each of these texts, the intended perlocutionary act is not mere conformity to a rule but a spoken *blessing that enables further service to God.*

In the second step of the theo-dramatic method, the reader must determine his or her place in the drama of the text, that is, one must understand how the world *in front of the text* relates to the worlds within it or behind it.[135] Theo-drama calls for creative

---

134. Thiselton, *New Horizons in Hermeneutics*, 304–5.
135. Vanhoozer, "A Drama-of-Redemption Model," 180.

understanding—looking at the canon as a whole as the script for God's redemptive drama and then projecting oneself into the story in order to determine how to improvise our role in new scenes. For Vanhoozer, Act One is creation; Act Two, the election, rejection, and redemption of Israel; Act Three, the climactic entrance of Jesus Christ; Act Four, the mission of the church; and Act Five is the eschaton and consummation of all things.[136] The propagation of the human race plays an important role in the first four acts of the theo-drama. In Act One, God blesses creation with progeny in order that in the second act, elect Israel, by its fruitfulness and multiplication, could be a blessing to the nations. In the climactic moment of Act Three, Israel blesses the world through her seed, who is Jesus Christ (Gal. 3:16). By Act Four, multiplication has taken on a new dimension in the church as believers are called *not only to make babies but also to make disciples.*

Once we recognize our place in the theo-drama, we must discern specific judgments from the canonical script in order that we may improvise rightly in our setting. This does not mean merely repeating previous performances. As participants in Act Four, we may be in a different "setting" in the sense that we are not the first human beings or those, like Noah and his family, who were responsible for repopulating the earth. We also have good reason to be wary of supersessionism or replacement theology that would confuse our role and scene with Israel's special casting. But these distinctions need not mean we as Act Four believers are not called to similar patterns of behavior.

First, by virtue of our humanity crafted in God's image (Gen. 1:27), we are blessed co-participants in God's global construction project, filling the earth and subduing it in such a way that reflects God's own

---

136. Vanhoozer, *The Drama of Doctrine*, 3.

reign (Gen. 1:28b). The earth serves humanity, not humanity the earth. This realization does not mean we should be reckless in how we tend to creation or utilize its resources, but we should remember that proper stewardship of it is vital for blessing its pinnacle creature. Second, the blessing of propagation goes hand-in-hand with an affirmation of the sanctity of human life that we as believers should continue to practice. Between the directives to "be fruitful and multiply" in the Noahic covenant of Genesis 9:1 and 9:7 God gives a solemn warning toward the person who would shed the blood of another—an act that is a rejection of God's blessing of copious human life (Gen. 9:6). In addressing the so-called population problem, we must insist on the sanctity of all human life and remember that a failure to do so is a dismissal of God's gift. Third, we who were grafted into Israel (Rom. 9:11–24) are called to join her in her mission to bless the nations as we are the mediators of God's blessing in our proclamation of the gospel.

In short, the theo-dramatic method calls attention to the illocutionary acts of "be fruitful and multiply" texts and calls on believers to use creative understanding and imagination in appropriating the canonical judgments of the text to contemporary questions about population. The speaker does *not* require that all persons procreate, nor does his instruction prohibit birth control or abstinence. Rather, the directive speech-act is a means through which God blesses his people and invites them to participate in his blessing the world. Most importantly for concerns about population control, this blessing asserts the importance and value of all human life and denounces any practice that would result in the murder of human beings created in God's image.

Conclusion

The real "problem" in doctrinal development is the issue of doctrinal continuity. If the Bible is the supreme authority in Christian faith and practice, how can an extra-biblical formulation of doctrine with terms and concepts markedly different from Scripture really be "Christian"? Many Catholic scholars of previous generations, especially those influenced by Romantic organicism, appealed to natural analogies in order to explain continuity. The approaches represented throughout this chapter make use of contemporary hermeneutical theory.

The relationships between *ipse*-selfhood and *idem*-sameness and between theological judgments and concepts appear to have untapped apologetic value in responding to the claims of historical critics. Bart Ehrman, for instance, has built a career popularizing the Bauer thesis and alleging corruptions in the New Testament textual tradition. He appears to expect something like *idem*-sameness across the transmission of manuscripts and does not appear to consider the possibility that continuity between doctrine and the New Testament can be framed in any other way than verbal repetition. This tendency is evident in his claim that "the apostles . . . did not teach the Nicene Creed or anything like it."[137] Yet what Yeago and Vanhoozer's respective comparisons of Philippians 2:5–11 and the Nicene Creed demonstrate Nicene fidelity to canonical patterns of judgment. Ehrman seems to hypothesize that Christian identity can only truly be preserved through static transmission—an idea that Vanhoozer and a choir of twentieth-century hermeneuticists strive to demythologize.

---

137. Bart D. Ehrman, *Lost Christianities: The Battles for Scripture and the Faiths We Never Knew* (New York: Oxford University Press, 2003), 176.

Vanhoozer's use of *ipse/idem* does raise other concerns. One might get the impression from reading Vanhoozer that Ricoeur views *idem*-sameness in an entirely negative light or that *ipse*-identity has replaced it entirely. Even Ricoeur acknowledges that while personal identity is more than *idem*-sameness, it certainly is not less. The same can be said for aspects of the Christian faith. Only *idem*-sameness makes it possible to speak of one Savior as opposed to a plurality of saviors or one God rather than a pantheon. Paul seems concerned with *idem*-sameness when he warns the Corinthians about false apostles proclaiming "another Jesus, "a different spirit," or "a different gospel" (2 Cor. 11:4). I also wonder whether Vanhoozer, in his dependency on Ricoeur's notion of self-constancy in personal identity, has left room open for personal conversion or *character development*. In other words, how can one retain some semblance of identity when she experiences a transformed life built on new promises and new behaviors? Some appeal to *idem*-sameness appears necessary.

Vanhoozer takes a twofold approach that is both descriptive and normative. On a descriptive level, he appeals to Ricoeur's differentiation between *idem*-sameness and *ipse*-identity. The value of the *ipse/idem* distinction for the identity problem is in the way it redirects the question. Continuity in the Christian tradition does not mean that the faith will have the exact same expressions and emphases in every place where it is practiced. Instead, *ipse*-identity is continuity of character and fulfillment of promises. This observation makes the identity question clearer: Is the Christian tradition throughout history consistent in its overall character? Even a cursory observation of the Christian tradition as it is practiced in different parts of the world throughout history reveals an unexpected degree of homogeneity, not *idem*-sameness, but a kind of constancy surprising to an information-age society. Even without shared language, mass media, and unified leadership, particular expressions of the church in every epoch and locality have been remarkably consistent in their shared convictions about God, Christ, canon, and their status as the people of God. The anchor of this cross-cultural constancy across the tradition appears to be Scripture, even in times and places where individual believers did not have access to it or ability to read it.

Thiselton also takes a descriptive approach to this question in his application of Price and Wittgenstein's respective observations about the dispositional nature of belief. As dispositions, Christian beliefs consist of networks of self-involving beliefs that involve many facets of the individual who holds them, including his or her noetic beliefs, emotions, will, and fortitude. These beliefs are also intersubjective in the sense that they are taught, practiced, and displayed publically. The dispositional account of Christian belief gives explanation to the historical phenomenon of development, as believers facing new challenges in new contexts respond in ways that are consistent with their trained dispositions. Thiselton's emphasis on dispositional belief is consistent with Vanhoozer's emphasis on phronetic theology as well. Both see theology as a task of cultivating practical wisdom (*phronēsis*) for action in varying settings.

The dispositional account also shows that one need not hold explicit, conscious belief in a doctrinal proposition in order to affirm it if said proposition can be shown to extend from another consciously held belief. One does not need to maintain consciously the proposition that Jesus shares the same metaphysical substance with God the Father (*homoousion to patri*) in order to affirm it when presented with it and its conceptual framework for the first time, particularly if that individual affirms that (1) there is one God and that (2) Jesus, like the Father, is God. In Vanhoozer's account of the continuity of Christian doctrine has similar features. For Vanhoozer, continuity is not in expressions or even shared conceptual frameworks or metaphors but in patterns of judgment and practice. To call Jesus *homoousion* with the Father is to make the same pattern of judgment practiced by the writers of the New Testament in a different setting and different conceptual world.

8

The Hermeneutics of Faithful and Fitting
Doctrinal Development

While the Lord tarries, doctrine develops. The progress and growth of ideas is an inevitable historical reality, even in religious traditions purportedly rooted in divine revelation. In post-critical Christian theology, attitudes toward this phenomenon are undergoing considerable change. Once met with contempt and anxiety from Protestants and Roman Catholics alike, the idea of postcanonical doctrinal development nowadays meets with a far more favorable, even enthusiastic consent in both circles. Evangelicals, however, meet with the prospect of doctrinal development in the tension between two poles: an unwavering commitment to the supreme authority of God's unchanging word (*sola scriptura*) and a need to be vigilant in self-reformation in ever-changing times (*Ecclesia semper reformanda est*).

Prima facie, the need for theories of development in Roman Catholicism is more evident than it is in Protestant and evangelical theology. As long as Catholics appeal to an open-ended ecclesiastical authority in the formulation and evolution of doctrine, they must formulate an apologetic that serves to alleviate the tension between closed biblical revelation and the introduction of new dogmas. The need for Protestant and evangelical discussions of development may be less pronounced but is no less urgent. Even with an evangelical commitment to Scripture's unrivaled authority, to the Protestant principle of *sola scriptura*, historical and hermeneutical consciousness requires considerable attention to the historical phenomenon of doctrinal development. Evangelicals committed to the unique authority and inspiration of Scripture need a defense of doctrine.

Throughout this book, I have addressed the theological problem of postcanonical doctrinal development with insights from contemporary hermeneutical theory and evangelical theology. As modeled by leading evangelical theologians and hermeneuticists, hermeneutical theory provides valuable insight in establishing a distinctly evangelical view of postcanonical development that acknowledges both (1) the sufficiency of revealed Scripture and (2) the ongoing need for constructive theology. In this concluding chapter, I will draw a few broad conclusions about the development of doctrine with reference to the insights acquired from hermeneutical theory throughout this book, addressing the implications of descriptive and normative hermeneutical approaches for various theological disciplines. This analysis will revisit issues related to the questions of authority, religious language, and continuity. In closing, I offer a few hermeneutical guidelines for doctrinal development that are faithful to Scripture and relevant to a contemporary setting.

The Value of Hermeneutical Models

An approach that is purely descriptive or prescriptive cannot address all the issues related to the so-called problem of development. No "one-size-fits-all" approach will suffice. Descriptive models based on natural analogies tender little or no normative value for doctrinal advancement or criteria for distinguishing faithful developments from heresy. Purely prescriptive models may advance helpful guidelines for ensuring fidelity to Scripture and tradition, but they offer little aid in explaining the historical development of doctrine. By contrast, describing the development of doctrine as a hermeneutical phenomenon can provide both explanatory theses of historical development and prescriptive guidelines for its continued practice. In the same way hermeneutical theory itself entails descriptive and normative dimensions, a comprehensive hermeneutical account of doctrinal development should keep the descriptive and normative poles in balance. As a second-order issue, the question of doctrinal development also has far-reaching implications for other disciplines in the broad spectrum of theological studies, including historical theology, Christian apologetics, missiology, and biblical studies.

A few specific benefits of a hermeneutical model of development are worth noting. First, a descriptive hermeneutical theory of development is helpful in the historical task of reverse engineering the Christian tradition. History and hermeneutics share a symbiotic relationship. On one side, the historical task is fundamentally hermeneutical in nature. All historical inquiry is reconstruction of past events that relies on the interpretation of texts and a critical evaluation of their meaning and significance (written history).[1] The

---

1. Again, I am using "text" in a very broad sense to describe any complex aggregate of signs employed in interpersonal communicative acts.

practice of hermeneutics is reciprocally historical in nature, as twentieth-century hermeneutical theory evidences. Readers and texts are products of their time and place in history (the events of history). This two-way relationship is important for describing the phenomenon of development. Doctrinal development is both a product of historically conditioned interpretation and a historical event studied with historical and hermeneutical tools.

Christian doctrine emerges in a hermeneutical conversation between at least two divergent, historically contingent horizons: the horizon of the text and the horizon of the present. This observation is the contribution of contemporary hermeneutics. Whereas the romanticists of the nineteenth-century aspired to close the gap between the past and the present through a hermeneutics of empathy and shared experience and to transcend the relativity of history made apparent by the rise of the historical consciousness, Gadamer and the twentieth-century hermeneutical tradition challenged this illusion of objectivity. These hermeneuticists call attention to the historically effected consciousness of the reader and the need for the interpreter to be consciously aware of the history of effects, to appreciate the distance between the interpreter and the text.

Historical distance, Gadamer and Bakhtin demonstrate, can be extremely beneficial to understanding. As Gadamer writes, "Often temporal distance can solve question [sic] of critique in hermeneutics, namely how to distinguish the true prejudices, by which we *understand*, from the *false* ones, by which we *misunderstand*."[2] When an interpreter recognizes the distance between himself and the text, he can appreciate the horizon of the text as something other. In the development of Christian doctrine, interpreters benefit from recognizing the otherness of the biblical horizon. Failure to

---

2. Gadamer, *Truth and Method*, 298.

acknowledge its otherness can result in the vision of an overly familiar god remade in the image of the reader. Distance or outsideness also grants fresh perspective. It often allows interpreters to see and hear things unseen and unheard by those closest to the original occurrence: historical context, the long-term effects of that occasion, and new questions that might emerge in different situations.

The New Testament is itself a witness to how historical distance shapes perspective. The disciples' experience of Jesus prior to the resurrection was quite different—and shrouded in much more mystery—than their apostolic, post-resurrection experiences of and reflections on Jesus. For example, historical distance may have explanatory power over the different emphases in the synoptic tradition and the Fourth Gospel. If John's gospel is, as most scholars concede, later than the Synoptic Gospels, then there is also time for a much more developed theological reflection on the identity of Christ, as could be evidenced by passages like the Johannine prologue. Furthermore, perhaps a particular occasion, like addressing the same strand of docetism addressed in 1 John, gave need for the fourth evangelist to draw out his particular selection of christological themes and material.

Second, descriptive hermeneutical approaches to development also can be beneficial to Christian apologetics. In the last several decades, some scholars and popular skeptics have claimed that many central facets of orthodox Christianity—the belief that Jesus was divine, the doctrine of the Trinity, and the unique authority of the biblical canon—are ideas that would have been alien to first-century followers of Jesus. How is it possible to say that the Nicene Creed or the Chalcedonian Creed represents the same Christian faith practiced by the apostles when the language and thought world of these creeds appears so different from first-century forms of the faith? Granted, these challenges are far to complex to leave entirely in the hands of systematic theologians like myself. Interdisciplinary engagement with New Testament scholars, historians, and classicists is necessary in order to establish the ancient setting, the self-understanding of the historical Jesus, the true meaning of the apostolic kerygma, and the early Christian worldview.[3] The systematic theologian, however, is tasked with a matter not bound to any particular historical or contextual examination. The theologian asks whether such development is logically possible: Can growing or developing doctrine retain continuity with the past or faithfulness to the established revelatory tradition?

In order to answer this question, the theologian must address the nature of doctrine and biblical interpretation. This task is descriptive. As a hermeneutical approach to these questions reveals, charges of "change" and "corruption" directed toward Christianity often thrive on modernistic assumptions about culture as frozen, closed systems beyond creative construction or interaction with the world. Many of these skeptics also neglect the historical and interpreted nature of all understanding—including their own historical projects. Descriptive

---

3. The conclusion to the Johannine epilogue (John 21:25) is sounding less and less hyperbolic with every passing year as more and more books about the historical Jesus surface. To misappropriate Qoheleth: "Of making many books [about Jesus] there is no end, and much [historical Jesus] research is wearying to the body" (Eccl. 12:12). A few notable Third Quest texts include James D. G. Dunn, *Jesus Remembered* (Grand Rapids, MI: Eerdmans, 2003); Craig Keener, *The Historical Jesus of the Gospels* (Grand Rapids, MI: Eerdmans, 2009); John P. Meier, *A Marginal Jew: Rethinking the Historical Jesus*, 4 vols. (New Haven: Yale University Press, 1991–2009); and Wright, *Jesus and the Victory of God*.Perhaps more relevant for the present concern are questions about early Christian belief. In recent years, historians and biblical scholars like Richard Bauckham (b. 1946), Larry W. Hurtado (b. 1943), and James D. G. Dunn (b. 1939) have produced noteworthy works about early Christian devotion to Jesus. See Richard Bauckham, *Jesus and the God of Israel: God Crucified and Other Studies on the New Testament's Christology of Divine Identity* (Grand Rapids, MI: Eerdmans, 2008); Larry W. Hurtado, *Lord Jesus Christ: Devotion to Jesus in Earliest Christianity* (Grand Rapids, MI: Eerdmans, 2005); idem, *How on Earth Did Jesus Become a God? Historical Questions about Earliest Devotion to Jesus* (Grand Rapids, MI: Eerdmans, 2005); and James D. G. Dunn, *Did the First Christians Worship Jesus? The New Testament Evidence* (Louisville: Westminster/John Knox, 2010).

hermeneutics provides a way to describe the nature of theological understanding and to establish continuity between different cultural expressions of the same theological judgments and dispositions.

Third, hermeneutical theory, partnered with the philosophy of language, can aid theologians in their understanding of the varying verbal expressions of doctrine over time. The insights of speech-act theory have great descriptive value in assessing the language of Scripture and Christian confessions, as well as demonstrating that doctrinal statements can (1) depict ontological realities and (2) "do" other things besides provide description. Fourth, normative hermeneutics provides important instruction for systematic theology as it points to the distinct genres of biblical literature. Fifth, hermeneutics shaped by the philosophy of science can demonstrate how Christian biblical interpretation can (1) strive for reality depiction and nevertheless (2) maintain a degree of provisionality in hermeneutical judgments.

Finally, hermeneutical theories of development also assist in the task of cross-cultural Christian mission. As Thiselton and Vanhoozer both illustrate, hermeneutical approaches to development need not result in formulaic, paint-by-number methodologies. (As we have seen, neither author offers a step-by-step outline of the process of theological formulation.) Nevertheless, a normative dimension is vital for rightly conceiving of theology's missiological task. Faithful, fitting development is an attempt to explain the message of Scripture to a contemporary setting, to transmit the gospel and Christian practice cross-culturally and cross-generationally. Development is not merely something that does happen; it is something that *should* happen in order for the church to fulfill her mission. It involves the hermeneutical task of discerning the judgments biblical authors make regarding God, Christ, and salvation history and to try to replicate those judgments in new settings, even utilizing new or different conceptual tools if necessary.

Development and the Authority of God

Not all developments are faithful to Scripture or fitting to the context. Some doctrinal developments truly are doctrinal downgrades, and some expressions of Christian doctrine can go stagnant or become irrelevant. In developing and formulating doctrine for new contexts, our goal is not to *transform* the Christian message to fit the context, thereby making it into something unrecognizable to biblical authors and believers throughout history, but to *translate* the message so that it is intelligible for contemporary audiences and new contexts.[4] With their commitment to the sufficiency of Scripture and the centrality of the gospel message, constructive theologians in the evangelical tradition strive to work between the extremes of stale traditionalism and theological neophilia—novelty for novelty's sake. Evangelical theologians aim to speak prophetically to an ever-changing cultural climate without resorting to innovation for the sake of innovation and most importantly, without transforming the message we have received into a "different gospel" (Gal. 1:6).

First, faithful doctrinal development begins with and ends in doxology, the praise and worship of God. For evangelicals, this is the hermeneutical starting point, the interpretive lens that should color the entire theological enterprise. Evangelicals believe that raison d'être of human beings is "to glorify God and enjoy him forever."[5] As a result, evangelical theologians of every denominational and traditional stripe contend that glory of God—not the praise of the

---

4. These two approaches of "transformation" and "translation" first appear in William Hordern, *New Directions in Theology Today*, vol. 1 (Philadelphia: Westminster, 1966).
5. Westminster Shorter Catechism (1646/1647), Q/A 1.

academy or the sale of books—takes precedence in the task of constructive theology. Scripture bears witness to this pattern of theological reflection. The psalmists return mediation on the word of God with praise and adoration (Ps. 19:8; 56:4; 119:14–16, 33–36, 111, 162). Paul frequently oscillates between explicating and extolling God (Rom. 1:25; 9:5; 11:33–36; Eph. 3:20–21; et al.). Doctrine that does not direct its hearers to the matchless splendor of God is at best the result of intellectual error and at worst a theological byproduct of sin. So whether they are teaching or writing, serving the church or exhorting the academy, whatever it is that theologians do, they should do it for the glory of God (1 Cor. 10:31).

Second, faithful doctrinal development is a response to the uniquely authoritative and truthful illocutionary acts of Scripture—i.e., what Scripture's divine and human authorship intends readers to do with these texts. Attention to biblical authority helps us distinguish between fitting and unfitting developments. Neither church nor extrabiblical tradition nor an ethical telos unforeseen by biblical authors has ultimate ruling authority in postcanonical development. Evangelicals who affirm a plenary-verbal view of biblical inspiration believe that the God expresses his revelation and authority through human communicative discourse. Once more, biblical authority is not the authority of a book or collection of books; it is God's authority expressed through books. If the Bible is, as evangelicals envision it, the written expression of God's word, then obedience to discourse of Scripture is obedience to God. To ignore the biblical text, or to envision a supplemental or interpretive authority that supersedes it, is to defy divine authority.

To recognize and to submit to the divine authority mediated through Scripture entails more than cherry-picking biblical texts for propositions, as some hard propositionalist theologians of the past described the task of biblical interpretation. Belief in biblical authority is more than a cognitive affirmation of the Bible's inspiration; it entails an orientation of obedience to the various illocutionary acts of Scripture—what the divine and human authors of Scripture of a particular unit of text expect as a response from their hearers and/or readers. As Thiselton and Vanhoozer demonstrate, this interpretive obedience means bearing in mind the plurality of voices and genres in Scripture. God uses some biblical authors to draft covenants and others to voice his promises. Some texts simply tell a story we need to know, while others elicit our awe and worship. Some offer general wisdom for daily living, others more specific advice for particular circumstances. No single interpretive or theological pattern with suffice when addressing the richness and diversity of Scripture.

While the divine and human illocutionary acts frequently overlap, there is, on occasion, a need for what Nicholas Wolterstorff calls a "second hermeneutic" that reads for meanings embedded by the Holy Spirit of which the human authors may not have been aware.[6] This is not a call for a return to allegorical readings or an endorsement of the reader-response approaches criticized in previous chapters. What this observation simply means is that we must seek to understand (1) what the text meant in an ancient setting and (2) what the text can mean when applied to a new setting. Meaning (2) does not change or deny meaning (1) but rather is a consideration of how the same, unchanging God might act or desire us to act in a new set of circumstances. We are not asking the question, "What does this passage mean to me?" We are asking, "What does the God who inspired this text then want me to do now?" Even without critical awareness of their hermeneutical approach, Christians throughout history instinctively have read the Bible this way. We draw

---

6. See Nicholas Wolterstorff, *Divine Discourse: Philosophical Reflections on the Claim that God Speaks* (Cambridge, MA: Cambridge University Press, 1995), 202–22.

inferences from ancient settings about what God might have us do in new and different settings. Christians traditionally have read the whole canon as a witness to Christ, even in Old Testament passages wherein their human authors may not have been able to anticipate the typological or prophetic similarities to the Christ story. Readers with a christocentric second hermeneutic recognize that we can learn more from the canonical whole than we can from its individual parts.

To some degree, the interpreter must practice something akin to what Ricoeur calls a "hermeneutics of suspicion," questioning interpretive motives and making a conscious effort to recognize the otherness of the text (in the case of Scripture, the holy otherness of the text).[7] Interpretive interests can be God honoring, such as the desire to read Scripture and obey it, but they can also be faulty assumptions shaped by theology, politics, or culture. Worse still, the motives of biblical readers can be sinful, shaped by the self-deception of the heart (Jer. 17:9). The Reformed tradition teaches that the depravity of human beings is all-encompassing, infecting every part of the human constitution—mind, will, and desires—with sinful, selfish desires. This depravity even extends to the way human beings read Scripture, and without the aid of the Spirit in illuminating the texts, would make reading the Bible without self-deception impossible. Every interpreter committed to the authority of Scripture asking questions like, "Do I come to the text in an attempt to defend a cherished doctrine or ethical soap box, or do I come with an open mind, willing to be transformed by the meaning intended by the Bible's divine-human authorship? Am I honestly ready to surrender to whatever the Spirit is saying through these texts?" Christians should seek transformation by the Spirit's illumination of Scripture's speech acts, not approval or affirmation of their ideologies or long-held positions.

7. See Paul Ricoeur, *Freud and Philosophy: An Essay on Interpretation*, trans. Denis Savage (New Haven: Yale University Press, 1970), 32–36; cf. Jeanrond, *Theological Hermeneutics*, 73–74.

Unlike a hermeneutics of suspicion that would distrust the motives and interests within the biblical text (e.g., to charge biblical authors with misogyny, homophobia, or imperialist interests) the bondservant of the Lord interprets illocutionary acts of Scripture with a *hermeneutics of submission*. To read the Bible as Scripture means capitulating one's own ideological interests to the will and intent of the divine author. This hermeneutical practice requires humility, teachable spirit, and a life surrendered to the Lord Jesus. This metaphor of submission does not mean that the text is enslaved to the past as if we must somehow recover the social, political, and cultural world of the Bible in order to be faithful to it. It means freely obeying the divine speech acts of Scripture in the present, taking desires of biblical authorship seriously in an ever-changing setting. After all, "while a slave, the bondservant is the Lord's freedman" (1 Cor. 7:22). In the same way, doctrinal development is *bound* to the authority of Scripture and *free* to respond to contemporary needs.

In addition to the hermeneutics of submission, the evangelical reader of the Bible also practices a *hermeneutics of trust*. To trust another individual means (1) believing that individual to possess a particular moral character and to be above consciously and purposely speaking mistruths and (2) believing that individual is capable of being entrusted with responsibility, particularly responsibility with things of great importance to the person trusting. I trust my wife completely. I have great confidence that I can believe what she says and that I can entrust my well-being and the well-being of my children to her wifely and motherly care.

As in any healthy interpersonal relationship, the relationship of the reader to the Bible involves personal trust. Trust in Scripture is not trust in an impersonal book or words on a page; it is personal trust in the One who speaks through them. First, trust in Scripture is a trust that the divine and human authors of the Bible do represent the world and theological realities competently and honestly. Second, trust in Scripture is trust in the ability of its instruction to carry one through life's circumstances, to believe that God knows better than we do. Denial of truthfulness and trustworthiness is evidence of dysfunction in a relationship. Interpreters of the Bible who reject its truthfulness have "trust issues" with its authorship.

Third, faithful doctrinal development is a product of the illumination of Scripture by the Holy Spirit. Admittedly, little has been said in this study about the role of the Holy Spirit in hermeneutics and doctrinal development. This lack of explicit emphasis need not lead to hasty conclusions about the diminution of his illuminating role. The Spirit, "who searches all things, even the depths of God," is the one who reveals the wisdom of God (1 Cor. 2:10). He is the teacher of "all things" (John 14:26), the "epistemic mediator" of the Godhead.[8] Yet Spirit-led interpretation is not a docetic affair; it involves enfleshed, historical hermeneutical practice. As Thiselton remarks, "The Holy Spirit may be said to work *through* human understanding, and not usually, if ever, through processes which bypass the considerations discussed under the heading of hermeneutics."[9] The work of the Spirit in illumination may be said to be as much as an illumination on the reader as it is on the text. Jesus stresses that the coming of the Spirit was necessary to "convict the world about sin and righteousness and judgment" (John 16:8) because "they do not believe me about sin" (John 16:9). The Spirit may work through the mechanisms of the mind and the tools of hermeneutics to help a reader understand a text, but the real "miracle" he performs is illuminating the reader's need for what the text says.

---

8. Graham A. Cole, *He Who Gives Life: The Doctrine of the Holy Spirit* (Wheaton, IL: Crossway, 2007), 261.
9. Anthony C. Thiselton, *The Two Horizons: New Testament Hermeneutics and Philosophical Description with Special Reference to Heidegger, Bultmann, Gadamer, and Wittgenstein* (Carlisle: Paternoster, 1980), 92.

Biblical texts with closed meanings do not change under the leadership of the Spirit, for this sort of change would be a *de novo* act of revelation. Instead, the Spirit illumines the divine–human authorial meaning of the text by directing its actualization in new settings. As Colin Gunton observes, the Spirit guides the living tradition or practice of the church and enables "the church to make radical and unexpected innovations in its missionary outreach."[10] Evangelicals insist on the qualitative difference between the Spirit's activities of illumination and inspiration. This insistence means that they also reject views of Scripture that merely describe the Bible a textual venue in which readers encounter the word of God. Evangelicals contend that the Bible is identical with the written word of God. In hermeneutical terms, the words of the Bible are God's speech acts. Most importantly, the Spirit trains and cultivates the hermeneutical practices of biblical interpreters in order to aid them in responding appropriately in new life situations. In faithful doctrinal development, we are not rewriting the illocutionary acts of Scripture but performing new perlocutionary acts in new cultural and historical settings.

Evangelicals may recognize the need for postcanonical doctrinal developments, but they do not afford them the same authoritative or normative status as inspired Scripture. While may explain away intracanonical developments as new stages in God's progressive revelation, evangelicals who affirm the unique inspiration and sufficiency of Scripture will not raise postcanonical doctrinal developments to the same heights. Evangelicals like me affirm the infallibility and inerrancy of revelation in Scripture but do not make the same assumptions about postcanonical doctrinal developments. The Bible may be true and trustworthy in everything its divine-

---

10. Colin E. Gunton, *Theology through the Theologians: Selected Essays 1972-1995* (Edinburgh: T&T Clark, 1996), 44.

human authorship affirms, but its interpreters are prone to error. Biblical inerrancy does not entail doctrinal inerrancy.

The fallibility of interpretation and doctrinal development suggests a third maxim for faithful development: faithful doctrinal development is a hermeneutical practice best carried out with a temperament of Christian humility. Critical hermeneutical realism means that doctrines derived from the interpretation of Scripture are held both provisionally and as cognitive statements about God and the world. As observed above, some texts are clearer than others, and some doctrines are held more confidently than others. A humble approach to development avoids two hermeneutical temperaments Vanhoozer identifies as "interpretive sins": hermeneutical pride that would claim complete mastery over the text and hermeneutical sloth that would ignore the responsibility of the reader to interpret texts faithfully.[11] Those who are guilty of interpretive pride confuse their interpretation of the text with the text itself, admonishing those who disagree with their interpretations and accusing them of rejecting the text itself. The hermeneutical skeptic who refuses any stable meaning to the text or any ability to understand such a meaning if it exists, much like a person suffering with depression or extreme anxiety, tends to "give up" on the task at hand because of individual or corporate self-doubt.

In hermeneutics as in life, pride and melancholy are two sides of the same coin: a self-centered refusal to acknowledge the good work that God has done in our lives. Humility entails godly, Christ-honoring confidence. We can be confident that are able to assess meaning of biblical texts with the aid and help of the Spirit and the interpretive tools with which God has blessed us, but we also recognize that we who are prone to error may need on occasion to

---

11. Kevin J. Vanhoozer, *Is There a Meaning in This Text?* (Grand Rapids, MI: Zondervan, 1998), 462–63.

correct our previously held assumptions. We need to be teachable interpreters of Scripture who hold our conclusions with varying degrees of provisionality and tentativeness. On some disagreements over biblical texts, evangelicals do well to practice what John Stott calls "humble agnosticism."[12] Other issues, especially those in which Scripture is clearer in meaning, should spark what John Piper more positively dubs "humble affirmation."[13]

Provisionality in the present moment is good news for evangelical theological hermeneutics. Worldviews can and do change. Genuine conversion is a real possibility! In this sense, the experience of gospel transformation is much like the fusion of horizons. When we who are shaped by the effects of providential history encounter the horizon of the gospel and seek to understand it, we enter a dialogue of question and answer where our experience of finitude and sin meets with the alterity of the claims of Christ. We consider what our lives are in relationship to this alternate horizon, and we forge a new horizon when we are transformed by the understanding of the gospel. The illumination of Scripture, guided by the same Spirit who regenerates us and initially changes our worldview, also entails new horizons and fusion events.

Ultimately, humility in doctrinal development means acknowledging that God has revealed himself, that we can have confidence in our ability to interpret his revelation with his guidance. We can admit, with Job, that as finite creatures we often speak hastily about things we do "not understand," "things too wonderful" for us, and things which we do not know (Job 42:3). We also can have confidence that God eventually will sort out our interpretive differences by giving complete disclosure: "For now we see in a

---

12. John Stott, *The Lausanne Covenant: Complete Text with Study Guide* (The Lausanne Movement, 2003), 56.
13. John Piper, *Let the Nations Be Glad! The Supremacy of God in Missions*, 2nd ed. (Grand Rapids, MI: Baker, 2003), 120n15.

mirror dimly but then face to face. Now [we] know [read, interpret] in part; then [we] shall know fully, even as [we] have been fully known" (1 Cor. 13:12). In that eschatological event, as Barth expects, our "present [indirect] knowing in faith will then be taken out of its isolation and taken up into a knowing in sight."[14]

Development Appropriate to Context

In some sense, theology is a universal human experience. While no one pursues fellowship with God apart from the aid of divine grace (Rom. 3:11; cf. Ps. 14:2), it is also true that God has endowed humanity with an indelible and insatiable curiosity and longing for him. As Qoheleth describes it, God has "set eternity in the human heart" (Eccl. 3:11, NIV). General revelation in creation, conscience, and history points all persons everywhere to their creator and life sustainer. So everyone, regardless of his or her worldview or religious affiliation, has questions and/or dispositional beliefs about God, meaning, and eschatology. The Christian believer and the atheist alike share in this universal theological experience, what Arthur F. Holmes calls a "'world-viewish' theology."[15]

In quite another sense, theology is not a universal human experience, nor does it affect every hearer in every context or worldview the same way. Theology must be context specific, appropriate to the "forms of life" (*Lebensformen*) it addresses. Theologians outside of evangelicalism have recognized this for a long time. As James Cone aptly observes,

Theology is not universal language about God. Rather, it is human

---

14. Karl Barth, *Church Dogmatics*, vol. 4, no. 2, *The Doctrine of Reconciliation*, trans. Geoffrey W. Bromiley (Edinburgh: T&T Clark, 1958), 840.
15. Arthur F. Holmes, *The Contours of a Christian World View* (Grand Rapids, MI: Eerdmans, 1983), 34–36, 39.

speech informed by historical and theological traditions, written for particular times and places. Theology is *contextual* language—that is, defined by the human situation that gives birth to it. No one can write theology for all times, places, and persons.[16]

Theology must be aware of cultural, geographical, and chronological contexts. Differing contexts mean differing horizons or cultural perspectives, and across time, cultural perspectives shift or change as well. As a result, no single systematic theology textbook—no matter how comprehensive or well argued—can address every doctrinal concern in every church and every time. Doctrine must develop in order to retain a voice in ever-changing settings.

Admittedly, consciousness of the contextual and constructive nature of Christian theology is a later feature in evangelical theology than in its Catholic and progressive Protestant counterparts. Evangelical theologians, however, have offered an important emendation to the concept of constructive theology: that constructive theology can be both contextual and subject to biblical authority. Contextual theology can be one of two things: transforming theology or transforming theology, theology that transforms the essence of the Christian faith or theology that transforms the lives and context of its recipients.[17] That is, theology can alter the substance and content of the Bible in order to be more relevant or appealing to a contemporary setting, or theology rooted in the substance and the content of the Bible can strive to transform the culture by projecting a new narrative world or worldview for the culture or individual to embrace. The relevant forms of theological

---

16. James H. Cone, *A Black Theology of Liberation*, Fortieth Anniversary Edition (Maryknoll, NY: Orbis, 2012), xv.
17. The former category of transforming theology is inspired by Millard Erickson's use of the term in his *Christian Theology*, 3d. ed. (Grand Rapids, MI: Baker, 2013), 76. The latter use takes its shape from the wordplay evoked by Thiselton in his *New Horizons in Hermeneutics: The Theory and Practice of Transforming Biblical Reading* (Grand Rapids, MI: Zondervan, 1992), 31–35.

discourse may vary from context to context, but the guiding norm of Scripture is universal and binding on all Christians.

Contextual theologies in liberal and progressive traditions often take the former approach to transforming theology. Take for example the most famous hermeneutical method in twentieth-century liberal theology: Rudolf Bultmann's method of demythologization. In making the case for demythologization, Bultmann argues that readers should learn to distinguish between elements specifically grounded in the outmoded worldviews of biblical authors and those existentially significant elements that transcend the limitations of those pre-scientific, pre-critical worldviews.[18] Bultmann believes that "kernels" of existential truth in the Bible can be found if the "husk" of its ancient *Weltanschauung* is shed. According to Bultmann, concepts such as heaven, hell, and resurrection are part of a pre-Enlightenment worldview better left in an ancient setting.

As an evangelical theologian committed to a hermeneutics of submission, I see the theological task very differently. Rather than adapting the biblical text to fit my world, I want to adapt my world to fit the biblical text. That is, rather than simply acknowledging and rejecting differences in worldviews between our horizons, I want to (1) recognize those places where I do not naturally think like biblical authors and (2) conform my thinking to their patterns of thought. I am, for example, aware that, often, much of the language utilized in Christian theology and preaching is tainted with the dualism of the Enlightenment, the distinction between *nature* and *super-nature*. In my own theological discourse, I try to avoid using the terms "natural" and "supernatural" to describe the different kinds of goings on in the

18. Rudolf Bultmann, *Jesus Christ and Mythology* (Upper Saddle River, NJ: Prentice Hall, 1958), 35–44; idem., "New Testament and Mythology: The Mythological Element of the Message of the New Testament and the Problem of its Re-interpretation," in *Kerygma and Myth: Rudolf Bultmann and Five Critics*, ed. Hans Werner Bartsch and trans. Reginald H. Fuller (New York: Harper & Row), 1–16.

world because biblical authors would not have thought in such terms. Biblical authors thought of the world as God's word and miracles not as violations of nature but rather as evidence of God's ongoing creative and new creative activity in the realm of his dominion.

Constructive theology can and should be theology faithful to the lordship of Christ working through the biblical text. The critical biblicist affirms with the author of Hebrews that the "word of God is living, vibrant, and sharper than any two-edged sword . . . discerning the thoughts and intentions of the human heart" (Heb. 4:12). The theologian practicing a hermeneutics of submission is in a better place to offer constructive solutions to context-specific "questions that arise" than a theologian who leaves biblical interpretation at the level of a hermeneutics of suspicion.

So what does contextual, faithful theology look like? First, for evangelicals, faithful and contextual theology is gospel-oriented and mission-minded. After all, evangelicals are so named for their commitment to the *euangelion*. We recognize, however, that despite the gospel's transcontexual power, it can never be presented in a transcontexual form. As Henry Knight III notes, "A gospel free of culture is not a human possibility."[19] The gospel message itself does not change, but its presentation is extremely context-sensitive. Its presentation is dependent upon language, storytelling structures, and metaphors contingent upon the culture receiving it. Missiologists who study the task of contextualization across cultures readily recognize this.

Second, the practice of contextual theology maintains an awareness of other theological traditions. Where there is diversity, there is development. Despite theological variety and polemical differences in the historic Christian tradition, the homogeneity of its central

---

19. Henry H. Knight III, *A Future for Truth: Evangelical Theology in a Postmodern World* (Nashville: Abingdon, 1997), 134.

features between traditions is astonishing. Anglican, Baptist, Catholic, Congregationalist, Lutheran, Mennonite, Methodist, Orthodox, Pentecostal, Presbyterian, and Reformed groups share a common core of convictions about the nature and activity of the one, triune God revealed in the Bible: the larger narrative of "God in Christ. . . reconciling the world to himself" (2 Cor. 5:19). These common convictions constitute the gospel, the shared network of beliefs Vincent of Lérins describes as "believed everywhere, always, and by all men,"[20] or what C. S. Lewis calls "mere Christianity."[21] This commonly held biblical gospel should be the focus of energies in faithful doctrinal development.

This commonality of gospel belief bears witness to the Reformation principle of the perspicuity of Scripture. For the Reformers, this doctrine of biblical clarity meant that no "authority of the dominant interpretive community" was necessary to interpret the "sufficiently unambiguous" Scriptures.[22] In promoting this idea, the Reformers and their heirs were aware of interpretive difficulties presented by some biblical texts. As the divines who drafted the Westminster Confession of Faith (1643) confess,

> All things in Scripture *are not alike plain in themselves*, nor alike clear unto all; yet those things which are necessary to be known, believed, and observed for salvation, are so clearly propounded, and opened in some place of Scripture or other, that not only the learned, but the unlearned, in a due use of the ordinary means, may attain unto a *sufficient understanding* of them.[23]

The development of doctrine should be a response to the authority of Scripture, but it should be practiced with an awareness of the

---

20. Vincent of Lérins *The Commonitory* §2.3.
21. See C. S. Lewis, *Mere Christianity* (San Francisco: HarperCollins, 2000), viii–xvi.
22. Vanhoozer, *Is There a Meaning in This Text?*, 315.
23. The Westminster Confession of Faith 1:7, italics mine.

difficulties certain biblical texts pose. Even among evangelicals where there is general agreement about the gospel and what constitutes evangelical identity (e.g., gospel-centeredness, the unique authority of the Bible, etc.), there is significant disagreement on secondary and tertiary issues. Browse the theology section of any seminary bookstore and expect to find several books with "Four Views" or "Five Views" in the title. While the disagreements contained within most of these books are quite stimulating and sometimes even brutal, there is a general recognition among these authors of their unity and fellowship on more significant issues. Evangelicals, far better than their fundamentalist counterparts, recognize diversity on issues important but less significant to the gospel's essence.

With the exception of groups who hold to additional material authorities other than Scripture, theological diversity in the broad Christian tradition is largely a result of interpretive differences of difficult texts in Scripture. Attempts to stratify the importance of doctrinal positions take their shape from the varying degrees of clarity in Scripture. Of essential importance is the doctrine of God and the gospel, the central message of the Scripture clearly and repeatedly rehearsed in the biblical texts. Differences in ecclesiology, eschatology, and the finer points of soteriology are interpretive in nature, either because Scripture lacks direct statements on these matters, because some biblical ideas are difficult to harmonize, or because contemporary interpreters lack the know-how to make sense of certain texts that assume contextual knowledge from their immediate audiences.

Third, contextual theology, like preaching, should be audience specific with its explanatory devices and use of metaphor. Within a homogenous church culture, there are different ways of preaching the same biblical texts. Even within my own predominately white, middle-class church culture, there are different ways of preaching the same biblical texts. This does not mean that the meaning of closed biblical texts varies from sermon to sermon or that all sermons with all their unique homiletical elements are somehow divinely and implicitly stored in the text. Rather, it means that the communication of the message varies from time to time and audience to audience. In my local church, I do not preach a sermon from the same text the same exact way to an audience entirely consisting of senior adults as I would to audiences primarily consisting of preschoolers or of preadolescents. The illustrations are different, as are the applications or rhetorical foci. Furthermore, I can preach different sermons from the same unit of text at different stages of my ministry that reflect different understandings of the biblical text and/or different questions that I bring to the text. With new cultures, new life situations, and new times, these changes in presentation and application can be much more drastic.

Finally, contextual theology should be prophetic in the sense that it should speak on behalf of God to the culture. In this way, the role of the theologian is not unlike the Old Testament prophet who acted as an "enforcer" of God's covenant law, who spoke and affirmed the word of God to the people of Israel. The new cultural crises that come with each successive generation in this fallen world present new challenges for the theologian, who must somehow explicate how Christian belief relates to Christian praxis. Whether the issue in question is abortion, gender roles, sexuality, slavery, or some future issue presently unforeseen by believers standing in the first quarter of the twenty-first century, evangelical theologians should be thinking about how to address these issues in a way that is faithful to Scripture and how Christians in the past have treated similar problems.

Take for example, the widespread legalization of abortion in Western culture forced evangelical theologians and ethicists to articulate theological anthropology in new ways. While Roman

Catholic theologians anticipated many of the issues in the abortion debate,[24] it was only after *Roe v. Wade* that many evangelicals began to reconsider the relationship between abortion and theological anthropology.[25] This evangelical doctrinal development also led to a reevaluation of a number of issues related to basic human dignity, including, but not limited to a theology of race relations.

These developments show that evangelicals speaking prophetically to their context can and should articulate their worldviews in new expressions of doctrinal language, testing these beliefs by the measuring rod of biblical authority, sound judgment, and internal consistency. When thinking about a prophetic theology, it is also crucial to remember the false prophets of Israel spoke to the desires of the people rather than speaking on behalf of God (Jer. 6:14; 8:11; 14:3 ; 23:17 ; 28:1–17; Ezek. 13:1–23; Mic. 3:5). Paul warned Timothy about a coming time when "people will not obey sound doctrine" because of their "itching ears" and their desire to appoint teachers that cater to their passions (2 Tim. 4:3). To be truly prophetic, a theologian must speak to the cultural needs and concerns in such a way that reinforces the word of God in Scripture, not amending or nullifying it to satisfy contemporary cultural desires.

24. The National Conference of Catholic Bishops established The National Right to Life Committee in 1967 in order to respond to shifting tides in legal and cultural thought about abortion. For a brief history of these developments, see Robert N. Karrer, "The National Right to Life Committee: Its Founding, Its History, and the Emergence of the Pro-Life Movement Prior to Roe v. Wade," *Catholic Historical Review* 97.3 (2011): 527–57.

25. My own Southern Baptist tradition underwent significant development in their understandings of abortion and personhood following *Roe v. Wade*. Whereas Southern Baptists in the 1970s allowed for "the possibility of abortion under such conditions as rape, incest, clear evidence of severe fetal deformity, and . . . damage to the emotional, mental, and physical health of the mother" ("Resolution On Abortion," adopted at the SBC convention, June 1971), they had, by 1980, moved to defend a "constitutional amendment prohibiting abortion except to save the life of the mother" ("Resolution on Abortion," adopted at the SBC Convention, June 1980). By 1982, Southern Baptists have moved from rejecting what they called an "indiscriminate attitude toward abortion" ("Resolution on Abortion," adopted at the SBC convention, June 1976) to rejecting abortion as "the practice of infanticide" ("Resolution on Abortion and Infanticide," adopted at the SBC convention, May 1982).

Conclusion

This book has addressed two key issues theological prolegomena through an explicitly evangelical lens: the so-called problem of doctrinal development and the role of hermeneutics. Doctrinal development can be described in hermeneutical terms and as the result of hermeneutical processes. Thus evangelicals can be said to live by biblical texts and always be reforming (*semper reformanda*). As engagement with Thiselton, Vanhoozer, and other hermeneutics specialists has shown, the formation and growth of Christian doctrine are akin to the development of literary knowledge, as texts can present new, deeper understandings and applications in changing settings. Theological understanding, like the understanding of texts, is historical in nature. Much like a classicist who seeks to understand the epic or a dramatist concerned with the most appropriate way to stage Shakespeare, the Christian theologian works to appropriate the communicative activity of God preserved in Scripture for a new setting. How one understands interpretive authority, the relationship between language and reality, and the nature of identity has considerable consequence for understanding developing ideas such as Christian doctrines.

Christianity is not a static, stagnant tradition but a living and active one. In some sense, Christian doctrine is settled and in another sense it is always being established. Christian beliefs must be defended anew in every successive generation. On occasion, this means revising or replacing previous metaphors or conceptual frameworks that are no longer germane to the contemporary context, or in other cases, rejecting those that are no longer considered consistent with the best knowledge contemporary readers have about the biblical text.

Every successive generation of Christian believers has a responsibility to the generation that came before it and the generation that lies ahead of it. They must be good stewards of the living tradition they have received, seeking always to be faithful to the authority of God revealed through Scripture. The development of doctrine is their attempt to "enrich" the discussion of Christian belief for present and future generations, to leave a legacy of thoughtfulness and devotion.[26] In their best moments, the people of God share in a vibrant, dynamic relationship with him, learning new things about him, and, as a result, love him more deeply. God has been incredibly gracious in preserving his self-disclosure for us in Scripture. This gracious self-disclosure, mediated through human speech acts, towers over all other human literary efforts. It is clear enough to change the lives of first-time readers and challenging enough to keep its life-long interpreters busy with the task of discovering its ongoing meaning and significance. This hermeneutical task goes hand-in-hand with the ongoing practice of doctrinal development.

26. Gunton, *Theology through the Theologians*, 47–49.

Bibliography

Primary Sources

Thiselton: Books

Bartholomew, Craig G., Joel B. Green, and Anthony C. Thiselton, eds. *Reading Luke: Interpretation, Reflection, and Formation*. Grand Rapids, MI: Zondervan, 2005.

Thiselton, Anthony C. *A Concise Encyclopedia of the Philosophy of Religion*. Grand Rapids, MI: Baker, 2002.

———. *1 & 2 Thessalonians through the Centuries*. Blackwell Bible Commentaries. Oxford: Wiley-Blackwell, 2010.

———. *The First Epistle to the Corinthians: A Commentary on the Greek Text*. The New International Greek New Testament Commentary. Grand Rapids, MI: Eerdmans, 2000.

———. *Hermeneutics: An Introduction*. Grand Rapids, MI: Eerdmans, 2009.

———. *The Hermeneutics of Doctrine*. Grand Rapids, MI: Eerdmans, 2007.

———. *Interpreting God and the Postmodern Self*. Grand Rapids, MI: Eerdmans, 1995.

———. *Life after Death: A New Approach to Last Things*. Grand Rapids, MI: Eerdmans, 2011.

———. *The Living Paul: An Introduction to the Apostle and His Thought*. Grand Rapids, MI: Eerdmans, 2009.

————. *New Horizons in Hermeneutics: The Theory and Practice of Transforming Biblical Reading.* Grand Rapids, MI: Zondervan 1992.

————. *Thiselton on Hermeneutics: Collected Works and New Essays.* Grand Rapids, MI: Eerdmans, 2006.

————. *The Two Horizons: New Testament Hermeneutics and Philosophical Description.* Exeter: Paternoster/Grand Rapids, MI: Eerdmans, 1980.

Thiselton, Anthony, Roger Lundin, and Clarence Walhout. *The Promise of Hermeneutics.* Grand Rapids, MI: Eerdmans, 1999.

————. *The Responsibility of Hermeneutics.* Grand Rapids, MI: Eerdmans, 1985.

Thiselton: Articles, Essays, and Reviews

Thiselton, Anthony C. "Authority and Hermeneutics: Some Proposals for a More Creative Agenda." In *A Pathway into the Holy Scripture*, ed. P. E. Satterthwaite and David F. Wright, 107–41. Grand Rapids, MI: Eerdmans, 1994.

————. "'Behind' and 'in Front' of the Text: Language, Reference, and Indeterminacy." In *After Pentecost: Language and Biblical Interpretation*, ed. Craig Bartholomew, Colin Green, and Karl Möller, 97–117. Grand Rapids, MI: Zondervan, 2001.

————. "Biblical Interpretation: Texts, Truth, and Signification." In *The Modern Theologians: An Introduction to Christian Theology since 1918*, ed. David F. Ford and Rachel Muers, 287–304. Malden, MA: Blackwell, 2005.

————. "Canon, Community and Theological Construction." In *Canon and Biblical Interpretation*, ed. Craig G. Bartholomew, Scott Hahn, Robin Parry, Christopher Seitz, and Al Wolters, 1–32. Grand Rapids, MI: Zondervan, 2006.

————. "Communicative Action and Promise in Interdisciplinary, Biblical, and Theological Hermeneutics." In *The Promise of Hermeneutics*, ed. Roger Lundin, Clarence Walhout, and Anthony C. Thiselton, 133–239. Grand Rapids, MI: Eerdmans, 1999.

————. "Explain, Interpret (*exēgeomai, hermēneuō*)." In *The New International Dictionary of New Testament Theology*, vol. 1, ed. Colin Brown, 573–84. Grand Rapids, MI: Zondervan, 1975.

————. "The Holy Spirit in 1 Corinthians: Exegesis and Reception-History in the Patristic Era." In *The Holy Spirit and Christian Origins: Essays in Honor of James D. G. Dunn*, ed. Graham N. Stanton, Bruce Longenecker, Stephen Barton, and James D. G. Dunn, 207–28. Grand Rapids, MI: Zondervan, 2004.

————. "The 'Interpretation' of Tongues? A New Suggestion in Light of Greek Usage in Philo and Josephus." *Journal of Theological Studies* 30 (1979): 15–36.

————. "Knowledge, Myth, and Corporate Memory." In *Believing in the Church: The Corporate Nature of Faith*. A Report by the Doctrine Commission of the Church of England, 45–78. Wilton, CT: Morehouse-Barlow, 1981.

————. "The Logical Role of the Liar Paradox in Titus 1:12, 13: A Dissent from the Commentaries in Light of Philosophical and Logical Analysis." *Biblical Interpretation* 2 (1994): 207–23.

————. "Luther on Barth in 1 Corinthians 15: Six Theses for Theology." In *The Bible, the Reformation, and the Church: Essays in Honour of James Atkinson*, ed. W. P. Stephens, 258–89. Sheffield: Sheffield, 1995.

————. "The Meaning of σάρξ in 1 Corinthians 5.5: A Fresh Approach in Light of Linguistic Philosophy." *Scottish Journal of Theology* 26 (1973): 204–28.

————. "The New Hermeneutic." In *New Testament Interpretation*, ed. I Howard Marshall, 308–33. Grand Rapids, MI: Eerdmans, 1977.

———. "The Parables as Language-Event: Some Comments on Fuch's Hermeneutics in Light of Linguistic Philosophy." *Scottish Journal of Theology* 23 (1970): 437–68.

———. "The Parousia in Modern Theology: Some Questions and Comments." *Tyndale Bulletin* 27 (1976): 27–54.

———. "Semantics and New Testament Interpretation." In *New Testament Interpretation*, ed. I. Howard Marshall, 75–104. Grand Rapids, MI: Eerdmans, 1977.

———. "The Semantics of Biblical Language as an Aspect of Hermeneutics." *Faith and Thought* 103 (1976): 108–20.

———. "Signs of the Times: Towards a Theology for the Year 2000 as a Grammar of Grace, Truth, and Eschatology in the Contexts of So-Called Postmodernity." In *The Future as God's Gift: Explorations in Christian Eschatology*, ed. David Fergusson and Marcel Sarot, 9–39. Edinburgh: T&T Clark, 2000.

———. "Speech-Act Theory and the Claim That God Speaks: Nicholas Wolterstorff's *Divine Discourse*." *Scottish Journal of Theology* 50 (1997): 97–110.

———. "The Supposed Power of Words in the Biblical Writings." *Journal of Theological Studies* 25 (1974): 283–99.

———. "Truth (*Alēthia*)." In *The New International Dictionary of New Testament Theology*, vol. 3, ed. Colin Brown, 874–902. Grand Rapids, MI: Zondervan, 1978.

———. "The Use of Philosophical Categories in New Testament Hermeneutics." *The Churchman* 87 (1973): 87–100.

———. "The Varied Hermeneutical Dynamics of Parables and Reader-Response Theory." In *The Responsibility of Hermeneutics*, ed. Roger Lundin, Anthony C. Thiselton, and Clarence Walhout, 83–106. Grand Rapids, MI: Eerdmans, 1985.

———. "Word (*Logos*): Language and Meaning in Religion." In *The New International Dictionary of New Testament Theology*, vol. 3, ed. Colin Brown, 1123–43. Grand Rapids: Zondervan, 1978.

Vanhoozer: Books

Adam, A. K. M., Stephen E. Fowl, Kevin J. Vanhoozer, and Francis Watson. *Reading Scripture with the Church: Toward a Hermeneutic of Theological Interpretation.* Grand Rapids, MI: Baker, 2006.

Vanhoozer, Kevin J. *Biblical Narrative in the Philosophy of Paul Ricoeur: A Study in Hermeneutics and Theology.* Cambridge University Press, 1990.

———. *The Drama of Doctrine: A Canonical-Linguistic Approach to Christian Theology.* Louisville: Westminster/John Knox, 2005.

———. *First Theology: God, Scripture, Hermeneutics.* Downers Grove, IL: InterVarsity, 2002.

———. *Is There a Meaning in This Text? The Bible, the Reader, and the Morality of Literary Knowledge.* Grand Rapids, MI: Zondervan, 1998.

———. *Remythologizing Theology: Divine Action, Passion, and Authorship.* Cambridge Studies in Christian Doctrine. Cambridge: Cambridge University Press, 2010.

———, ed. *The Cambridge Companion to Postmodern Theology.* Cambridge: Cambridge University Press, 2003.

———, ed. *Dictionary for the Theological Interpretation of the Bible.* Grand Rapids, MI: Baker, 2005.

———, ed. *Nothing Greater, Nothing Better: Theological Essays on the Love of God.* Grand Rapids, MI: Eerdmans, 2001.

———, ed. *The Trinity in a Pluralistic Age: Theological Essays on Culture and Religion.* Grand Rapids, MI: Eerdmans, 1997.

Vanhoozer, Kevin J., Charles A. Anderson, and Michael J. Sleasman, eds. *Everyday Theology: How to Read Cultural Texts and Interpret Trends.* Grand Rapids, MI: Baker, 2007.

Vanhoozer, Kevin J., and Andrew Kirk, eds. *To Stake a Claim: Mission and the Western Crisis of Knowledge.* Maryknoll, NY: Orbis, 1999.

Vanhoozer, Kevin J., James K. A. Smith, and Bruce Ellis Benson, eds. *Hermeneutics at the Crossroads.* Indiana Series in the Philosophy of Religion. Bloomington: Indiana University Press, 2006.

Vanhoozer, Kevin J., and Owen Strachan. *The Pastor as Public Theologian: Reclaiming a Lost Vision.* Grand Rapids, MI: Brazos, 2014.

Vanhoozer, Kevin J., and Martin Warner, eds. *Transcending Boundaries in Philosophy*
and Theology: Reason, Meaning, and Experience. Aldershott: Ashgate, 2007.

Vanhoozer: Articles, Essays, and Reviews

Vanhoozer, Kevin J. "The Apostolic Discourse and Its Developments." In *Scripture's Doctrine and Theology's Bible*, ed. Markus Bockmuehl and Alan J. Torrance, 191–207. Grand Rapids, MI: Baker, 2008.

———. "Bernard Ramm." In *Dictionary of Evangelical Theologians*, ed. Walter Elwell, 290–306. Grand Rapids, MI: Zondervan, 1993.

———. "'But That's Your Interpretation': Realism, Reading, and Reformation." *Modern Reformation* 8 (1999): 281–85.

———. "Christ and Concept: Doing Theology and the 'Ministry' of Philosophy." In *Doing Theology in Today's World*, ed. John D. Woodbridge and T. McComiskey, 99–146. Grand Rapids, MI: Zondervan, 1991.

———. "Discourse on Matter: Hermeneutics and the 'Miracle' of Understanding." In *Hermeneutics at the Crossroads*, ed. Kevin J.

Vanhoozer, James K. A. Smith, and Bruce Ellis Benson, 3–34. Bloomington: Indiana University Press, 2006.

———. "Disputing about Words? Of Fallible Foundations and Modest Metanarratives." In *Christianity and the Postmodern Turn: Six Views*, ed. Myron Penner, 187–200. Grand Rapids, MI: Brazos, 2005.

———. "Does the Trinity Belong in a Theology of Religions? On Angling in the Rubicon and the 'Identity' of God." In *The Trinity in a Pluralistic Age: Theological Essays on Culture and Religion*, ed. Kevin J. Vanhoozer, 41–71. Grand Rapids, MI: Eerdmans, 1997.

Vanhoozer, Kevin J. "A Drama-of-Redemption Model." In *Four Views on Moving beyond the Bible to Theology*, ed. Gary T. Meadors, 151–99. Grand Rapids, MI: Zondervan, 2009.

———. "Effectual Call or Causal Effect? Summons, Sovereignty, and Supervenient Grace." *Tyndale Bulletin* 48 (1998): 213–51.

———. "Evangelicalism and the Church: The Company of the Gospel." In *The Futures of Evangelicalism*, ed. Craig Bartholomew, Robin Parry, and Andrew West, 40–99. Grand Rapids, MI: Kregel, 2004.

———. "Exploring the World, Following the Word: the Credibility of Evangelical Theology in an Incredulous Age." *Trinity Journal* 16 (1995): 3–27.

———. "Forming the Performers: How Christians Can Use Canon Sense to Bring Us to Our (Theodramatic) Senses." *Edification: The Transdisciplinary Journal of Christian Psychology* 4 (2010): 5–16.

———. "Four Theological Faces of Biblical Interpretation." In *Reading Scripture with the Church: Toward a Hermeneutic of Theological Interpretation*, ed. A. K. M. Adam, Stephen E. Fowl, Kevin J. Vanhoozer, and Francis Watson, 131–42. Grand Rapids, MI: Baker, 2006.

———. "From Canon to Concept: 'Same' and 'Other' in the Relation between Biblical and Systematic Theology." *Scottish Bulletin of Evangelical Theology* 12 (1994): 96–124.

————. "From Speech Acts to Scripture Acts: The Covenant of Discourse and the Discourse of Covenant." In *After Pentecost: Language and Biblical Interpretation*, ed. Craig Bartholomew, Colin Green, and Karl Möller, 1–49. Grand Rapids, MI: Zondervan, 2001.

————. "God's Mighty Speech-Acts: The Doctrine of Scripture Today." In *A Pathway into the Holy Scripture*, ed. P. E. Satterthwaite and David F. Wright, 143–82. Grand Rapids, MI: Eerdmans, 1994.

Vanhoozer, Kevin J. "Human Being, Individual and Social." In *The Cambridge Companion to Christian Doctrine*, ed. Colin Gunton, 158–88. Cambridge: Cambridge University Press, 1997.

————. "Hyperactive Hermeneutics." *Catalyst* 19 (April 1993): 3–4.

————. "Imprisoned or Free? Text, Status, and Theological Interpretation in the Master/Slave Discourse of *Philemon*." In *Reading Scripture with the Church: Toward a Hermeneutic of Theological Interpretation*, ed. A. K. M. Adam, Stephen E. Fowl, Kevin J. Vanhoozer, and Francis Watson, 51–94. Grand Rapids, MI: Baker, 2006.

————. "Intention/Intentional Fallacy." In *Dictionary for Theological Interpretation of the Bible*, ed. Kevin J. Vanhoozer, 327–30. Grand Rapids, MI: Zondervan, 2005.

————. "Into the Great 'Beyond': A Theologian's Response to the Marshall Plan." In *Beyond the Bible: Moving from Scripture to Theology*, by I. Howard Marshall, 81–96. Grand Rapids, MI: Baker, 2004.

————. "A Lamp in the Labyrinth: The Hermeneutics of Aesthetic Theology." *Trinity Journal* 8 (1987): 25–56.

————. "Linguistics, Literary Theory, Hermeneutics and Biblical Theology: What's Theological about a Theological Dictionary?" In *The New International Dictionary of Old Testament Theology and Exegesis*, vol. 1, ed. Willem A. VanGemeren, 15–51. Grand Rapids, MI: Zondervan, 1997.

————. "Lost in Interpretation? Truth, Scripture, and Hermeneutics." In *Whatever Happened to Truth*, ed. *Andreas Köstenberger, 93–129. Wheaton, IL: Crossway, 2005.*

————. "May We Go Beyond What Is Written After All? The Pattern of Theological Authority and the Problem of Doctrinal Development." In *"But My Words Will Never Pass Away": The Enduring Authority of the Christian Scriptures*, ed. D. A. Carson. Grand Rapids, MI: Eerdmans, Forthcoming.

Vanhoozer, Kevin J. "'One Rule to Rule Them All?' Theological Method in an Era of World Christianity." In *Doing Theology in a Globalized World*, ed. Craig Ott and Harold Netland, 85–126. Grand Rapids, MI: Baker, 2006.

————. "On the Very Idea of a Theological System: An Essay in Aid of Triangulating Scripture, Church, and World." In *Always Reforming: Explorations in Systematic Theology*, ed. Andrew McGowan, 125–82. Leicester: InterVarsity UK, 2006.

————. "A Person of the Book? Barth on Biblical Authority and Interpretation." In *Karl Barth and Evangelical Theology: Convergences and Divergences*, 26–59. Grand Rapids, MI: Baker, 2007.

————. "Philosophical Antecedents to Ricoeur's *Time and Narrative*." In *On Paul Ricoeur: Narrative and Interpretation*, ed. David Wood, 34–54. London: Routledge, 1991.

————. "Pilgrim's Digress: Christian Thinking on and about the Post/Modern Way." In *Christianity and the Postmodern Turn: Six Views*, ed. Myron Penner, 71–103. Grand Rapids, MI: Brazos, 2005.

————. "Providence." In *Dictionary for Theological Interpretation of the Bible*, ed. Kevin J. Vanhoozer, 641–45. Grand Rapids, MI: Zondervan, 2005.

————. "The Reader in New Testament Study." In *Hearing the New Testament: Strategies for Interpretation*, ed. Joel B. Green, 301–28. Grand Rapids, MI: Eerdmans, 1995.

———. "Ricoeur, Paul." In *Dictionary for Theological Interpretation of the Bible*, ed. Kevin J. Vanhoozer, 692–95. Grand Rapids, MI: Zondervan, 2005.

———. "Scripture and Tradition." In *The Cambridge Companion to Postmodern Theology*, ed. Kevin J. Vanhoozer, 149–69. Cambridge: Cambridge University Press, 2003.

———. "The Semantics of Biblical Literature: Truth and Scripture's Diverse Literary Forms." In *Hermeneutics, Authority, and Canon*, ed. D. A. Carson and John Woodbridge, 49–104. Grand Rapids, MI: Zondervan, 1986.

Vanhoozer, Kevin J. "The Spirit of Understanding: Special Revelation and General Hermeneutics." In *Disciplining Hermeneutics: Interpretation in Christian Perspective*, ed. Roger Lundin, 131–65. Grand Rapids, MI: Eerdmans, 1997.

———. "Systematic Theology." In *Dictionary for Theological Interpretation of the Bible*, ed. Kevin J. Vanhoozer, 773–79. Grand Rapids, MI: Zondervan, 2005.

———. "Theology and Apologetics." In *The New Dictionary of Christian Apologetics*, ed. Campbell Campbell-Jack and Gavin McGrath, 35–43. London: Routledge, 2006.

———. "Theology and the Condition of Postmodernity: A Report on Knowledge (of God)." In *The Cambridge Companion to Postmodern Theology*, ed. Kevin J. Vanhoozer, 3–25. Cambridge: Cambridge University Press, 2003.

———. "Truth." In *Dictionary for Theological Interpretation of the Bible*, ed. Kevin J. Vanhoozer, 818–22. Grand Rapids, MI: Zondervan, 2005.

———. "The Voice and the Actor." In *Evangelical Futures: A Conversation on Theological Method*, ed. John G. Stackhouse, 61–106. Grand Rapids, MI: Baker, 2000.

———. "What Is Theological Interpretation of the Bible?" In *Dictionary for Theological Interpretation of the Bible*, ed. Kevin J. Vanhoozer, 19–25. Grand Rapids, MI: Zondervan, 2005.

—————. "Word of God." In *Dictionary for Theological Interpretation of the Bible*, ed. Kevin J. Vanhoozer, 850–54. Grand Rapids, MI: Zondervan, 2005.

—————. "The World Well-Staged? Theology, Hermeneutics, and Culture." In *God and Culture*, ed. D. A. Carson and John Woodbridge, 1–30. Grand Rapids, MI: Eerdmans, 1993.

Secondary Sources

Adler, Mortimer J., and Charles van Doren. *How to Read a Book*. 2nd ed. New York: Touchstone, 1972.

Agarwal, R. R. *The Medieval Revival and Its Influence on the Romantic Movement*. New Delhi: Abhinav, 1990.

Aland, Kurt. *Did the Early Church Baptize Infants?* Translated by George Raymond Beasley-Murray. Eugene, OR: Wipf & Stock, 2004.

Alston, William P. *Divine Nature and Human Language*. Ithaca, NY: Cornell University Press, 1989.

—————. *A Realist Conception of Truth*. Ithaca, NY: Cornell University Press, 1996.

—————. "Substance and the Trinity." In *The Trinity: An Interdisciplinary Symposium on the Trinity*, ed. Stephen T. Davis, Daniel Kendall, and Gerald O'Collins, 179–201. Oxford: Oxford University Press, 1999.

Archer, Margaret S., Andrew Collier, and Douglas V. Porpora. *Transcendence: Critical Realism and God*. New York: Routledge, 2004.

Aristotle. *On Interpretation*. Loeb Classical Library. Translated by Harold P. Cooke. Cambridge, MA: Harvard University Press, 1938.

Armstrong, Charles I. *Romantic Organicism: From Idealist Origins to Ambivalent Afterlife*. New York: Palgrave Macmillan, 2003.

Armstrong, David Malet, Charles Burton Martin, and Ullin Thomas Place. *Dispositions: A Debate*. Edited by Tim Crane. London: Routledge, 1966.

Ashford, Bruce R. "Wittgenstein's Theologians? A Survey of Ludwig Wittgenstein's Impact on Theology." *Journal of the Evangelical Theological Society* 50/2 (June 2007): 357–75.

Austin, J. L. *How to Do Things with Words.* 2nd ed. Edited by J. O. Urmson and Marina Sbisà. Cambridge, MA: Harvard University Press, 1962.

———. *Philosophical Papers*, 3d ed., ed. J. O. Urmson and G. J. Warnock. Oxford: Oxford University Press, 1979.

Ayer, Alfred Jules. *Language, Truth and Logic.* New York: Dover, 1992.

Babcock, Maltbie Davenport. "This Is My Father's World." In *The Baptist Hymnal*, 43. Nashville: Convention Press, 1991.

Baillie, John. *The Idea of Revelation in Recent Thought.* New York: Columbia University Press, 1956.

Bakhtin, Mikhail Mikhailovich. *The Dialogic Imagination*, ed. Michael Holquist. Translated by Caryl Emerson and Michael Holquist. Austin: University of Texas Press, 1981.

———. *Speech Genres and Other Late Essays.* Translated by Vern McGee, ed. Caryl Emerson and Michael Holquist. Austin: University of Texas Press, 1986.

———. *Toward a Philosophy of the Act*, ed. Vadim Liapunov and Michael Holquist. Translated by Vadim Liapunov. Austin: University of Texas Press, 1993.

Balthasar, Hans Urs von. *The Glory of the Lord: A Theological Aesthetics.* 7 vols. San Francisco: Ignatius, 1986–1990.

———. *Theo-Drama: Theological Dramatic Theory.* 5 vols. San Francisco: Ignatius, 1988.

———. *Theo-Logic.* 3 vols. San Francisco: Ignatius, 2001–2005.

Bann, Stephen, and John E. Bowlt, eds. *Russian Formalism: A Collection of Articles and Texts in Translation.* Edinburgh: Scottish Academic Press, 1973.

Barkun, Michael. *Religion and the Racist Right: The Origins of the Christian Identity Movement.* Chapel Hill: University of North Carolina Press, 1997.

Barr, James. *The Bible in the Modern World.* London: SCM, 1973.

———. *The Concept of Biblical Theology: An Old Testament Perspective.* Minneapolis: Fortress Press, 1999.

Barth, Karl. *Church Dogmatics*, vol. 1, no. 1. *The Doctrine of the Word of God.* Translated by G. T. Thomson and Harold Knight. Edinburgh: T&T Clark, 1975.

———. *Church Dogmatics*, vol. 1, no. 2. *The Doctrine of the Word of God.* Translated by G. T. Thomson and Harold Knight. Edinburgh: T&T Clark, 1956.

———.*Church Dogmatics*, vol. 2, no. 1. *The Doctrine of God.* Translated by G. T. Thomson and Harold Knight. Edinburgh: T&T Clark, 1957.

———.*Church Dogmatics*, vol. 4, no. 2. *The Doctrine of Reconciliation.* Translated by Geoffrey W. Bromiley. Edinburgh: T&T Clark, 1958.

———. *The Epistle to the Romans.* 6th ed. Translated by Edwyn C. Hoskyns. Oxford: Oxford University Press, 1933.

———. *Protestant Theology in the Nineteenth Century.* Translated by Brian Cozens and John Bowden. Grand Rapids, MI: Eerdmans, 2002.

Bartholomew, Craig G. "Three Horizons: Hermeneutics from the Other End—An Evaluation of Anthony Thiselton's Hermeneutic Proposals." *European Journal of Theology* 5 (1996): 121–35.

Bartlett, David L. *The Shape of Scriptural Authority.* Philadelphia: Fortress Press, 1983.

Barton, John, ed. *The Cambridge Companion to Biblical Interpretation.* Cambridge: Cambridge University Press, 1998.

Barton, Stephen C. "New Testament Interpretation as Performance." *Scottish Journal of Theology* 52 (1999): 179–208.

Bauckham, Richard. *Jesus and the God of Israel: God Crucified and Other Studies on the New Testament's Christology of Divine Identity.* Grand Rapids, MI: Eerdmans, 2008.

Bauer, Walter. *Orthodoxy and Heresy in Earliest Christianity.* Edited by Robert A. Craft and Gerhard Krodel. Philadelphia: Fortress Press, 1991.

Bebbington, David W. *Evangelicalism in Modern Britain: A History from the 1730s to the 1980s.* London: Routledge, 1989.

Beiser, Frederick C. *Enlightenment, Revolution and Romanticism: The Genesis of Modern German Political Thought 1790–1800.* Cambridge, MA: Harvard University Press, 1992.

Berger, Peter L. *The Sacred Canopy: Elements of a Sociological Theory of Religion.* New York: Doubleday, 1967.

Berger, Peter L., and Thomas Luckmann. *The Social Construction of Reality.* New York: Anchor, 1966.

Berger, Peter L., and Anton Zijderveld. *In Praise of Doubt: How to Have Convictions without Becoming a Fanatic.* New York: HarperOne, 2009.

Berkhof, Louis. *Systematic Theology.* 2nd ed. Grand Rapids, MI: Eerdmans, 1974.

Berry, Everett. "Theological vs. Methodological Post-Conservatism: Stanley Grenz and Kevin Vanhoozer as Test Cases." *Westminster Theological Journal* 69 (2007): 105–26.

Bhaskar, Roy. *Reclaiming Reality: A Critical Introduction to Contemporary Philosophy.* London: Verso, 1989.

Bird, Michael F. *Evangelical Theology: A Biblical and Systematic Introduction.* Grand Rapids, MI: Zondervan, 2013.

———. "Inerrancy is Not Necessary for Evangelicalism Outside the USA." In *Five Views on Biblical Inerrancy,* ed. J. Merrick and Steven M. Garrett, 145–73. Grand Rapids, MI: Zondervan, 2013.

Bird, Michael F. Craig A. Evans, Simon Gathercole, Charles E. Hill, and Chris Tilling, *How God Became Jesus: The Real Origins of Belief in Jesus'*

Divine Nature—A Response to Bart D. Ehrman. Grand Rapids, MI: Zondervan, 2014.

Blackburn, Simon. *The Oxford Dictionary of Philosophy.* Oxford: Oxford University Press, 1994.

Bleicher, Josef. *Contemporary Hermeneutics: Hermeneutics as Method, Philosophy and Critique.* London: Routledge, 1980.

Blomberg, Craig L. Review of *The Bible Made Impossible: Why Biblicism is Not a Truly Evangelical Reading of Scripture,* by Christian Smith, *Review of Biblical Literature* (August 2012). Accessed May 17, 2013. http://www.bookreviews.org/pdf/8205_8969.pdf.

Booth, Wayne C. *The Company We Keep: An Ethics of Fiction.* Berkeley: University of California Press, 1989.

Bossuet, Jacques-Bénigne. *Exposition de la Doctrine de L'église Catholique sur les Matières de Controverse.* Paris, 1686.

———. *Première Instruction Pastorale sur les Promesses de l'Eglise,* no. 28. *Oeuvres complètes de Bossuet,* vol. 22. Besançon, 1815.

Bousset, Wilhelm. *Kyrios Christos: A History of the Belief in Christ from the Beginnings of Christianity to Irenaeus.* Translated by John E. Steely. Nashville: Abingdon, 1970.

———. *Religionsgeschichtliche Studien: Aufsätze zur Religionsgeschichte des Hellenistischen Zeitalters,* ed. Anthonie F. Verheule. London: Brill, 1979.

Boyd, Gregory A. "Christian Love and Academic Dialogue: A Reply to Bruce Ware." *Journal of the Evangelical Theological Society* 45/2 (June 2002) 233–43.

———. *God of the Possible: A Biblical Introduction to the Open View of God.* Grand Rapids, MI: Baker, 2000.

Brainwaithe, Richard B. *An Empiricist's View of the Nature of Religious Belief.* Cambridge: Cambridge University Press, 1955.

Briggs, Richard S. *Words in Action: Speech-Act Theory and Biblical Interpretation, Toward a Hermeneutic of Self-Involvement.* New York: T&T Clark, 2001.

Bright, Michael H. "English Literary Romanticism and the Oxford Movement." *Journal of the History of Ideas* 40 (1979): 385–404.

Brissett, Dennis, and Charles Edgley, eds. *Life as Theatre: A Dramaturgical Sourcebook.* Chicago: Aldine, 1975.

Brown, Dan. *The Da Vinci Code.* New York: Doubleday, 2003.

Brown, David. *Discipleship and Imagination: Christian Tradition and Truth.* Oxford: Oxford University Press, 2000.

———. *Tradition and Imagination: Revelation and Change.* Oxford: Oxford University Press, 1999.

Brown, Harold O. J. *Heresies: The Image of Christ in the Mirror of Heresy and Orthodoxy.* Grand Rapids, MI: Baker, 1988.

Bühler, Karl. *Sprachtheorie: Die Darstellungsfunktion der Sprache.* Jena: Verlag von Gustav Fischer, 1965.

Bultmann, Rudolf K. *Existence and Faith: Shorter Writings of Rudolf Bultmann.* Meridian, NY: Merdian, 1960.

———. *Jesus Christ and Mythology.* Upper Saddle River, NJ: Prentice Hall, 1958.

———. "New Testament and Mythology." In *Kerygma and Myth: A Theological Debate,* ed. Hans Werner Bartsch, 1–44. Translated by Reginald H. Fuller. London: SPCK, 1953.

———. *New Testament and Mythology and Other Basic Writings.* Edited and translated by Schubert M. Ogden. Philadelphia: Fortress Press, 1984.

———. *Theology of the New Testament.* Translated by Kendrick Grobel. 2 vols. Waco, TX: Baylor University Press, 2007.

Burnett, Richard E. *Karl Barth's Theological Exegesis: The Hermeneutical Principles of the Römerbrief Period.* Grand Rapids, MI: Eerdmans, 2004.

Butler, Joseph. *Analogy of Religion: Natural and Revealed to the Constitution and Course of Nature*, ed. Robert Emory and G. R. Brooks. New York: Harper and Brothers, 1860.

Butler, William Archer. *Lectures on Romanism in Reply to Mr. Newman's Essay on Development.* 2nd ed. Edited by Charles Hardwick. Cambridge: Macmillan, 1858.

Caird, George B. *The Language and Imagery of the Bible.* London: The Trinity Press, 1980.

Calvin, John. *Commentary on Genesis.*

———. *Institutes of the Christian Religion.*

Carnap, Rudolf. "The Elimination of Metaphysics through Logical Analysis of Language." In *Logical Positivism*, ed. A. J. Ayer, 60–81. New York: Free Press, 1959.

———. *Logical Syntax of Language.* Translated by Amethe Smeaton. London: Kegan Paul, Trench, Trubner & Co., 1949.

Carpenter, John A. *Revive Us Again: The Reawakening of American Fundamentalism.* New York: Oxford University Press, 1999.

Carr, Thomas K. *Newman & Gadamer: Toward a Hermeneutics of Religious Knowledge.* American Academy of Religion Reflection and Theory in the Study of Religion 10. Atlanta: Scholars, 1996.

Carroll, Benajah Harvey. *The Inspiration of the Bible.* New York: Revell, 1930.

Carson, D. A. *Collected Writings on Scripture.* Edited by Andrew David Naselli. Wheaton, IL: Crossway, 2010.

———. "Theological Interpretation of Scripture: Yes, But . . ." In *Theological Commentary: Evangelical Perspectives*, ed. R. Michael Allen, 187–207. London: T&T Clark, 2011.

Cartwright, Nancy, Jordi Cat, Lola Fleck, and Thomas E. Uebel. *Otto Neurath: Philosophy between Science and Politics.* Cambridge: Cambridge University Press, 1996.

Cattaneo, Arturo, Manfred Hauke, André-Marie Jerumanis, and Ernesto William Volonté, eds. *Married Priests? 30 Crucial Questions about Celibacy.* San Francisco: Ignatius, 2012.

Chadwick, Owen. *From Bossuet to Newman.* 2nd ed. Cambridge: Cambridge University Press, 1987.

———. *The Mind of the Oxford Movement.* Stanford: Stanford University Press, 1967.

———. *Newman.* Oxford: Oxford University Press, 1983.

Chalybäus, Heinrich Moritz. *Historical Development of Speculative Philosophy from Kant to Hegel.* Translated by Alfred Edersheim. Edinburgh: T&T Clark, 1854.

Chesterton, Gilbert K. *The Napoleon of Notting Hill.* London: William Clowes and Sons, 1904.

Chillingworth, William. *The Religion of Protestants a Safe Way to Salvation.* Oxford: Leonard Lichfield, 1638.

Church, R. W. *The Oxford Movement: Twelve Years, 1833-1845.* London: Macmillan, 1892.

Clark, David K. *To Know and Love God: Method for Theology.* Wheaton, IL: Crossway, 2003.

Cole, Graham A. *He Who Gives Life: The Doctrine of the Holy Spirit.* Wheaton, IL: Crossway, 2007.

Collier, Andrew. *Critical Realism: An Introduction to Roy Bhaskar's Philosophy.* London: Verso, 1994.

Collingwood, R. G. *An Autobiography.* Oxford: Oxford University Press, 2002.

———. *Denken: Eine Autobiographie.* Edited and introduced by Hans-Georg Gadamer. Stuttgart: K. F. Koehler, 1955.

———. *The Idea of History.* Oxford: Oxford University Press, 1946.

Congar, Yves. "La 'réception' comme réalité ecclésiologique." *Revue des sciences philosophiques et théologiques* 56 (1972): 369–403.

————. *La tradition et la vie de l' Eglise*. 2nd ed. Paris: Janvier, 1984.

Cooper, John W. *Panentheism: The Other God of the Philosophers*. Grand Rapids, MI: Baker, 2006.

Costigan, Richard F. "Bossuet and the Consensus of the Church." *Theological Studies* 56 (1995): 652–72.

Criswell, Wallie Amos. *Why I Preach That the Bible Is Literally True*. Nashville: Broadman, 1969.

Cunningham, Mary Kathleen. *What Is Theological Exegesis? Interpretation and Use of Scripture in Barth's Doctrine of Election*. Valley Forge, PA: Trinity, 1995.

D'Holbach, Paul-Henri. *Christianity Unveiled: Being an Examination of the Principles and Effects of the Christian Religion*, trans. W. M. Johnson. New York, 1835.

————. *Le christianisme devoile, ou examination of principes et des effets de la religion chrétienne*. Paris, 1766.

Dawkins, Richard. "The Future Looks Bright," *The Guardian*, June 20, 2003, Accessed May 9, 2013. http://www.theguardian.com/books/2003/jun/21/society.richarddawkins.

————. *The God Delusion*. New York: Houghton Mifflin, 2006.

Day, Adian. *Romanticism*. The New Critical Idiom. Oxford: Routledge, 1996.

Davidson, Edward H. and William J. Scheick. *Paine, Scripture, and Authority: The Age of Reason as Political and Religious Idea*. Cranbury, NJ: Associated University Press, 1994.

Dennett, Daniel C. *Breaking the Spell: Religion as Natural Phenomenon*. New York: Penguin, 2006.

Derrida, Jacques. *Of Grammatology*. Baltimore: John Hopkins University Press, 1976.

————. *Speech and Phenomena, and Other Essays on Husserl's Theory of Signs*. Evanston, IL: Northwestern University Press, 1973.

———. *Writing and Difference.* London: Routledge, 1978.

Descartes, René. *Discourse on the Method for Rightly Conducting One's Reason and for Seeking Truth in the Sciences.* Translated by Donald A. Cress. Indianapolis: Hackett, 1980.

———. *Meditations on First Philosophy in Which the Existence of God and the Distinction of the Soul from the Body Are Demonstrated.* Translated by Donald A. Cress. 3d ed. Indianapolis: Hackett, 1993.

Dockery, David S. *Christian Scripture: An Evangelical Perspective on Inspiration, Authority, and Interpretation.* Nashville: Broadman & Holman, 1995.

The Doctrinal Commission of the Church of England. *Christian Believing: The Nature of the Christian Faith and Its Expression in Holy Scripture and Creeds: A Report of the Doctrinal Commission of the Church of England.* London: SPCK, 1976.

Dogmatic Constitution on Divine Revelation. Boston: St. Paul Books and Media, 1965.

Doriani, Daniel M. *Putting the Truth to Work: The Theory and Practice of Biblical Application.* Phillipsburg, NJ: Presbyterian & Reformed, 2001.

Draper, James T., Jr., and Kenneth Keathley. *Biblical Authority: The Critical Issue for the Body of Christ.* Nashville: Broadman & Holman, 2001.

Drey, Johann Sebastian. *Die Apologetik als Wissenschaftliche Nachweisung der Göttlichkeit des Christentums in seiner Erscheinung.* 3 vols. Mainz: Fl. Kupferberg, 1838–1847.

———. *Brief Introduction to the Study of Theology with Reference to the Scientific Standpoint and the Catholic System.* Notre Dame Studies in Theology, vol. 1. Translated by Michael J. Himes. Notre Dame: University of Notre Dame Press, 1994.

———. *Dissertatio Historico-Theologica Originem et Vicissitudinem Exomologeseos in Ecclesiâ Catholicâ ex Documentis Ecclesiasticis Illustrans.* Ellwangen: Typis Johann, Georg Ritter, 1815.

———. *Kurze Einleitung in das Studium der Theologie, mit Rücksicht auf den wissenschaftlichen Standpunct und das katholische System.* Tübingen: Heinrich Laupp, 1819.

———. "Toward the Revision of the Present State of Theology." In *Romance and the Rock: Nineteenth-Century Catholics in Faith and Reason*, ed. Joseph Fitzer, 62–73. Minneapolis: Fortress Press, 1989.

Dulles, Avery. *John Henry Newman.* 2nd ed. London: Continuum, 2009.

———. *Models of Revelation.* Maryknoll, NY: Orbis, 1992.

Duncan III, J. Ligon, Mark E. Dever, C. J. Mahaney, and R. Albert Mohler, Jr. "Together for the Gospel: Affirmations and Denials." April 2006. Accessed April 13, 2014. http://t4g.org/about/affirmations-and-denials-2/.

Dunn, James D. G. *Did the First Christians Worship Jesus? The New Testament Evidence.* Louisville: Westminster/John Knox, 2010.

———. *Jesus Remembered.* Grand Rapids, MI: Eerdmans, 2003.

Ebeling, Gerhard. "Time and Word." In *The Future of Our Religious Past: Essays in Honour of Rudolf Bultmann*, ed. James M. Robinson, trans. Charles E. Carlston and Robert P. Scharlemann, 247–66. London: SCM, 1971.

———. *Word and Faith.* Translated by James W. Leitch. Philadelphia: Fortress Press, 1963.

———. *The Word of God and Tradition: Historical Studies Interpreting the Divisions of Christianity.* Translated by S. H. Hooke. London: Collins, 1968.

Eco, Umberto. *The Role of the Reader: Explorations in the Semiotics of Texts.* Bloomington: Indiana University Press, 1979.

Edwards, Michael. *Towards a Christian Poetics.* Grand Rapids, MI: Eerdmans, 1984.

Ehrman, Bart D. *Lost Christianities: The Battles for Scripture and the Faiths We Never Knew.* New York: Oxford University Press, 2003.

————. *The Orthodox Corruption of Scripture: The Effect of Early Christological Controversies on the Text of the New Testament.* New York: Oxford University Press, 1993.

Erickson, Millard J. *Christian Theology.* 2nd ed. Grand Rapids, MI: Baker, 1998.

————. *Christian Theology.* 3d ed. Grand Rapids, MI: Baker, 2013.

Ernesti, Johann August. *Elementary Principles of Interpretation.* 4th ed. Translated by Moses Stuart. Andover, UK: Allen, Morrill, and Wardwell, 1842.

Evans, Donald D. *The Logic of Self-Involvement: A Philosophy Study of Everyday Language with Special Reference to the Christian Use of Language about God as Creator.* London: SCM, 1963.

Fairweather, Eugene R., ed. *The Oxford Movement.* New York: Oxford University Press, 1964.

Fehr, Wayne L. *The Birth of the Catholic Tübingen School.* AAR Academy Series, no. 37. Ann Arbor, MI: American Academy of Religion, 1971.

Felch, Susan M. "Dialogism." In *Dictionary for Theological Interpretation of the Bible,* ed. Kevin J. Vanhoozer, 174–75. Grand Rapids, MI: Baker, 2005.

Felch, Susan M., and Paul J. Contino, eds. *Bakhtin and Religion: A Feeling for Faith.* Evanston, IL: Northwestern University Press, 2001.

Feuerbach, Ludwig. *The Essence of Christianity.* 2nd ed. Translated by George Elliot [Marian Evans]. London: Trübner & Company, 1881.

Fiorenza, Francis Schüssler. *Foundational Theology: Jesus and the Church.* New York: Crossroad, 1992.

Fish, Stanley. *Is There a Text in This Class? The Authority of Interpretive Communities.* Cambridge: Harvard University Press, 1980.

Fitzer, Joseph. *Möhler and Baur in Controversy, 1832-1838.* Tallahassee: American Academy of Religion, 1974.

Forstman, Jack. *A Romantic Triangle: Schleiermacher and Early German Romanticism.* Atlanta: Scholar's Press, 1977.

Fowl, Stephen E. *Engaging Scripture: A Model for Theological Interpretation.* Challenges in Contemporary Theology. Oxford: Blackwell, 1998.

———. *The Story of Christ in the Ethics of Paul: An Analysis of the Function of the Hymnic Material in the Pauline Corpus.* Sheffield: Sheffield Academic Press, 1990.

Frei, Hans. *The Eclipse of Biblical Narrative.* New Haven: Yale University Press, 1974.

———. *The Identity of Jesus Christ.* Philadelphia: Fortress Press, 1975.

———. *Types of Christian Theology.* New Haven: Yale University Press, 1992.

Fries, Heinrich. *Fundamental Theology.* Translated by Robert J. Daly. Washington, DC: Catholic University of America Press, 1996.

Fuchs, Ernst. *Hermeneutik.* 4th ed. Tübingen: Mohr, 1970.

Funk, Robert W. *Language, Hermeneutic, and Word of God: The Problem of Language in the New Testament and Contemporary Theology.* New York: Harper & Row, 1966.

Gabler, Johann P. "An Oration on the Proper Distinction between Biblical and Dogmatic Theology and the Specific Objectives of Each." In *The Flowering of Old Testament Theology: A Reader in Twentieth-Century Old Testament Theology, 1930-1990,* ed. Ben C. Ollenburger, E. A. Martens, and Gerhard F. Hasel, 493–502. Winona Lake, IN: Eisenbrauns, 1992.

Gadamer, Hans-Georg. *Philosophical Hermeneutics.* 2nd ed. Translated and edited by David E. Linge. Berkeley: University of California Press, 2008.

———. "The Problem of Historical Consciousness." Translated by Jeff L. Close. *Graduate Faculty Philosophy Journal* 5 (1975): 8–52.

———. *Truth and Method.* Translated by Joel Weinsheimer and Donald G. Marshall. 2nd ed. New York: Continuum, 2004.

———. *Wahrheit und Methode: Grundzüge einer philosophischen Hermeneutik.* Gesammelte Werke 1. Tübingen: Mohr Siebeck, 2010.

Gagnon, Robert A. J. *The Bible and Homosexual Practice: Texts and Hermeneutics.* Nashville: Abingdon, 2001.

Gardeil, Ambroise. *Le donné révélé et la théologie*. Paris: Editions du Cerf, 1932.

Garrett, James Leo. *Systematic Theology*. Vol. 1. 3d ed. North Richland Hills, TX: B.I.B.A.L., 2007.

Gaull, Marilyn. *English Romanticism: The Human Context*. New York: W. W. Norton, 1988.

Geertz, Clifford. *The Interpretation of Cultures*. New York: Basic, 1973.

Geiselmann, Josef Rupert. "Die Glaubenswissenschaft der katholischen Tübinger Schule in ihrer Grundlegung durch Johann Sebastian v. Drey." *Tübinger Theologische Quartalschrift* 111 (1930): 49–117.

———. *Lebendiger Glaube aus geheiligter Überlieferung: Der Grundgedanke der Theologie J. A. Möhlers und ker katholischen Tübinger Schule*. Freiburg: Herder, 1964.

———. *The Meaning of Tradition*. Quaestiones Disputatae, no. 15. Translated by W. J. O'Hara. New York: Herder and Herder, 1962.

Gilkey, Landon. "Cosmology, Ontology, and the Travail of Biblical Language." *The Journal of Religion* 41 (1961): 194–205.

Glock, Hans-Johann. *A Wittgensteinian Dictionary*. The Blackwell Philosopher Dictionaries. Oxford: Blackwell, 1996.

Goldingay, John. *Models for Interpretation of Scripture*. Grand Rapids, MI: Eerdmans, 1995.

Gonzáles, Justo L. *A Concise History of Christian Doctrine*. Nashville: Abingdon, 2005.

Gratian. *The Treatise on the Laws* (with *The Ordinary Gloss*). Studies in Medieval and Early Modern Canon Law, no. 2. Translated by Augustine P. Thompson and James Gordley. Washington, DC: Catholic University of America Press, 1993.

Green, Joel B., and Max Turner, eds. *Between Two Horizons: Spanning New Testament Studies and Systematic Theology*. Grand Rapids, MI: Eerdmans, 1999.

Gregg, Robert C., ed. *Arianism: Historical and Theological Reassessments: Papers from the Ninth International Conference on Patristic Studies, September 5-10, 1983, Oxford, England.* Philadelphia: Philadelphia Patristic Association, Ltd., 1985.

Gregg, Robert C., and Dennis E. Groh. *Early Arianism: A View of Salvation.* Philadelphia: Fortress Press, 1981.

Grenz, Stanley J. *Revisioning Evangelical Theology: A Fresh Agenda for the Twenty-First Century.* Downers Grove, IL: InterVarsity, 1993.

Grenz, Stanley J., and John R. Franke. *Beyond Foundationalism: Shaping Theology in a Postmodern Context.* Louisville: Westminster/John Knox, 2001.

Grenz, Stanley J., and Roger E. Olson. *20th-Century Theology: God and the World in a Transitional Age.* Downers Grove, IL: InterVarsity, 1992.

———. *Who Needs Theology? An Invitation to the Study of God.* Downers Grove, IL: InterVarsity, 1996.

Gritsch, Eric W. "Introduction to *On the Councils and the Church*, 1539." In *Luther's Works*, vol. 41, ed. Jaroslav Pelikan, 5–8. Philadelphia: Fortress Press, 1966.

Grondin, Jean. "Gadamer's Basic Understanding of Understanding." In *The Cambridge Companion to Gadamer*, ed. Robert J. Dostal, 36–51. Cambridge: Cambridge University Press, 2002.

———. *Hans-Georg Gadamer: A Biography.* Translated by Joel Weinsheimer. New Haven: Yale University Press, 2003.

———. *The Philosophy of Gadamer.* Translated by Kathryn Plant. Montreal: McGill University Press, 2003.

———. *Introduction to Philosophical Hermeneutics.* Translated by Joel Weinsheimer. New Haven: Yale University Press, 1997.

———. *The Philosophy of Gadamer.* Translated by Kathryn Plant. New York: McGill-Queens University Press, 2002.

Grudem, Wayne. *Systematic Theology.* Grand Rapids, MI: Zondervan, 2009.

Grunberger, Richard. *The 12-Year Reich: A Social History of Nazi Germany 1933-1945.* New York: De Capo, 1995.

Guarino, Thomas G. *The Foundations of Systematic Theology.* London: T&T Clark, 2005.

———. *Vincent of Lérins and the Development of Christian Doctrine.* Grand Rapids, MI: Baker, 2013.

Gunton, Colin. *A Brief Theology of Revelation.* Edinburgh: T&T Clark, 1995.

———. *Theology through the Theologians: Selected Essays 1972-1995.* Edinburgh: T&T Clark, 1996.

Hagner, Donald A. *Matthew 1-13.* Word Biblical Commentary 33a. Nashville: Thomas Nelson, 2000.

Hammans, Herbert. "Recent Catholic Views on the Development of Dogma." *Concilium* (1967): 53–63.

Hanfling, Oswald. *Philosophy and Ordinary Language: The Bent and Genius of Our Tongue.* New York: Routledge, 2000.

Hanson, R. P. C. *The Continuity of Christian Doctrine.* New York: Seabury, 1981.

———. *The Search for the Christian Doctrine of God: The Arian Controversy, 318-381.* London: T&T Clark, 1988.

Hanson, R. P. C., and Reginald H. Fuller. *The Church of Rome: A Dissuasive.* London: SCM, 1948.

Harnack, Adolf von. *History of Dogma.* Translated by Neil Buchanan. 7 vols. Eugene, OR: Wipf & Stock, 1997.

Harris, Harriet A. *Fundamentalism and Evangelicals.* Oxford: Oxford University Press, 1998.

Harris, Horton. *The Tübingen School: A Historical and Theological Investigation of the School of F. C. Baur.* Oxford: Clarendon, 1975.

Harris, Sam. *The End of Faith: Religion, Terror, and the Future of Faith.* New York: W. W. Norton, 2005.

Hart, D. G. *That Old-Time Religion in Modern America: Evangelical Protestantism in the Twentieth Century.* Chicago: Ivan R. Dee, 2003.

Hasel, Gerhard. *New Testament Theology: Basic Issues in the Current Debate.* Grand Rapids, MI: Eerdmans, 1978

———. *Old Testament Theology: Basic Issues in the Current Debate.* 4th ed. Grand Rapids, MI: Eerdmans, 1991.

Hasker, William. *God, Time, and Knowledge.* Ithaca, NY: Cornell University Press, 1998.

Heidegger, Martin. *Being and Time.* Translated by John Stambaugh. Albany: State University of New York Press, 1996.

Helm, Paul. "Analysis 2 – Propositions and Speech Acts." *Helm's Deep* (May 1 2007). Accessed December 10, 2013. http://paulhelmsdeep.blogspot.com/ 2007/05/analysis-2-propositions-and-speech-acts.html.

Henry, Carl F. H. *God, Revelation, and Authority.* 5 vols. Waco, TX: Word, 1976–1983.

———. *The Uneasy Conscience of Modern Fundamentalism.* Grand Rapids, MI: Eerdmans, 1947.

Herder, Johann Gottfried. *Against Pure Reason: Writings on Religion, Language, and History.* Translated by Marcia Bunge. Minneapolis: Fortress Press, 1993.

———. *Reflections on the Philosophy of History of Mankind.* Translated by F. E. Manuel. Chicago: University of Chicago Press, 1968.

———. "Vom Erkennen und Empfinden der menschlichen Seele." In *Herders Werke* Berlin: Aufbau-Verlag, 1982, 3:331–405.

Heyduck, Richard. *The Recovery of Doctrine in the Contemporary Church: An Essay in Philosophical Ecclesiology.* Waco, TX: Baylor University Press, 2002.

Hick, John. *Faith and Knowledge.* 2nd ed. Ithaca, NY: Cornell University Press, 1966.

———. *An Interpretation of Religion.* New Haven, CT: Yale, 1989.

————. "Theology and Verification." *Theology Today* 17 (1960): 12–31.

Hinze, Bradford E. "Johann Sebastian Drey's Critique of Schleiermacher's Theology," *The Heythrop Journal* 37 (1996): 1–23.

————. *Narrating History, Developing Doctrine: Friedrich Schleiermacher and Johann Sebastian Drey.* Atlanta: Scholars Press, 1993.

Hirsch, Eric D., Jr. *The Aims of Interpretation.* Chicago: University of Chicago Press, 1976.

————. "Meaning and Significance Reinterpreted." *Critical Inquiry* 11 (1984): 202–24.

————. *Validity in Interpretation.* New Haven: Yale University Press, 1967.

Hitchens, Christopher. *God is Not Great: How Religion Poisons Everything.* New York: Twelve, 2007.

Hock, Ronald F. *The Infancy Gospels of James and Thomas.* Santa Rosa, CA: Polebridge Press, 1995.

Hodge, Charles. *Systematic Theology.* Vol. 1. Peabody, MA: Hendrickson, 2003.

Hodgson, Bernard. "Logical Positivism and the Vienna Circle." In *Columbia Companion to Twentieth-Century Philosophers*, ed. Contantin V. Boundas, 96-115. New York: Columbia University Press, 2007.

Holmes, Arthur F. *Contours of a World View.* Grand Rapids, MI: Eerdmans, 1983.

Hordern, William. *New Directions in Theology Today.* Vol. 1. Philadelphia: Westminster, 1966.

Horton, Michael Scott. *The Christian Faith: A Systematic Theology for Pilgrims along the Way.* Grand Rapids, MI: Zondervan, 2011.

Hughes, Philip E. "The Truth of Scripture and the Problem of Historical Relativity." In *Scripture and Truth*, ed. D. A. Carson and John D. Woodbridge, 173–94. Grand Rapids, MI: Baker, 1992.

Hultgren, Arland J. "Being Faithful to the Scriptures: Romans 1:26–27 as a Case in Point." *Word and World* 14 (1994): 315–25.

————. *The Rise of Normative Christianity.* Minneapolis: Fortress Press, 1994.

Hunsinger, George. "Postliberal Theology." In *The Cambridge Companion to Postmodern Theology,* ed. Kevin J. Vanhoozer, 42–57. Cambridge: Cambridge University Press, 2003.

Hurtado, Larry W. *How on Earth Did Jesus Become a God? Historical Questions about Earliest Devotion to Jesus.* Grand Rapids, MI: Eerdmans, 2005.

————. *Lord Jesus Christ: Devotion to Jesus in Earliest Christianity.* Grand Rapids, MI: Eerdmans, 2005.

Inwood, M. J. "Schelling, Friedrich Wilhelm Joseph von." In *The Oxford Guide to Philosophy,* ed. Ted Honderich, 843–44. Oxford: Oxford University Press, 1990.

The International Council on Biblical Inerrancy. *The Chicago Statement on Biblical Hermeneutics.* 1982.

————. *The Chicago Statement on Biblical Inerrancy.* 1978.

Jakobson, Roman. "Closing Statement: Linguistics and Poetics." In *Style in Language,* ed. Thomas A. Sebeok, 350–77. New York: Wiley, 1960.

Jasper, David. *A Short Introduction to Hermeneutics.* Louisville: Westminster/John Knox, 2004.

Jauss, Hans Robert. *Question and Answer: Forms of Dialogic Understanding.* Translated by M. Hays. Theological History of Literature, no. 68. Minneapolis: University of Minnesota Press, 1989.

————. *Toward an Aesthetic of Reception.* Translated by T. Bahti. Theory and History of Literature, no. 2. Minneapolis: University of Minnesota Press, 1982.

Jeanrond, Werner G. *Text and Interpretation as Categories of Theological Thinking.* Dublin: Gill and MacMillan, 1988.

————. *Theological Hermeneutics: Development and Significance.* New York: Crossroads, 1991.

Jeremias, Joachim. *Infant Baptism in the First Four Centuries.* Translated by David Cairns. Eugene, OR: Wipf & Stock, 2004.

————. *The Origins of Infant Baptism: A Further Study in Reply to Kurt Aland.* Translated by D. M. Burton. Eugene, OR: Wipf & Stock, 2004.

Johnson, Luke Timothy. *Scripture and Discernment: Decision Making in the Church,* rev. ed. Nashville: Abingdon, 1996.

Johnson, Luke Timothy and Eve Tushnet. "Homosexuality and the Church: Two Views." *Commonweal* (June 15, 2007). Accessed November 23, 2013. http://commonwealmagazine.org/homosexuality-church-1.

Johnston, Paul. *Wittgenstein: Rethinking the Inner.* New York: Routledge, 1993.

Jones, O. R., ed. *The Private Language Argument.* London: Macmillan, 1971.

Jowett, Benjamin. *Essays and Reviews.* London: John W. Parker and Son, 1860.

Kaiser, Walter C. "Issues in Contemporary Hermeneutics." In *Rightly Divided: Readings in Biblical Hermeneutics,* ed. Roy B. Zuck, 47–52. Grand Rapids, MI: Kregel, 1996.

————. "A Principlizing Model." In *Four Views on Moving beyond the Bible to Theology,* ed. Gary T. Meadors, 19–50. Grand Rapids, MI: Zondervan, 2009.

————. "A Response to Kevin J. Vanhoozer." In *Four Views on Moving beyond the Bible to Theology,* ed. Gary T. Meadors, 200–04. Grand Rapids, MI: Zondervan, 2009.

Kaiser, Walter C. and Moisés Silva. *An Introduction to Biblical Hermeneutics: The Search for Meaning.* Grand Rapids, MI: Zondervan, 1994.

Kaczor, Christopher. "Thomas Aquinas and the Development of Doctrine." *Theological Studies* 62 (2001): 283–302.

Kant, Immanuel. *The Critique of Pure Reason.* Translated by Werner S. Pluhar. Indianapolis: Hackett, 1996.

Karrer, Robert N. "The National Right to Life Committee: Its Founding, Its History, and the Emergence of the Pro-Life Movement Prior to Roe v. Wade." *Catholic Historical Review* 97.3 (2011): 527–57.

Keener, Craig. *The Historical Jesus of the Gospels*. Grand Rapids, MI: Eerdmans, 2009.

Kelly, J. N. D. *Early Christian Creeds*. 3d ed. New York: Longman, 1972.

————. *Early Christian Doctrines*. 4th ed. San Francisco: HarperCollins, 1978.

Kelsey, David H. *Proving Doctrine: The Uses of Scripture in Modern Theology*. Harrisburg, PA: Trinity, 1999.

Ker, Ian. *John Henry Newman: A Biography*. Oxford: Oxford University Press, 1990.

Kerr, Fergus. *Theology after Wittgenstein*. 2nd. ed. London: SPCK, 1997.

Klein, Julie Thompson. *Humanities, Culture, and Interdisciplinarity: The Changing American Academy*. New York: State University of New York Press, 2005.

————. *Interdisciplinarity: History, Theory, and Practice*. Detroit: Wayne State University Press, 1991.

Klink III, Edward and Darian R. Lockett. *Understanding Biblical Theology: A Comparison of Theory and Practice*. Grand Rapids, MI: Zondervan, 2012.

Knight, Henry H. III. *A Future for Truth: Evangelical Theology in a Postmodern World*. Nashville: Abingdon, 1997.

Knowles, Robert. *Anthony C. Thiselton and the Grammar of Hermeneutics: The Search for a Unified Theory, A Study Presented to Anthony C. Thiselton in Recognition of Fifty Years of Outstanding Contribution to the Discipline of Hermeneutics*. Milton Keynes, UK: Paternoster, 2012.

Köstenberger, Andreas J., and Michael Kruger. *The Heresy of Orthodoxy: How Contemporary Culture's Fascination with Diversity Has Reshaped Our Understanding of Early Christianity*. Wheaton, IL: Crossway, 2010.

Kowalski, Anthony P. *Married Catholic Priests: Their History, Their Journey, Their Reflections*. New York: Crossroad, 2005.

Kripke, Saul A. *Wittgenstein on Rules and Private Language*. Oxford: Blackwell, 1962.

Kübler-Ross, Elisabeth. *On Death and Dying*. New York: Macmillan, 1969.

Kuhn, Thomas S. *The Structure of Scientific Revolutions.* 3d ed. Chicago: University of Chicago Press, 1996.

Lane, Anthony N. S. "*Sola Scriptura?* Making Sense of a Post-Reformation Slogan." In *A Pathway into the Holy Scripture,* ed. Philip E. Satterthwaite and David F. Wright, 297–327. Grand Rapids, MI: Eerdmans, 1994.

Lash, Nicholas. *Change in Focus: A Study of Doctrinal Change and Continuity.* London: Sheed and Ward, 1981.

———. "Development of Doctrine: Smokescreen or Explanation?" *New Blackfriars* 52 (1971): 101–8.

———. "Faith and History: Some Reflections on Newman's 'Essay on the Development of Christian Doctrine.'" *Theological Quarterly* 38 (1971): 224–41.

———. "How Large Is a Language Game?" *Theology* 87 (1984): 19–28.

———. "Literature and Theory: Did Newman Have a 'Theory' of Development?" In *Newman and Gladstone: Centennial Essays,* ed. James D. Bastable, 161–73. Dublin: Veritas, 1978.

———. *Newman on Development: The Search for an Explanation in History.* Shepherdstown, WV: Patmos, 1975.

———. *Theology on the Way to Emmaus.* London: SCM, 1986.

———, ed. *Doctrinal Development and Christian Unity.* London: Sheed and Ward, 1967.

Lessing, Gotthold Ephraim. *The Education of the Human Race.* London: Smith, Elder, and Co., 1858.

———. *Lessing's Theological Writings.* Translated and edited by Henry Chadwick. London: Adam and Charles Black, 1956.

Lewis, C. S. *Mere Christianity.* San Francisco: Harper Collins, 2000.

———. *Reflections on the Psalms.* New York: Hartcourt, 1986.

Lindbeck, George A. "Atonement and the Hermeneutics of Intratextual Social Embodiment." In *The Nature of Confession,* ed. Timothy Phillips and Dennis Okholm, 221–40. Downers Grove, IL: InterVarsity, 1996.

————. "The Bible as Realistic Narrative." *Journal of Ecumenical Studies* 17 (1980): 80–85.

————. *The Future of Roman Catholic Theology: Vatican II—Catalyst for Change.* Philadelphia: Fortress Press, 1970.

————. *Infallibility.* Milwaukee, WI: Marquette University Press, 1972.

————. "The 'Literal Reading' of Biblical Narrative in Christian Tradition: Does It Stretch or Will It Break?" In *The Bible and the Narrative Tradition,* ed. Frank D. McConnell, 36–77. New York: Oxford University Press, 1986.

————. *The Nature of Doctrine.* Louisville: Westminster/John Knox, 1984.

————. "The Postcritical Canonical Interpretation: Three Modes of Retrieval." In *Theological Exegesis: Essays in Honor of Brevard Childs,* ed. Christopher Seitz and Kathryn Green-McCreight, 26–51. Grand Rapids, MI: Eerdmans, 1999.

————. "The Problem of Doctrinal Development and Contemporary Protestant Theology." In *Man as Man and Believer, Concilium,* vol. 21, ed. Edward Schillebeeckx and Boniface Willems, 133–46. New York: Paulist, 1967.

————. "Protestant Problems with Lonergan on Development of Dogma." In *Foundations of Theology,* ed. Phillip McShane, 115–23. Notre Dame, IN: University of Notre Dame Press, 1971.

————. "The Story-Shaped Church: Critical Exegesis and Theological Interpretation." In *Scriptural Authority and Narrative Tradition,* ed. Garrett Green, 161–78. Philadelphia: Fortress Press, 1987.

————. "Toward a Postliberal Theology: Faithfulness as Intertexuality." In *The Return to Scripture in Judaism and Christianity,* ed. Peter Ochs, 83–103. New York: Paulist Press, 1993.

Lindsell, Harold. *The Battle for the Bible.* Grand Rapids, MI: Zondervan, 1976.

Lints, Richard. *The Fabric of Theology: A Prolegomenon to Evangelical Theology.* Grand Rapids, MI: Eerdmans, 1993.

Livingston, James C. *Modern Christian Thought.* 2 vols. Minneapolis: Fortress Press, 2006.

Locke, John. *Essay Concerning Human Understanding,* ed. Peter H. Nidditch. Oxford: Oxford University Press, 1977.

Lotman, Jurij. *The Structure of the Artistic Text.* Ann Arbor: University of Michigan Press, 1977.

Lovejoy, Arthur O. *Essays in the History of Ideas.* Baltimore: John Hopkins University Press, 1948.

Lundin, Roger. *The Culture of Interpretation.* Grand Rapids, MI: Eerdmans, 1993.

———. *From Nature to Experience: The American Search for Cultural Authority.* Lanham, MD: Rowman & Littlefield, 2005.

———, ed. *Disciplining Hermeneutics: Interpretation in Christian Perspective.* Grand Rapids, MI: Eerdmans, 1997.

Luther, Martin. "On the Councils and the Church." In *Luther's Works,* vol. 41, ed. Jaroslav Pelikan, 95–106. Philadelphia: Fortress Press, 1966.

Luz, Ulrich. *Matthew in History: Interpretation, Influence, and Effects.* Minneapolis: Fortress Press, 1994.

———. *Matthew 1-7: A Commentary.* Translated by W. C. Linss. Minneapolis: Fortress Press, 1989.

———. *Matthew 8-20: A Commentary.* Translated by W. C. Linss. Minneapolis: Fortress Press, 2001.

———. *Matthew 21-28: A Commentary.* Translated by J. E. Crouch. Minneapolis: Fortress Press, 2005.

Mackie, J. L. *Truth, Probability, and Paradox: Studies in Philosophical Logic.* Oxford: Oxford University Press, 1973.

MacIntyre, Alasdair. *Whose Justice? Which Rationality?* Notre Dame: University of Notre Dame Press, 1988.

Macquarrie, John. *An Existentialist Theology: A Comparison of Heidegger and Bultmann.* New York: Harper Torchbooks, 1960.

Malina, Bruce J. *The New Testament World: Insights from Cultural Anthropology*. 3d ed. Louisville: Westminster/John Knox, 2001.

Marsden, George M. *Fundamentalism and American Culture*, rev. ed. New York: Oxford University Press, 2006.

———. *Understanding Fundamentalism and Evangelicalism*. Grand Rapids, MI: Eerdmans, 1990.

Marshall, Bruce D. "Introduction: *The Nature of Doctrine* after 25 Years." In George A. Lindbeck, *The Nature of Doctrine: Religion and Theology in a Postliberal Age*, rev. ed., vii–xxviii. Louisville: Westminster/John Knox, 2009.

Marshall, Ian Howard. *Beyond the Bible: Moving from Scripture to Theology*, with essays by Kevin J. Vanhoozer and Stanley E. Porter. Grand Rapids, MI: Baker, 2004.

———. "Climbing Ropes, Ellipses and Symphonies: The Relation between Biblical and Systematic Theology." In *A Pathway into the Holy Scripture*, ed. P. E. Satterthwaite and David F. Wright, 199–220. Grand Rapids, MI: Eerdmans, 1994.

Martin, Dale B. *Sex and the Single Savior: Gender and Sexuality in Biblical Interpretation*. Louisville: Westminster/John Knox, 2006.

Martin, John Jeffries. *Myths of Renaissance Individualism*. New York: Palgrave Macmillan, 2006.

Marx, Karl. "Preface to *A Contribution to the Critique of Political Economy*." In *The Marx-Engels Reader*, ed. Robert C. Tucker, 3–6. New York: Norton, 1978.

McClendon, James Wm., Jr., and James M. Smith. *Convictions: Defusing Religious Relativism*. 2nd ed. Valley Forge, PA: Trinity, 1994.

———. *Understanding Religious Convictions*. Notre Dame: University of Notre Dame Press, 1975.

McFague, Sallie. *The Body of God: An Ecological Theology*. Minneapolis: Fortress Press, 1993.

————. *Metaphorical Theology: Models of God in Religious Language.* Philadelphia: Fortress Press, 1982.

————. *Models of God: Theology for an Ecological, Nuclear Age.* Philadelphia: Fortress Press, 1987.

McGrath, Alister E. *Christian Theology.* 5th ed. Malden, MA: Wiley-Blackwell, 2011.

————. *Christianity's Dangerous Idea.* New York: HarperOne, 2007.

————. "Engaging the Great Tradition: Evangelical Theology and the Role of Tradition." In *Evangelical Futures: A Conversation on Theological Method,* ed. John G. Stackhouse Jr., 139–58. Grand Rapids, MI: Baker, 2000.

————. "Evangelical Theological Method: The State of the Art." In *Evangelical Futures: A Conversation on Theological Method,* ed. John G. Stackhouse Jr., 15–38. Grand Rapids, MI: Baker, 2000.

————. *Evangelicalism and the Future of Christianity.* Downers Grove, IL: InterVarsity, 1995.

————. *The Genesis of Doctrine: A Study in the Foundation of Doctrinal Criticism.* Grand Rapids, MI: Eerdmans, 1990.

————. *Heresy: A History of Defending Truth.* New York: HarperOne, 2009.

————. *The Intellectual Origins of the European Reformation.* 2nd ed. Oxford: Blackwell, 2004.

————. *Iustitia Dei: A History of the Christian Doctrine of Justification.* 3d ed. Cambridge: Cambridge University Press, 2005.

————. *J. I. Packer: A Biography.* Grand Rapids, MI: Baker, 1997.

————. *The Making of a Modern German Christology: From the Enlightenement to Pannenberg.* Oxford: Blackwell, 1986.

————. *The Order of Things: Explorations in Scientific Theology.* Oxford: Blackwell, 1996.

————. *Reformation Thought: An Introduction.* 3d ed. Malden, MA: Blackwell, 1999.

————. *A Scientific Theology.* 3 vols. Grand Rapids, MI: Eerdmans, 2001–2003.

McGrath, Mark G. *The Vatican Council's Teaching on the Evolution of Dogma.* Rome: Pontificium Athenaeum Angelicum, 1960.

McHann, James Clark, Jr. *The Three Horizons: A Study in Biblical Hermeneutics with Special Reference to Wolfhart Pannenberg.* Ph.D. diss., University of Aberdeen, 1987.

McKim, Donald. *A Guide to Contemporary Hermeneutics: Major Trends in Biblical Interpretation.* Grand Rapids, MI: Eerdmans, 1986.

————. *What Christians Believe about the Bible.* Nashville: Thomas Nelson, 1985.

McKnight, Edgar V. "Old and New Horizons in Hermeneutics: Anthony C Thiselton on Contemporary Developments in Hermeneutics." *Perspectives in Religious Studies* 20, no. 3 (1993): 289–302.

McKnight, Scot and Joseph B. Modica, eds. *Jesus Is Lord, Caesar Is Not: Evaluating Empire in New Testament Studies.* Downers Grove, IL: InterVarsity, 2013.

Meadors, Gary T., ed. *Four Views on Moving from the Bible to Theology.* Grand Rapids, MI: Zondervan, 2009.

Meier, John P. *A Marginal Jew: Rethinking the Historical Jesus.* 4 vols. New Haven: Yale University Press, 1991–2009.

Meyer, Ben F. *Critical Realism & The New Testament.* Allison Park, Pennsylvania: Pickwick Publications, 1989.

Mendelson, Jack. "The Habermas-Gadamer Debate." *New German Critique* 18 (1979): 44–73.

Metzger, Bruce M. *The Canon of the New Testament: Its Origin, Development, and Significance.* New York: Oxford University Press, 1987.

Möhler, Johann Adam. *Symbolik: Oder Darstellung der Dogmatischen Gegensätze der Katholiken und Protestanten.* Mainz, 1833.

Mohler, R. Albert, Jr. "Confessional Evangelicalism." In *Four Views on the Spectrum of Evangelicalism*, ed. Andrew David Naselli and Collin Hansen, 68–96. Grand Rapids, MI: Zondervan, 2011.

———. "What is Truth? Truth and Contemporary Culture." *Journal of the Evangelical Theological Society* 48/1 (March 2005): 63–75.

Moltmann, Jürgen. *The Crucified God*. Translated by R. A. Wilson and John Bowden (New York: Harper & Row, 1974);

———. *God in Creation: A New Theology of Creation and the Spirit of God*. Translated by Margaret Kohl. San Francisco: Harper & Row, 1985.

———. *Theology of Hope: On the Ground and the Implications of a Christian Eschatology*. Translated by James W. Leitch. New York: Harper & Row, 1967.

———. *The Trinity and the Kingdom*. Translated by Margaret Kohl. San Francisco: Harper & Row, 1981.

Moore, G. E. "Moore's Paradox." In *G. E. Moore: Selected Writings*, ed. Thomas Baldwin, 207–12. London: Routledge, 1993.

Moran, Joe. *Interdisciplinarity*. The New Critical Idiom. New York: Routledge, 2001.

Morgan, Robert, and John Barton. *Biblical Interpretation*. Oxford: Oxford University Press, 1988.

Mouw, Richard J. *The Smell of Sawdust: What Evangelicals Can Learn From Their Fundamentalist Heritage*. Grand Rapids, MI: Zondervan, 2000.

Mozley, James Bowling. *The Theory of Development: A Criticism of Dr. Newman's Essay on the Development of Christian Doctrine*. London: Rivingtons, 1888.

Mumford, Stephen. *Dispositions*. Oxford: Oxford University Press, 2003.

Murfin, Ross, and Supryia M. Ray. *The Bedford Glossary of Critical and Literary Terms* Boston: Bedford/St. Martin's, 1998.

Murphy, Nancey C. *Beyond Liberalism and Fundamentalism: How Modern and Postmodern Philosophy Set the Theological Agenda.* Valley Forge, PA: Trinity, 1996.

Murphy, Nancey C., and Brad J. Kallenberg. "Anglo-American Postmodernity: A Theology of Communal Practice." In *The Cambridge Companion to Postmodern Theology,* ed. Kevin J. Vanhoozer, 26–41.

Murphy, Nancey C., and James Wm. McClendon. "Distinguishing Modern and Postmodern Theologies." *Modern Theology* 5, no. 3 (1989): 191–214.

Murray, John Courtney. *The Problem of God: Yesterday and Today.* New Haven: Yale University Press, 1964.

Mussner, Franz. *The Historical Jesus in the Gospel of John.* London: Burns & Oates, 1967.

Neufield, Vernon H. *The Earliest Christian Confessions.* Grand Rapids, MI: Eerdmans, 1963.

Neurath, Otto. *Philosophical Papers 1913-1946.* Vienna Circle Collection, no. 16. Edited and translated by Robert S. Cohen and Marie Neurath. Dordecht: D. Reidel, 1983.

———. "Protokollsätze." *Erkenntnis* 3 (1932): 204–14.

Newman, John Henry. *Apologia Pro Vita Sua.* London: Longmans, Green, and Co., 1864.

———. *The Arians of the Fourth Century.* 3d ed. London: E. Lumney, 1871.

———. *An Essay in Aid of a Grammar of Assent.* London: Burns, Oates, and Co., 1870.

———. *An Essay on the Development of Christian Doctrine.* London: James Toovey, 1845.

———. *An Essay on the Development of Doctrine.* 2nd ed. Notre Dame, IN: University of Notre Dame Press, 1989.

———. *Fifteen Sermons Preached before the University of Oxford.* New York: Scribner, Welford, and Company, 1872.

————. *The Via Media of the Anglican Church.* Vol. 1. London: Longman, Green, and Co., 1891.

————. *The Via Media of the Anglican Church.* Vol. 2. London: Basil Montagu Pickering, 1877.

Newport, John P. "Contemporary Philosophical, Literary, and Sociological Hermeneutics." In *Biblical Hermeneutics: A Comprehensive Introduction to Interpreting Scripture*, 2nd ed., ed. Bruce Corley, Steve W. Lemke, and Grant I. Lovejoy, 163–75. Nashville: Broadman & Holman, 2002.

Ngien, Dennis. "Chalcedonian Christology and Beyond: Luther's Understanding of the *Communicatio Idiomatum.*" *The Heythrop Journal* 45, no. 1 (2004): 54–68.

Nichols, Aidan. *From Newman to Congar: The Idea of Doctrinal Development from the Victorians to the Second Vatican Council.* Edinburgh: T&T Clark, 1990.

Nielsen, Kai. "Wittgensteinian Fideism." *Philosophy* 42 (1967): 191–209.

Nineham, Dennis E., ed. *The Church's Use of the Bible Past and Present.* London: SPCK, 1963.

Noll, Mark A. *A History of Christianity in the United States and Canada.* Grand Rapids, MI: Eerdmans, 1992.

Oberman, Heiko. *Forerunners of the Reformation: The Shape of Late Medieval Thought.* New York: Holt, Rinehart, and Winston, 1966.

O'Collins, Gerald, and Daniel Kendall. *The Bible for Theology: Ten Principles for the Theological Use of Scripture.* New York: Paulist, 1997.

O'Connell, Marvin R. *The Oxford Conspirators: A History of the Oxford Movement.* New York: Macmillan, 1969.

Oden, Thomas C. *The Rebirth of Orthodoxy: Signs of New Life in Christianity.* San Francisco: HarperCollins, 2003.

Oldham, Steven L. "Alister E. McGrath and Evangelical Theories of Doctrinal Development." Ph.D. diss., Baylor University, 2000.

Ollenburger, Ben C. "What Krister Stendahl 'Meant': A Normative Critique of 'Descriptive Biblical Theology.'" *Horizons in Biblical Theology* 8 (1986): 61–98.

————, ed. *Old Testament Theology: Flowering and Future.* Winona Lake, IN: Eisenbrauns, 2004.

Olson, Roger E. "Open Theism: A Test Case for Evangelicals." August 23, 2010. Accessed December 9, 2012. http://www.patheos.com/blogs/ rogereolson/2010/08/open-theism-a-test-case-for-evangelicals/.

Orminston, Gayle L., and Alan D. Schrift, eds. *The Hermeneutic Tradition: From Ast to Ricoeur.* New York: State University of New York Press, 1990.

Orr, James. *The Process of Dogma.* 3d ed. London: Hodder and Stoughton, 1908.

————. *Revelation and Inspiration.* New York: Charles Scribner's and Sons, 1910.

Osborne, Grant R. *The Hermeneutical Spiral: A Comprehensive Introduction to Biblical Interpretation.* Downers Grove, IL: InterVarsity, 1991.

Outler, Albert C. "John Wesley's Heritage and the Future of Systematic Theology." In *Wesleyan Theology Today*, ed. Theodore H. Runyon, 38–46. Nashville: Kingswood, 1985.

————. *The Wesleyan Theological Heritage: Essays of Albert C. Outler.* Edited by Thomas C. Oden and Leicester R. Longden. Grand Rapids, MI: Zondervan, 1991.

Packer, J. I. *"Fundamentalism" and the Word of God.* Grand Rapids, MI: Eerdmans, 1958.

————. "Infallible Scripture and the Role of Hermeneutics." In *Scripture and Truth*, ed. D. A. Carson and John D. Woodbridge, 325–56. Grand Rapids, MI: Baker, 1992.

Paine, Thomas. *The Age of Reason; Being an Investigation of True and Fabulous Theology.* 1794, 1795, 1807.

Palmer, Richard E. *Hermeneutics.* Evanston, IL: Northwestern University Press, 1969.

Pannenberg, Wolfhart. *Basic Questions in Theology: Collected Essays.* Translated by George H. Kehm. Philadelphia: Fortress Press, 1970.

———. *Jesus: God and Man.* 2nd ed. Translated by Lewis L. Wilkins and Duane A. Priebe. Philadelphia: Westminster, 1977.

———. *Systematic Theology.* 3 vols. Translated by Geoffrey W. Bromiley. Grand Rapids, MI: Eerdmans, 1991–1998.

———. *Theology and the Philosophy of Science.* Translated by Francis McDonagh. Philadelphia: Westminster, 1976.

Pascal, Blaise. *Pensées.* Edited by Jean-Frédéric Astié. Paris, 1857.

———. *Pensées and Other Writings.* Edited by Anthony Levi. Translated by Honor Levi. New York: Oxford University Press, 1995.

Patte, Daniel. *Ethics of Biblical Interpretation: A Reevaluation.* Louisville: Westminster/John Knox, 1995.

———. "Speech Act Theory and Biblical Exegesis." *Semeia* 41 (1988): 85–102.

Patterson, Sue. *Realist Christian Theology in a Postmodern Age.* Cambridge Studies in Christian Doctrine. Cambridge: Cambridge University Press, 1999.

Pauck, Wilhelm. *Harnack and Troeltsch: Two Historical Theologians.* New York: Oxford University Press, 1968.

Peacocke, Arthur. *Imitations of Reality: Critical Realism in Science and Religion.* Notre Dame, IN: University of Notre Dame Press, 1984.

Pears, David. *Ludwig Wittgenstein.* New York: Viking Press, 1970.

Pelikan, Jaroslav. *The Christian Tradition: A History of the Development of Doctrine.* 5 vols. Chicago: University of Chicago, 1975–1991.

———. *Development of Doctrine: Some Historical Prolegomena.* New Haven: Yale University Press, 1969.

———. *Historical Theology: Continuity and Change in Christian Doctrine.* Philadelphia: Westminster, 1971.

————. *Obedient Rebels: Catholic Substance and Protestant Principle in Luther's Reformation*. New York: Harper & Row, 1964.

————. *The Vindication of Tradition: The 1983 Jefferson Lecture in the Humanities*. New Haven: Yale University Press, 1986.

Perdue, Leo G. *The Collapse of History: Reconstructing Old Testament Theology*. Minneapolis: Fortress Press, 1994.

————. *Reconstructing Biblical Theology: After the Collapse of History*. Minneapolis: Fortress Press, 2005.

Phillips, D. Z. *Belief, Change, and the Forms of Life*. Atlantic Highlands, NJ: Humanities Press International, 1986.

Phillips, Timothy R., and Dennis L. Okholm, eds. *The Nature of Confession*. Downers Grove, IL: InterVarsity, 1996.

Pinnock, Clark H. *Most Moved Mover: A Theology of God's Openness*. Grand Rapids, MI: Baker, 2001.

————. *The Scripture Principle*. San Francisco: Harper & Row, 1984.

————. "There is Room for Us: A Reply To Bruce Ware." *Journal of the Evangelical Theological Society* 45/2 (June 2002): 213–19

Piper, John. *Let the Nations Be Glad! The Supremacy of God in Missions*. 2nd ed. Grand Rapids, MI: Baker, 2003.

Plantinga, Alvin. "Two (or More) Kinds of Scripture Scholarship." *Modern Theology* 14 (April 1998): 243–78.

————. *Warrant and Proper Function*. Oxford: Oxford University Press, 1993.

Plantinga, Alvin, and Nicholas Wolterstorff. *Faith and Rationality*. Notre Dame, IN: University of Notre Dame Press, 1983.

Pöhler, Rolf J. *Continuity and Change in Adventist Teaching*. Friedensauer Schriftenreihe. Reihe A: Theologie, vol. 3. Berlin: Peter Lang, 2000.

————. *Continuity and Change in Christian Doctrine*. Friedensauer Schriftenreihe, Reihe A: Theologie, vol. 2. Berlin: Peter Lang, 1999.

Pojman, Louis P. *What Can We Know? An Introduction to the Theory of Knowledge*. 2nd ed. Belmont, CA: Wadsworth, 2001.

Pokorny, Petr, and Jan Roskovec, eds. *Philosophical Hermeneutics and Biblical Exegesis*. Wissenschaftliche Untersuchungen zum Neuen Testament, no. 153. Tübingen: Mohr Siebeck, 2002.

Polanyi, Michael. *Personal Knowledge: Towards a Post-Critical Philosophy.* London: Routledge & Kegan Paul, 1958.

Polkinghorne, John. *One World: The Interaction of Science and Theology.* Princeton: Princeton University Press, 1986.

Popper, Karl. *The Logic of Scientific Discovery.* New York: Routledge, 1992.

———. "Normal Science and Its Dangers." In *Criticism and the Growth of Knowledge : Proceedings of the International Colloquium in the Philosophy of Science, London, 1965, Vol. 4*, ed. Imre Lakatos and Alan Musgrave, 51–58. Cambridge: Cambridge University Press, 1970.

———. *The Poverty of Historicism.* Boston: Beacon, 1957.

Porter, Stanley E. "Reader-Response Criticism and New Testament Study: A Response to A. C. Thiselton's *New Horizons in Hermeneutics.*" *Literature and Theology* 8 (1994): 94–102.

———. "Why Hasn't Reader-Response Theory Caught On in New Testament Studies?" *Literature and Theology* 4 (1990): 278–92.

———. "Wittgenstein's Classes of Utterance and Pauline Ethical Texts." *Journal of the Evangelical Theological Society* 32 (1989): 85–97.

Powell, Mark Alan. *What Is Narrative Criticism?* Minneapolis: Fortress Press, 1990.

Quash, Ben. *Theology and the Drama of History.* Cambridge: Cambridge University Press, 2005.

Poythress, Vern S. "Canon and Speech Act: Limitations in Speech-Act Theory, with Implications for a Putative Theory of Canonical Speech Acts." *Westminster Theological Journal* 70 (2008): 337–54.

———. "Divine Meaning of Scripture." *Westminster Theological Journal* 48 (1986): 241–79.

———. "Ground-Rules of New Testament Interpretation." *Westminster Theological Journal* 41 (1979): 190–201.

———. "Philosophical Roots of Phenomenological and Structuralist Literary Criticism." *Westminster Theological Journal* 41 (1978): 165–71.

———. *Science and Hermeneutics: Implications of the Scientific Method for Biblical Interpretation.* Grand Rapids, MI: Zondervan, 1988.

———. *Symphonic Theology: The Validity of Multiple Perspectives in Theology.* Grand Rapids, MI: Zondervan, 1987.

Price, H. H. *Belief.* New York: Humanities, 1969.

Raab, Kelley A. *When Women Become Priests: The Catholic Women's Ordination Debate.* New York: Columbia University Press, 2000.

Rahner, Karl. *Theological Investigations.* Vol. 1. Translated by Cornelius Ernst. New York: Seabury, 1961.

Rahner, Karl, and Joseph Ratzinger [Benedict XVI]. *Revelation and Tradition.* Translated by W. J. O'Hara. New York: Herder and Herder, 1966.

Rambach, Johann J. *Institutiones Hermeneuticae Sacrae.* Jena, 1723.

Ramm, Bernard. *The Devil, Seven Wormwoods, and God.* Waco, TX: Word, 1977.

Ramsey, Frank P. *Philosophical Papers.* Edited by D. H. Mellor. Cambridge: Cambridge University Press, 1990.

Randall, Hastings. *The Idea of the Atonement in Christian Theology.* London: Macmillan, 1919.

Randall, J. H. Jr. *The Role of Knowledge in Western Religion.* Boston: Beacon Press, 1958.

Ransom, John Crowe. *The New Criticism.* Westport, CT: Greenwood, 1979.

Redeker, Martin. *Schleiermacher: Life and Thought.* Translated by J. Wallhauser. Philadelphia: Fortress Press, 1973.

Richardson, Alan. *The Bible in the Age of Science.* London: SCM, 1961.

Ricoeur, Paul. *The Conflict of Interpretations.* Evanson, IL: Northwestern University Press, 1974.

————. *Essays in Biblical Interpretation.* Philadelphia: Fortress Press, 1980.

————. *Fallible Man.* Translated by Charles Kelbley. Chicago: Henry Regnery, 1967.

————. *Freud and Philosophy: An Essay on Interpretation.* Translated by Denis Savage. New Haven: Yale University Press, 1970.

————. "Hermeneutics and the Critique of Ideology." In *The Hermeneutic Tradition: From Ast to Ricoeur,* ed. Gayle L. Orminston and Alan D. Schrift, 298–334. New York: State University of New York Press, 1990.

————. *Hermeneutics and the Human Sciences: Essays on Language, Action, and Interpretation.* Translated by John B. Thompson. Cambridge: Cambridge University Press, 1981.

————. *Interpretation Theory: Discourse and the Surplus of Meaning.* Fort Worth: Texas Christian University Press, 1976.

————. *Oneself as Another.* Translated by Kathleen Blamey. Chicago: University of Chicago Press, 1992.

————. *The Rule of Metaphor: Multi-disciplinary Studies of the Creation of Meaning in Language.* Translated by Robert Czerny, Kathleen McLaughlin, and John Costello. Toronto: University of Toronto Press, 1975.

————. *The Symbolism of Evil.* Boston: Beacon, 1969.

————. *Thinking Biblically.* Chicago: University of Chicago Press, 1998.

————. *Time and Narrative.* Translated by K. McLaughlin and D. Peliauer. Vols. 1–3. Chicago: University of Chicago Press, 1984–88.

————. "World of the Text, World of the Reader." In *A Ricoeur Reader: Reflection and Imagination,* ed. Mario J. Valdés, 491–98. Toronto: University of Toronto Press, 1991.

Rizzuto, Ana-Maria. *The Birth of the Living God: A Psychoanalytic Study.* Chicago: University of Chicago Press, 1979.

————. *Why Did Freud Reject God?: A Psychodynamic Interpretation.* New Haven: Yale, 1998.

Rogers, Jack B. ed. *Biblical Authority.* Waco: Word, 1977.

Rogers, Jack B., and Donald K. McKim. *The Authority and Interpretation of the Bible.* San Francisco: Harper & Row, 1979.

Rohrbaugh, Richard L., ed. *The Social Sciences and New Testament Interpretation.* Grand Rapids, MI: Baker, 2003.

Rorty, Richard M. ed. *The Linguistic Turn: Essays in Philosophical Method.* Chicago: University of Chicago Press, 1967.

————. "Metaphilosophical Difficulties of Linguistic Philosophy." In *The Linguistic Turn,* ed. Richard M. Rorty, 1–39. Chicago: University of Chicago Press, 1992.

Rowell, Geoffrey. *The Vision Glorious: Themes and Personalities of the Catholic Revival in Anglicanism.* Oxford: Oxford University Press, 1983.

Rush, Osmond. *The Reception of Doctrine: An Appropriation of Hans Robert Jauss' Reception Aesthetics and Literary Hermeneutics.* Tesi Gregorianna, Serie Teologia, no. 19. Rome: Pontifical Gregorian University Press, 1997.

Sanders, Fred. *The Deep Things of God: How the Trinity Changes Everything.* Wheaton, IL: Crossway, 2010.

Sanders, John. "Be Wary of Ware: A Reply to Bruce Ware." *Journal of the Evangelical Theological Society* 45/2 (June 2002): 221–31.

Sawyer, M. James. *The Survivor's Guide to Theology: Investigation of the Critical Issues, Survey of Key Traditions, Biography of Major Theologians, Glossary of Terms.* Grand Rapids, MI: Zondervan, 2006.

Schaff, Philip. *History of the Christian Church.* Vol. 2. New York: Charles Scribner, 1910.

Schelstrate, Emmanuel. *Antiquitas Illustrata Circa Concillia Generalia.* Antwerp: Marcelli Parys, 1678.

————. *De Disciplina Arcani.* Rome: Sac. Congregat. de Propagandâ Fide, 1685.

Schick, Edgar B. *Metaphorical Organicism in Herder's Early Works: A Study of the Relation of Herder's Literary Idiom To His World-View*. The Hague: Mouton, 1971.

Schillebeeckx, Edward. *God the Future of Man*. Translated by N. D. Smith. New York: Sheed and Ward, 1968.

Schleiermacher, Friedrich. D. E. *Brief Outline of Theology as a Field of Study*. 3d ed. Translated by Terrence N. Tice. Louisville: Westminster/John Knox, 2011.

———. *The Christian Faith*. 2nd ed. Translated and edited by H. R. Mackintosh and J. S. Stewart. Edinburgh: T&T Clark, 1928.

———. *Hermeneutics and Criticism: And Other Writings*. Cambridge Texts in the History of Philosophy. Edited by Andrew Bowie. Cambridge: Cambridge University Press, 1998.

———. *Hermeneutics: The Handwritten Manuscripts*. American Academy of Religion Texts and Translation Series. Edited by Heinz Kimmerle. Translated by James Duke and Jack Forstman. Atlanta: Scholars Press, 1999.

Schökel, Luis Alonso. *The Inspired Word: Scripture in the Light of Language and Literature*. Translated by Francis Martin. New York: Herder and Herder, 1965.

Schweitzer, Albert. *The Mysticism of Paul the Apostle*. Translated by William Montgomery. Baltimore: John Hopkins University Press, 1998.

———. *The Quest of the Historical Jesus: A Critical Study of Its Progress from Reimarus to Wrede*. Translated by William Montgomery. London: Adam and Charles Black, 1910.

Searle, John R. *Expression and Meaning: Studies in the Theory of Speech Acts*. Cambridge: Cambridge University Press, 1979.

———. *Speech Acts: An Essay in the Philosophy of Language*. Cambridge: Cambridge University Press, 1969.

Seixas, Peter C. "Collective Memory, History Education, and Historical Consciousness." In *Recent Themes in Historical Thinking: Historians in Conversation*, ed. Donald A. Yerxa, 28–34. Columbia: University of South Carolina Press, 2008.

———. "Introduction." In *Theorizing Historical Consciousness*, ed. Peter C. Sexias, 5–10. Toronto: University of Toronto Press, 2004.

Sellars, Roy Wood. "A Statement of Critical Realism." *Revue internationale de philosophie* 1 (1938–9): 474–6.

Sherry, Patrick. "Is Religion a 'Form of Life'?" *American Philosophical Quarterly* 9 (1972): 159–67.

Smend, Rudolf. *Die Mitte des Alten Testaments: Exegetische Aufsätze.* Tübingen: Mohr Siebeck, 2002.

Smith, Christian. *The Bible Made Impossible: Why Biblicism is Not a Truly Evangelical Reading of Scripture.* Grand Rapids, MI: Brazos, 2012.

Smith, Joseph, Jr. "An Epistle of the Prophet to the Twelve." In *History of the Church of Jesus Christ of Latter-day Saints*, vol. 4, ed. B. H. Roberts, 226–32. Salt Lake City: Deseret, 1978.

Smith, Wilfred Cantwell. *The Meaning and End of Religion: A New Approach to the Religious Traditions of Mankind.* New York: Macmillan, 1963.

Soskice, Janet Martin. *Metaphor and Religious Language.* Oxford: Clarendon, 1985.

Spinks, D. Christopher. "The Meaning of Scripture: Thinking Theologically about Scriptural Interpretation with Special Reference to Stephen E. Fowl and Kevin J. Vanhoozer." Ph.D. diss., Fuller Theological Seminary, 2006.

Steiner, George. *After Babel: Aspects of Language and Translation.* 3d ed. Oxford: Oxford University Press, 1998.

———. *Real Presences.* Chicago: University of Chicago Press, 1991.

Stendahl, Krister. "Biblical Theology, Contemporary." In *Interpreter's Dictionary of the Bible*, ed. G. A. Buttrick, 1:418–32. New York: Abingdon, 1962.

Stenger, Victor J. *God: The Failed Hypothesis—How Science Shows That God Does Not Exist.* Amherst, NY: Prometheus, 2007.

Stewart, Robert B. *The Quest of the Hermeneutical Jesus: The Impact of Hermeneutics on the Jesus Research of John Dominic Crossan and N. T. Wright.* Lanham, MD: University Press of America, 2008.

———, ed. *The Reliability of the New Testament: Bart Ehrman and Daniel Wallace in Dialogue.* Minneapolis: Fortress Press, 2011.

———, ed. *The Resurrection of Jesus: John Dominic Crossan and N. T. Wright in Dialogue.* Minneapolis: Fortress Press, 2006.

Stiver, Dan R. *The Philosophy of Religious Language: Sign, Symbol, and Story.* Cambridge, MA: Blackwell, 1996.

———. *Theology after Ricoeur: New Directions in Hermeneutical Theology.* Louisville: Westminster/John Knox, 2001.

Stott, John. *The Lausanne Covenant: Complete Text with Study Guide.* The Lausanne Movement, 2003.

Strange, Roderick. *John Henry Newman: A Mind Alive.* London: Darton, Longman and Todd, 2008.

Swinburne, Richard. *The Coherence of Theism.* 2nd ed. Oxford: Clarendon, 1993.

Tanner, Kathryn. *Theories of Culture: A New Agenda for Theology.* Minneapolis: Fortress Press, 1997.

Tate, W. Randolph. *Biblical Interpretation: An Integrated Approach.* Peabody, MA: Hendrickson, 1991.

Temple, William. *Nature, God, and Man.* Edinburgh: R&R Clark, 1934.

Tentzel, Wilhelm Ernst. *Dissertatio de Disciplina Arcani.* Leipsic, 1683.

Thiel, John E. *Senses of Tradition: Continuity and Development in Catholic Faith.* Oxford: Oxford University Press, 2000.

Thielicke, Helmut. *The Evangelical Faith.* Vol. 1. *Prolegomena: The Relation of Theology to Modern Thought Forms.* Translated and edited by Geoffrey W. Bromiley. Grand Rapids, MI: Eerdmans, 1974.

————. *How Modern Should Theology Be?* Translated by H. George Anderson. Philadelphia: Fortress Press, 1969.

Thomas, Robert L. *Evangelical Hermeneutics: The New versus the Old.* Grand Rapids, MI: Kregel, 2002.

Thompson, Daniel P. "Schillebeeckx and the Development of Doctrine." *Theological Studies* 62 (2001): 303–21.

Thompson, James L. *Reading the Bible with the Dead: What You Can Learn from the History of Exegesis That You Can't Learn from Exegesis Alone.* Grand Rapids, MI: Eerdmans, 2007.

Thornbury, Gregory Alan. *Recovering Classical Evangelicalism: Applying the Wisdom and Vision of Carl F. H. Henry.* Wheaton, IL: Crossway, 2013.

Tilley, Terrence W. *The Evils of Theodicy.* Washington, DC: Georgetown University Press, 1991.

————. *History, Theology, and Faith: Dissolving the Modern Problematic.* Maryknoll, NY: Orbis, 2004.

Tillich, Paul. *A History of Christian Thought: From Its Judaic and Hellenistic Origins to Existentialism.* New York: Touchstone, 1972.

————. *The Interpretation of History.* New York: Schribner's, 1936.

————. *The Protestant Era.* Chicago: University of Chicago Press, 1966.

————. *Systematic Theology.* 3 vols. Chicago: University of Chicago Press, 1951–1967.

Toon, Peter. *The Development of Doctrine in the Church.* Grand Rapids, MI: Eerdmans, 1979.

Torrance, Thomas F. *The Christian Doctrine of God, One Being Three Persons.* Edinburgh: T&T Clark, 1996.

————. *Christian Theology and Scientific Culture.* New York: Oxford University Press, 1981.

————. *The Ground and Grammar of Theology.* Charlottesville: University Press of Virginia, 1980.

————. *Reality and Evangelical Theology: The Realism of Christian Revelation.* 2nd ed. Downers Grove, IL: InterVarsity Press, 1999.

————. *Theological Science.* Oxford: Oxford University Press, 1969.

————. "The Transcendental Role of Wisdom in Science." In *Science et sagesse: Entretiens de l'Académie Internationale de Philosophie des Sciences, 1990,* ed. Evandro Agazzi, 63–80. Friboug: Universiätsverlag Freiburg Schweiz, 1991.

Tracy, David. *The Analogical Imagination: Christian Theology and the Culture of Pluralism.* New York: Crossroad, 1998.

————. *Blessed Rage for Order: The New Pluralism in Theology.* New York: Seabury, 1975.

————. *Plurality and Ambiguity: Hermeneutics, Religion, Hope.* Chicago: University of Chicago, 1994.

Treier, Daniel J. "Bakhtin's Chronotopes for Doing Theology in Time: Or, We Never Metanarrative We Didn't Like." Paper presented at the annual meeting of the Evangelical Theological Society, Boston, MA, 17 November 1999.

————. "Biblical Theology and/or Theological Interpretation of Scripture? Redefining the Relationship." *Scottish Journal of Theology* 61 (2008): 16–31.

————. *Introducing Theological Interpretation of Scripture: Recovering a Christian Practice.* Grand Rapids, MI: Baker, 2008.

————. Review of *The Hermeneutics of Doctrine,* by Anthony C. Thiselton. *International Journal of Systematic Theology* 11 (2009): 225–27.

————. "The Superiority of Pre-Critical Exegesis? *Sic et Non.*" *Trinity Journal* 24 (2003) 77–103.

————. "Virtue and the Voice of God: Toward a Postcritical, Sapiential Understanding of Theology." Ph.D. diss., Trinity Evangelical Divinity School, 2002.

Trigg, Robert. "Theological Realism and Antirealism." In *A Companion to the Philosophy of Religion*, ed. Philip L. Quinn and Charles Taliaferro, 213–20. Oxford: Blackwell, 1999.

Tristam, Henry. "J. A. Moehler et J. H. Newman. La pensée allemande et la renaissance catholique en Angleterre." *Revue des sciences philosophiques et théologiques* 27 (1938): 184–204.

Turner, Max. "Historical Criticism and Theological Hermeneutics of the New Testament." In *Between Two Horizons: Spanning New Testament Studies and Systematic Theology*, ed. Joel B. Green and Max Turner, 44–70. Grand Rapids, MI: Eerdmans, 2000.

Van Huyssteen, J. Wentzel. *Essays in Postfoundationalist Theology*. Grand Rapids, MI: Eerdmans, 1997.

———. *Theology and the Justification of Faith: Constructing Theories in Systematic Theology*. Translated by H. F. Snijders. Grand Rapids, MI: Eerdmans, 1989.

Via, Dan O. and Robert A. J. Gagnon. *Homosexuality and the Bible: Two Views*. Minneapolis: Fortress Press, 2003.

Vico, Giambattista B. *New Science*. Translated by David Marsh. New York: Penguin, 2000.

Vidu, Adonis. *Postliberal Theological Method*. Carlisle: Paternoster, 2007.

Vincent of Lérins. *The Commonitory*. Translated and edited by George E. McCracken and Allen Cabaniss. The Library of Christian Classics, vol. 9. Philadelphia: Westminster, 1957.

Virkler, Henry A. *Hermeneutics: Principles and Processes of Biblical Interpretation*. Grand Rapids, MI: Baker, 1995.

Vitz, Paul C. *The Faith of the Fatherless: The Psychology of Atheism*. 2nd ed. San Francisco: Ignatius, 2013.

Von Rad, Gerhard. *Old Testament Theology*. Vol. 2. Translated by D. M. G. Stalker. Edinburgh: Oliver and Boyd, 1965.

Voss, Gustav. "Johann Adam Möhler and the Development of Dogma." *Theological Studies* 4 (1943): 420–44.

Walgrave, Jan Henrik. *Unfolding Revelation: The Nature of Doctrinal Development*. Philadelphia: Westminster, 1972.

Wallace, Daniel B. "Is Intra-Canonical Development Compatible with a High Bibliology?" Paper presented at the Evangelical Theological Society Southwestern Regional Meeting. Dallas, TX, March 1, 2002.

Walsh, Brian J. "Anthony Thiselton's Contribution to Biblical Hermeneutics." *Christian Scholar's Review* 14, no. 3 (1985): 224–35.

Walton, John H. and D. Brent Sandy. *The Lost World of Scripture: Ancient Literary Culture and Biblical Authority*. Grand Rapids, MI: InterVarsity, 2013.

Walvoord, John F. "A Response to William V. Crockett." In *Four Views on Hell*, ed. William Crockett, 77–81. Grand Rapids, MI: Zondervan, 1996.

Ward, Wilfrid. *The Life of John Henry Newman*. 2 vols. London: Longmans, Green, and Co., 1912.

Ware, Bruce A. "Defining Evangelicalism's Boundaries Theologically: Is Open Theism Evangelical?" *Journal of the Evangelical Theological Society* 45/2 (June 2002): 193–212.

———. "Rejoinder to Replies by Clark H. Pinnock, John Sanders, And Gregory A. Boyd." *Journal of the Evangelical Theological Society* 45/2 (June 2002): 245–56.

Warfield, Benjamin Breckenridge. *The Inspiration and Authority of the Bible*, ed. Samuel G. Craig. Philadelphia: Presbyterian and Reformed, 1948.

Watson, Francis. *Text and Truth: Redefining Biblical Theology*. Grand Rapids, MI: Eerdmans, 1997.

———. *Text, Church, and World: Biblical Interpretation in Theological Perspective*. Grand Rapids, MI: Eerdmans, 1994.

Webb, William J. *Corporal Punishment in the Bible: A Redemptive-Movement Hermeneutic for Troubling Texts*. Downers Grove, IL: InterVarsity, 2011.

———. *Slaves, Women & Homosexuals: Exploring the Hermeneutics of Cultural Analysis.* Downers Grove, IL: InterVarsity, 2001.

Webster, John B. "Introduction: Systematic Theology." In *The Oxford Handbook of Systematic Theology,* ed. John B. Webster, Kathryn Tanner, and Iain Torrance (Oxford: Oxford University Press, 2009),

Weidhorn, Manfred. *The Person of the Millennium: The Unique Impact of Galileo on World History.* Lincoln, NE: iUniverse, 2005.

Wells, Samuel. *Improvisation: The Drama of Christian Ethics.* Grand Rapids, MI: Brazos, 2004.

Werner, Martin. *The Formation of Christian Dogma: A Historical Study of Its Problem.* New York: Harper, 1957.

Westphal, Merold. *Overcoming Onto-Theology: Toward a Postmodern Christian Faith.* New York: Fordham University Press, 2001.

———. *Whose Community? Which Interpretation? Philosophical Hermeneutics for the Church.* The Church and Postmodern Culture. Grand Rapids, MI: Baker, 2009.

Whorf, Benjamin Lee. *Language, Thought, and Reality: Selected Writings of Benjamin Lee Whorf.* Edited by John B. Carroll. Cambridge: MIT Press, 1956.

Wiles, Maurice F. *Archetypal Heresy: Arianism through the Centuries.* Oxford: Oxford University Press, 1996.

———. "In Defence of Arius." *The Journal of Theological Studies* 13 (1962): 339–47.

———. *The Making of Christian Doctrine: A Study in the Principles of Doctrinal Development.* Cambridge: Cambridge University Press, 1967.

———. *Working Papers in Doctrine.* Naperville, IL: Allenson, 1976.

Williams, Daniel H. *Retrieving the Tradition and Renewing Evangelicalism: A Primer for Suspicious Protestants.* Grand Rapids, MI: Eerdmans, 1999.

Williams, Rowan. *Arius: Heresy & Tradition.* 2nd ed. Grand Rapids, MI: Eerdmans, 2002.

Wimsatt, William K., and Monroe C. Beardsley. "The Intentional Fallacy." *The Sewanee Review* 4 (1946): 468–88.

Winch, Peter. *The Idea of a Social Science and Its Relationship to Philosophy.* 2nd ed. London: Routledge, 1990.

Witherington, Ben, III. *The Indelible Image: The Theological and Ethical Thought World of the New Testament.* Vol. 2. *The Collective Witness.* Downers Grove, IL: InterVarsity, 2010.

———. *The Living Word of God: Rethinking the Theology of the Bible.* Waco, TX: Baylor University Press, 2007.

———. "The Truth Will Win Out: An Historian's Perspective on the Inerrancy Controversy," *Journal of the Evangelical Theological Society* 57/1 (March 2014): 19–27.

Wittgenstein, Ludwig. *The Brown and Blue Books: Preliminary Studies for the "Philosophical Investigations."* 2nd ed. New York: Harper & Row, 1965.

———. *Culture and Value.* Translated by Peter Winch. Chicago: University of Chicago Press, 1984.

———. *On Certainty.* Translated and edited by G. E. M. Anscombe and George Hendrik von Wright. New York: Harper Perennial, 1972.

———. *Philosophical Investigations* [*Philosophische Untersuchungen*]. 4th ed. Translated by G. E. M. Anscombe, P. M. S. Hacker, and Joachim Schulte. Oxford: Blackwell, 2009.

———. *Tractatus Logico-Philosophicus.* Translated by C. K. Ogden. London: Kegan Paul, Trench, Trübner & Co., 1933.

———. *Zettel.* Translated and edited by G. E. M. Anscombe and George Hendrik von Wright. Oxford: Blackwell, 1967.

Wooddell, Joseph D. "Article I: The Scriptures." In *Baptist Faith and Message 2000: Critical Issues in America's Largest Protestant Denomination,* ed. Douglas K. Blount and Joseph D. Wooddell, 1–12. Lanham, MD: Rowman and Littlefield, 2007.

Wolterstorff, Nicholas. *Divine Discourse: Philosophical Reflections on the Claim That God Speaks*. Cambridge: Cambridge University Press, 1995.

———. "The Importance of Hermeneutics for a Christian Worldview." In *Disciplining Hermeneutics: Interpretation in Christian Perspective*, ed. Roger Lundin, 25–47. Grand Rapids, MI: Eerdmans, 1997.

Wood, Charles M. *The Formation of Christian Understanding: An Essay in Theological Hermeneutics*. Philadelphia: Westminster, 1981.

Wood, W. Jay. *Epistemology: Becoming Intellectually Virtuous*. Downers Grove, IL: InterVarsity, 1998.

Wright, N. T. *Evil and the Justice of God*. Downers Grove, IL: InterVarsity, 2006.

———. "How Can the Bible Be Authoritative?" *Vox Evangelica* 21 (1991): 7–32.

———. *Jesus and the Victory of God*. Minneapolis: Fortress Press, 1997.

———. *The Last Word: Beyond the Bible Wars to a New Understanding of the Authority of Scripture*. San Francisco: HarperSanFrancisco, 2005.

———. *The New Testament and the People of God*. Minneapolis: Fortress Press Press, 1992.

———. "Reading Paul, Thinking Scripture." In *Scripture's Doctrine and Theology's Bible: How the New Testament Shapes Christian Dogmatics*, ed. Markus Bockmuehl and Alan J. Torrance, 59–71. Grand Rapids, MI: Baker, 2008.

———. *The Resurrection of the Son of God*. Minneapolis: Fortress Press, 2003.

———. *Surprised by Hope: Rethinking Heaven, the Resurrection, and the Mission of the Church*. San Francisco: HarperOne, 2008.

———. "Whence and Whither Historical Jesus Studies in the Life of the Church?" In *Jesus, Paul and the People of God: A Theological Dialogue with N. T. Wright*, ed. Nicholas Perrin and Richard B. Hays, 114–58. Downers Grove, IL: InterVarsity, 2011.

Yarnell, Malcolm B., III. *The Formation of Christian Doctrine*. Nashville: Broadman and Holman, 2007.

Yeago, David S. "The New Testament and Nicene Dogma: A Contribution to the Recovery of Theological Exegesis." In *Theological Interpretation of Scripture: Classic and Contemporary Readings*, ed. Stephen E. Fowl, 87–100. Cambridge, MA: Blackwell, 1997.

Young, Frances. *The Art of Performance: Towards a Theology of Holy Scripture*. London: Darton, Longman, & Todd, 1990.

Zimmerman, Jens. "Ignoramus: Gadamer's 'Religious Turn.'" In *Gadamer's Hermeneutics and the Art of Conversation*, International Studies in Hermeneutics and Phenomenology 2, ed. Andrzej Wierciński, 209–222. London: Transaction, 2011.

———. *Recovering Theological Hermeneutics: An Incarnational-Trinitarian Theory of Interpretation*. Grand Rapids, MI: Baker, 2004.

Index